THE FABER BOOK OF LETTERS

THE FABER BOOK OF LETTERS

Letters written in the
English language
1578–1939

Edited by Felix Pryor

faber and faber
LONDON · BOSTON

First published in 1988
by Faber and Faber Limited
3 Queen Square London WCIN 3AU
Reprinted 1988

Photoset by Wilmaset Birkenhead Wirral
Printed in Great Britain by
Mackays of Chatham PLC, Chatham, Kent
All rights reserved

British Library Cataloguing in Publication Data

The Faber book of letters.
1. Letters in English, 1400–. Anthologies
I. Pryor, Felix
826'.008
ISBN 0-571-15269-4

for
Julia Hamilton

Contents

Introduction	ix
A Note on the text	xv
THE LETTERS 1578–1939	I
Index of letter-writers	285
Index of recipients	288
Index of selected subjects	291
Sources	294
Acknowledgements	316

Introduction

Most letters are very boring. It is perhaps for this reason that, contrary to popular belief, more are being written today than at any other time in history. Even in the early seventeenth century letters seem to have been regarded as something of a nuisance. A fragment from an otherwise lost tragedy attributed to John Webster (to be published in The Cambridge Edition of his Works) has recently come to light, and here the point is made with some panache. In it, a prince's favourite is shown a letter which exposes his treacherous double-dealing. But before the favourite has a chance to read it, he assumes that the letter must be of the sort that awaits us on our return from holiday:

> What's this? Some bill exhibited by my tailor against me for not discharging his bill? Why I hope favourites may remain in debt, and not be forced to pay them, but be borne out in greater matters then petty trifles: or is it a complaint of some of my taverners for his reckonings? 'Slid! if it be I'll clapperclaw the villain, I'll brain him with his own pottle pots; besides withdrawing of my roaring quaffers from him, his house shall stand more empty then ever it did in the time of a visitation . . . Or may [be] 'tis some oppress'd damosel . . . would have me compell'd by the title of a father to legitimate the unlawfully begotten progeny; why if these things should go by compulsion I should have as many wives as Solomon . . .

Webster was a younger contemporary of Shakespeare. The only part of Shakespeare's correspondence that survives is a letter addressed to him, but never delivered. It is not written by Anne Hathaway or Queen Elizabeth (these gaps in his correspondence were filled by the eighteenth-century forger W. H. Ireland), but by a kinsman who was trying to touch him for some money. It stands as representative of the typical letter written through the ages, the type of letter this anthology does its best to ignore. It is also representative of most letters that have survived. Old love letters have no practical value but, alas, letters from solicitors do. Piety demands that we burn the one and preserve the other.

One other category of letter has tended to survive: those written by the famous. It requires a praiseworthy degree of sang-froid to throw a letter from the Queen, Poet Laureate or President into the waste-paper basket. This is one reason why this anthology is populated by famous people. Of these most, but by no means all, are professional writers. Those who are able to write good books are usually the ones best able to write good letters. They are at home in the medium. It comes, in a sense, as an unexpected bonus that those who were good at doing other things – who, like Van Gogh, Gainsborough or Nelson, pursued other professions – could also write brilliant letters.

Alexander Pope took letter-writing very seriously. In the 1730s he wrote to his correspondents asking them to return the letters he had sent them. After covering his tracks through a tortuous series of transactions, he then re-wrote and published his own letters. On the other hand Lord Chesterfield, who is probably the best known of all eighteenth-century letter-writers, did not write with publication in mind. But his letters read exactly as if he had. I am reminded of a modern, high-quality glass factory, where all the pieces are hand-made, but finished to such a pitch of perfection that they look as if they were made by machine. Some Spirit of the Age has demanded that all irregularities be ironed out.

Alexander Pope had a right to tidy up his own letters, but I do not feel that I have the same right when it comes to the letters I have chosen. I have, therefore, decided to print all letters in their entirety: having made this rule, I have stuck to it.

The uneven quality of most letters reminds us of the fact that we are reading a private communication. The famous letter written by Wilfred Owen to his mother on New Year's Eve 1917 opens with a discussion of Christmas cards. But this beginning sets the scene for what is to follow. We can hear the audience coughing and the orchestra tuning up before the symphony breaks upon us.

In the past it has often been the practice to regard letters as exercises in charm, as a minor, even genteel, branch of literature. One of the most successful anthologies published in the early years of this century is that by E. V. Lucas. This he called *The Gentlest Art*. A contemporary of Lucas, C. E. Vulliamy, claimed in his *English Letter Writers* that

The English Letter Writers, properly speaking, are those men and women whose fame as writers of prose is chiefly or wholly dependent upon their published epistles. Of these, Lady Mary Wortley Montagu, Chesterfield, and Horace Walpole are conspicuous and obvious types, and there can be no doubt of Cowper's position in the same category. The group is not a large one: it could have been assembled easily in a drawing room of moderate size.

I find this notion off-putting. Wherever possible I have sought material from outside the drawing room. I have even ventured into the lunatic asylum.

Some letters – even some drawing-room letters – convey a sense of immediacy. In a letter to his brother George, Keats describes this better than anyone else:

> the fire is at its last click – I am sitting with my back to it with one foot rather askew upon the rug and the other with the heel a little elevated from the carpet . . . These are trifles – but . . . Could I see the same thing done of any great Man long since dead it would be a great delight: as to know in what position Shakespeare sat when he wrote 'To be or not to be' . . .

This sense of living presence can be so vivid as to be almost startling: Keats going for a walk in Winchester in the early autumn, Emily Dickinson on her sick-bed, T. E. Lawrence wintering in a Yorkshire resort, Dickens at Chelmsford on a rainy Sunday morning or interrupting his letter to 'whop' the over-sexed family dog, Tolstoy dying in the station master's house at Astapovo.

Lying behind the popular belief that letters are no longer being written is the realization that the telephone has taken over. If more letters are being written today it is because credit-card companies and solicitors have inherited the earth. Lovers now speak to one another on the telephone and their conversations are no longer recorded. Some letters of the past are no more than the briefest of telephone calls, moments frozen in time. On 7 May 1707, the essayist Richard Steele, obviously aware that he was due back at home, called his wife from the Coffee House

> Dear Prue
>   I am just drinking a Pint of Wine and will come home forthwith.
> I am with Mr. Elliot settling things. Yrs Ever Ever
>   Richd Steele

I have, on the whole, not included those letters whose chief interest lies in the historical event described, a type of interest already catered for by John Carey in his pioneering *Faber Book of Reportage*. Of course many of the letters chosen here will contain an element of reportage but some, such as the worried letter by John Barrow of the Admiralty speculating on the whereabouts of Napoleon in the days after Waterloo, act in a more direct way. Instead of hearing the actors described, we hear them speak.

Unlike newspaper reports, which are generally intended for a wide public, letters are usually intended for a single recipient, or at most a small group of recipients: and it can make a considerable difference if we know who that recipient is. A case in point is a series of letters by Dora Wordsworth to her father, part of a group of family papers which were discovered ten years ago. The excitement of reading Dora's letters, fresh from the solicitor's trunk where they had been stored for over a hundred years, was heightened by the realization that the last person to have read them might well have been Wordsworth himself.

> Father I must not forget to tell you how strangely your lines or rather your 'dancing Daffodils' were brought to my 'heart' yesterday m[ornin]g . . . As Mr Q. & I were returning from the City by the low road – and tide was out – we turned a point in the road which presents a pretty half moon bay fringed with pine trees . . . beneath these trees was a bright yellow bed (may be a yard wide) of flowers [–] daffodils as I chose to fancy running along the whole line of the bay – & what think you my daffodils proved – oranges left there by the tide – they are lying in hundreds green & yellow all along the sea coast – but seeing them in that way by the rivers side under the deep shade of those pine trees I was carried at once to your picture by the side of Ullswater & though I could not say my heart danced *with* the daffodils for these were motionless it certainly did dance *through* them . . .

Reading the printed text of a letter is sometimes a poor substitute for reading the original. The telephone receiver is no longer placed in your hand.

Although letters rejoice in – and celebrate – the ephemeral, I see no sense in distinguishing between Letters and Literature. Great letters (such as those by Keats or Emily Dickinson) are great literature; bad letters, bad literature. We all speak in prose, and all write letters.

I have deliberately blurred the distinction between letters-as-fact and literature-as-fiction. One of the letters included here, that describing Ralph Hamilton's wartime burial in 1918, has been incorporated in a recent work of fiction (Julia Hamilton's *The Idle Hill of Summer*), the novel's fiction adding to this letter's power to move the reader. Another of my letters was later absorbed into a poem written by its recipient. In 1915 Henry James wrote to W. B. Yeats thanking him for a poem contributed to an anthology:

> happy you poets who can be present, & *so* present by a simple flicker of your genius, & not, like the clumsier race, have to lay a train & pile up faggots that may not after prove in the least combustible!

Yeats gave this letter to his friend Lady Gregory, who pasted it into an album containing drawings by her son. When that son was killed in the war, Yeats recalled James's letter in his poem 'In Memory of Major Robert Gregory':

> Some burn damp faggots, others may consume
> The entire combustible world in one small room
> As though dried straw, and if we turn about
> The bare chimney is gone black out
> Because the work had finished in that flare . . .

It may be thought that I have blurred the distinction too much by including Hamlet's letter to Ophelia. While I have excluded purely fictional letters from this anthology, I have included this one on the no doubt specious grounds that the letter at some time actually existed as a bit of paper handed from one actor to another at the Globe Theatre. The similarity of Hamlet's letter to that written in real life only a month or two earlier by the love-lorn 'Mr V' has not, I think, been remarked on before. But in pointing this out, I hasten to add that I am not casting Mr V. into the role of Mr W. H., or suggesting that Shakespeare had any knowledge of his letter.

It may be wondered why I have included foreigners such as Voltaire and Tolstoy. I have done so because they sometimes took the trouble to write in English. Were I to exclude them on the grounds of nationality I should also have to exclude Joseph Conrad (born Teodor Josef Konrad Korzeniowski) and introduce strict racial criteria for admittance. I have, on the other hand, included no foreigners writing in their native tongue as their letters would have to be translated and any pretence to authenticity sacrificed. We would be presented with the absurd spectacle of Sir Philip Sidney in his original Elizabethan garb rubbing shoulders with Montaigne in a modern translator's suit.

Many of the letters that I have included are well known. Quite a few are published here for the first time: among these are Nelson's earliest-known love letter to Lady Hamilton, describing an erotic dream (one feels almost ashamed at eavesdropping on such intensity of emotion); the extraordinary letter by Oscar Wilde's wife about her husband and her own impending death (Ophelia, as it were, giving us her view of Hamlet), with its touching echo of Keats's last letter; Swinburne's exercise in Gladstonian oratory in which he explains to Burne-Jones why he has felt forced to decline the Archbishopric of Canterbury; and the letter by Lewis Carroll to the little girl who was clearly unimpressed by *Alice Through the Looking Glass*. From the twentieth century there is the letter by Henry James to Yeats, the unbowdlerized version of Yeats's letter to Ethel Mannin, the full text of T. E. Lawrence's famous dispatch from Arabia describing the destruction of a Turkish train, his letter to Siegfried Sassoon, and the letter to him from E. M. Forster.

Most anthologists end their prefaces by reiterating the pious hope that the reader will be encouraged to seek out the originals. In an anthology such as this, however, there are obvious practical difficulties. Nor is it always advisable that readers seek out editions of Collected Letters. In some cases (Keats, Byron, Dickens) such diligence will pay handsome dividends – but not all. The Collected Letters, for example, of Anthony Trollope (who usually confined himself to business) are only for those interested in the economic consequences of authorship.

My hope is rather that some of the letters collected here will be read and re-read. That I have found letters to gloat over. And that, occasionally, the numinous breaks through.

A Note on the text

The original spelling of the letters printed here has, as far as possible, been preserved. Certain obsolete conventions have, however, been brought into line with modern practice: thus the use of 'v's and 'u's and of 'i's and 'j's has been standardized, 'y^e' expanded into 'the', 'y^t' into 'that', 'xxx *li* given as '£30', 'nacon' (where 'c' is equivalent to the modern 'ti') replaced by 'nation' etc. All superscript letters have been lowered, and contractions silently expanded whenever they threaten to be tiresome. Generally speaking, the principles followed are those set out by G. H. Healey in his edition of Defoe's letters (1955).

One must often be content with a compromise. In the case of Emily Dickinson, for example, the originals of the first three letters by her to be included in this anthology survive, and these preserve her idiosyncratic but expressive punctuation. But the originals of the last two letters have been destroyed, and one has had to rely on nineteenth-century transcripts in which conventional punctuation has been used. In other cases surviving transcripts leave passages or words out and sometimes even an original, such as Byron's letter to Augusta, has been censored. Subject to these limitations, I have tried to print the text of each letter in its original form and in its entirety.

Much of the unpublished material in this anthology is drawn from the manuscript collection of Harry and Brigitte Spiro, who have not only allowed me to use whatever I want, but have put themselves to considerable trouble to make it accessible to me. The Book and Manuscript Department at Sotheby's kindly allowed me a free run of their library and records, and helped me in many other ways. The London Library has, as usual, proved itself invaluable.

I should also like to thank all those who have made suggestions, attempted to answer tiresome queries or helped secure texts, including Mark Amory, Graham Baird, Peter Beal, Robert Booth, Stephen Brook, Gerald Burdon, Asya Chorley, Nest Cleverdon, John Creasey, Jo Currie, Tim d'Arch Smith, Roy Davids, E. E. Duncan-Jones, Stanley

Eaker, Arthur Freeman, Victoria Glendinning, Jeremy Griffiths, Sophie Gurney, Julia Hamilton, Kate Hedworth, Merlin Holland, Catriona Howatson, Hilton Kelliher, John Kelly, the late Sir Geoffrey Keynes, Quentin Keynes, Stephen Keynes, Mary-Jo Kline, Allan Lazarus, Nigel Lewis, Timothy McCann, Roger McGough, John Manners, Michael Mitchell, John and Caroline Montagu, Ann Moore, Bryan Oates, Tom Pocock, Jean Pryor, Alan Rawlings, Stephen Roe, Hinda Rose, Anthony Rota, Edward Saunders, Colin Smythe, Caroline Stroude, Will Sulkin, Terence de Vere White, William and Sarah Ward, Susan Wharton, John Wilson and Joan Winterkorn. The late Richard Ellmann took a kindly interest in my speculations about Henry James, W. B. Yeats, Ophelia, and Constance Wilde; Harold Jenkins in my speculations about the love letters of Hamlet and Mr V.

This book owes its existence to the support of Craig Raine and to Simon Rae who introduced the fledgling to him. John Molony thought up the idea in the first place: so it owes more to him than to anyone.

T.F.M.P.

The Letters
1578–1939

SIR PHILIP SIDNEY to Edmund Molyneux, 31 May 1578

Sir Philip Sidney, 1554–86, poet, politician and soldier; Edmund Molyneux, secretary to his father, Sir Henry Sidney, the Lord Deputy Governor of Ireland.

Mr Mollineax

Few woordes are beste. My lettres to my Father have come to the eys of some. Neither can I condemne any but yow for it. If it be so yow have plaide the very knave with me; and so I will make yow know if I have good proofe of it. But that for so muche as is past. For that is to come, I assure yow before God, that if ever I know yow do so muche as reede any lettre I wryte to my Father, without his commandement, or my consente, I will thruste my Dagger into yow. And truste to it, for I speake it in earnest. In the meane time farwell. From Courte this laste of May 1578.

By me

Philippe Sidney.

SIR RALPH LANE to Sir Philip Sidney, 12 August 1585

Sir Ralph Lane, d.1603, first Governor of Virginia; Sir Philip Sidney, poet, politician and soldier. The Queen had issued Sidney with letters patent authorizing him to discover new land in America and hold 'such and so much quantity of ground as should amount to the number of thirty hundred thousand acres'.

My moost Noble Generalle.

Albeyt in the myddest of infynytt busynesses, As havyng, emungst savvages, the chardge of wylde menn of myne owene natione, Whose unrulynes ys suche as not to gyve leasure to the goovernour to bee all most at eny tyme from them. Neverthelesse I wolde not omytte, to wryte thes fewe lynes of dewety, and affectione unto you; In the which I am to leave you to the letre which I wrotte to your most honorable father in

3

lawe Master Secrettary, touchyng the advertysementes of thys her Majestes newe kingedom of Verginia, and the singularityes thereof, and to advertyese you alltogether (but bryefely) of sume such matter as in our coursse hytherwardes wee have found worthye of your partycpatione: Which in fewe wordes ys thys, that yf her majeste shall at eny tyme finde her selfe burthened with the King of Spayene, wee have by our dwellyng uppon the llande of St Jhon and Hyspagniola for the space of 5, weekes, soo dyscoveredde the forces thereof with the infynytt ryches of the same, As that I find yt an attempt most honorable and fesible, and proffytable, and only fytte for your selfe to bee cheefe commaunder in. Thys entry wolde soo gaulle the king of Spayene, as yt wolde dyverte hys forces that hee troublethe these partes of Chrystendom with, into thos partes where hee canne not gretely annoye us with them. And how gretely a small force woulde garboyelle hym here, when ii of hys most rychest and strongest Ilandes St John, and Hyspagnyola, tooke suche alarmes of us not only landyng but dwellyng upon them with only 120, menn, I referre yt to your Judgement.

To conclude, findynge by myne owene vyewe, hys forces at Lande to bee soo meane, and hys terror made soo grete emongeste us in England, consyderyng that the reputatione thereof dothe alltogeather growe from the mynes of his threasor and the same in places which wee see here are soo easye bothe to bee taken and kepte by eny small force sent by hyr Majeste, I colde not but wryte these ylle fasshyoned lynes unto you, and to exhorte you my Noble Generalle by occasyone not to refuse the good oportunyty of suche a servyce, to the churche of Chryste, of greate releyffe from many callamytyes that thys threasor in Spanyardes handes, dothe inflycte unto the members thereof, veary honorable and proffytable for her majeste and our countrey, and moost commendable and fytte for yourselfe to bee the Enterpryser of: And even soo for thys tyme ceasyng further to trouble you, with my humble commendatyones to my lady your wyffe, I commytt you, my Noble Generalle, to the mercie of the Allmyghty.

From the Porte FerdyNando in Verginia, the 12th of Auguste: 1585

Your poore soldyoure,
and assured at Commandement,

Rafe Lane

SIR PHILIP SIDNEY to Queen Elizabeth I, 10 November 1585

Sir Philip Sidney, 1554–86, poet, politician and soldier; Elizabeth, Queen of England and Ireland. On 16 November 1585 Sidney embarked from Gravesend for the Low Countries, where he was to join the Earl of Leicester in his campaign against the Spanish. He met his death at Zutphen a year later.

Most gratious soverein.

This rude peece of paper shall presume becaws of your Majesties commandement, most humbly to present such a cypher as little leysure coold afoord me. If there come any matter to my knowledg the importance whereof shall deserv to be so masked I will not fail (since yowr pleasure is my onely boldnes) to your own handes to recommend it. In the mean tyme I beseech yowr Majesty will vouchsafe legibly to reed my hart in the cource of my life, and though it self bee but of a mean worth, yet to esteem it lyke a poor hows well sett. I most lowly kis yowr handes and prai to God yowr enemies mai then onely have peace when thei are weery of knowing your force. At Gravesend this 10th of November.

Your Majesties most humble servant

Ph. Sidnei

To the Queenes most
Excellent Majesty

QUEEN ELIZABETH I to the Lady Elizabeth Southwell, 16 October 1598

Elizabeth I, 1533–1603, Queen of England and Ireland; Elizabeth Southwell, Lady-in-Waiting, cousin of the poet and martyr Robert Southwell. Elizabeth Southwell later attended the Queen on her death-bed and wrote a well-known account of the scene.

Your lovinge Soveraine
Elizabeth R

Good Bess. As we could not but be very sory at the dolefull woord brought us of the deceasse of your late husband, in respect of the loss we receave of so good a servant to us; So our knowledge and remembrance of your tender and deere Love ever to him, hath wrought a more feeling in us by participating with you in greefe: which we being desirous & carefull to mitigate in you, wold not but shew the same, by putting you in minde cusin by these affectionate and loving lynes from our self, that Natures common woork being now don in him by the divine providence of the Allmighty, You are first and above all by quiett yerlding to his unresistable ordenance, to call for comfort of him, And then to remember unto you, That besides your good father and mother whom God is pleasid to suffer you to enjoye, You shall be sure of us your gracious Souverain to have a contynuall and loving care of you for your best good. And so good Bess remayne comforted in God and us.

Richmond xvith of October 1598

QUEEN ELIZABETH I to William Shakespeare, undated

Elizabeth I, 1533–1603, Queen of England and Ireland; William Shakespeare, playwright and poet. This letter is an eighteenth-century fake by William Henry Ireland (1777–1835).

Wee didde receive youre prettye Verses goode Masterre William through the hands off oure Lorde Chamberlayne ande wee doe Complemente thee onne theyre greate excellence Wee shalle departe fromme Londonne toe Hamptowne forre the holydayes where wee Shalle expecte thee withe thye beste Actorres thatte thou mayste playe before oureselfe toe amuse usse bee notte slowe butte comme toe usse bye Tuesdaye nexte asse the lorde Leiscesterre wille bee withe usse

Elizabeth R.

Thys Letterre I dydde receyve fromme mye moste gracyouse Ladye Elyzabethe ande I doe requeste itte maye bee kepte withe alle care possyble

Wm Shakspeare

For Master William Shakspeare atte the Globe bye Thames.

RICHARD QUINEY to William Shakespeare, 25 October 1598

Richard Quiney, d. 1602, bailiff of Stratford-upon-Avon; William Shakespeare, playwright and poet. This letter was written while Quiney was on a mission on behalf of Stratford Corporation which was having difficulty meeting its tax liabilities: the money Quiney asks for, however, was for his own use. The letter was never delivered, and passed into the corporation archives on his death.

To my loveinge good ffrend and contreymann Mr. Wm. Shackespere deliver thees

Loveinge contreyman, I am bolde of yow, as of a ffrende, craveinge yowr helpe with £30 uppon Mr. Bushells and my securytee, or Mr. Myttons with me. Mr. Rosswell is nott come to London as yeate, and I have especiall cawse. Yow shall ffrende me muche in helpeing me out of all the debettes I owe in London, I thancke God, & muche quiet my mynde, which wolde nott be indebeted. I am nowe towardes the Courte, in hope of answer for the dispatche of my buysenes. Yow shal nether loase creddytt nor monney by me, the Lorde wyllinge; & nowe but perswade yowrselfe soe, as I hope, & yow shall nott need to feare, butt, with all hartie thanckefullenes, I wyll holde my tyme, & content yowr ffrende, & yf we bargaine farther, yow shal be the paie-master yowrselfe. My tyme biddes me hastene to an ende, & soe I committ thys to yowr care & hope of yowr helpe. I feare I shall nott be backe thys night ffrom the Cowrte. Haste. The Lorde be with yow & with us all, Amen! ffrom the Bell in Carter Lane, the 25 October, 1598.

Yowrs in all kyndenes

Ryc. Quyney

'MR V.' to Mistress Mary Loveringe, [May 1599]

When this letter was first published in the *Daily Mail* on 8 October 1902, a note was with it, which has since disappeared, identifying the sender as 'a Mr V—, a landed proprietor, then residing near South Molton'.

To his lovinge frinde, Mres Mary Loveringe, give this

O my sweete harte the longe absence of your persone hath constraynede me to expresse unto you my deere, the inwarde griefes, the secrete sorrowes, the pinchinge paynes, that my poor appressed harte pitifullye endureth, my tremblinge hand is scarce able to holde the penne neither dare my stammeringe tongue to expresse that which my afflicted harte desireth to manifest unto you

[signature removed]

> Take this girdell sweetehart though [the gift] be small,
> take hart take hand take body and all,
> you have my hart and sha[ll] have ever,
> change when you will but I will never.

HAMLET, PRINCE OF DENMARK, to Ophelia, [summer or autumn 1599]

Hamlet was probably drafted in the summer or autumn of 1599 and put into production at the end of the year.

To the Celestiall, and my Soules Idoll, the most beautified Ophelia.

> Doubt thou, the Starres are fire,
> Doubt, that the Sunne doth move:
> Doubt Truth to be a Lier,
> But never Doubt, I love.

O deere Ophelia, I am ill at these Numbers: I have not Art to reckon my grones; but that I love thee best, oh most Best beleeve it. Adieu.

> Thine evermore most deere Lady, whilst this
> Machine is to him, Hamlet.

JOHN WILLOUGHBY to Humphrey Spurway, 1 June 1600

John Willoughby, 1571–1658, gentleman lawyer; Humphrey Spurway, author of newsletters (the forerunners of newspapers).

Mr. Spurway, comendations remembred, &c. I am bolde to praye (yf your leasure serve) to go unto a widdow woman's howse (her name I know not) at the hether end of Powles Churchyeard; the howse is adjonyng to my Lord Byshopp of London's gate: she doth sell worsted stockings. I praye you to enquire there for her sonne called Frauncis. At my being in London the laste terme, I lefte a payre of worsted stockinges with him to have them new dyed. He promysed me to bring them to you the laste terme, which I perceyve he did not; wherefore I pray you to be earnest with him to have them. From Peyhembury, this fyrst of June, 1600.

I pray you deliver these 2 enclosed letters according to the direction.

Your loving frend.

Jo. Willoughbye.

SIR WALTER RALEGH to his wife Elizabeth, [December 1603]

Sir Walter Ralegh, ?1554–1618, poet, historian, colonist, soldier and courtier; Elizabeth Ralegh, formerly Maid-of-Honour to the Queen. Ralegh had fallen out of favour on James I's accession in 1603 and was sentenced to be executed on 11 December. He was reprieved on 10 December, after having written this letter of farewell to his wife. The sentence was eventually carried out in 1618.

You shall receave, deare wief, my last words in these my last lynes. My love I send you, that you may keepe it when I am dead; and my councell, that you may remember it when I am noe more. I would not, with my last Will, present you with sorrowes, deare Besse. Lett them goe to the grave with me, and be buried in the dust. And, seeing it is not the will of God that ever I shall see you in this lief, beare my destruccion gentlie and with a hart like yourself.

First, I send you all the thanks my hart cann conceive, or my penn

9

expresse, for your many troubles and cares taken for me, which – though they have not taken effect as you wished – yet my debt is to you never the lesse; but pay it I never shall in this world.

Secondlie, I beseich you, for the love you bare me living, that you doe not hide yourself many dayes, but by your travell seeke to helpe your miserable fortunes, and the right of your poore childe. Your mourning cannot avayle me that am but dust.

You shall understand that my lands were conveyed to my child, *bonâ fide*. The wrightings were drawn at Midsummer was twelvemonethes, as divers can wittnesse. My honest cosen Brett can testifie so much, and Dalberie, too, cann remember somewhat therein. And I trust my bloud will quench their mallice that desire my slaughter; and that they will not alsoe seeke to kill you and yours with extreame poverty. To what frind to direct thee I knowe not, for all mine have left mee in the true tyme of triall: and I plainly perceive that my death was determyned from the first day. Most sorry I am (as God knoweth) that, being thus surprised with death, I can leave you noe better estate. I meant you all myne office of wynes, or that I could purchase by selling it; half my stuffe, the jewells, but some few, for my boy. But God hath prevented all my determinations; the great God that worketh all in all. If you can live free from want, care for no more; for the rest is but vanity. Love God, and beginne betymes to repose yourself on Him; therein shall you find true and lastinge ritches, and endles comfort. For the rest, when you have travelled and wearied your thoughts on all sorts of worldly cogitations, you shall sit downe by Sorrow in the end. Teach your sonne alsoe to serve and feare God, while he is young; that the feare of God may grow upp in him. Then will God be a husband unto you, and a father unto him; a husband and a father which can never be taken from you.

Bayly oweth me two hundred pounds, and Adrion six hundred pounds. In Gersey, alsoe, I have much owinge me. The arrearages of the wynes will pay my debts. And, howsoever, for my soul's healthe, I beseech you pay all poore men. When I am gonne, no doubt you shalbe sought unto by many, for the world thinks that I was very ritch; but take heed of the pretences of men and of their affections; for they laste but in honest and worthy men. And no greater misery cann befall you in this life then to become a pray, and after to be despised. I speak it (God knowes) not to disswad you from marriage – for that willbe best for you – both in respect of God and the world. As for me, I am no more your's, nor you myne. Death hath cutt us asunder; and God hath devided me from the world, and you from me.

Remember your poore childe for his father's sake, that comforted you and loved you in his happiest tymes.

Gett those letters (if it bee possible) which I writt to the Lords, wherein I sued for my lief, but God knoweth that itt was for you and yours that I desired it, but itt is true that I disdaine myself for begging itt. And know itt (deare wief) that your sonne is the childe of a true man, and who, in his own respect, despiseth Death, and all his misshapen and ouglie formes.

I cannot wright much. God knowes howe hardlie I stole this tyme, when all sleep; and it is tyme to separate my thoughts from the world. Begg my dead body, which living was denyed you; and either lay itt att Sherborne if the land continue, or in Exiter church, by my father and mother. I can wright noe more. Tyme and Death call me awaye.

The everlasting, infinite powerfull, and inscrutable God, that Almightie God that is goodnes itself, mercy itself, the true lief and light, keep and yours, and have mercy on me, and teach me to forgeve my persecutors and false accusers; and send us to meete in His glorious kingdome. My true wief, farewell. Blesse my poore boye; pray for me. My true God hold you both in His armes.

Written with the dyeing hand of sometyme thy husband, but now (alasse!) overthrowne.

Your's that was; but nowe not my owne,

W. Ralegh.

SIR ROBERT CECIL to Sir Thomas Edmondes, 9 November 1605

Sir Robert Cecil, First Earl of Salisbury, ?1563–1612, Secretary of State to Elizabeth I and James I; Sir Thomas Edmondes, diplomat. The 'moiles' referred to are, of course, mules.

Mr Edmonds,

Hearing of this post his departure, and being loth to send of purpose, I have thoght good to intreate you by this lettre to do me so much courtesy, if possibly you can, to procure me some Spanish gloves of the same perfume which you sent Sir John Stanhop for the Queen. My meaning therin is thus, that you will lern of some person about him or those which went with him to Bruxells whyther any such gloves be to be had there or no. If there be, then I desire that you will write to Bodery to bestow £40 sterling in them, for all the gloves that ever I saw come out of Spaine these ar the most delicate and do the most please the Queen, as I believe Mr Stanhop will shortly write unto you, for she is much pleased that an English man (as she sayth) had the witt to gett any good thing from a French man.

These which you have sent ar of two sorts, and so I desire both black and whyte. I have often seen out of Spaine and Portingall gloves, but they be oyly and ill-favored. If you think that in France any such be to be had, I pray you in any wise provyde me some, whatsoever they cost you, and I will answer it here, where you shall apoint me.

For Gondys offer of moyles, Sir, this I say. If he will procure me to [i.e. two] goodly moiles indead, such as you remember Madame Beauforth had one, a dapple grey, I will furnish him with as faire geldings as wever he had in his lyfe; but I wold be glad to have you carry this matter so as to undermine how he will valew our geldings with his moyles. And thus having made you no waighty dispatch at this time but about these toyes, I will end with this assurance that at your coming home you need not doubt of your desire and therewith I end,

Your loving assured friend,
Ro: Cecyll.

SIR FRANCIS BEAUMONT to Ben Jonson,
undated [?between 1605 and 1613]

Sir Francis Beaumont, 1584–1616, playwright, collaborator with John Fletcher; Ben Jonson, playwright and poet. When first printed in 1640, this verse epistle in praise of the Mermaid Tavern was headed: 'Mr. Francis Beaumonts Letter to Ben Jonson, written before he and Mr. Fletcher came to London with two of the precedent Comedies then not finisht, which deferrd their merry meetings at the Mermaid'.

> The sun which doth the greatest comfort bring
> To absent friends, because the self-same thing
> They know they see however absent, is
> Here our best Hay-maker (forgive me this,

It is our Countreys style). In this warme shine,
I lie and dreame of your full Mermaid wine.
Oh we have water mixt with Claret Lees,
Drinke apt to bring in dryer heresies
Than beere, good only for the Sonnets strain,
With fustian metaphors to stuffe the brain,
So mixt, that given to the thirstiest one,
'Twill not prove almes, unlesse he have the stone:
I thinke with one draught mans invention fades,
Two Cups had quite spoil'd Homers *Illiads*;
'Tis Liquor that will find out Sutcliffs wit,
Lie where he will, and make him write worse yet;
Fill'd with such moisture in most grievous qualmes,
Did Robert Wisdome write his singing Psalmes;
And so must I doe this, and yet I thinke
It is a potion sent us down to drink
By special Providence, keeps us from fights,
Makes us not laugh, when we make legs to Knights.
'Tis this that keeps our minds fit for our States,
A Medicine to obey our Magistrates:
For we do live more free than you, no hate,
No envy at one anothers *happy* State
Moves us, we are all equal every whit:
Of Land that God gives men here is their wit,
If we consider fully: for our best
And gravest man will, with his main house jest,
Scarce please you; we want subtilty to do
The Citie tricks, lie, hate, and flatter too:
Here are none that can bear a painted show,
Strike when you winch, and then lament the blow:
Who like Mills set the right way for to grind,
Can make their gaines alike with every wind:
Only some fellows with the subtil'st pate
Amongst us, may perchance æquivocate
At selling of a Horse, and that's the most.
Methinks the little wit I had is lost
Since I saw you, for wit is like a rest
Held up at Tennis, which men doe the best,
With the best gamesters: What things have we seen,
Done at the Mermaid! heard words that have been

13

So nimble, and so full of subtill flame,
As if that every one from whence they came,
Had meant to put his whole wit in a jest,
And had resolv'd to live a foole, the rest
Of his dull life; then when there hath been throwne
Wit able enough to justifie the Towne
For three dayes past, wit that might warrant be
For the whole City to talk foolishly
Till that were cancel'd, and when that was gone,
We left an aire behind us, which alone,
Was able to make the two next companies
Right witty; though but downright fools, more wise.
When I remember this, and see that now
The Country gentelman begin to allow
My wit for dry bobs, then I needs must cry,
I see my days of ballating grow nigh;
I can already riddle, and can sing
Catches, sell bargains, and I feare shall bring
My self to speak the hardest words I find,
Over as oft as any, with one wind,
That takes no medicines: But one thought of thee
Makes me remember all these things to be
The wit of our young men, fellows that show
No part of good, yet utter all they know:
Who like trees of the Guard, have growing soules.
Only strong destiny, which all controules,
I hope hath left a better fate in store,
For me thy friend, than to live ever poor,
Banisht unto this home; fate once againe
Bring me to thee, who canst make smooth and plain
The way of Knowledge for me, and then I,
Who have no good but in thy company,
Protest it will my greatest comfort be
To acknowledge all I have to flow from thee.
Ben, when these Scænes are perfect, we'll taste wine;
I'll drink thy Muses health, thou shalt quaff mine.

JOHN DONNE to Sir Henry Goodyer, [c. 1609]

John Donne, 1572–1631, poet, Dean of St Paul's; Sir Henry Goodyer, literary patron. The identity of the recipient of this letter is not certain.

Sir

I write not to you out of my poor Library, where to cast mine eye upon good Authors kindles or refreshes sometimes meditations not unfit to communicate to near friends; nor from the high way, where I am contracted, and inverted into my self; which are my two ordinary forges of Letters to you. But I write from the fire side in my Parler, and in the noise of three gamesome children; and by the side of her, whom because I have transplanted into a wretched fortune, I must labour to disguise that from her by all such honest devices, as giving her my company, and discourse, therefore I steal from her, all the time which I give this Letter, and it is therefore that I take so short a list, and gallop so fast over it; I have not been out of my house since I received your pacquet. As I have much quenched my senses, and disused my body from pleasure, and so tried how I can indure to be mine own grave, so I try now how I can suffer a prison. And since it is but to build one wall more about our soul, she is still in her own Center, how many circumferences soever fortune or our own perversnesse cast about her. I would I could as well intreat her to go out, as she knows wither to go. But if I melt into a melancholy whilest I write, I shall be taken in the manner: and I sit by one too tender towards these impressions, and it is so much our duty, to avoid all occasions of giving them sad apprehensions, as S. Hierome accuses Adam of no other fault in eating the Apple, but that he did it *Ne contristaretur delicias suas*. I am not carefull what I write, because the inclosed Letters may dignifie this ill-favoured bark, and they need not grudge so coarse a countenance, because they are now to accompany themselves, my man fetched them, and therefore I can say no more of them than themselves say. Mistress Meauly intreated me by her Letter to hasten hers; as I think, for by my troth I cannot read it. My Lady was dispatching in so much haste for Twicknam, as she gave no word to a Letter which I sent with yours; of Sir Tho. Bartlet, I can say nothing, nor of the plague, though your Letter bid me: but that he diminishes, the other increases, but in what proportion I am not clear. To them at Hammersmith, and Mistress Herbert I will do your command. If I have been good in hope, or can promise any little offices in the future probably, it is comfortable, for I am the worst present man in the world; yet the instant, though it be nothing, joynes times together, and therefore this unprofitableness, since I have been, and will still indevour to be so, shall not interrupt me now from being

Your servant and lover
J. Donne.

NATHAN FIELD AND OTHERS to Philip Henslowe, [early July 1613]

Nathan Field, 1587–1619/20, Robert Daborne, d. 1628, Philip Massinger, 1583–1640, playwrights; Philip Henslowe, landlord and financier of the Fortune Theatre. An endorsement on the letter shows that £5 was sent to Daborne as requested.

Mr Hinchlow

you understand our unfortunate extremitie, and I doe not thincke you so void of christianitie, but that you would throw so much money into the Thames as wee request now of you; rather then endanger so many innocent lives; you know there is £10 more at least to be receaved of you, for the play, wee desire you to lend us £5 of that, which shall be allowed to you without which wee cannot be bayled, nor I play any more till this be dispatch'd, it will loose you, £20 ere the end of the next weeke, beside the hinderance of the next new play, pray Sir Consider our Cases with humanitie, and now give us cause to acknowledge you our true freind in time of neede; wee have entreated Mr Davison to deliver this note, as well to wittnesse your love, as our promises, and allwayes acknowledgment to be ever

your most thanckfull; and loving freinds,
Nat: Field

The money shall be abated out of the mony remayns for the play of mr Fletcher & owrs
Rob: Daborne

I have ever founde yow a true lovinge freinde to mee & in soe small a suite it beeinge honest I hope yow will not faile us. Philip Massinger

JOHN DONNE to Sir H[?enry Goodyer], 4 October 1622

John Donne, 1572–1631, poet, Dean of St Paul's; Sir Henry Goodyer, literary patron.

Octob. the 4th 1622. almost at midnight.

Sir,

All our moralities are but our outworks, our Christianity is our Citadel; a man who considers duty but the dignity of his being a man, is not easily beat from his outworks, but from his Christianity never; and therefore I dare trust you, who contemplates them both. Every distemper of the body now, is complicated with the spleen, and when we were young men we scarce ever heard of the spleen. In our declinations now, every accident is accompanied with heavy clouds of melancholy; and in our youth we never admitted any. It is the spleen of the minde, and we are affected with vapors from thence; yet truly, even this sadnesse that overtakes us, and this yeelding to the sadnesse, is not so vehement a poison (though it be no Physick neither) as those false waies, in which we sought our comforts in our looser daies. You are able to make rules to your self, and our B. Saviour continue to you an ability to keep within those rules. And this particular occasion of your present sadnesse must be helped by the rule, for, examples you will scarce finde any, scarce any that is not encombred and distressed in his fortunes. I had locked my self, sealed and secured my self against all possibilities of falling into new debts, and in good faith, this year hath thrown me £400 lower than when I entred this house. I am a Father as well as you, and of children (I humbly thank God) of as good dispositions; and in saying so, I make account that I have taken my comparison as high as I could goe; for in good faith, I beleeve yours to be so: but as those my daughters (who are capable of such considerations) cannot but see my desire to accommodate them in this world, so I think they will not murmure if heaven must be their Nunnery, and they associated to the B. virgins there: I know they would be content to passe their lives in a Prison, rather than I should macerate my self for them, much more to suffer the mediocrity of my house, and my means, though that cannot preferre them: yours are such too, and it need not that patience, for your fortune doth not so farre exercise their patience. But to leave all in Gods hands, from whose hands nothing can be wrung by whining but by praying, nor by praying without the *Fiat voluntas tua.* Sir, you are used to my hand, and, I think have leisure to spend some time in picking out sense, in ragges; else I had written lesse, and in longer time. Here is room for an *Amen*; the prayer – so I am going to my bedside to make for all you and all yours, with

Your true friend and servant in Christ Jesus

J. Donne.

THE DUKE OF BUCKINGHAM to James I, 25 April 1623

George Villiers, First Duke of Buckingham, 1592–1628, favourite of James; James I, King of England and Ireland, James VI of Scotland. Buckingham had gone to Spain with Prince Charles (later Charles I) to seek for him the hand of Princess Maria of Spain. Their mission was unsuccessful.

Dere dad, gossope, and steward,

Though your babie him selfe hath sent word what neede he hath of more jewells, yeet will I by this berer, who can make more speede then Carlile, againe acquaint your majestie therewith and give my poure and sausie opinion what will be fittest more to send. Hetherto you have bine so spareing that, whereas you thought to have sent him suffitientlie for his one wareing, to present his mistris, who I ame sure shall shortlie now louse that title, and to lend me, that I to the contrarie have bine forsed to lend him. You neede not aske who made me able to doe it. Sir, he hath neyther chaine nor hattband, and I beseech you consider first how rich they are in jewells here, then in what a poure equipage he came in, how he hath no other meanes to appere like a kings sonne, how they are usefullests at such a time as this, when they may doe your selfe, your sone and the nation honor, and lastlie how it will neyther caust nor hasard you anie thinge. These resons I hope, since you have ventured allredie your cheefest jewell, your sonne, will serve to perswade you to lett louse theese more after him, first your best hattband, the Portingall dimond, the rest of the pendant dimonds to make up a necles to give his mistris, and the best rope of perle, with a rich chaine or tow for him selfe to waire, or els your doge must want a coller, which is the redie way to put him into it. There are manie other jewells which are of so meane qualitie as they deserve not that name, but will save much in your purs and serve verie well for presents. They had never so good and great an occation to take the aire out of there boxses as at this time. God knowes when they shall have such another, and they had neede some times to gett nerer the sonne to continue them in their perfection. Here give me leave humbly on my knees to give your majestie thankes for that rich jewell you sent me in a box by my lord Vahan; and give him leave to kiss your hands from me, who tooke the paines to draw it. My reward to him is this: he spent his time well, which is the thinge wee should all most desier and is the glorie I covett most here in your service, which sweet Jesus grant me and your blessing.

Your majestie's most humble slave
and doge,

Steenie.

Madrill, the 25 of April 1623.

Sir,

 Foure asses I have sent you, tow hees and tow shees, five cameles, too hees, tow shees, with a yong one, and one ellefant, which is worth your seeing. Thees I have impudentlie beged for you. There is a Barbarie hors comes with them, I thinke, from Watt Aston. My lord Bristow sayeth he will send you more camills. When wee come oure selves, wee will bringe you horses and asses anoughe. If I may know whether you desier mules or not, I will bringe them, or dere of this cuntrie eyther, and I will lay waite for all the rare coler burds that can be hard of. But if you doe not send your babie jewells eneugh, Ile stope all other presents. Therefore louke to it.

EDMUND WALLER to Lady Lucy Sidney, July 1639

Edmund Waller, 1606–87, poet; Lady Lucy Sidney, daughter of Lord Leicester. Lucy was the sister of Lady Dorothy Sidney, courted by Waller as 'Saccherissa' in his poems. Waller's courtship was in vain, and Lady Dorothy married Henry, Lord Spencer on 20 July 1639. Penshurst Place is the Sidney family seat.

Madam,

 In this Common Joy at Penshurst I know none to whom Complaints may come less unseasonable than to your Ladyship, the Loss of a Bed-fellow being almost equal to that of a Mistress; and therefore you ought at least to pardon, if you consent not to the Imprecations of the Deserted, which just Heaven no doubt will hear.

May my Lady Dorothy, if we may yet call her so, suffer as much, and have the like Passion for this young Lord, whom she has preferr'd to the rest of Mankind, as others have had for her; and may this Love, before the Year go about, make her taste of the first Curse impos'd on Womankind, the Pains of becoming a Mother. May her first-born be none of her own Sex, nor so like her, but that he may resemble her Lord as much as her self.

May she that always affected Silence and Retiredness, have the House fill'd with the Noise and Number of her Children, and hereafter of her Grand-Children, and then may she arrive at that great Curse so much declin'd by fair Ladies, Old Age: May she live to be very old, and yet seem young, be told so by her Glass, and have no Aches to inform her of the Truth: And when she shall appear to be mortal, may her Lord not mourn for her, but go Hand in Hand with her to that Place, where we are told there is neither marrying nor giving in Marriage, that being there divorced, we may all have an equal Interest in her again. My Revenge being immortal, I wish all this may also befall their Posterity to the World's End, and afterwards.

To you, Madam, I wish all good things, and that this Loss may in good Time be happily supplyed with a more constant Bed-fellow of the other Sex.

Madam, I humbly kiss your Hands, and beg Pardon for this Trouble, from

Your Ladyship's most humble Servant,

E. Waller.

OLIVER CROMWELL to the Speaker of the House of Commons, 14 June 1645

Oliver Cromwell, 1599–1658, Parliamentary general, later Lord Protector; William Lenthall, Speaker of the House of Commons. The King had been defeated at Naseby, near Market Harborough, by the Parliamentary forces under Sir Thomas Fairfax, Cromwell himself commanding the right wing. This letter was written from Market Harborough on the day of the battle.

Sir,

Beinge commanded by you to this service, I thinke my selfe bound to acquaint you with the good hand of God towards you and us.

Wee marched yesterday after the Kinge, whoe went before us from Daventree to Haverbrowe, and quartered about six miles from him. This day wee marched towards him. Hee drew out to meet us; both Armies engaged; wee after 3 howers fight, very doubtful, att last routed his Armie, killed and tooke about 5000, very many officers, but of what quallitye wee yett know not. Wee tooke alsoe about 200 carrages, all hee had, and all his gunns, beinge 12 in number, wherof 2 were demmie cannon, 2 demmie culveringes, and (I thinke) the rest sacers. Wee persued the enimie from three miles short of Haverbro to nine beyond, even to sight of Leicester, whether the Kinge fled. Sir, this is non other but the hand of God, and to him aloane belongs the Glorie, wherin non are to share with him. The Generall served you with all fayethfullnesse and honor, and the best commendations I can give him is that I dare say Hee attributes all to God, and would rather perish then assume to him selfe, which is an honest and a thrivinge way, and yett as much for bravery may bee given to him in this action as to a man. Honest men served you faythfully in this action. Sir, they are trustye; I beseech you in the name of God not to discorage them. I wish this action may begett thankfullnesse and humilitye in all that are concerned in itt. Hee that venters his life for the libertye of his cuntrie, I wish Hee trust God for the libertye of his conscience and you for the libertye Hee fights for. In this Hee rests whoe is

Your most humble servant,
Oliver Cromwell.

June 14th, 1645.
Haverbrowe.

CHARLES I to Prince Rupert, 14 September 1645

Charles I, 1600–49, King of Great Britain and Ireland; Prince Rupert, his nephew and Commander-in-Chief of his forces during the Civil War. Fairfax had stormed Bristol on 10 September, and its surrender by Rupert put paid to Royalist hopes in the south of England. Charles held him personally responsible and revoked all his commissions.

Hereford 14: Sep. 1645

Nepueu/though the losse of Bristol be a great blow to me, yet your surrendering it as you did, is of so much Affliction to me, that it makes me forget, not only, the consideration of that place, but is lykewais the greatest tryall of my constancy that hath yet befalen me; for, what is to be done? after one, that is so neer me as you ar, both in Blood & Frendship, submits himselfe to so meane an Action (I give it the easiest Terme) such; I have so much to say, that I will say no more of it; only, least rasheness of Judgement be layed to my Charge, I must remember you of your letter of the 12: of Aug: wheby you asseured me, (that if no Muteny hapned) you would keepe Bristol for fower Monthes; did you keepe it fower Dayes? was there anything lyke a Muteny? more Questions might be asked but now, I confesse, to litle purpose: my Conclusion is, to desyre you to seeke your subsistance (untill it shall please God to determine of my Condition) somewhere beyond Sease, to which end, I send you heere-with a Passe, & I pray God to make you sencible, of your present Condition, & give you meanes, to redime what you have lost; for I shall have no greater Joy in a Victory, then a just occasion, without blushing, to asseure you of my being

Your loving Oncle & most faithfull frend
Charles R

GERRARD WINSTANLEY to Lord Fairfax and the Army Council, 8 December 1649

Gerrard Winstanley, *c.* 1609–76, radical pamphleteer and leader of the Diggers or True Levellers; Thomas, Lord Fairfax, Commander-in-Chief of the Army. The Diggers were one of a number of radical sects that sprang up during the period after the execution of Charles I in 1649. Winstanley and his fellows had, as an expression of their communistic beliefs, started digging and planting crops on St George's Hill, Surrey. For this they were brought before the Court at Kingston for infringing the rights of Mr Drake, Lord of the Manor; Winstanley was ordered to pay £11 9s. 1d. as a fine with costs, and his four cows were seized.

Sir,

I understand that Mr. Parson Platt with some other Gentlemen, have made report to you, and the Councell of State, that wee that are called

Diggers are a riotous people, and that wee will not bee ruled by the Justices, and that wee hold a mans house by violence from him, and that wee have 4 guns in it, to secure ourselves, and that wee are drunkards, and Cavaleers waiteing an opportunity to helpe to bringe in the Prince, and such like.

Truely Sir, these are all untrue reports, and as false as those which Haman of old raised against sincere harted Mordecay to incense Kinge Ahasuerus against him. The conversation of the diggers is not such as they report, wee are peaceable men, and walke in the light of righteousness to the utmost of our power. Our enemies have sent divers tymes to beate us, and to pull downe our houses, yet wee never gave them bad language, nor resisted againe, but tooke all their abuses patiently, waiteing upon God till hee make their harts quiett, that wee may live in peace by them; but truely the same things which they falsely report of us, wee and all the people round about us, can and would prove to their faces, if yow should call us face to face, some of them were alwayes Cavaleers, and had a hand in the Kentish riseing, and were cheife promoters of the offensive Surry petition; but wee doe not speake this to ripp up old quarrells, neither doe I desire to mention their names, least yow should thinke wee were enemies; for truely it is our desire to conquer them with love, though they much abuse us that have always bin your freinds, as the enemy themselves, if they were face to face, can say not otherwise.

Now Sir, the end of our digging and ploughing upon the common land is this, that wee and all the impoverisht poore in the land may gett a comfortable livelyhood by our righteous labours thereupon; which wee conceive wee have a true right unto, (I speake in the name of all the poore commoners) by vertue of the conquest over the King, for while hee was in power hee was the successour of William the Conquerour, and held the land as a conquerour from us, and all Lords of Mannours held tytle to the common lands from him; but seeing the common people of England by joynt consent of person and purse, have caste out Charles our Norman oppressour, wee have by this victory recovered ourselves from under his Norman yoake, and the land now is to returne into the joynt hands of those who have conquered, that is the commonours, and the land is to bee held noe longer from the use of them by the hand of anye whose those will uphold the Norman and kingly power still; and if soe, then wee that are impoverished by sticking to the Parliament and you, shall loose the benefitt of all our taxes, free quarter, and blood, and remayne slaves still to the kingly power in the hands of Lords of Mannours, which wee have cast out of the hands of Charles.

Therefore wee poore opporessed Commoners claime freedome in the common land, by virtue of the Parliaments promises and ingagement, and of the armies actinge; for wee did beleive and rely thereupon, being as wee conceive it a firme bargaine betweene you and us; for you and the Parliament in effect said to us, 'Give us your taxes, free quarter, excise, and adventure your lives with us to cast out the oppressour Charles, and wee will make yow a free people', therefore by the law of contract as wee expected was firmly made and confirmed on our part by performance, wee claime this freedom to enjoy the common land for our livelihood, for wee have bought it by our bloud and money.

Secondly, wee claime this freedome by equality in the conquest over the Kinge, for the Parliament told us what they did they did it for the safety and peace of the whole nation, the army told us they fought not for themselves, but for the safety and peace of the whole Nation, and yow and wee joyned our forces togeather to procure our freedome, and have obteyned it; therefore if there bee a spoyle of the common land to be gathered, as there is, it is to bee equally devided betweene yow that went to warr, and wee that stay'd at home and paid you, that is, as the Gentry have their inclosure free to themselves, soe wee the poore impoverisht commoners claime freedome in the common land by vertue of this conquest over the Kinge, which is gotten by our joynt consent.

Thirdly, wee know that England cannott bee a free Commonwealth, unless all the poore commoners have a free use and benefitt of the land; for if this freedome bee not granted, wee that are the poore commoners are in a worse case then we were in the King's dayes, for then wee had some estate about us, though wee were under oppression, but now our estates are spent to purchase freedome, and wee are under oppression still of Lords of Mannours tyranny; therefore unless wee that are poore commoners have some part of the land to live upon freely, as well as the Gentry it cannott bee a common wealth, neither can the kingly power bee removed soe longe as this kingly power in the hands of Lords of Mannours rules over us.

Now Sir, if you and the Counsell will quietly grant us this freedome, which is our owne right, and sett us free from the kingly power of Lords of Mannours, that violently now as in the Kings dayes holde the commons from us, (as if wee had obteyned noe conquest at all over the kingly power), then the poore that ly under the great burden of poverty, and are alwayes complayning for want, and their miseries increased because they see noe meanes of releife found out, and therefore cry out continually to you and the Parliament for releife and to make good your promises, wilbe quietted.

Wee desire noe more of yow then freedome to worke, and to enjoy the benefitt of our labours – for here is wast land enough and to spare to supply all our wants – but if yow deny this freedome, then in righteousness wee must raise collections for the poore out of the estates, and a mass of money will not supply their wants; because many are in want that are ashamed to take collection money, and therefore they are desperate, and will rather robb and steale, and disturb the land, and others that are ashamed to beg would doe any worke for to live, as it is the case of many of our diggers that have bin good housekeepers; but if this freedome were granted to improve the common lands then there would bee a supply to answer every ones inquire, and the murmurings of the people against yow and the Parliament would cease, and within a few yeares wee should have noe beggers nor idle persons in the land.

Secondly, hereby England would bee enriched with all commodity with in it selfe which they each would afford; and truely this is a stayne to Christian religion in England, that wee have soe much land ly wast, and soe many starve for want; and further, if this freedome bee granted, the whole land wilbee united in love and strength, that if a forraigne enemy like an army of ratts and mice come to take our inheritance from us, wee shall all rise as one man to defend it.

Then lastly, if yow will grant the poore comoners this quiett freedome to improve the common land for our livelyhood, wee shall rejoyce in yow and the army in protecting our worke, and wee and our worke wilbee ready to secure that, and wee hope there will not bee any kingly power over us, to rule at will and wee to bee slaves, as the power has bin, but that you will rule in love as Moses and Joshua did the Children of Israell before any kingly power came in, and that the Parliament wilbe as the Elders of Israell, chosen freely by the people to advise for and assist both yow and us.

And thus in the name of the rest of these called Diggers and Commonours through the land, I have in short declared our mynde and cause to you in the light of righteousness, which will prove all these reports made against us to bee false and distructive to the uniteing of England into peace.

Per me Gerrard Winstanley for my selfe and in the behalfe of my fellow Commoners.

December the 8th,
     1649.

DOROTHY OSBORNE to Sir William Temple, [5 or 6 March 1653]

Dorothy Osborne, 1627–95; Sir William Temple, diplomat. This is one of the famous series of letters written by Dorothy Osborne to Sir William Temple before their marriage.

Sir

Your last letter came like a pardon to one upon the block. I had given over hopes on't, haveing received my letters by the other Carrier, whoe uses alway's to bee last. The losse put mee hugely out of order, and you would both have pittyed and laught at mee, if you could have seen how woddenly I entertain'd the widdow whoe came hither the day before, and surprised mee very much. Not being able to say any thing, I gott her to Card's, and there with a great deal of Patience lost my Mony to her, or rather I gave it as my Ransome. In the middest of our Play in comes my blessed Boy with your letter, and in Earnest I was not able to disguise the Joy it gave mee, though one was by that is not much your freind, and took notice of a blush that for my life I could not keep back. I putt up the letter in my Pockett, and made what hast I could to loose the mony I had left, that I might take occasion to goe fetch some more, but I did not make such hast back againe I can assure you, I tooke time enough to have Coyned my self some mony if I had had the Art on't, and left my Brother enough to make all his addresses to her, if hee were soe disposed. I know not whither he was pleased or not, but I am sure I was.

You make soe reasonable demandes, that 'tis not fitt you should bee deny'd, you aske my thought's but at one hower. You will think me bountifull I hope, when I shall tell you, that I know noe hower when you have them not. Noe, in Earnest my very dream's are yours, and I have

26

gott such a habitt of thinking of You, that any other thought intrudes and grow's uneasy to mee. I drink your health every morning in a drench that would Poyson a horse I beleeve, and 'tis the only way I have to perswade my self to take it, 'tis the infusion of steell, and makes mee soe horridly sick that every day at ten a clock I am makeing my will, and takeing leave of all my friend's, you will beleeve you are not forgot then. They tell mee I must take this ugly drink a fortnight, and then begin another as Bad, but unlesse you say soe too I do not thinke I shall, 'tis worse then dyeing, by the halfe.

I am glad your father is soe kinde to you, I shall not dispute it with him because 'tis much more in his power then in myne, but I shall never yeeld that tis more in his desyr's. Sure hee was much pleased with that which was a truth when you told it him but would have bin none if hee had asked the question sooner, hee thought there was noe danger of you since you were more ignorant and lesse concern'd in my being in Towne then hee; if I were Mrs Cl: hee would bee more my friend but howsoever I am much his Servant as hee is your father.

I have sent you your booke, and since you are at Leasure to consider the moone you may bee enough to reade Cleopatra, therefore I have sent you three Tomes. When you have done with those you shall have the rest, and I beleeve they will please, there is a story of Artemise that I will recomende to you, her disposition I like extreamly, it has a great deal of Gratitude int, and if you meet with one Brittomart pray send mee word how you like him.

I am not displeased that my Lord makes noe more hast for though I am very willing you should goe the Journy for many reason's, yet two or three months hence sure will bee soone enough to visett soe cold a Country and I would not have you indure two winters in one year, besydes I looke for my Eldest brother and my Cousen Molle heer shortly and I should bee glad to have noe body to entertaine but you, whilest you are heer, Lord that you had the invisible Ring, or Fortunatas his Wisheing hatt, now, at this instante you should bee heer. My Brother is gon to wayte upon the widdow homeward's, She that was borne to persecute you and I, I think. She has soe tyred mee with being heer (but two days) that I doe not think I shall accept of the offer she has made mee of liveing with her in case my Father dy's before I have disposed of my self, yet wee are very great, and for my comfort she say's she will come againe about the latter ende of June, and stay longer with mee.

My Aunt is still in Towne, kept by her buisnesse which I am affrayde will not goe well, they doe soe delay it, and my pretious Uncle do's soe visett her, and is soe kinde that without doubt some Mischeife will follow. Doe you know his sonne my Cousen Harry, tis a handsome youth, and well natured but such a goose, and hee has bred him soe strangly, that hee needs all his ten thousand pound a yeer. I would faine have him marry my Lady Diana, she was his Mistresse when hee was a boy. Hee had more witt then, then hee has now I think, and I have lesse witt then hee sure for spending my paper upon when I have soe litle. Heer is hardly Roome for Your affectionate freind and Servant

JOHN DRYDEN to Honor Dryden, [May 1653 or 1655]

John Dryden, 1631–1700, poet, critic and playwright; Honor Dryden, his cousin.

Madame,

If you have received the lines I sent by the reverend Levite, I doubt not but they have exceedingly wrought upon you; for beeing so longe in a Clergymans pocket, assuredly they have acquired more Sanctity then theire Author meant them. Alasse Madame, for ought I know they may become a Sermon ere they could arrive at you; and believe it having you for the text it could scarcely proove bad, if it light upon one that could handle it indifferently. But I am so miserable a preacher that though I have so sweet and copious a subject, I still fall short in my expressions And instead of an use of thanksgiveing I am allways makeing one of comfort, that I may one day againe have the happinesse to kisse your faire hand. but that is a message I would not so willingly do by letter as by word of mouth. This is a point I must confesse I could willingly dwell longer on, and in this case what ever I say you may confidently take for gospell. But I must hasten. And indeed Madame (Beloved I had almost sayd) hee had need hasten who treats of you; for to speake fully to evry part of your excellencyes requires a longer houre then most persons have allotted them. But in a word your selfe hath been the best Expositor upon the text of your own worth, in that admirable Comment you wrote upon it, I meane your incomparable letter. By all thats good (and you Madame are a great part of my Oath) it hath put me so farre besides my selfe that I have scarce patience to write prose: my pen is stealing into verse every time I kisse your letter. I am sure the poore paper smarts for my Idolatry, which by wearing it continually neere my brest will at last bee burnt and martyrd in those flames of adoration it hath kindled in mee. But I forgett Madame what rarityes your letter came fraught with besides words; You are such a Deity that commands worship by provideing the Sacrifice: you are pleasd Madame to force mee to write by sending me Materialls, and compell mee to my greatest happinesse. Yet though I highly vallue your Magnificent presents, pardon mee if I must tell the world they are but imperfect Emblemes of your beauty; For the white and red of waxe and paper are but shaddowes of that vermillion and snowe in your lips and forehead. And the silver of the Inkhorne if it presume to vye whiteness with your purer Skinne, must confesse it selfe blacker than the liquor it containes. What then do I more than retrieve your own guifts? and present you that paper adulterated with blotts which you gave spotlesse?

> For since t'was mine the white hath lost its hiew
> To show t'was n'ere it selfe but whilst in you;
> The Virgin Waxe hath blusht it selfe to red
> Since it with mee hath lost its Maydenhead.
> You (fairest Nymph) are waxe; oh may you bee
> As well in softnesse so as purity;
> Till Fate and your own happy choise reveale
> Whom you so farre shall blesse to make you seale.

Fairest Valentine the unfeigned wishe of your humble votary,

Jo: Dryden.

Cambridge
May the
To the faire hands
of Madame Honor Dryden
these crave admittance

LORD CHESTERFIELD to an unknown correspondent, December 1656

Philip Stanhope, second Earl of Chesterfield, 1633–1713, politician, patron of Dryden. This letter is taken from the letterbook in which Chesterfield kept copies of his outgoing and incoming correspondence.

Bretby Decm: 1656

Sir:

I would sooner have returned you my most humble thanks for your last favour, had I not been tormented with such a cold as I think is attended with a Legion of Devils, I mean, head:ake, touthake, coff, and defluction in my Eyes &c which makes me often wish, that there were some body now as there was formerly, that could send them all into a herd of Swine. Seriously, I am not only obliged to keep my chamber, but to be the most part of the day up on my bed, and therefore I know you will not expect a long letter at this time from

Sir:
Your most humble servant

BARBARA VILLIERS AND LADY ANN HAMBLETON to Lord Chesterfield, 1657

Barbara Villiers, 1641–1709, later Countess of Castlemaine and Duchess of Cleveland, mistress to Charles II; Philip Stanhope, second Earl of Chesterfield, politician.

My Lord

My freind and I are now a bed to gether a contriving how to have your company this after noune. If you deserve this favour, you will come and seek us at Ludgate hill a bout three a clock at Butlers shop, where wee will expect you, but least wee should give you to much satisfaction at once, wee will say no more, expect the rest when you see

Your &c

JEREMY TAYLOR to John Evelyn, 17 February 1658

Jeremy Taylor, 1613–67, Bishop, author of *Holy Living* and *Holy Dying*; John
Evelyn, diarist and virtuoso. Evelyn's son Richard, who was five years and three
days old when he died on 27 January 1658, was a child of extraordinary precocity.
According to Evelyn's diary he could read English, Latin and French when only
two and a half.

Deare Sir,

If dividing & sharing greifes were like the cutting of rivers, I dare say to
you, you would find your streame much abated; for I account my selfe to
have a great cause of sorrow not onely in the diminution of the numbers
of your joyes & hopes, but in the losse of that pretty person, your
strangely hopeful boy. I cannot tell all my owne sorrowes without adding
to yours; & the causes of my real sadnesse in your losse are so just and so
reasonable, that I can no otherwise comfort you but by telling you, that
you have very great cause to mourne: So certaine it is that greife does
propagate as fire does. You have enkindled my funeral torch, & by
joyning mine to yours, I doe but encrease the flame. *Hoc me malè urit*, is
the best signification of my apprehension of your sad story. But, Sir, I
cannot choose but I must hold another & a brighter flame to you – it is
already burning in your breast; & if I can but remoove the dark side of
the lanthorne, you have enough within you to warme yourselfe, & to
shine to others. Remember, Sir, your two boyes are two bright starres, &
their innocence is secur'd, & you shall never heare evil of them agayne.
Their state is safe, & heaven is given to them upon very easy termes;
nothing but to be borne and die. It will cost you more trouble to get
where they are; and amongst other things one of the hardnesses will be,
that you must overcome even this just and reasonable greife; and indeed,
though the greife hath but too reasonable a cause, yet it is much more
reasonable that you master it. For besides that they are no loosers, but
you are the person that complaines, doe but consider what you would
have suffer'd for their interest; you have suffer'd them to goe from you,
to be great Princes in a strange country; and if you can be content to
suffer your owne inconvenience for their interest, you command your
worthiest love, the question of mourning is at an end. But you have said
and done well, when you looke upon it as a rod of God; and He that so
smites here, will spare hereafter; & if you by patience & submission
imprint the discipline upon your owne flesh, you kill the cause, & make

31

the effect very tolerable; because it is in some sense chosen, & therefore in no sense unsufferable. Sir, if you doe not looke to it, time will snatch your honour from you, & reproach you for not effecting that by Christian philosophy which time will doe alone. And if you consider that of the bravest men in the world, we find the seldomest stories of their children, & the Apostles had none, & thousands of the worthiest persons that sound most in story died childlesse; you will find that is a rare act of Providence so to impose upon worthy men a necessity of perpetuating their names by worthy actions & discourses, governments, & reasoning. – If the breach be never repair'd it is because God does not see it fitt to be; and if you will be of his mind it will be much the better. But, Sir, if you will pardon my zeale and passion for your comfort, I will readily confesse that you have no need of any discourse from me to comfort you. Sir, now you have an opportunity of serving God by passive graces; strive to be an example & a comfort to your lady, & by your wise counsel & comfort stand in the breaches of your owne family, and make it appeare that you are more to her than ten sons. Sir, by the assistance of Almighty God, I purpose to wait on you some time next weeke, that I may be a witnesse of your Christian courage and bravery; & that I may see that God never displeases you as long as the maine stake is preserv'd, I meane your hopes & confidences of heaven. Sir, I shal pray for all that you can want, that is, some degrees of comfort & a present mind; and shal alwayes doe you honour, & faine also would doe you service, if it were in the power, as it is in the affections & desires of,

Deare Sir,
Your most affectionate & obliged
freind & servant,
Jer. Taylor.

Feb. 17, 1657–8.

LORD WINDSOR to Lord Hatton, [October 1658]

Thomas Windsor, seventh Baron Windsor, ?1627–87, Royalist; Christopher Hatton, first Viscount Hatton, Royalist. Oliver Cromwell, the Lord Protector, had died on 3 September 1658 and was buried on 22 October; he was succeeded by his son Richard.

Dear Kitt,

I thought you would have been in the country before this time, and therefore did not wright untell Charles Lytleton assured mee you were in London, which puts mee in fear you will not have time to see us here, synce you wilbe invited to see the manifficent funerall of his late Highnes and the instolling of the present Protector; which, with your owne building, will deprive us of seeing you here before the tearme. I observe all gentlemen were swords; and that I may not looke more lyke a bumking then the rest, I desire you will bwy mee a lytle wryding sword and belt. I would not exced five pound price. I did see Andrew Newport's, which hee baught over against the Temple. At the same time Nor: Phill: Howard baught such a one in the same place. If there be another of the same to be had, I desire it, and that you will send it downe by the Sturbridge horse carrier who lyes at the Castle in Wood streete and comes oute of the towne on Saterday. This will give you trouble enough, therefore I aught to begg your pardon, and conclude with the assurance of ever being,

Dear Kitt,

Your most affectionate and obliged servant,

Tho: Windsor.

LORD CHESTERFIELD to an unknown lady, [*c.* 1660]

Philip Stanhope, second Earl of Chesterfield, 1633–1713, politician. This letter is headed in Chesterfield's letterbook: 'To one who walked 4 whole days with mee in St Jeamses Park and yet I never knew who shee was'.

Madam

Though I did never think it possible (at least for mee) to be in love with any person without seeing their face, or knowing who they were, yet you have convinced mee of that mistake, for the perfections of your Shape, the beauty of your Neck, the delicacy of your hands, the charms of an admirable voice, the pleasantness of your humour, and a grace that attends all your motions, have soe captivated my sence that I am forst to confess your Victory and declare I never yet found so absolute a Conqueror; for my thoughts doe represent you as a Deity that mankind ought to worship. but why (if your face be sutable to all the rest (which I can hardly doubt of) doe you refuse to have it seen, and deny the King, the Duke, and all the court, to know who it is they so much admire; or how come I to be honoured four nights together with your company which you seem to refuse all other men, and yet at the same time you protest that I shall never know who you are, which is in effect to take away a mans hart and never to let him know who has it; certainly this is a new piece of cruelty that was never before known to your sex, and so malitious an invention must needs proceed from a very dangerous person, but all this can not hinder mee from being, My Deare I know not who

Your most passionat obedient servant

JOHN EVELYN to Sir Christopher Wren, 4 April 1665

John Evelyn, 1620–1706, diarist and virtuoso; Sir Christopher Wren, architect. Evelyn's only surviving son, also called John, was born on 19 January 1655; a Dr Bohun was appointed his tutor in 1665. He died in 1699.

Sir,

You may please to remember that some tyme since I begg'd a favour of you in behalfe of my little boy: he is now susceptible of instruction, a pleasant, and (though I speake it) a most ingenious and pregnant child. My designe is to give him good education; he is past many initial difficulties, and conquers all things with incredible industry: do me that eternal obligation, as to enquire out and recom'end me some young man for a preceptor. I will give him £20 per ann. sallary, and such other accom'odations as shall be no ways disagreeable to an ingenious spirit; and possibly I may do him other advantages: in all cases he will find his condition with us easy, his scholar a delight, & the conversation not to be despised: this obliges me to wish he may not be a morose, or severe person, but of an agreeable temper. The qualities I require are, that he be a perfect Grecian, and if more than vulgarly mathematical, so much the more accomplish'd for my designe: myne owne defects in the Greeke tongue and knowledge of its usefulnesse, obliges me to mention that particular with an extraordinary note: in sum I would have him as well furnish'd as might be for the laying of a permanent & solid foundation: the boy is capable beyond his yeares; and if you encounter one thus qualified, I shall receive it amongst the greate good fortunes of my life that I obtain'd it by the benefit of your friendship, for which I have ever had so perfect an esteeme. There is no more to be said, but that when you have found the person, you direct him im'ediately to me, that I may receive, and value him.

Sir, I am told by Sir Jo: Denham that you looke towards France this somer: be assur'd I will charge you with some addresses to friends of mine there, that shall exceedingly cherish you; and though you will stand in no neede of my recom'endations, yet I am confident you will not refuse the offer of those civilities which I shall bespeake you.

There has layne at Dr Needham's a copy of the Parallel bound up for you, & long since design'd you, which I shall entreate you to accept; not as a recompence of your many favours to mee, much lesse a thing in the least assistant to you (who are yourselfe a master), but as a toaken of my respect, as the booke itselfe is of the affection I beare to an art which you so happily cultivate.

Dear Sir, I am

Yr&c.

Says-Court, 4 Apr. 1665.

CHARLES II to Louise de Kéroualle, [*c.* 1670]

Charles II, King of Great Britain and Ireland; Louise de Kéroualle, Duchess of Portsmouth and Aubigny, his mistress. 'Fubs' was Charles's nickname for her.

Newmarket
Saturday

I shall not be out of paine till I know how my dearest gott to London, and for that purpose I send this expresse to come away to morrow morning to bring me word how you have rested after your journey. I will not trouble you with a long letter now, knowing how troublesome that is to one indisposed, and pray do not answer this your selfe, except you are quite out of paine, all I will add is, that I should do my selfe wrong if I toulld you that I love you better than all the world besides, for that were making a comparison where tis impossible to expresse the true passion and kindnesse I have for my dearest dearest fubs

CR

LORD ROCHESTER to Henry Savile, [1673–4]

John Wilmot, second Earl of Rochester, 1647–80, poet and rake; Henry Savile, diplomat.

Dear Savile,
Do a charity becoming one of your pious principles, in preserving your humble servant Rochester from the imminent peril of sobriety, which, for want of good wine more than company (for I drink like a hermit betwixt God and my own conscience) is very like to befall me. Remember what pains I have formerly taken to wean you from your pernicious resolutions of discretion and wisdom. And, if you have a grateful heart (which is a miracle amongst you statesmen), show it by directing the bearer to the best wine in town, and pray let not this highest point of sacred friendship be performed slightly, but go about it with all due deliberation and care, as holy priests to sacrifice, or as discreet thieves to the wary performance of burglary and shop-lifting. Let your well-discerning palate (the best judge about you) travel from cellar to cellar and then from piece to piece till it has lighted on wine fit for its noble choice and my approbation. To engage you the more in this matter, know, I have laid a plot may very probably betray you to the drinking of it. My Lord — will inform you at large.

Dear Savile, as ever thou dost hope to out-do Machiavel or equal me, send some good wine! So may thy wearied soul at last find rest, no longer hovering 'twixt th' unequal choice of politics and lewdness! May'st thou be admired and loved for thy domestic wit; beloved and cherished for thy foreign interest and intelligence.

Rochester.

SIR THOMAS BROWNE to his son Edward, 14 June [1676]

Sir Thomas Browne, 1605–82, author of the *Religio Medici* and *Urn Burial*, physician; his son Edward, physician. This letter was written from Norwich, where Browne had his practice; his son had his in London.

Dear Son

I am sorry to heare Mr Bishop is so much his owne foe. Surely his brayne is not right. Probably you may heare agayne of him before hee returnes into his country. Hee seemed to bee fayre conditiond when hee was in these parts, though very hypochondriacall sometimes. Mr Hombarston whenever his brayne is distemper'd, resolves upon a journey to London, & there showes himself, acts his part & returnes home better composed, as hee did the last time. Hee would not bee persuaded to bleed agayne before hee went. If the dolphin were to bee showed for money in Norwich, litle would bee gott. If they showed it in London, they are like to take out the viscera & salt the fish & then the dissection will bee inconsiderable. You may remember the dolphin opened when the King was heere & Dr Clark was at my howse, when you tooke a draught of severall parts very well, which Dr Clark had sent unto him. Bartholinus hath the Anatome of one in his centuries. You may observe therein the odde muscle whereby it spouts out water, the odde Larynx like a goose head, the flattish heart, the Lungs, the *Renes racemosi*, the penis, the multiple stomack &c. When wee wasshed that fish a kind of cuticule came of in severall places on the sides & back. Your mother hath an art to dresse & cooke the flesh so as to make an excellent savory dish of it, & the King being at Newmarket I sent collars thereof to his table, which were well liked of.

Though you must take the paynes to compose a new sett of Lectures, yet I do not see why you should not retaine the greatest and necessarie part for information of the Auditors, allthough you may alter or adde

37

some things as observation or reading shall informe you, or as you find they are not cleare enough or fully enough expressed, & some remarkable observations may bee retained, as that of the *papillae pyramidalis* in the elephants skinne, with some hint that the appositenesse & aptnesse therein would not bee omitted, though showne & produced to serve for illustration before, for there will bee many present next time which were not nowe, & some absent which were now present.

De pulmone

The Lungs taking up a considerable part of the chest, it may seeme something strange that the chest may bee runne through, or traversely peirced through both sides, & yet the Lungs escape & have no hurt, butt this notwithstanding may happen, if the thrust bee made at the expiration and when the Lungs subside.

De pene.

Some have queried why since nature hath been so sollicitous about the provisions for generation, this penis is only single and not double in masles, which Sinibaldus thincks sufficiently answered when hee sayth, *Absit certe, nimius est unus.* O no, God forbid, one is to much. However, the question is not altogether groundlesse, for in some animals this part is double, as in the viper, Sinibaldus, *lib. 3, tractat. 1, cap. 3*, which you need not quote as to the place.

de cuticula aut cute.

Many, especially yong persons, are sayd to bee goose skinned, wherein the parts are a litle elevated, whereof I have heard an odde observation, which I cannot as yet confirme, that those who have such skinns have not had the *lues venerea.*

You have also divers parts to handle which were not treated in your last, as the *Mesenterium*, Thymus, Larynx & its cartilages, wherein you may help yourself in Casserius also *de dentibus*, for the barber chirurgeons sake that they may have a Theoricall knowledge of those parts wherin they are often practicall.

I shall returne the lect. upon the first good opportunity that you may have them by you to make use of & send hints as they occurre.

Your loving father

T.B.

June 14.

PRINCESS MARY to Frances Apsley, [*c.* 1676]

Princess Mary, 1662–94, later Queen Mary II, wife of William III; Frances Apsley, her girlhood friend, daughter of Sir Allen Apsley. In their letters Mary posed as 'Mary Clorine' and Frances as 'Aurelia', her husband. Their correspondence was carried by Richard Gibson, the Princess's dwarf drawing-master.

Who can imagin that my dear husband can be so love sike for fear I do not love her but I have more reson to think that she is sike of being wery of me for in tow or three years men are alwais wery of thier wifes and look for Mistresses as sone as thay can gett them but I think I am pretty wel asured of the love of my dear but if I had al that is to be had in the world I shold never have anufe if my dearest oh! dearest Aurelia did but show half the love to me as I if I had speech to declare shold do to her I shold be the hapest creature in the world as now I am but in indeferant hapines for nothing in the world I am sure can soe much ad to my plesure as to love and to be loved again for my part I have more love for you than I can posible have for al the world besids you do not expect from me a letter like your own this morning for I am sure Mr. Draden [i.e. Dryden] and al the poets in the world put together could not make such another. I pretend to nothing in this world but if it be posibel to tell my love I have for my Aurelia to my dearest dearest husband & ever beg of her to except me as her most obedaint wife

Mary
Clorine

From al things in this world my hart
has escaped but from cupits blody dart
I no resistance could find
love is the noblest frialty of the mind

HENRY SAVILE to his brother Lord Halifax, 16 April 1677

Henry Savile, 1642–87, diplomat, friend of Rochester; his brother George Savile, first Marquess of Halifax, politician, author of the *Character of a Trimmer*. During parliamentary elections of the time, much depended on a candidate's capacity for withstanding and returning their constitutents' hospitality: on this occasion Savile was successful and was elected to Parliament as Burgess for Newark.

Newarke, April 16, '77.

Sir Rob. and I came hither on Thursday morning last; since which time I have been so continually drunk that I could never have time either to write to London or ride to Rufford. Sir Richard Rothwell had been at so great an expense before we came, that we found it impossible to hope for a voice in this town if we stuck to the new order of the House of Commons, and not to the old custom of England; nay we were fain to double our reckonings to them. We were not the contrivers of that damn'd vote, as was particularly laid to my charge; but I hope I have pretty well convinced them of the contrary, but at so dear a rate that I doubt, whether I succeed or not, I have quite broken my back, and shall do my heart if I return unsuccessfull to London, after pains and trouble taken that I would not undergoe again to be an emperor instead of a burgess. But I find whatever is undertaken out of the pride of a man's heart brings great anxiety's at long run; and, though I should succeed, which is far from a certainty, I have reason to wish I had never seen nor heard of this town; but our measures now at court are so taken that it is esentiall to a man's succeeding there to be of the parliament, which if I am destin'd not to be, I must be content with my poverty without any remedy but patience, and every man allowing that no man living ever had so many ugly accidents to prevent what he aimed at. Because of the mart at Gainsborough, the day of election could not be till Thursday, which is the day I wish for more than a lover ever did for a wedding night to be at an end of more noise and tumult than ever poor mortal was troubled with; I have been all this day sick to agonyes with four day's swallowing more good ale and ill sack than one would have thought a country town could have held; and this worthy employment must be begun again tomorrow though I burst for it; therefore pray for me and pity me, for I would gladly change my next three days with any slave at Algiers.

DR FELL to Lady Hatton, 3 July [1680]

Dr John Fell, 1625–86, Dean of Christ Church and Bishop of Oxford, promoter of the Oxford University Press; Elizabeth, second wife of Viscount Hatton, Royalist. John Fell is the subject of Thomas Brown's well-known rhyme: 'I do not love thee, Dr Fell, / The reason why I cannot tell, / But this one thing I know full well: / I do not love thee, Dr Fell.' All but one of Lady Hatton's children died in infancy.

Most Honord Madam,   July 3

I perceive it lies upon your mind that you are a person remarkable for misfortunes; therefore I pray let us consider the thing a a little first, whither your observation be truly made, and then whither it ought to be matter of trouble to you. As to the former part, I think it not evident that any thing singularly calamitous has befaln you. It is very sure that you have lost several of your neerest relations before you attaind to a full age; but surely this is no unusual thing; for children to be orphans, and of a numerous family several to dye early, is the event of every day. On the other side, to how many is it exceedingly unfortunate that their parents have lived long, have wasted the fortunes, disgraced the families, and debaucht the manners of their relations, so that the life of parents and kindred is very far from being in itself a blessing. But, dearest Madam, the friends which you have lost were persons of vertue; and is that the calamity that, when you had received the benefits of education and example from them, Almighty God took them from this miserable world to give them the rewards of eternity? Do you envy them their happiness? Or do you count it an injury that you have not them continued here to their infinit disadvantage, so long as it would answer your convenience? Tho your dear father lived not long after you could understand the tenderness due to that relation, it pleasd God to continue your incomparable mother till you were not only fully instituted in all christian duties but till you were married and put into obligations of leaving father and mother; and indeed, if you remember well, you had, even in my most honord ladies life time, a prospect of being calld to attend your husband at Guernesey. And I pray think, had that bin the case, nay had you bin settled at Kirby and my lady but at Easton, would you not for a great part of your time be deprived of each other?

In like manner I could reason with you concerning my dearest Lord, your brother. But to go forward, let us consider whither the loss of friends be the only calamity of the world. What think you of poverty;

what think you of sickness; what think you of being debaucht in vice? When you number your misfortunes, I pray put on the other side your blessings and advantages, and consider that whatever ill of any kind you are freed from, whatever blessing is continued to you, is the meer bounty and free mercy of a gracious God. Whatever innocence you have that may recommend you to His favor is itself the greatest of favors.

And now, dearest Madam, let us consider the second point, whither, taking it for granted that you are this remarkably unfortunate person which you esteem yourself, this ought to be so much resented by you. I am sure, upon all the measures which christianity teaches, afflictions are placed under a better character; we are told it is the mark of sonship, the sign that we are not bastards, nay, that we are children whom the Father of spirits loves and chastises. Accordingly we are commanded to think it all joy when we fall into diverse temtations, to rejoice and to be exceeding glad, and be assured therefrom that great is our reward in Heaven. If you have any argument to justify your grief and trouble, I pray let me hear it, and let us debate the matter at large. But if upon an equal view your condition be not extraordinarily calamitous; that if it be tis sent by an alwise and gracious Providence that designs it for your real and certain advantage, I hope you will be so just to that Fatherly hand, and so just to your own interest, as with cheerfullness to acquiesce in your condition and resolve yourself to be, as I verily believe you are, very happy. I will not lay before you the large receits which you have had from God's hand, of fortune, honor, understanding, education, friends, health, and the like; but I will tell you why I think my Lady Hatton very happy. She is removed from the infectious conversation of the town, where the precious time designed for the great purposes of eternity is to be wasted in impertinent and uncharitable visits and unseasonable meals; where the estate designd for the infinite emprovements of charity is to be wasted in gaudy furniture, expensive dressings, and ridicule equipags; where the reputation, our best tresure next to innocence, must be in perpetual hasards, and is impossible by any care or forecast to be preserved entire. And she is also in the station where Providence has placed hir in the country, where she has free opportunities for devotion and retirement into hir own soul, for frugal care of the interests of hir family, for charities to hir poor neighbours, and retird from the stroke of malicious tongues; and with all this dares be alone, dare look into hirself, and esteems a conversation with God and vertue superior to all the frolics with men or vice.

My most honord Madam, cast up your accounts, and, when you have don so, tell me plainly whither you would change your condition with any of the gay ladies of the age, nay, with any one whom you know in the whole world. And if upon just reflection you cannot pitch anywhere to better your condition, then determine whether you ought to be dissatisfied with that which is assigned you. God Almighty bless you in all your interests and relations.

I remain, honord Madam,

Your most faithfull servt in our Lord,

Jo. Oxon.

I shall be glad to hear that my little Lord and Kitty are well at Eton.

WILLIAM PENN to Colonel Henry Sidney, 29 March 1681

William Penn, 1644–1718, founder of Pennsylvania; Henry Sidney, Earl of Romney, general of British regiments in the Dutch service. Penn had been granted his patent for the new colony on 4 March; Sidney's brother Algernon helped frame its constitution.

My kind friend,

The world thus chaing'd and chaingeing makes me mighty careless of the comforts of it, and you courtiers must and will learn to think so too, when your disapointments come home; and if I have any prospect, your turn may be next. 'Tis a pretty thing to see how finely the great monarchs of the world play at ninepins with their ministers, distroy their creatures that they may create again. The corruption of one thing is the generation of another, if philosophy be true, and perhaps order may arise from our confusion. If one could be sure of yt, 'twould mittigate the pain. Which of us two shall be embassador then, I cant tell. Well, I perceive the Dutch aire is takeing, and that thou art resolv'd to keep out of harms way. So shall I too, when I am gott to my new granted province in America, where the charge of the voyage will secure me from the revenge of my enimys. But not to be tedious, lett me begg a letter to Coll. Russell in Lt. Cooks behalf. He has faild of his promess; the place is gone and the man ruin'd, if he will not give him the vallue of the colours of that ensigne of the regiment that has it. He professes to do it. Till then, that the man may

have his pay seems reasonable. Perhaps this is like to be the last trouble
thou willt receive by the means of

Thy very true ould friend,

Wm. Penn.

For me at one Fords in Bow-lane, London.

NELL GWYN to (?) Laurence Hyde, [? May or June 1682]

Eleanor Gwyn, 1650–87, orange-seller, actress, mistress of Charles II; Laurence
Hyde, later Lord Rochester (of a new creation), politican. This letter was
possibly written to Hyde while he was at The Hague on diplomatic business.
Among those mentioned in it are: Sir Carr Scrope, companion of Charles II and
minor poet; Mrs Knight, a singer and rival of Nell Gwyn for the King's affections;
John Wilmot, Earl of Rochester; the poet, Henry Savile; his friend and MP for
Newark, the Earl of Dorset; Nell Gwyn's former lover, Thomas Shadwell, the
poet later ridiculed by Dryden ('The rest to some faint meaning make pretence, /
But Shadwell never deviates into sense'); Joseph Harris, actor and dramatist; and
Lords Burford and Beauclerk, her children by the King.

pray Deare Mr. Hide forgive me for not writeing to you before now for
the reasone is I have bin sick thre months & sinse I recovered I have had
nothing to intertaine you withall nor have nothing now worth writing but
that I can holde no longer to let you know I never have ben in any
companie wethout drinking your health. for I love you with all my soule.
the pel mel is now to me a dismale plase sinse I have uterly lost Sir Car
Scrope never to be recovred agane for he tould me he could not live
allwayes at this rate & so begune to be a littel uncivil, which I could not
sufer from an uglye *baux garscon*. Ms Knights Lady mothers dead & she
has put up a scrutchin no beiger then my Lady grins scunchis. My lord
Rochester is gon in the cuntrei. Mr Savil has got a misfortune, but is upon
recovery & is to mary an hairres, who I thinke wont wont have an ill time
ont if he holds up his thumb. My lord of Dorscit apiers wonse in thre
munths, for he drinkes aile with Shadwell & Mr Haris at the Dukes house
all day long. my Lord Burford remimbers his sarvis to you. my Lord
Bauclaire isis goeing into france. we are a goeing to supe with the king at
whithall & my lady Harvie. the King remembers his sarvis to you. now
lets talke of state affairs, for we never caried things so cunningly as now

for we dont know whether we shall have pesce or war, but I am for war and for no other reason but that you may come home. I have a thousand merry conseets, but I cant make her write um & therfore you must take the will for the deed. god bye. your most loveing obedunt faithfull & humbel

sarvant

E. G.

DR FELL to Lady Hatton, 25 January [1684]

Dr John Fell, 1625–86, Dean of Christ Church and Bishop of Oxford; Elizabeth, second wife of Viscount Hatton. Lord Hatton was Governor of Guernsey.

Most Honord Madam,   25 Jan.

   You will allow me to give myself the satisfaction of constant writing, tho I am deprivd of that of hearing. The severity of cold continues still upon us; but I look down upon it as one of the worst effects of the rigor of the season that all commerce and intercourse are frozen up. We are told strange stories of several streets built upon the river of Thames that have joined Southwark to London. I should be glad if the practice could be emproved to make a road to Guernsay and join it unto our continent, that there might be an easier passage for letters to you and for your honors return to us. In the meantime this new city upon the river is a lively embleme of the designes and business of this world, where the foundation is water and the first thaw drowns the whole fabric. That your honor may build upon the unmoveable foundations of piety and vertue, which no change of weather or affairs can undermine, is the praier of,

honord Madam,

Your

Most faithfull servt in our Lord,

Jo. Oxon.

EDMUND HALLEY to Isaac Newton, 22 May 1686

Edmund Halley, 1656–1742, astronomer; Sir Isaac Newton, scientist. Without Halley, Newton's great *Principia Mathematica* would not have been published: it was he 'who tracked Newton to his College, who drew from him his great discoveries, and who generously gave them to the world' (Brewster, *Life of Newton*). When the manuscript was presented to the Royal Society, Hooke claimed to have been the first to discover the gravitational Law of Inverse Squares. Wishing to avoid controversy, Newton wanted the third part of the *Principia* suppressed, but was dissuaded by Halley. In an attempt to conciliate Hooke ten years earlier Newton had written, 'If I have seen further it is by standing on the shoulders of Giants.'

Sir   London Maii 22° 1686.

Your Incomparable treatise intituled *Philosophiæ Naturalis Principia Mathematica*, was by Dr Vincent presented to the R. Society on the 28th past, and they were so very sensible of the Great Honour you do them by your Dedication, that they immediately ordered you their most hearty thanks, and that a Councell should be summon'd to consider about the printing thereof; but by reason of the Presidents attendance upon the King, and the absence of our Vice-Presidents, whom the good weather had drawn out of Town, there has not since been any Authentick Councell to resolve what to do in the matter; so that on Wednesday last the Society in their meeting, judging that so excellent a work ought not to have its publication any longer delayd, resolved to print it at their own charge, in a large Quarto, of a fair letter; and that this their resolution should be signified to you and your opinion therin be desired, that so it might be gone about with all speed. I am intrusted to look after the printing it, and will take care that it shall be performed as well as possible, only I would first have your directions in what you shall think necessary for the embellishing therof, and particularly whether you think it not better, that the Schemes should be enlarged, which is the opinion of some here; but what you signifie as your desire shall be punctually observed.

There is one thing more that I ought to informe you of, viz, that Mr Hook has some pretensions upon the invention of the rule of the decrease of Gravity, being reciprocally as the squares of the distances from the Center. He sais you had the notion from him, though he owns the Demonstration of the Curves generated thereby to be wholly your own; how much of this is so, you know best, as likewise what you have to do in this matter, only Mr Hook seems to expect you should make some mention of him, in the preface, which, it is possible, you may see reason to praefix. I must beg your pardon that it is I, that send you this account, but I thought it my duty to let you know it, that so you may act accordingly; being in myself fully satisfied, that nothing but the greatest Candour imaginable, is to be expected from a person, who of all men has the least need to borrow reputation. When I shall have received your directions, the printing shall be pushed on with all expedition, which therfore I entreat you to send me, as soon as may be. You may please to direct to me to be left with Mr Hunt at Gresham College, and your letter will come to the hands of Sir

Your most affectionate humble
Servant
Edm. Halley

To his honoured friend
Mr Isaac Newton
Professor of Mathematicks
  in the University of
    Cambridg.

LORD MULGRAVE to Sir George Etherege, 7 March 1687

John Sheffield, third Earl of Mulgrave, first Duke of Buckingham and Normanby, 1648–1721, statesman, poet, patron of Dryden and friend of Pope; Sir George Etherege, playwright. This letter was written when Etherege was serving as the envoy of James II in Ratisbon and Mulgrave was Lord Chamberlain.

March 7, 1687
Whitehall

I saw t'other day by chance a letter of yours to Mr. Dryden, which put me in mind of one I received from you a good while ago, as well as of the Lady in the Garret. For the last memorandum I thank you with all my heart, the remembrance of her being very sweet, both as a pleasure enjoy'd and a danger escap'd, and I am not so young now but that I can chew the Cud of Lechery with some sorte of Satisfaction. You who are so amorous and vigorous may have your minde wholely taken up with the present, but we grave, decayd people, alas, are glad to steal a thought some times towards the passt and then are to ask God forgiveness for it too. This is a little revenge for your suspicion of my being alter'd, as well as a vindication of my innocency in that particular. But to speak more seriously you shall never find me chang'd, whenever there is any occasion of employing Your humble servant

Mulgrave

SIR GEORGE ETHEREGE to Robert Corbet, April 1687

Sir George Etherege, ?1634–91, playwright; Robert Corbet, a gentleman gambler. Like the previous letter, this was written during Etherege's service in Ratisbon.

Sir.

Yesterday your letter of the 30th of March came to my hands and gave me a pleasure which nothing but the like proof of your kindness can give me here. If my Ghost be as restless when I am in the other world as my minde is now I am in an other Countrey, my friends must expect to be much haunted. It will cost them some frights and it may be some money to lay me. There is not a day but my thoughts dog you from the Coffee-house to the Play, from thence to Marribone, allways concern'd for your good luck and in paine I cannot make one with you in the Sports you follow. Some of the ancients have imagin'd that the greatest torment of the dead was an Impatient longing after what they delighted most in while they were living, and I can swear by my damnation in Germany this Hell is no jesting matter.

Now Mr. B— is promoted, I hope Mr. Swan will be mounted. I am sorry on so good an occasion I have not a quibble in my head which wou'd pass muster. I pitty Mrs. Debora's loss in Mr. Whitakers being gone to board in an other quarter. If he happens into a house with Mr. Crowne, John's songs and Josephs voice will charme the whole family. I find the Collonel is resolv'd to blaze to the last as well as my self. Methinks I see in a Triumph of our present loves a Cupid, for fear of burning his fingers, with a little piece of a Torch on a Save-all. He has beauty, the strongest cordiall, to keep up his Spirits. I have only a plain Bavarian with her sandy coulor'd locks, brawny limbs and a brick complection, and yet I find myself often very hearty.

Pray remember me kindly to all my friends and particularly to Tom Maule. I am very sensible of the Trouble the Correspondence you have with me gives you. I shall not tire you with any tedious acknowledgements but onely assure you, you oblige one who cannot be ungratefull and is extreamly. Sir etc.

JOHN DRYDEN to Mrs Steward, 2 February 1698[/99]

John Dryden, 1631–1700, poet, critic and playwright; Elizabeth Steward, Dryden's cousin.

Candlemass-Day, 1698[/99]

Madam,

Old Men are not so insensible of beauty, as it may be, you young ladies think. For my own part, I must needs ackowledge that your fair eyes had made me your slave before I receivd your fine presents. Your letter puts me out of doubt that they have lost nothing of their lustre, because it was written with your own hand; and not heareing of a feavour or an ague, I will please my self with the thoughts that they have wholly left you. I wou'd also flatter my self with the hopes of waiting on you in Cotterstock some time next summer; but my want of health may perhaps hinder me. But if I am well enough to travell as farr north as Northamptonshyre, you are sure of a guest, who has been too well us'd, not to trouble you again.

My sonn, of whom you have done me the favour to enquire, mends of his indisposition very slowly; the ayr of England not agreeing with him hetherto so well as that of Italy. The Bath is propos'd by the Doctours, both to him and me: but we have not yet resolv'd absolutely on that journey; for that city is so closs and so ill situated, that perhaps the ayr may do us more harm then the waters can do us good: for which reason we intend to try them heer first; and if we find not the good effect which is promis'd of them, we will save our selves the pains of goeing thether. In the mean time, betwixt my intervalls of physique and other remedies which I am useing for my gravell, I am still drudging on: always a Poet,

49

ery vulgar stomach. – My wife and your Cousin, Charles, give you their
most humble service, and thanks for your remembrance of them. I
present my own to my worthy Cousin, your husband, and am, with all
respect,

Madam,
Your most obliged Servant,
John Dryden.

For Mrs. Stewart,
att Cotterstock,
in Northamptonshyre,
These.
To be left with the Postmaster of Oundle.

SIR RICHARD STEELE to Mary Scurlock, 1 September 1707

Richard Steele, 1672–1729, essayist, founder of the *Tatler*. Steele met Mary
Scurlock at the funeral of his first wife; they married on 9 September.

Snt James's Coffee-house, Sepbr 1st, 1707

Madam,
  It is the hardest thing in the World to be in Love and yet attend
businesse. As for Me, all who speake to Me find Me out, and I must Lock
my self up, or other people will do it for Me.
  A Gentleman ask'd Me this Morning what news from Lisbon, and I
answer'd, She's Exquisitely handsome. Another desir'd to know when I
had been last at Hampton-Court, I reply'd Twill be on Tuesday come
se'nnight. Prithee Allow Me at least to Kisse Your hand before that day,
that my mind may be in some Composure. Oh Love!

50

A thousand Torments dwell about Thee,
Yet who would Live to Live without Thee?

   Methinks I could write a Volume to You, but all the Language on earth
would fail in saying how much, and with what disinterested passion, I am
Ever Yrs,

                                                             Richd Steele

DANIEL DEFOE to Robert Harley, 11 September 1707

Daniel Defoe, 1660–1731, novelist and journalist; Robert Harley, first Earl of
Oxford, Secretary of State for the Northern Department. This letter was written
from Edinburgh where Defoe was, as Harley's agent, promoting the Act of
Union between England and Scotland; he had not been paid for five months.

Sir
   You have Allways Allow'd me The Freedome of a plain and Direct
Stateing things to you. If I Should Not do it Now I should Not be just to
you, Much less Faithfull to My Self; and I Entreat your Pardon for This
from the True and Necessary part of it.
   If I Were where I have had the honor to be Sir, in your Parlour, Telling
you my Own Case, and what a Posture my Affaires are in here, it would
be too Moveing a Story; you Could Not, I am Perswaded, *pardon my
Vanity*, you have too much Concerne for me and too much Generosity in
your Nature, you Could Not bear it – I have allwayes Sir been bred like a
Man, I Would Say a Gentleman if Circumstances Did Not of late Alter
that Denomination, and tho' my Missfortunes and Enemies have
Reduced me, yet I allwayes struggled with the World So as Never to
want, till Now – Again Sir I had the honour to Come hither in a Figure
Suitable to your Design, whom I have the honor to Serv; while you
Supply'd me Sir, I can Appeal to him that knows all things, I Faithfully
Serv'd. I baulk't No Cases, I Appeard in print when Others Dared not to
Open Their Mouths, and without boasting I Ran as Much Risq of my life
as a Grenadr in storming a Counterscarp; – It is Now five Months since
you were pleased to Withdraw your Supply; – and yet I had Never your
Ordr to Return; – I knew My Duty better Than to quitt my post without
your Command; But Really Sir if you supposed, I had lay'd up a Bank
Out of your former, It is my Great Missfortune That such a Mistake

happens; I Depended too much on your Goodness to withold any Reasonable Expence, to form a Magazine for my Last Resort.

Tis true I spend you a Large Summe. But you will Remember how often I Entreated your Restraint in that Case, and perticular Directions, but as left to my liberty, I acted as I Concluded I Ought to Do, Pushing Every work as Thoro'ly as I Could, – And in stead of Forming a Magazine for My Self. If you were to See Me Now, Entertaind of Courtisy, without Subsistence, allmost Grown shabby in Cloths, Dejected &c, what I Care Not to Mention; you would be Mov'd to hasten My Relief, in a Manner Suitable to that Regard you were Allways pleased to show for me.

I Was Sir Just on the brink of Returning, and that of Meer Necessity, when Like life From the Dead I Recd your last, with My Ld Treasurers Letter; But Sir Hitherto, his Ldships Goodness to Me, Seems like Messages from an Army to a Town besieged, That Relief is Comeing; which heartns and Encourages the Famished Garrison, but does not Feed them; and at Last They Are Obliged to Surrender for want, when perhaps One week would ha' Delivred them.

What shall I farther liken my Case to? Tis like a Man hang'd, Upon an Appeal, with the Queens Pardon in his Pocket; Tis Really the Most Disscourageing Circumstance that Ever I was in; I Need Not Tell you Sir that this is Not a place to Get Money in. Pen and Ink and Printing will Do Nothing here. Men Do Not live here by Their Witts – When I look on my present Condition, and Reflect that I am Thus, with my Ld T—s Letter promiseing Me an Allowance for Subsistence in My Pocket, and Offring me Comfortable Things, Tis a Very Mortifying Thought that I have Not One friend in the World to Support me Till his Ldship shall think Fitt to begin That allowance.

The prayer of this Petition Sir is Very Brief, That I may be helped to wait, or that you will please Sir to Move my Ld T—r That Since his Ldship has thought Fitt to Encourage Me to Expect Assistance in Order to Serve the Governmt in this place; – his Ldship will be pleased to Make Such steps Towards it, as may prevent My being Oblig'd to abandone an Employ of Such Consequence, to My Own Ruine and the loss of the Capascity I am Now in of Doeing his Ldship Service.

I Need Say No More to Move you to This Sir. I entreat a speedy Reply and Supply to

Sir, Your Faithfull Tho' Discouragd Servt
D F

Sept. 11. 1707

LADY MARY WORTLEY MONTAGU, to Edward Wortley Montagu, 28 March 1710

Lady Mary Pierrepont afterwards Montagu, 1689–1762, author and traveller; Edward Wortley Montagu, politician, later her husband. Steele, who wrote under the name of Bickerstaff, had dedicated the second number of the *Tatler* to Montagu. In the first, he had declared that the journal was named in honour of the fair sex. Lady Mary, who wrote Montagu many further letters, married him in 1712.

Perhaps you'l be surprizd at this Letter. I have had manny debates with my selfe before I could resolve on it. I know it is not Acting in Form, but I do not look upon you as I do upon the rest of the world, and by what I do for you, you are not to judge my manner of acting with others. You are Brother to a Women I tenderly lov'd. My protestations of freindship are not like other people's. I never speak but what I mean, and when I say I love, it is for ever. I had that real concern for Mrs. Wortley I look with some regard on every one that is related to her. This and my long Acquaintance with you may in some measure excuse what I am now doing.

I am surprizd at one of the Tatlers you sent me. Is it possible to have any sort of Esteem for a person one beleives capable of having such triffling Inclinations? Mr. Bickerstaff has very wrong notions of our sex. I can say there are some of us that despises charms of show, and all the pageantry of Greatnesse, perhaps with more ease than any of the Philosophers. In contemning the world they seem to take pains to contemn it. We dispise it, without takeing the pains to read lessons of Morrality to make us do it. At least I know I have allwaies look'd upon it with contempt without being at the Expence of one serious refflection to oblige me to it. I carry the matter yet farther. Was I to chuse of £2,000 a year or twenty thousand, the first would be my choice. There is something of an unavoidable embarras in makeing what is calld a great figure in the world, that takes off from the happynesse of Life. I hate the noise and hurry inseparable from great Estates and Titles, and look upon both as blessings that ought only to be given to Fools, for tis only to them that they are blessings.

The pritty Fellows you speak of, I own entertain me sometimes, but is it impossible to be diverted with what one dispises? I can laugh at a puppet shew, at the same time I know there is nothing in it worth my attention or regard. General Notions are generally wrong. Ignorance and

Folly are thought the best foundations for Virtue, as if not knowing what a Good Wife is was necessary to make one so. I confesse that can never be my way of reasoning. As I allwaies forgive an Injury when I think it not done out of malice, I can never think my selfe oblig'd by what is done without design. Give me leave to say it (I know it sounds Vain): I know how to make a Man of sense happy, but then that man must resolve to contribute something towards it himselfe. I have so much Esteem for you I should be very sorry to hear you was unhappy, but for the world I would not be the Instrument of makeing you so, which (of the humour you are) is hardly to be avoided if I am your Wife. You distrust me. I can neither be easy nor lov'd where I am distrusted, nor do I believe your passion for me is what you pretend it; at least I'm sure, was I in love I could not talk as you do.

Few Women would have spoke so plainly as I have done, but to dissemble is among the things I never do. I take more pains to approve my conduct to my selfe than to the world, and would not have to accuse my selfe of a minute's deceit. I wish I lov'd you enough to devote my selfe to be for Ever miserable for the pleasure of a day or two's happynesse. I cannot resolve upon it – You must think otherwise of me or not at all.

I don't injoin you to burn this Letter. I know you will. Tis the first I ever writ to one of your sex and shall be the last. You must never expect another. I resolve against all correspondence of this kind. My resolutions are seldom made and never broken.

JONATHAN SWIFT to Benjamin Motte, 8 August 1726

Jonathan Swift, 1667–1745, satirist, Dean of St Patrick's cathedral, Dublin; Benjamin Motte, bookseller. Afraid of government prosecution, Swift published *Gulliver's Travels* under the name of its hero, Lemuel Gulliver. Even when dealing with Benjamin Motte, the book's publisher, he covered himself by adopting the pseudonym Richard Sympson; presumably as an added precaution he got his friend John Gay, author of *The Beggar's Opera*, to write out this letter which was sent to Motte with the manuscript. Alexander Pope helped arrange the book's publication.

London Augt 8th. 1726

Sir
    My Cousin Mr Lemuel Gulliver entrusted me some Years ago with a

Copy of his Travels, whereof that which I here send you is about a fourth part, for I shortned them very much as you will find in my Preface to the Reader. I have shewn them to several persons of great Judgment and Distinction, who are confident they will sell very well. And although some parts of this and the following Volumes may be thought in one or two places to be a little Satyrical, yet it is agreed they will give no Offence, but in that you must Judge for your self, and take the Advice of your Friends, and if they or you be of another opinion, you may let me know it when you return these Papers, which I expect shall be in three Days at furthest. The good Report I have received of you makes me put so great a trust into your Hands, which I hope you will give me no Reason to repent, and in that Confidence I require that you will never suffer these Papers to be once out of your Sight.

As the printing these Travels will probably be of great value to you, so as a Manager for my Friend and Cousin I expect you will give a due consideration for it, because I know the Author intends the Profit for the use of poor Sea-men, and I am advised to say that two Hundred pounds is the least Summ I will receive on his account, but if it shall happen that the Sale will not answer as I expect and believe, then whatever shall be thought too much even upon your own word shall be duly repaid.

Perhaps you will think this a strange way of proceeding to a man of Trade, but since I begin with so great a trust to you, whom I never saw, I think it not hard that you should trust me as much. Therefore if after three days reading and consulting these Papers, you think it proper to stand to my agreement, you may begin to print them, and the subsequent parts shall be all sent to you one after another in less than a week, provided that immediately upon your Resolution to print them, you do within three days deliver a Bank Bill of two hundred pounds, wrapt up so as to make a parcel to the Hand from whence you receive this, who will come in the same manner exactly at 9 a clock at night on Thursday which will be the 11th Instant.

If you do not aprove of this proposal deliver these Papers to the person who will come on thursday.

If you chuse rather to send the Papers make no other Proposal of your own but just barely write on a piece of paper that you do not accept my offer.

I am
Sir
your humble Servant
Richard Sympson

ALEXANDER POPE to Jonathan Swift, 28 June 1728

Alexander Pope, 1688–1744, poet; Jonathan Swift, satirist. Pope was staying with the Tory politician and literary patron Lord Bolingbroke. Fearful of prosecution for libel, he had published his *Dunciad*, which gave a great deal of offence to a great many people, anonymously and under a false Dublin imprint (possibly in the hopes of implicating Swift) on 18 May 1728. An enlarged edition appeared in the following year.

Dawley, June 28, 1728

I now hold the pen for my Lord Bolingbroke, who is reading your letter between two Haycocks, but his attention is sometimes diverted by casting his eyes on the clouds, not in admiration of what you say, but for fear of a shower. He is pleas'd with your placing him in the Triumvirate between your self and me; tho' he says that he doubts he shall fare like Lepidus, while one of us runs away with all the power like Augustus, and another with all the pleasures like Anthony. It is upon a forsight of this, that he has fitted up his farm, and you will agree, that this scheme of retreat at least is not founded upon weak appearances. Upon his return from the Bath, all peccant humours, he finds, are purg'd out of him; and his great Temperance and Oeconomy are so signal, that the first is fit for my constitution, and the latter would enable you to lay up so much mony, as to buy a Bishoprick in England. As to the return of his health and vigour, were you here, you might enquire of his Hay-makers; but as to his temperance, I can answer that (for one whole day) we have had nothing for dinner but mutton-broth, beans and bacon, and a Barn-door fowl.

Now his Lordship is run after his Cart, I have a moment left to my self to tell you, that I overheard him yesterday agree with a Painter for £200 to paint his country-hall with Trophies of Rakes, spades, prongs, &c. and other ornaments merely to countenance his calling this place a Farm – now turn over a new leaf –

He bids me assure you he should be sorry not to have more schemes of kindness for his friends, than of ambition for himself: There, tho' his schemes may be weak, the motives at least are strong; and he says further, if you could bear as great a fall, and decrease of your revenues, as he knows by experience he can, you wou'd not live in Ireland an hour.

The Dunciad is going to be printed in all pomp, with the inscription, which makes me proudest. It will be attended with *Proeme, Prologomena, Testimonia Scriptorum, Index Authorum,* and Notes *Variorum.* As to the latter, I desire you to read over the Text, and make a few in any way you like best, whether dry raillery, upon the stile and way of commenting of trivial Critics; or humorous, upon the authors in the poem; or historical, of persons, places, times; or explanatory, or collecting the parallel passages of the Ancients. Adieu. I am pretty well, my Mother not ill, Dr. Arbuthnot vex'd with his fever by intervals; I am afraid he declines, and we shall lose a worthy man: I am troubled about him very much. I am, &c.

ANTHONY HENLEY, MP, to his Constituents, [1734]

Anthony Henley, d. 1745, elder brother of Robert Henley, afterwards Lord Chancellor and first Earl of Northington. Henley was Member of Parliament for Southampton from 1727 to 1734. The year before relinquishing his seat, he had made a runaway match with a fifteen-year-old heiress, Lady Betty Berkeley. His constituents had complained to him about the Excise Bill, an unpopular measure which Sir Robert Walpole had failed to carry.

Gentlemen,

I received yours and am suprised by your insolence in troubling me about the Excise. You know, what I very well know, that I bought you. And I know, what perhaps you think I don't know, you are now selling yourselves to Somebody Else; and I know, what you do not know, that I am buying another borough. May God's curse light upon you all: may your houses be as open and common to all Excise Officers as your wifes and daughter were to me, when I stood for your scoundrell corporation.

Yours, etc.,
Anthony Henley

SIR ROBERT WALPOLE to Charles Churchill, 24 June 1743

Sir Robert Walpole, first Earl of Orford, 1676–1745, Prime Minister; Charles Churchill, General, father of an illegitimate son who married Walpole's illegitimate daughter in 1746. This letter was written after Walpole's enforced retirement from politics early in 1742 and was later converted into a Latin ode by Nicholas Hardinge, Clerk of the House of Commons.

Houghton, June 24 1743

Dear Charles

I have now wrote to Capt: Jackson to Give Lord Tyrawley a Ticket as you desired. I am very Glad to oblige him with it. This place affords no news, no Subjects of Amusement, or Entertainment to fine Men; Men of wit & pleasure about Town Understand not the Language; nor taste, the Charms of the Inanimate World. My Flatterers here are all mutes. The Oaks, the Beaches, the Chesnuts seem to Contend, who shall best please the Lord of the Mannor. They Cannot deceive, They will not lye. I in Return with Sincerity admire them, and have as many Beauties about me, as fill up all my hours of Dangling, and no disgrace attends me from 67 years of Age. Within doors we Come a little nearer to Real Life, and Admir upon almost Speaking Canvass, all, Town Ladies can Boast, with them I am Satisfied, beause they gratify me, with all I wish, and all I wont, and Expect nothing in Return, which I cannot give. If these Dear Charles, are any temptations, I heartily invite you to Come and partake of them. Shifting the Scene has sometimes its Recommendation, and from Countrey fare you may possibly Return with a Better Appetite, to the more delicate Entertainments, of a Refined Life.

Since I wrote what is above, we have been Surprised with the Good News from Abroad. to much Cannot be said upon it. for it is truly matter of Infinite Joy. because of Infinite Consequence;

I am truly Dear Charles
yours most Affectionately
Orford

THE DUKE OF MONTAGU to Charles Frederick, 9 April 1749

John Montagu, second Duke of Montagu, ?1688–1749, Master General of the Ordnance; Charles Frederick, Comptroller of His Majesty's Fireworks. Handel's *Music for the Royal Fireworks* had been written to celebrate the Peace of Aix-la-Chapelle the previous year. As the music was ready before the fireworks, Jonathan Tyers, owner of the Vauxhall Gardens, requested to be allowed to hold a public rehearsal there. Handel's objections to this were overruled and the rehearsal was held on 21 April 1749 before an immense crowd. The celebrations themselves took place in Green Park on 29 April. Some fireworks went off at the wrong moment, others failed to go off at all, rockets fell among the crowd, and the pavilion caught fire.

Sunday, 9 April, 1749.

Sir, – In answer to Mr. Hendel's letter to you (which by the stile of it I am shure is impossible to be of his inditing) I can say no more but this, that this morning at court the King did me the honor to talke to me conserning the fireworks, and in the course of the conversation his Majesty was pleased to aske me when Mr. Hendel's overture was to be rehersed; I told his Majesty I really coud not say anything conserning it from the difficulty Mr. Hendel made about it, for that the master of Voxhall, having offered to lend us all his lanterns, lamps, &c. to the value of seven hundred pounds, whereby we woud save just so much money to the office of Ordnance, besides thirty of his servants to assist in the illuminations, upon condition that Mr. Hendel's overture shoud be rehersed at Voxhall, Mr. Hendel has hetherto refused to let it be at Foxhall, which his Majesty seemed to think he was in the wrong of; and I am shure I think him extreamly so, and extreamly indifferent whether we have his overture or not, for it may very easily be suplyed by another, and I shall have the satisfaction that his Majesty will know the reason why we have it not; therefore, as Mr. Hendel knows the reason, and the great benefit and saving it will be to the publick to have the rehersal at Voxhall, if he continues to express his zeal for his Majesty's service by doing what is so contrary to it, in not letting the rehersal be there, I shall intirely give over any further thoughts of his overture and shall take care to have an other,

I am, Sir
Your most humble
servant,

Montague.

WILLIAM HOGARTH to his wife, Jenny, 6 June 1749

William Hogarth, 1697–1764, painter and engraver; Jenny, daughter of the painter, Sir James Thornhill.

Dear Jenny   June 6 1749

I write to you now, not because I think you may expect it only, but because I find a pleasure in it, which is more than I can say of writing to any body else, and I insist on it you don't take it as a mere complement, your last letter pleased more than I'll say, but this I will own if the postman should knock at the door in a weeks time after the receipt of this I shall think there is more musick in't than the beat of a Kettle Drum, & if the words to the tune are made by you, (to carry on metafor) and brings news of your all coming so soon to town I shall think the words much better than the musick, but dont hasten out of a scene of Pleasure to make me one (I wish I could contribute to it) you'l see by the Enclosed that I shall be glad to make a small contributer to it. I dont know whether or no you knew that Garrick was going to be married to the Violette when you went away. I supt with him last night and had a deal of talk about her. I can't write any more than what this side will contain, you know I wont turn over a new leaf I am so obstinate, but then I am no less obstinate in being your affectionate Husband

                                                        Wm Hogarth

THOMAS GRAY to Horace Walpole, 11 February 1751

Thomas Gray, 1716–71, poet; Horace Walpole, author, connoisseur and builder of Strawberry Hill. Gray and Walpole had formed their friendship during their schooldays at Eton. Faced with the threat of piracy, Walpole managed to have Gray's *Elegy* published by Dodsley on 16 February, and it went through four editions in two months.

My dear Sir
As you have brought me into a little Sort of Distress, you must assist me, I believe, to get out of it, as well as I can. yesterday I had the Misfortune of receiving a Letter from certain Gentlemen (as their Bookseller

expresses it) who have taken the *Magazine of Magazines* into their Hands. they tell me, that an *ingenious* Poem, call'd, *Reflections* in a Country-Churchyard, has been communicated to them, which they are printing forthwith: that they are inform'd, that the *excellent* Author of it is I by name, & that they beg not only his *Indulgence*, but the *Honor of his Correspondence*, &c: as I am not at all disposed to be either so indulgent, or so correspondent, as they desire; I have but one bad Way left to escape the Honour they would inflict upon me. & therefore am obliged to desire you would make Dodsley print it immediately (which may be done in less than a Week's time) from your Copy, but without my Name, in what Form is most convenient for him, but in his best Paper & Character. he must correct the Press himself, & print it without any Interval between the Stanza's, because the Sense is in some Places continued beyond them; & the Title must be, Elegy, wrote in a Country Church-yard. if he would add a Line or two to say it came into his Hands by Accident, I should like it better. if you think fit, the 102d Line may be read

> Awake, & Faithful to her wonted Fires.

but if this be worse than before; it must go, as it was. in the 126th, for *ancient* Thorn, read *aged*.

If you behold the Mag: of Mag:s in the Light that I do, you will not refuse to give yourself this Trouble on my Account, which you have taken of your own Accord before now. Adieu, Sir, I am

> Yours ever
>
> T G:

If Dodsley don't do this immediately, he may as well let it alone.

SAMUEL JOHNSON to Lord Chesterfield, February 1755

Samuel Johnson, 1709–84, author; Philip Stanhope, fourth Earl of Chesterfield, letter-writer. The prospectus for Johnson's famous *Dictionary of the English Language* had been issued in 1747, bearing a dedication to Lord Chesterfield. Late in 1754 Chesterfield, from whom Johnson had in the meantime heard little, published two papers recommending the work, then nearing completion. Soon after Chesterfield received this letter, he was visited by the publisher Dodsley who recalled later that he, 'read it to me, said this man has great powers, pointed out the severest passages, and observed how well they were expressed'.

February 1755

My Lord

I have been lately informed by the proprietor of The World that two Papers in which my Dictionary is recommended to the Public were written by your Lordship. To be so distinguished is an honour which, being very little accustomed to favours from the Great, I know not well how to receive, or in what terms to acknowledge.

When upon some slight encouragement I first visited your Lordship I was overpowered like the rest of Mankind by the enchantment of your adress, and could not forbear to wish that I might boast myself Le Vainqueur du Vainqueur de la Terre, that I might obtain that regard for which I saw the world contending, but I found my attendance so little incouraged, that neither pride nor modesty would suffer me to continue it. When I had once addressed your Lordship in public, I had exhausted all the art of pleasing which a retired and uncourtly Scholar can possess. I had done all that I could, and no Man is well pleased to have his all neglected, be it ever so little.

Seven years, My Lord, have now past since I waited in your outward Rooms or was repulsed from your Door, during which time I have been pushing on my work through difficulties of which It is useless to complain, and have brought it at last to the verge of Publication without one Act of assistance, one word of encouragement, or one smile of favour. Such treatment I did not expect, for I never had a patron before.

The Shepherd in Virgil grew at last acquainted with Love, and found him a Native of the Rocks. Is not a Patron, My Lord, one who looks with unconcern on a Man struggling for Life in the water and when he has reached ground encumbers him with help. The notice which you have been pleased to take of my Labours, had it been early, had been kind; but it has been delayed till I am indifferent and cannot enjoy it, till I am solitary and cannot impart it, till I am known and do not want it.

I hope it is no very cinical asperity not to confess obligation where no benefit has been received, or to be unwilling that the Public should consider me as owing that to a Patron, which Providence has enabled me to do for myself.

Having carried on my work thus far with so little obligation to any Favourer of Learning I shall not be disappointed though I should conclude it, if less be possible, with less, for I have been long wakened from that Dream of hope, in which I once boasted myself with so much exultation, My lord Your Lordship's Most humble Most Obedient Servant,

Sam: Johnson

HORACE WALPOLE to George Montagu, 24 October 1758

Horace Walpole, fourth Earl of Orford, 1717–97, author, connoisseur and builder of Strawberry Hill; George Montagu, a friend of Walpole's from Eton. Walpole's self-deprecating remark about the sons of heroes is made in reference to his father, Sir Robert Walpole. The seventeeth-century French politicians mentioned by him stand for some of those prominent in British eighteenth-century politics: Retz for Walpole himself, 'Mazarine' (Mazarin) for Newcastle, the Prime Minister, Louvois for Henry Fox, first Lord Holland, Colbert for the elder Pitt, and Rigbière for Richard Rigby who, even by the standards of his day, was notably corrupt.

Arlington Street, Oct. 24, 1758.

I am a little sorry that my preface, like the show-cloth to a sight, entertained you more than the *Bears* that it invited you in to see. I don't mean that I am not glad to have written anything that meets your approbation; but if Lord Whitworth's work is not better than my preface, I fear he has much less merit than I thought he had.

Your complaint of your eyes makes me feel for you: mine have been very weak again, and I am taking the bark, which did them so much service last year. I don't know how to give up the employment of them, I mean, reading – for as to writing, I am absolutely winding up my bottom, for twenty reasons. The first and perhaps the best, I have writ enough – the next; by what I have writ, the world thinks I am not a fool, which was just what I wished them to think, having always lived in terror of that oracular saying, Ἡρώων παῖδες λῶβοῖ, which Mr Bentley translated with so much more parts than the vain and malicious *Hero* could have done that set him the task, I mean his father, 'The sons of heroes are loobies.' My last reason is, I find my little stock of reputation very troublesome, both to maintain, and to undergo the consequences – it has dipped me in *erudite* correspondences – I receive letters every week that compliment my learning – now as there is nothing I hold so cheap as a learned man, except an unlearned one, this title is unsupportable to me; if I have not a care, I shall be called learned, till somebody abuses me, for *not* being learned, as they, not I, fancied I was. In short, I propose to have nothing more to do with the world, but divert myself in it as an obscure passenger – pleasure, virtu, politics, and literature, I have tried them all, and have had enough of them – content and tranquillity with now and then a little of three of them, that I may not grow morose, shall satisfy the rest of a life that is to have much idleness and I hope a little goodness – for politics – a long adieu! With some of the Cardinal de Retz's experience, though with none of his genius, I see the folly of taking a violent part without any view (I don't mean to commend a violent part *with* a view, that is still worse). I leave the state to be scrambled for by Mazarine, at once cowardly and enterprising, ostentatious, jealous and false; by Louvois, rash and dark; by Colbert, the affector of national interest, with designs, not much better; and I leave the Abbé de la Rigbière to sell the weak Duke of Orleans, to whoever has money to buy him, or would buy him to get money – at least these are my present reflections – if I should change them tomorrow, remember, I am not only a human creature, but that I am I, that is, one of the weakest of human creatures; and so sensible of my fickleness, that I am sometimes inclined to keep a diary of my mind, as people do of the weather – Today, you see it is temperate – tomorrow, it may again blow, politics and be stormy – for while I have so much quicksilver left, I fear my Passionometer will be susceptible of sudden changes. What do years give one? Experience. Experience, what? Reflections, what? – nothing that ever I could find – nor can I well agree with Waller that

> The soul's dark cottage batter'd and decay'd
> Lets in new light through chinks that Time has made –

chinks I am afraid there are, but instead of new light, I find nothing but darkness visible, that serves only to discover sights of woe! I look back through my chinks – I find errors, follies, faults – forwards, old age and death; pleasures fleeting from me, no virtues succeeding to their place – *il faut avouer*, I want all my quicksilver to make such a background receive any other objects!

I am glad Mr Frederick Montagu thinks so well of me as to be sure I shall be glad to see him without an invitation. For you, I had already perceived that you would not come to Strawberry this year – adieu!

Remember, nobody is to see this letter, but yourself and the clerks of the post office.

Yours ever
H.W.

WILLIAM HENRY LYTTELTON to Emperor Old Hop and the Little Carpenter, 22 May 1759

William Henry Lyttelton, first Baron Lyttelton, 1724–1808, Governor of South Carolina; Emperor Old Hop and the Little Carpenter, Cherokee Indian chiefs. Relations between white colonists and the local Indians had been deteriorating since 1757, when four Indians had been scalped by settlers. A few months after the date of this letter Fort Loudoun (in what is now Tennessee) fell, and open war broke out.

>   To the Emperor Old Hop, and the Little Carpenter
>   The Governor of South Carolina sends Greeting.

     Friends and Brothers,

Since the Day when the Great King George our common Father was pleased to send me to be his Governor of this Province, it has been my constant Desire to preserve a firm Peace and Friendship with the Cherokee Nation; and to that End I have not ceased to do Acts of brotherly Love & Kindness to you & your People, supplying you liberaly with Goods not only from the Stores of private Traders, but also with others, which I freely gave you to a very great Value.

When you, the Little Carpenter, was lately here, I brighten'd the Chain of Friendship between the two Nations; & you then told me that as long as you lived, you would be an Enemy to the French & hue to your Father the great King George, and that you would use your utmost Endeavours that all your Countrymen should be so too. You have likewise sent a Talk by Richard Smith to the Governor of Virginia, in which you assure him that for the Time to come, the Path shall be clear and good for his People and your People. & that no more Blood shall be spilt there; and you desire that he will send Traders into your Nation from his Government.

But notwithstanding all these Things I have received Intelligence that Moitoi of Settico with a Gang of twenty five Men has lately kill'd & scalp'd nineteen White People, Subjects of the great King George, so that the Path is now fouler than ever; and stinks with their Blood; nor can the Traders from Virginia pass for the Stench of it. I learn also that twenty more of your Men from the Towns over the Hills are still outlying in Wait to do more mischief & many Complaints have come to me from the People of those Parts, whose Relations are murdered, & who apply to me for Redress. This Evil has happen'd while you, the Little Carpenter, and I were eating like brothers out of the same Dish, and while my Hand was stretch'd out to put Arms into the Hands of you & your People.

I now dispatch this Letter to you, Old Hop, as Emperor of the Nation to inform you of these Matters, & to require you to take them into Consideration with your Headmen & Warriors, & to give me Satisfaction; and I shall expect your Answer by the next Messanger that Capt. Demerè shall send to me, after you have received this.

When you, the Little Carpenter, your last Talk offer'd to go to War against the French, I desired you to stay in the Nation, that you might keep all Things quiet there, and if any of your Countrymen were guilty of any Outrages against the White People, that you might procure them Satisfaction, & prevent any more Violences for the future; all which you assured me you would do, & I now look for the Performance of your Promises. I am

> your Friend & Brother.
> W.H.L.
> Charles Town. May 22. 1759.

HORACE WALPOLE to George Montagu, 21 October 1759

Horace Walpole, fourth Earl of Orford, 1717–97, author, connoisseur and builder of Strawberry Hill; George Montagu, a friend of Walpole's from Eton. This was the period of the elder Pitt's great ministry (which had Newcastle as its nominal head). The year 1759 saw the defeat of the French at the Battle of Minden, the fall of Louisburg and Fort Duquesne in French America, the destruction of the French Navy at the battles of Lagos and Quiberon and, on 13 September, the fall of Quebec to Wolfe.

> Strawberry Hill, Oct. 21, 1759.

Your pictures shall be sent as soon as any of us go to London, but I think that will not be till the Parliament meets. Can one easily leave the remains of such a year as this? It is still all gold. I have not dined or gone to bed by a fire till the day before yesterday. Instead of the glorious and ever-memorable year 1759, as the newspapers call it, I call it this ever-warm and victorious year. We have not had more conquest than fine weather: one would think we had plundered East and West Indies of sunshine. Our bells are worn threadbare with ringing for victories. I believe it will require ten votes of the House of Commons before people will believe that it is the Duke of Newcastle that has done all this and not Mr Pitt. One thing is very fatiguing; all the world is made knights or generals. Adieu! I don't know a word of news less than the conquest of America.

Yours ever
H. W.

PS. You shall hear from me again if we take Mexico or China before Christmas.

PPS. I had sealed my letter, but break it open again, having forgot to tell you that Mr Cowslade has the pictures of Lord and Lady Cutts, and is willing to sell them.

LAURENCE STERNE to Catherine Fourmantel, 8 March 176[0]

Laurence Sterne, 1713–68, novelist; Catherine Fourmantel, singer. While working on *Tristram Shandy* Sterne began a flirtation with Catherine Fourmantel, a young and intelligent French girl who was lodging near him with her mother at Stonegate, York. Tradition holds that she appears in the book as 'dear dear Jenny'. The first two volumes were published in York late in 1759. In a few months Sterne was famous. He went to London, had his portrait painted by Reynolds, and was fêted by society.

London [March] 8th 176[0]

My dear Kitty.

I have arrived here safe, & sound, except for the Hole in my heart, which you have made, like a dear enchanting Slut as you are. – I shall take Lodgings this morning in Picadilly or the Hay market, & before I seal this Letter will let you know where to direct a Letter to me; which Letter I shall wait for by the return of the post with great impatience – so write my dear Love without fail. I have the greatest honors paid me, & most civilities shewn me, that were ever known, from the Great; & am engaged allready to ten Noble men & men of fashion to dine. Mr Garrick pays me all & more honour than I could look for, I dined with him to day – & he has promised Numbers of great People to carry me to dine wth'em – he has given me an Order for the Liberty of his Boxes, and of every part of his house for the whole Season; & indeed leaves nothing undone that can do me either Serevice or Credit. he has undertaken the whole Management of the Booksellers, & will procure me a great price – but more of this in my next.

And now my dear dear Girl let me assure you of the truest friendship for you, that ever Man bore towards a Woman – where ever I am, my heart is warm towards you & ever shall be, till it is cold for ever. I thank you for the kind of proof you gave me of your Love and of yr desire to make my heart easy, in ordering yrself to be denied to You know who – whilst I am so miserable to be separated from my dear dear Kitty, it would have stabb'd my Soul, to have thought such a fellow could have the Liberty of coming near you – I therefore take this proof of yr Love & good principles, most kindly – & have as much faith & dependence upon You in it, as if I was at yr Elbow – would to God, I was at it this moment, – for I am sitting solitary & alone in my bed Chamber (ten o'Clock at night, after the play) – & would give a Guinea for a Squeeze of yr hand – I send my Soul perpetually out to see what you are a doing – wish I could convey my Body with it – Adieu dear & kind Girl, & believe me ever yr kind friend & most Affectionate Admirer. – I go to the Oratorio this night.

Adieu, adieu.

PS
my Service to yr Mama
  Direct for me in the Pell Mell
  at the 2d house from St Albans street.

VOLTAIRE to Lord Chesterfield, 5 August 1761

Voltaire, pseudonym of François-Marie Arouet, 1694–1778, author; Philip Dormer Stanhope, fourth Earl of Chesterfield, letter-writer. Chesterfield subscribed for one copy of the book.

à Ferney par Geneve 5 august 1761

Mylord,
  Give me leave to apply from the foot of the alps to the english noble

man whose wit is the most adapted to the taste of every nation. I have in my old age a sort of conformity with you. T'is not in point of wit, but in point of ears. Mine are much hard too. The consolidation of deaf people is to read, and some times to scrible. I have a'[s] a scribler, made a pretty curious commentary on many tragedies of Corneille. T'is my duty since the gran daughter of Corneille is in my house.

If there was a gran daugter of Shakespear, I would subscribe for her. I hope those who take Pontichéri will take subscriptions too.

The work is prodigiously cheap, and no money is to be given but at the reception of the book.

Nurse receives the names of the subscribers. Yr name will be the most honourable and the dearest to me.

I wish yr lordship long life, good eyes and good stomak.

Mylord souvenez vous de votre ancien serviteur Voltaire qui vous est attaché comme s'il était né à Londres.

THOMAS GAINSBOROUGH to David Garrick, 22 August 1768

Thomas Gainsborough, 1727–88, painter; David Garrick, actor. Mrs Pritchard was an actress who had recently died; in her farewell performance a few months earlier she had spoken an epilogue composed by Garrick. A year later Garrick staged his famous Shakespeare Jubilee at Stratford. Torrential rain fell throughout the proceedings.

Dear Sir,

I doubt I stand accused (if not accursed) all this time of my neglect for not going to Stratford, and giving you a Line from thence as I promised; but, Lord, what can one do such Weather as this, continual Rains; My Genius is so dampt by it that I can do nothing to please me. I have been several days rubbing in & rubbing out my design for Shakespeare and damme if I think I shall let it go or let you see it at last – I was willing like an Ass as I am, to expose myself a little out of the simple Portrait way, and had a notion of showing where that inimitable Poet had his Ideas from, by an immediate Ray darting down upon his Eye turn'd up for the purpose; but G— damn it I can make nothing of my Ideas there has been such a fall of rain from the same quarter – you shall not see it for I'll cut it

out before you can come – tell me Dear Sir when you purpose coming to
Bath, that I may be quick enough in my Motions. Shakespeare's Bust is a
silly smiling thing, and I have not sense enough to make him more
sensible in the Picture and so I tell ye you shan't see it. I must make a
plain Picture of Him standing erect, and give it an old look as if it had
been Painted at the time he lived and there we shall fling 'em Damme.

Poor Mrs. Pritchard died here on Saturday night 11 o'clock – so now
her performance being no longer present to those who must see and hear,
before they can believe, will you know my dear sir – but I beg pardon, I
forgot – Time puts us all into his Fobb, as I do my Timekeeper, *watch*
that my dear.

Who am I but the same

Think you
T.G.

'Impudent scoundrel says Mr. G. – Blackguard.'
Bath 22nd Agst. 1768

LORD CHESTERFIELD to his godson, Philip Stanhope, 15 September 1768

Philip Dormer Stanhope, fourth Earl of Chesterfield, 1694–1773, author of the
Letters to his Son; Philip Stanhope, his godson, afterwards fifth Earl of
Chesterfield. The Dr Dodd mentioned in the postscript was the Revd William
Dodd, a fashionable preacher and Philip Stanhope's tutor. Nine years later he
forged a bond in his pupil's name, for which (notwithstanding the efforts of Dr
Johnson and others) he was executed.

Black-heath, Septr the 15th 1768.

My Dear Boy,

I send you enclosed a letter from your friend young Mr. Chenevix,
which you should answer in about a month. Politeness is as much
concerned in answering letters within a reasonable time, as it is in
returning a bowe, immediately. *A propos* of letters, let us consider the
various kinds of letters, and the general rules concerning them. Letters of
business must be answered immediately, and are the easiest either to
write or to answer, for the subject is ready and only requires great
clearness and perspicuity in the treating. There must be no prettynesses,

no quaintnesses, no Antitheses, nor even wit. *Non est his Locus*. The letters that are the hardest to write, are those that are upon no subject at all, and which are like *Small Talk* in conversation. They admit of wit if you have any, and of agreable trifling or *badinage*. For as they are nothing in themselves, their whole merit turns upon their ornaments; but they should seem easy and natural, and not smell of the lamp, as most of the letters I have seen printed do, and probably because they were wrote, in the intention of printing them. Letters between real intimate friends are of course frequent, but then they require no care nor trouble, for there the heart leaves the understanding little or nothing to do. Matter and expression present themselves. There are two other sorts of letters, but both pretty much of the same nature. These are letters to great Men your superiors, and *Lettres galantes*, I do not mean love letters, to fine women. Put flattery enough in them both, and they will be sure to please. I can assure you that men, especially great men, are not in the least behind hand with women in their love of Flattery. Whenever you write to persons greatly your inferiors; and by way of giving orders, let your letters speak, what I hope in God, you will always feell, the utmost gentleness and humanity. If you happen to write to your *Valet de Chambre*, or your Bailif, it is no great trouble to say *Pray do such a thing*, it will be taken kindly, and your orders will be the better executed for it. What good heart would roughly exert the power and superiority, which chance more than merit has given him over many of his fellow creatures? I pray God to bless you, but remember at the same time, that probably he will only bless you in proportion to your deserts.

P.S. I have left a Dictionary in two volumes of German, French, and English, for you at Dr Dodd's house in London, but notwithstanding that, I flatter myself that I shall win my wager of you next Lady Day.

HORACE WALPOLE to Thomas Chatterton, 28 March 1769

Horace Walpole, fourth Earl of Orford, 1717–97, author, connoisseur and builder of Strawberry Hill; Thomas Chatterton, poet. Chatterton had passed off much of his own poetry as the work of Thomas Rowley, a fifteenth-century monk from Bristol. Earlier that month he had sent Walpole a treatise entitled 'The Ryse of Peyncteynge in Englande bie T. Rowley'. The first two volumes of Walpole's *Anecdotes of Painting in England*, a survey of English art from medieval times, had appeared in 1762–3.

Arlington Street, March 28, 1769.

Sir,

I cannot but think myself singularly obliged by a gentleman with whom I have not the pleasure of being acquainted, when I read your very curious and kind letter, which I have this minute received. I give you a thousand thanks for it, and for the very obliging offer you make me of communicating your MSS to me. What you have already sent me is very valuable and full of information; but instead of correcting you, Sir, you are far more able to correct me. I have not the happiness of understanding the Saxon language, and without your learned notes, should not have been able to comprehend Rowley's text.

As a second edition of my *Anecdotes* was published but last year, I must not flatter myself that a third will be wanted soon; but I shall be happy to lay up any notices you will be so good as to extract for me and send me at your leisure; for as it is uncertain when I may use them, I would by no means borrow and detain your MSS.

Give me leave to ask you where Rowley's poems are to be found. I should not be sorry to print them, or at least a specimen of them, if they have never been printed.

The Abbot John's verses, that you have given me, are wonderful for their harmony and spirit, though there are some words I do not understand. You do not point out exactly the time when he lived, which I wish to know, as I suppose it was long before John ab Eyck's discovery of oil painting. If so, it confirms what I had guessed, and have hinted in my *Anecdotes*, that oil painting was known here much earlier than that discovery or revival.

I will not trouble you with more questions now, Sir; but flatter myself from the humanity and politeness you have already shown me, that you will sometimes give me leave to consult you. I hope too you will forgive the simplicity of my direction, as you have favoured me with no other. I am, Sir,

> Your much obliged and obedient humble servant,
> Hor. Walpole

PS. Be so good as to direct to Mr Walpole in Arlington Street.

THOMAS CHATTERTON to William Barrett,
[February or March 1770]

Thomas Chatterton, 1752–70, poet; William Barrett, Bristol antiquary. Horace Walpole had broken off his correspondence with Chatterton when he discovered the true identity of his Rowleian treatise on painting. This so upset Chatterton that he set about satirizing not only Walpole, but all the leading citizens of his native town & Bristol, the sole exception being Michael Clayfield, who had befriended him and lent him books. Chatterton suffered further insult at the hands of the attorney John Lambert, to whom he was apprenticed, who had threatened to burn any manuscript he found by him which were not on business.

Sir

Upon recollection, I don't know how Mr. Clayfield, could come by his Letter, as I intended to have given him a Letter but did not. In regard to my Motives for the supposed rashness, I shall observe that I keep no worse Company than *myself*; I never drink to Excess, and have, without Vanity, too much Sense to be attached, to the mercentary retailers of Iniquity. – No; It is my Pride, my damn'd, native, unconquerable Pride, that plunges me into Distraction. You must know that the 19/20th of my Composition is Pride – I must either live a Slave, a Servant; to have no Will of my own, no Sentiments of my own which I may freely declare as such; – or Die – Perplexing Alternative! but it distracts me to think of it – I will endeavour to learn Humility, but it cannot be here. What it may cost me in the trial Heaven knows! – I am

Your much Obliged unhappy
humble Servant
T.C.
Thursday Eveng.

3 April 1770

ESTHER SAUNDERS to Thomas Chatterton, with Chatterton's reply, 3 April 1770

Esther Saunders, an admirer of Chatterton; Thomas Chatterton, poet. Chatterton left Bristol for London on 24 April. He committed suicide by arsenic poisoning on 25 August 1770, three months short of his nineteenth birthday.

Sir

to a Blage you I wright a few Lines to you But have not the weakness to be Believe all you Say of me for you may Say as much to other young Ladys for all I kno But I Cant go out of a Sunday with you for I ham a fraid we Shall be Seen to go Sir if it agreeble to you I had Take a walk with you in the morning for I be Belive we Shant be Seen a bout 6 a Clock But we must wait with patient for ther is a Time for all Things.

April 3 1770
Esther Saunders

There is a time for all things – Except Marriage my dear

And so your humble Servant
T: Chatterton
April 9th—

CHRISTOPHER SMART to Dr Burney, 26 April 1770

Christopher Smart, 1722–71, poet; Charles Burney, musical historian. Smart and Burney had been friends since 1744 when both were new to London. After Smart was released from Bedlam, where he had been confined for religious mania, Burney helped organize a relief fund for him. Despite Burney's efforts, he was confined to the debtors' prison, from where this letter was written, and where he died in 1771.

King's Bench Prison
April 26th 1770.

Dr Sir

After being a fortnight at a spunging house, one week at the Marshalsea in the event of all things, I am this day safely arrived at the

King's Bench – Seven years in Madhouses, eight times arrested in six years, I beg leave to commend myself to a benevolent & providing friend
Yrs affectionately
Christopher Smart.

THE DUKE OF QUEENSBERRY to his Negro servant, Soubise, 8 November 1772

Charles Douglas, third Duke of Queensberry, 1698–1778, Lord Justice General; Soubise, his servant. The Mr Angelo referred to is presumably Dominic Angelo who at this time was a fashionable riding instructor and who later ran a famous fencing school. The Duke is said to have been attracted to Angelo's wife, the actress Peg Woffington. Soubise's reaction to Queensberry's letter is not recorded.

Amresbury, November 8th, 1772

Soubise (I wish I could call you good Soubise), I desire you will tell Mr Angelo that I am much obliged to him for his kind offer of a shooting horse, which I will very readily accept of on condition that he will give me leave to pay for him when we meet.

I will now say a few words to you about yourself. You may have observed that I have never of late said much to you on that subject, not that I was blind to your faults nor imposed upon by your cunning false professions, but that I found advice made no impression on you, & therefore for some time I have expected no good from it. The unmerited kindness & indulgence you have met with ought, from gratitude as well as from self-interest, to have induced you to endeavour by good behaviour to deserve the continuance of the goodness of your friends. You may still regain my good opinion (which you have forfeited) if you can get the better of an evil disposition you have given way to. In order to correct one's faults it is necessary in the first place to be sensible of them, I will therefore tell you what yours are. Prosperity seems really to have turned your head. You are full of pride and arrogance, which are despicable qualities even in persons of high rank & fortune, & in you are quite ridiculous. Reflect what your condition would have been if Captain Douglas had not brought you here from Jamaica. You would probably

75

have been at this very time a slave, working half-naked among sugar-canes. You are now, by the kindness of your friends, in a situation much above what you had any pretensions to, but that should rather inspire you with modest gratitude than with foolish pride. You are self-conceited, & aim at being on a level with the fashionable fine gentleman of the age, which must lead into all the vices and follies of it, and must soon bring distress and ruin upon you. Accustom yourself to speak truth, and to adhere strictly to it at all times & upon all occasions, even in the confession of a fault, for endeavouring to disguise guilt by lying is an aggravation of it. In short, a liar is a shameful and dishonest character, detested & distrusted by all mankind. I have now laid your faults open before you, & if you have a grain of reason and common sense you must be convinced of the necessity of a total change to prevent the fatal consequences of an inconsiderate dissipated course of life. After the trouble I have now taken for your sake, you cannot doubt of my being

Your well-wisher
Queensberry &c

Our own waggon goes to London with some goods, and will be there on Wednesday next, & will set out from thence either that night or Thursday morning early. If Mr Angelo will send the horse to our house on Wednesday care will be taken of him to bring him safe here.

DAVID HUME to the Comtesse de Boufflers, 20 August 1776

David Hume, 1711–76, philosopher; the Comtesse de Boufflers, mistress of the Prince de Conti and friend of Hume since 1761. Hume, who had been suffering from cancer of the liver, died five days later on 25 August.

Edinburgh, 20 August, 1776.

Tho I am certainly within a few weeks, dear Madam, and perhaps within a few days, of my own death, I could not forbear being struck with the death of the Prince of Conti – so great a loss in every particular. My reflection carried me immediately to your situation in this melancholy incident. What a difference to you in your whole plan of life! Pray write me some particulars; but in such terms that you need not care, in case of decease, into whose hands your letter may fall.

My distemper is a diarrhoea, or disorder in my bowels, which has been gradually undermining me these two years; but, within these six months, has been visibly hastening me to my end. I see death approach gradually, without any anxiety or regret. I salute you, with great affection and regard, for the last time.

David Hume.

CAPTAIN COOK to Lord Sandwich, 26 November 1776

James Cook, 1728–79, circumnavigator, charted New Zealand and the east coast of Australia; John Montagu, fourth Earl of Sandwich, First Lord of the Admiralty. This is the last letter sent by Cook to his patron Lord Sandwich, and his last communication with the outside world before setting off on his final voyage of exploration. Omai, a native of Huahine in the Society Islands, had been brought back to England by Cook on his previous voyage, where he had been much fêted.

Cape of Good Hope Novr 26th 1776

My Lord

Captain Clerke joined me on the 10th Inst. and we are at length ready to put to sea and proceed on the Voyage, having on board Provisions for two years and upwards. Nothing is wanting but a few females of our own species to make the Resolution a Compleate ark, for I have taken the liberty to add considerably to the number of animals your Lordship was pleased to order to be put on board in England: as my intention for so doing is for the good of posterity, I have no doubt but it will meet with your Lordships approbation.

The takeing on board some horses has made Omai compleatly happy, he consented with raptures to give up his Cabbin to make room for them, his only concern now is that we shall not have food for all the stock we have got on board. He continues to injoy a good state of health and great flow of Spirits and on every occasion expresses a thankfull rememberence of your Lordships great kindness to him. I have the pleasure to assure your Lordship that they have not been lost upon him, and that he has obtained during his stay in England a far greater knowlidge of things than any one could expect or will perhaps believe. Sence he has been with me I have not had the least reason to find fault with any part of his conduct and the people here are surprised at his genteel behaviour and deportment.

Permit me to assure your Lordship that my endeavours shall not be wanting to accomplish the great object of the Voyage and to render my self in some degree worthy of the honors and great bounty your Lordship have confered on –

My Lord
Your Lordships Most faithfull
and devoted humble Servant
Jams: Cook

Earl of Sandwich –

GEORGE III to Lord Sandwich, 3 August 1777

George III, 1738–1820, King of Great Britain and Ireland; John Montagu, fourth Earl of Sandwich, First Lord of the Admiralty. Burgoyne had captured Ticonderoga on 6 July 1777. He surrendered himself and his army to the Americans at Saratoga on 17 October.

Kew, August 3rd 1777, 30 m. past 4 p.m.

Lord Sandwich – Appearances cannot be more favourable than those of success at Ticonderoga, which will I trust enable Burgoyne to get soon to Albany, and must put Washington into a most unpleasant situation; and I am not yet so much convinced of the prowess of the Americans as to think they will persist when they find but little chance of success.

THOMAS GAINSBOROUGH to William Jackson, 4 June [before 1778]

Thomas Gainsborough, 1727–88, painter; William Jackson, composer and amateur painter. Karl Friedrich Abel was a virtuoso on the viola da gamba and gave concerts with J. C. Bach; his portrait was painted twice by Gainsborough, who used to exchange drawings for his music.

My Dear Jackson,

I am much obliged to you for your last Letter, and the Lessons recd. before; I think I now begin to see a little into the nature of Modulation and the introduction of flats and sharps; and when we meet you shall hear me play extempore – My Friend Abel has been to visit me, but he made but a short stay, being obliged to go to Paris for a Month or six weeks, after which He has promised to come again. There never was a poor Devil so fond of Harmony, with so little knowledge of it, so that what you have done is pure Charity – I dined with Mr. Duntze in expectation (and indeed full assurance) of hearing your scholar Miss Floud play a little, but was for the second time *flung*. She had best beware of the third time, lest I *fling* Her, and if I do I'll have a Kiss before she is up again. I'm sick of Portraits and wish very much to take my Viol da Gamba and walk off to some sweet Village when I can paint Landskips and enjoy the fag End of Life in quietness and ease. But these fine Ladies and their Tea drinkings, Dancings, *Husband huntings* and such will fob me out of the last ten years, & I fear miss getting Husbands too – But we can say nothing to these things you know Jackson, we must jogg on and be content with the jingling of the Bells, only d-mn it I hate a dust, the Kicking up of a dust, and being confined *in Harness* to follow the track, whilst others ride in the waggons, under cover, stretching their Legs in the straw at Ease, and gazing at Green Trees & Blue skies without half my *Taste*, that's damn'd hard. My Comfort is, I have 5 Viols da Gamba 3 Jayes and two Barak Normans.

Adieu dear Jackson
and believe me ever & sincerely yours

Bath June 4th   Tho. Gainsborough

WILLIAM COWPER to William Unwin, 6 August 1780

William Cowper, 1731–1800, poet; William, the son of Mary Unwin, Cowper's protectress.

My dear Friend,

You like to hear from me – this is a very good Reason why I should Write – but I have nothing to say – this seems equally a good Reason why I should not. Yet if you had alighted from your Horse at our Door this Morning, and at this present Writing, being 5 o'clock in the Afternoon, had found Occasion to say to me, Mr. Cowper you have not Spoke since I came in, have you resolved never to speak again? It would be but a poor Reply, if in Answer to the Summons I should Plead Inability as my best & only Excuse. And this by the way, suggests to me a Seasonable Piece of Instruction, and reminds me of what I am very apt to forget when I have my Epistolary Business in Hand: that a Letter may be written upon any thing or Nothing, just as that any thing or Nothing happens to Occurr. A man that has a Journey before him, 20 Miles in Length, which he is to perform on Foot, will not Hesitate & doubt whether he shall set out or not, because he does not readily conceive how he shall ever reach the End of it; for he knows that by the simple Operation of moving one Foot forward first, and then the other, he shall be sure to Accomplish it. So it is in the present Case, and so it is in every similar Case. A Letter is Written, as a Conversation is maintained, or a Journey perform'd, not by preconcerted, or premeditated Means, by a New Contrivance, or an Invention never heard of before, but merely by maintaining a Progress, and resolving as a Postillion does, having once Set out, never to Stop 'till we reach the appointed End. If a Man may Talk without thinking, why may he not Write upon the same Terms? A Grave Gentleman of the last Century, a Tie Wig, Square:toes, Steinkirk Figure would say – my good Sir, a man has no right to do either. But it is to be hoped that the present Century has nothing to do with the Mouldy Opinions of the last, and so good Sir Launcelot, or Sir Paul or whatever be your Name, Step into your Picture Frame again, and Look as if you Thought for another Century, & leave us Moderns in the mean time, to think when we can, & to Write whether we can or not, else we might as well be as Dead as you are.

When we Look back upon our Forefathers, we seem to Look back upon the People of another Nation, almost upon Creatures of another

Species. Their vast rambling Mansions, Spacious Halls, and painted Casements, the Gothic Porch smother'd with Honey Suckles, their little Gardens and high Walls, their Box Edgings, Balls of Holly, and yew Tree Statues, are become so entirely unfashionable now, that we can hardly believe it possible that a People who resembled us so little in their Taste, should Resemble us in any thing else. But in every thing else I suppose they were our Counterparts exactly, and Time that has Sewed up the Slashed Sleeve, and reduced the large Trunk Hose to a neat pair of Silk Stockings, has left Human Nature just where it found it. The Inside of the Man at least has undergone no Change, His Passions, Appetites & Aims are just what they ever were: they Wear perhaps a handsomer Disguise than they did in Days of Yore, for Philosophy and Literature will have their Effect upon the Exterior, but in every other respect, a Modern is only an Ancient in a different Dress.

When you can send me some Franks, I can send you some Verses. And shall be glad of my Translations of Bourne, when you can conveniently restore them, for I am making a Collection, not for the Public, but for Myself.

> Our Love attends Yourself & all your Family.
> Yours affectionately Wm Cowper.

Augt. 6. 1780.

DR JOHNSON to Mrs Thrale, 28 June 1783

Samuel Johnson, 1709–84, author; Hester Lynch Thrale, afterwards Piozzi, friend of Dr Johnson, author of the *Anecdotes of the late Samuel Johnson*. Johnson had taken Anna Williams, who was totally blind, into his house after his wife's death.

Dear Madam

Your letter is just such as I desire, and as from you I hope always to deserve.

The black Dog I hope always to resist, and in time to drive though I am deprived of almost all those that used to help me. The neighbourhood is impoverished. I had once Richardson and Laurence in my reach. Mrs Allen is dead. My house has lost Levet, a man who took interest in every thing and therefore was very ready at conversation. Mrs Williams is so weak that she can be a companion no longer. When I rise my breakfast is solitary, the black dog waits to share it, from breakfast to dinner he continues barking, except that Dr Brocklesby for a little keeps him at a distance. Dinner with a sick woman you may venture to suppose not much better than solitary. After Dinner what remains but to count the clock, and hope for that sleep which I can scarce expect. Night comes at last, and some hours of restlessness and confusion bring me again to a day of solitude. What shall exclude the black dog from a habitation like this? If I were a little richer I would perhaps take some cheerful Female into the House.

Your Bath news shews me new calamities. I am afraid Mrs. Lewis is left with a numerous family very slenderly supplied. Mrs. Sheward is an old maid, I am afraid, yet sur le pavé.

Welch, if he were well, would be well enough liked, his Daughter has powers and knowledge, but no art of making them agreeable.

I must touch my Journal. Last night fresh flies were put to my head, and hindred me from sleeping. To day I fancy myself incommoded by heat.

I have however watered the garden both yesterday and to day, just as I watered the laurel in the Island.

I am Madam Your most humble servant

London June 28. 1783   Sam: Johnson.

BENJAMIN FRANKLIN to Sir Joseph Banks, 27 July 1783

Benjamin Franklin, 1706–90, author, scientist and statesman; Sir Joseph Banks, President of the Royal Society. Franklin was in France as United States Commissioner during the peace negotiations with Great Britain, the Provisional Articles having been signed on 30 November 1782. The Montgolfier brothers had sent up the first successful hot-air balloon from Annonay in June, and repeated the experiment before a large crowd at Paris the following month.

Passy, July 27, 1783.

Dear Sir,

I received your very kind letter by Dr. Blagden, and esteem myself much honour'd by your friendly remembrance. I have been too much and too closely engag'd in public affairs since his being here, to enjoy all the benefit of his conversation you were so good as to intend me. I hope soon to have more leisure, and to spend a part of it in those studies that are much more agreeable to me than political operations.

I join with you most cordially in rejoicing at the return of Peace. I hope it will be lasting, and that mankind will at length, as they call themselves reasonable creatures, have reason and sense enough to settle their differences without cutting throats. For in my opinion *there never was a good War, or a bad Peace.*

What vast additions to the conveniences and comforts of living might mankind have acquired, if the money spent in wars had been employ'd in Works of public utility; what an extention of agriculture even to the tops of our Mountains; what Rivers rendered navigable, or joined by canals; what Bridges, Acqueducts, new Roads, and other public Works, Edifices, and Improvements, rendering England a compleat Paradise, might not have been obtain'd by spending those millions in doing good, which in the last War have been spent in doing mischief; in bringing misery into thousands of families, and destroying the lives of so many thousands of working people who might have perform'd the useful labour.

I am pleas'd with the late astronomical discoveries made by our Society. Furnish'd as all Europe now is with Academies of Science, with nice instruments and the spirit of Experiment, the progress of human knowledge will be rapid, and discoveries made of which we have at present no conception. I begin to be almost sorry I was born so soon, since I cannot have the happiness of knowing what will be known a hundred years hence.

I wish continued success to the labours of the Royal Society, and that you may long adorn their chair, being with the highest esteem,

> Dear Sir,
> > your most obedient
> > > and most humble servant,
> > > > B. Franklin.

Dr. Blagden will acquaint you with the experiment of a vast Globe sent up into the air, much talk'd of here at present, and which if prosecuted may furnish means of new knowledge.

SAMUEL JOHNSON to Lucy Porter, 2 December 1784

Samuel Johnson, 1709–84, author; Lucy Porter, daughter of Johnson's wife Elizabeth by her first marriage. Johnson died eleven days later, on 13 December.

Dear Madam

I am very ill, and desire your prayers. I have sent Mr Green the epitaph, and a power to call on You for ten pounds.

I laid this summer a stone over Tetty in the chapel of Bromley in Kent. The Inscription is in Latin of which this is the English.

Here lie the remains of Elizabeth, descended from the ancient house of Jarvis at Peatling in Leicestershire; a Woman of beauty, elegance, ingenuity, and piety. Her first Husband was Henry Porter; her second, Samuel Johnson, who having loved her much, and lamented her long, laid this stone upon her.

She died in March. 1752.

That this is done, I thought it fit that You should know; what care will be taken of us, who can tell? May God pardon and bless us, for Jesus Christs sake. Amen.

I am, Madam, Your most humble Servant

Dec. 2. 1784   Sam: Johnson.

ROBERT BURNS to Robert Ainslie, 3 March 1788

Robert Burns, 1759–96, poet; Robert Ainslie, lawyer. Burns had several children by Jean Armour. 'Clarinda' was Mrs M'Lehose, with whom he indulged in a high-flown and sentimental correspondence.

Mauchline, 3d March, 1788

My dear Friend,

I am just returned from Mr. Miller's farm. My old friend whom I took with me was highly pleased with the bargain, and advised me to accept of it. He is the most intelligent, sensible farmer in the county, and his advice has staggered me a good deal. I have the two plans before me: I shall endeavour to balance them to the best of my judgment, and fix on the most eligible. On the whole, if I find Mr. Miller in the same favorable disposition as when I saw him last, I shall in all probability turn farmer.

I have been through sore tribulation, and under much buffeting of the Wicked One, since I came to this country. Jean I found banished like a martyr – forlorn, destitute, and friendless; all for the good old cause: I have reconciled her to her fate: I have reconciled her to her mother: I have taken her a room: I have taken her to my arms: I have given her a mahogany bed: I have given her a guinea; and I have f—d her till she rejoiced with joy unspeakable and full of glory. But – as I always am on every occasion – I have been prudent and cautious to an astounding degree; I swore her, privately and solemnly, never to attempt any claim on me as a husband, even though anybody should persuade her she had such a claim, which she has not, neither during my life, nor after my death. She did all this like a good girl, and I took the opportunity of some dry horselitter, and gave her such a thundering scalade that electrified the very marrow of her bones. O, what a peacemaker is a guid weel-willy p—le! It is the mediator, the guarantee, the umpire, the bond of union, the solemn league and covenant, the plenipotentiary, the Aaron's rod, the Jacob's staff, the prophet Elisha's pot of oil, the Ahasuerus' sceptre, the sword of mercy, the philosopher's stone, the horn of plenty, and Tree of Life between Man and Woman.

I shall be in Edinburgh the middle of next week. My farming ideas I shall keep quiet till I see. I got a letter from Clarinda yesterday, and she tells me she has got no letter of mine but one. Tell her that I wrote to her from Glasgow, from Kilmarnock, from Mauchline, and yesterday from Cumnock, as I returned from Dumfries. Indeed, she is the only person in Edinburgh I have written to till this day. How are your soul and body putting up? – a little like man and wife, I suppose.

Your faithful Friend,
R.B.

WILLIAM COWPER to Samuel Rose, 24 April 1792

William Cowper, 1731–1800, poet; Samuel Rose, lawyer and Cowper's trustee.
Cowper was at this time editing Milton.

The Lodge
April 24. 1792

My dear friend –
The Cheese and the Rose-water arrived safe at Weston yesterday.
Safe, but not all; for alas! one bottle

> Denied its due investiture of Hay,
> Got a sad blow, and perish'd by the way.

I think myself happy however to have received the rest of the cargo
uninjured, for I was not without fear that the whole might suffer wreck,
the floods in this country having lately swept carts, waggons and drivers
away without mercy. You will perhaps think me premature in writing
before I have had opportunity to taste your purchase. But the reason is,
that Cheese is a diet which at present does not suit me, neither am I sure
that my palate is just now in a condition to judge of it. For you must know
that I have been confined to the house and almost to my chair this
fortnight, by a most excruciating disorder, synonimous with those things
on which they sometimes lay the foundations of bridges. But the name is
the only point of resemblance, since instead of serving me with a
foundation, it deprived me even of that which nature gave me, making it
impossible for me to *sit* still a moment.
I am glad that you have introduced Mr. Mackenzie to my Cousin, and
especially as she was so much pleased by his visit. He seems, she says, to
be a very amiable man, she liked his conversation much, and only wished
that he could have stay'd longer. This is much for her to say who is rather
nice in her choice, and feels with the quickness of a sensitive plant both
the agreeable and disagreeable of her acquaintance. It argues accordingly great merit on the part of Mr. Mackenzie.
You do well, I hope, to resolve on employing two Printers, though two
perhaps can be as idle as one, and twenty as idle as either. In which case
the vexation will encrease exactly in proportion to the number. But may
it prove otherwise with you, who I suppose have been already sufficiently
tormented.

I should have told you, though my letter, being not very melancholy, may have suggested it to you already, that I am now nearly recover'd from my aukward malady. But it has been a sad hindrance to me in my literary labours; I had proceeded in my commentary almost through the 1st. book of the Paradise Lost, when it brought me to a stand, and from contemplating a lake of brimstone I was obliged to pass at once into a brimstone regimen.

So now farewell – you have, and yours, our united best wishes, with many thanks for the Cheese and its pleasant accompaniments, and I remain

Sincerely yours Wm Cowper.

WILLIAM COWPER to John Newton, 11 April 1799

William Cowper, 1731–1800, poet; the Revd John Newton, former slave trader, author with Cowper of *The Olney Hymns*. Cowper had long suffered from intermittent bouts of acute depression, characterized by a dream experienced in 1773 'before the recollection of which every consolation vanishes' in which he heard the sentence pronounced '*Actum est de te, periisti*' ('It is all over with thee, thou hast perished'). He suffered his final attack in 1794 and although he lived for another six years, never recovered. This is his last known letter.

Dereham –
Apr: 11. 1799.

Dear Sir –

Your last letter so long unanswer'd may, and indeed must, have proved sufficiently, that my state of mind is not now more favourable to the purpose of writing than it was when I received it; for had any alteration in that respect taken place, I should certainly have acknowledged it long since, or at whatsoever time the change had happen'd, and should not have waited for the present call upon me to return you my thanks at the same time for the letter and for the book which you have been so kind as to send me. Mr. Johnson has read it to me. If it afforded me any amusement, or suggested to me any reflections, they were only such as served to imbitter, if possible, still more the present moment, by a sad retrospect to those days when I thought myself secure of an eternity to be spent with the Spirits of such men as He whose life afforded the subject of it. But I was little aware of what I had to expect, and that a storm was at hand which is one terrible moment would darken, and in another still more terrible, blot out that prospect for ever. – Adieu Dear Sir, whom in those days I call'd Dear friend, with feelings that justified the appellation –

I remain yours
Wm Cowper.

WILLIAM BLAKE to John Trusler, 23 August 1799

William Blake, 1757–1827, poet, painter, and engraver; John Trusler, 'eccentric divine, literary compiler, and medical empiric' (*Dictionary of National Biography*). Trusler, author of *Hogarth Moralized* (1768), had commissioned some designs from Blake. These, it seems, did not meet with his approval.

Revd Sir,

I really am sorry that you are fall'n out with the Spiritual World, Especially if I should have to answer for it. I feel very sorry that your Ideas & Mine on Moral Painting differ so much as to have made you angry with my method of Study. If I am wrong, I am wrong in good company. I had hoped your plan comprehended All Species of this Art, & Expecially that you would not regret that Species which gives Existence to Every other, namely, Visions of Eternity. You say that I want somebody to Elucidate my Ideas. But you ought to know that What is Grand is necessarily obscure to Weak men. That which can be made Explicit to the Idiot is not worth my care. The wisest of the Ancients consider'd what is not too Explicit as the fittest for Instruction, because it rouzes the faculties to act. I name Moses, Solomon, Esop, Homer, Plato.

But as you have favor'd me with your remarks on my Design, permit me in return to defend it against a mistaken one, which is, That I have supposed Malevolence without a Cause. Is not Merit in one a Cause of Envy in another, & Serenity & Happiness & Beauty a Cause of Malevolence? But Want of Money & the Distress of A Thief can never be alledged as the Cause of his Thieving, for many honest people endure greater hardships with Fortitude. We must therefore seek the Cause elsewhere than in want of Money, for that is the Miser's passion, not the Thief's.

I have therefore proved your Reasonings Ill proportion'd, which you can never prove my figures to be; they are those of Michael Angelo, Rafael & the Antique, & of the best living Models. I percieve that your Eye is perverted by Caricature Prints, which ought not to abound so much as they do. Fun I love, but too much Fun is of all things the most loathsom. Mirth is better than Fun, & Happiness is better than Mirth. I feel that a Man may be happy in This World. And I know that This World Is a World of imagination & Vision. I see Every thing I paint In This World, but Every body does not see alike. To the Eyes of a Miser a Guinea is more beautiful than the Sun, & a bag worn with the use of Money has more beautiful proportions than a Vine filled with Grapes. The tree which moves some to tears of joy is in the Eyes of others only a green thing that stands in the way. Some See Nature all Ridicule & Deformity, & by these I shall not regulate my proportions; & Some Scarce see Nature at all. But to the Eyes of the Man of Imagination, Nature is Imagination itself. As a man is, So he Sees. As the Eye is formed, such are its Powers. You certainly Mistake, when you say that the Visions of Fancy are not to be found in This World. To Me This World is all One continued Vision of Fancy or Imagination, & I feel Flatter'd when I am told so. What is it sets Homer, Virgil & Milton in so high a rank of Art? Why is the Bible more Entertaining & Instructive than any other book? Is it not because they are addressed to the Imagination, which is Spiritual Sensation, & but mediately to the Understanding or Reason? Such is True Painting, and such was alone valued by the Greeks & the best modern Artists. Consider what Lord Bacon says: 'Sense sends over to Imagination before Reason have judged, & Reason sends over to Imagination before the Decree can be acted.' See Advancement of Learning, Part 2, P. 47 of first Edition.

But I am happy to find a Great Majority of Fellow Mortals who can Elucidate My Visions, & Particularly they have been Elucidated by Children, who have taken a greater delight in contemplating my Pictures than I even hoped. Neither Youth nor Childhood is Folly or Incapacity. Some Children are Fools & so are some Old Men. But There is a vast Majority on the side of Imagination or Spiritual Sensation.

To Engrave after another Painter is infinitely more laborious than to Engrave one's own Inventions. And of the size you require my price has been Thirty Guineas, & I cannot afford to do it for less. I had Twelve for the Head I sent you as a Specimen; but after my own designs I could do at least Six times the quantity of labour in the same time, which will account for the difference of price as also that Chalk Engraving is at least six times as laborious as Aqua tinta. I have no objection to Engraving after another Artist. Engraving is the profession I was apprenticed to, & should never have attempted to live by any thing else, If orders had not come in for my Designs & Paintings, which I have the pleasure to tell you are Increasing Every Day. Thus If I am a Painter it is not to be attributed to Seeking after. But I am contented whether I live by Painting or Engraving.

I am, Revd Sir, your very obedient servant,

William Blake

13 Hercules Buildings
Lambeth
August 23. 1799

LORD NELSON to Lady Hamilton, 29 January–2 February [1800]

Horatio Nelson, 1758–1805, Admiral; Emma Hamilton, Nelson's mistress, wife of Sir William Hamilton, British Plenipotentiary at Naples. This is the earliest known love letter from Nelson to Lady Hamilton. Although not dated by year, it was clearly written in 1800, when 29 January fell on a Wednesday. At that time Nelson was cruising in the Mediterranean and fretting under the command of Admiral Keith, the 'Commander In Chief' referred to in the letter. Nelson arrived at Palermo on 3 February, and sent his servant Tom Allen to Lady Hamilton with a more discretely worded note (published in *The Despatches*). The present letter, which bears neither salutation, signature nor address-panel, was no doubt sent with the note as an enclosure. His next letter to her (published in *The Morrison Collection*) was written when once again at sea on 13 February. In it he explains why he has re-adopted the more guarded tone which distinguishes all the other letters written to her at this time and for some time afterwards: 'I do not send you any news or opinions, as this letter goes by post and may be opened.'

Wednesday 29th Janry

Separated from all I hold dear in this world what is the use of living if indeed such an existance can be called so, nothing could alleviate such a Separation but the call of our Country but loitering time away with *nonsense* is too much, no Seperation no time my only beloved Emma can alter my love and affection for You, it is founded on the truest principles of honor, and it only remains for us to regret which I do with the bitterest anguish that there are any obstacles to our being united in the closest ties of this Worlds rigid rules, as We are in those of real love. Continue only to love Your faithful Nelson as he loves his Emma. You are my guide I submit to You, let me find all My fond heart hopes and wishes with the risk of my life I have been faithful to my word never to partake of any amusement or to sleep on Shore. Thursday Janry 30th We have been Six days from Leghorn and no prospect of our making a passage to Palermo, to me it is worse than death. I can neither Eat or Sleep for thinking of You my dearest love, I never touch even pudding You know the reason. No I would Starve sooner. My only hope is to find You have Equally kept Your promises to Me, for I never made You a promise that I did not as strictly keep as if made in the presence of heaven, but I rest perfectly confident of the reallity of Your love and that You would die sooner than be false in the smallest thing to Your Own faithful Nelson who lives only for his Emma, friday I shall run Mad we have had a gale of Wind that is nothing but I am 20 Leagues farther from You than Yesterday noon. Was I master notwithstanding the weather I would have been 20 Leagues nearer but my Commander In Chief knows not what I feel by absence, last Night I did nothing but dream of You altho' I woke 20 times in the Night. In one of my dreams I thought I was at a large Table You was not present, Sitting between a Princess who I detest and another. They both tried to Seduce Me and the first wanted to take those liberties with Me which no Woman in this World but Yourself ever did. The consequence was I knocked her down and in the moment of bustle You came in and taking Me in Your embrace wispered I love nothing but You My Nelson. I kissed You fervently And we enjoy'd the height of love. Ah Emma I pour out my Soul to You. If you love any thing but Me You love those who feel not like your N. Sunday Noon fair Wind which makes me a little better in hopes of seeing You my love My Emma to morrow. Just 138 Miles distant, and I trust to find You like myself. for no love is like Mine towards You.

[3 March 1800]

SAMUEL TAYLOR COLERIDGE to William Godwin, [3 March 1800]

Samuel Taylor Coleridge, 1772–1834, poet and critic; William Godwin, philosopher, Shelley's father-in-law.

Mr Lamb's No / 36 Chapel Street Pentonville –
8, Monday Morning

Dear Godwin

The Punch after the Wine made me tipsy last night – this I mention, not that my head aches, or that I felt after I quitted you, any unpleasantness, or titubancy – ; but because tipsiness has, and has always, one unpleasant effect – that of making me talk *very* extravagantly / & as when sober, I talk extravagantly enough for any *common* Tipsiness, it becomes a matter of nicety in discrimination to know when I am or am not affected. – An idea starts up in my hand [head?] – away I follow it thro' thick & thin, Wood & Marsh, Brake and Briar – with all the apparent Interest of a man who was defending one of his old and long-established Principles – Exactly of this kind was the Conversation, with which I quitted you / I do not believe it possible for a human Being to have a greater horror of the Feelings that usually accompany such principles as I then supported, or a deeper Conviction of their irrationality than myself – but the whole Thinking of my Life will not bear me up against the accidental Press & Crowd of my mind, when it is elevated beyond it's natural Pitch / . –

We shall talk wiselier with the Ladies on Tuesday – God bless you, & give your dear little ones a kiss a piece for me –

The Agnus Dei & the Virgin Mary desire their kind respects to *you*, you sad Atheist – !

Your's with affectionate
Esteem
S. T. Coleridge

SAMUEL TAYLOR COLERIDGE to James West Tobin, 25 July 1800

Samuel Taylor Coleridge, 1772–1834, poet and critic; James West Tobin, a member of Wordsworth and Davy's Bristol circle. Coleridge had just moved to Keswick; Wordsworth, with whom he was still on intimate terms, had moved to Dove Cottage with his sister at the end of the previous year. Davy, to whom Coleridge refers, is the scientist Sir Humphry Davy, whom he had met in Bristol; Hartley is Coleridge's son.

> Friday, July 25, 1800
> From the leads on the housetop of Greta Hall,
> Keswick, Cumberland, at the present time in the
> occupancy and usufruct-possession of S. T. Coleridge,
> Esq., Gentleman-poet and Philosopher in a mist.

Yes, my dear Tobin, here I am, with Skiddaw behind my back; the Lake of Bassenthwaite, with its simple and majestic *case* of mountains, on my right hand; on my left, and stretching far away into the fantastic mountains of Borrowdale, the Lake of Derwentwater; straight before me a whole camp of giants' tents, – or is it an ocean rushing in, in billows that, even in the serene sky, reach halfway to heaven? When I look at the feathery top of this scoundrel pen, with which I am making desperate attempts to write, I see (in that slant direction) the sun almost setting, – in ten minutes it will touch the top of the crag; the vale of Keswick lies between us, so much for the topography of the letter; as to the chronology, it is half past seven in the evening.

I left Wordsworth yesterday; he was tolerably well, and meditates more than his side permits him even to attempt. He has a bed for you; but I absolutely stipulate that you shall be half the time at Keswick. We have house-room enough, and I am sure I need say nothing of anything else. What should prevent you from coming and spending the next brace of months here? I will suppose you to set off in the second week of August, and Davy will be here in the first week of September at the farthest; and then, my dear fellow, for physiopathy and phileleutherism – sympathy lemonaded with a little argument – punning and green peas with bacon, or *very ham*; rowing and sailing on the lake (there is a nice boat obsequious to my purposes). Then, as to chemistry, there will be Davy with us. We shall be as rich with reflected light as yon cloud which the sun has taken to his very bosom!

When you come, I pray you do not forget to bring Bartram's Travels with you. Where is John Pinny? He talked of accompanying you.

Wordsworth builds on his coming down this autumn; if I knew his present address, I would write to him. Wordworth remains at Grasmere till next summer (perhaps longer). His cottage is indeed in every respect so delightful a residence, the walks so dry after the longest rains, the heath and a silky kind of fern so luxurious a bedding on every hilltop, and the whole vicinity so tossed about on those little hills at the feet of the majestic mountains, that he moves in an eddy; he cannot get out of it.

In the way of books, we are extraordinarily well off for a country place. My landlord has a respectable library, full of dictionaries and useful modern things; *ex. gr.*, the Scotch Encyclopaedia, the authors of which may the devil scotch, for toothless serpents that poison with dribble! But there is at some distance Sir Wilfred Lawson's magnificent library, and Sir Wilfred talks of calling upon me, and of course I keep the man in good humor with me, and gain the use of his books.

Hartley returns his love to you; he talks often about you. I hear his voice at this moment distinctly; he is below in the garden, shouting to some foxgloves and fern, which he has transplanted, and telling them what he will do for them if they grow like good boys! This afternoon I sent him naked into a shallow of the river Greta; he trembled with the novelty, yet you cannot conceive his raptures.

God bless you!

I remain, with affectionate esteem,
Yours sincerely,
S. T. Coleridge.

I open the letter, and make a new fold, to tell you that I have bit the wafer [seal] into the very shape of the young moon that is just above the opposite hill.

GEORGE MORLAND to John Graham, 6 May 1801

George Morland, 1763–1804, painter; John Graham, a patron. Morland's epitaph on himself was, 'Here lies a drunken dog'.

Dear Graham I am worse than ever. Had an opium pill to take last night, and as I thought two must do me more good than one, I took them both, I expected it was *up*.

However I am not quite so bad but I will use my best endeavour to get on for you this week. the whole of which I must keep quiet.

Good bie

G. Morland

Wednesday

LORD NELSON to Lady Hamilton, 19 and 20 October 1805

Horatio Nelson, 1758–1805, Admiral; Emma Hamilton, his mistress. This famous letter, Nelson's last, was written on the eve of the Battle of Trafalgar, fought on 21st October, and left unfinished at his death. At the end of it Lady Hamilton has written, 'This letter was found open on His desk, & brought to Lady Hamilton by Capt Hardy. Oh, miserable, wretched Emma! Oh, glorious & happy Nelson!'

Victory Octr. 19th: 1805 Noon Cadiz ESE 16 Leagues

My Dearest beloved Emma the dear friend of my bosom the Signal has been made that the Enemys Combined fleet are coming out of Port. We have very little Wind so that I have no hopes of seeing them before to-morrow May the God of Battles crown my endeavours with success at all events I will take care that my name shall ever be most dear to you and Horatio both of whom I love as much as my own life. and as my last writing before the battle will be to you so I hope in God that I shall live to finish my letter after the Battle. May Heaven bless you prays your Nelson & Bronte. Octr. 20th, in the morning we were close to the mouth of the Streights but the Wind had not come far enough to the Westward to allow the Combined Fleets to Weather the shoals off Traflagar but they were counted as far as forty Sail of Ships of War which I suppose to be 34 of the Line and six frigates, a Group of them was seen off the Lighthouse of Cadiz this Morng but it blows so very fresh & thick weather that I rather believe they will go into the Harbour before night. May God Almighty give us success over these fellows and enable us to get a Peace.

'SAM' to his father, [October or November 1805]

'Sam', surname unknown, a sailor on board the *Royal Sovereign*, the flagship of Admiral Collingwood, second-in-command at the Battle of Trafalgar.

Honoured Fathre,
This comes to tell you that I am alive and hearty except three fingers; but that's not much, it might have been my head. I told brother Tom I should like to see a greadly battle, and I have seen one, and we have peppered the Combined rarely (off Trafalgar); and for the matter of that, they fought us pretty tightish for French and Spanish. Three of our mess are killed, and four more of us winged. But to tell you the truth of it, when the game began, I wished myself at Warnborough with my plough again; but when they had given us one duster, and I found myself snug and tight, I set to in good earnest, and thought no more about being killed than if I were at Murrell Green Fair, and I was presently as busy and as black as a collier. How my fingers got knocked overboard I don't know, but off they are, and I never missed them till I wanted them. You see, by my writing, it was my left hand, so I can write to you and fight for my King yet. We have taken a rare parcel of ships, but the wind is so rough we cannot bring them home, else I should roll in money, so we are busy smashing 'em, and blowing 'em up wholesale.

Our dear Admiral Nelson is killed! so we have paid pretty sharply for licking 'em. I never set eyes on him, for which I am both sorry and glad; for to be sure, I should like to have seen him – but then, all the men in our ship are such soft toads, they have done nothing but blast their eyes, and cry, ever since he was killed. God bless you! chaps that fought like the devil, sit down and cry like a wench. I am still in the *Royal Sovereign*, but the Admiral has left her, for she is like a horse without a bridle, so he is in a frigate that he may be here and there and everywhere, for he's as *cute* as here and there one, and as bold as a lion, for all he can cry! I saw his tears with my own eyes, when the boat hailed and said my Lord was dead. So no more at present from

Your dutiful Son,
Sam

LORD BYRON to the Revd J. T. Becher, 26 February 1808

George Gordon, Lord Byron, 1788–1824, poet; the Revd John Thomas Becher, Vicar-General of Southwell Minster, Byron's early literary advisor. Byron had come down from Cambridge that Christmas. The January number of the *Edinburgh Review*, which appeared in late February, contained a cutting and sarcastic review of Byron's *Hours of Idleness*. Byron was later to become part of the Whig circle centred around Lord and Lady Holland in whose favour, as he correctly surmised, the *Edinburgh* was biased. Mrs Byron was his mother.

Dorant's [Hotel]. February 26th. 1808

My dear Becher, – Just rising from my Bed, having been up till six at a Masquerade, I find your Letter, and in the midst of this dissipated Chaos it is no small pleasure to discover I have some *distant* friends in their Senses, though mine are rather out of repair. – Indeed, I am worse than ever, to give you some idea of my late life, I have this moment received a prescription from Pearson, not for any *complaint* but from *debility*, and literally *too much Love*. – You know my devotion to woman, but indeed Southwell was much mistaken in conceiving my adorations were paid to any Shrine there, no, my Paphian Goddesses are elsewhere, and I have sacrificed at their altar rather too liberally. – In fact, my blue eyed Caroline, who is only sixteen, has been lately so *charming*, that though we are both in perfect health, we are at present commanded to *repose*, being nearly worn out. – So much for Venus, now for Apollo, – I am happy you still retain your predilection, and that the public allow me some share of praise, I am of so much importance, that a most violent attack is preparing for me in the next number of the Edinburgh Review, this I have from the authority of a friend who has seen the proof and manuscript of the Critique, you know the System of the Edinburgh Gentlemen is universal attack, they praise none, and neither the public or the author expects praise from them, it is however something to be noticed, as they profess to pass judgment only on works requiring the public attention. – You will see this when it comes out, it is I understand of the most unmerciful description, but I am aware of it, and I hope *you* will not be hurt by its severity. – Tell *Mrs. Byron* not to be out of humour with them, and to prepare her mind for the greatest hostility on their part, it will do no injury however, and I trust her mind will not be ruffled. – They defeat their object by indiscriminate abuse, and they never praise except the partizans of Ld. Holland & Co. – It is nothing to be abused, when Southey, Moore, Lauderedale, Strangford, and Payne Knight share the same fate. – I am sorry, but C— Recollections must be suppressed during this edition, I have altered at your Suggestion the *obnoxious allusions* in the 6th Stanza of my last ode. – And now, Becher I must return my best acknowledgments for the interest you have taken in me and my poetical Bantlings, and I shall ever be proud to show how much I esteem the *advice* and the *Adviser*. – Believe me

most truly yours
Byron

P.S. – Write soon.

BENJAMIN ROBERT HAYDON to Lord Elgin, December 1808

Benjamin Robert Haydon, 1786–1846, painter and diarist; Thomas Bruce, seventh Earl of Elgin. Haydon first saw the Parthenon Marbles in 1808 at Elgin's house in Park Lane, and spent three months drawing them. He was later instrumental in having them purchased by the nation.

My dear Lord Elgin,

I hope you will excuse my troubling you once more about the marbles. You said you intended to offer premiums to those who would produce the best *restorations*. Now, to restore the mutilated parts of any figure, as they ought to be restored, pre-supposes a thorough knowledge of the character of what remains. This could not be expected from students on their first admission. I would venture, therefore, to propose, that a twelvemonth should be given to them to model and investigate before they commenced restoring, and then I think your Lordship would have better chance of their succeeding. I am so interested in anything that concerns the marbles, that they are become part of my existence.

I am, my dear Lord Elgin,
Your grateful and faithful servant.
B. R. Haydon.

PERCY BYSSHE SHELLEY to Thomas Hitchener, 14 May 1812

Percy Bysshe Shelley, 1792–1822, poet; Thomas Hitchener, father of Elizabeth Hitchener. Shelley had formed an intense friendship – which was intellectual rather than amatory – with Elizabeth Hitchener, who ran a school near Hurstpierpoint. Her father was a retired smuggler who kept a public house.

Nantgwillt, May 14. 1812

Sir

If you have always considered *character* a posession of the first consequence you & I essentially differ. If you think that an admission of your inferiority to the world leaves any corner by which yourself & character may aspire beyond it's reach, we differ there again. In short, to be candid, I am deceived in my conception of your character. –

I had some difficulty in stifling an indignant surprise on reading the sentence of your letter in which *you* refuse my invitation to your daughter. How are you entitled to do this? who made you her governor? did you receive this refusal from her to communicate to me? No you have not. – How are *you* then constituted to answer a question which can only be addressed to *her*? believe me such an assumption is as impotent as it is immoral, you may cause your daughter much anxiety many troubles, you may stretch her on a bed of sickness, you may destroy her body, but you are defied to shake her mind. – She is now very ill. *You* have agitated her mind until her frame is seriously deranged – take care Sir, you may destroy her by disease, but her mind is free, *that* you cannot hurt. – Your ideas of *Propriety* (or to express myself clearer, of *morals*) are all founded on considerations of *profit*. I do not mean money but profit in its extended sense: – As to your daughter's welfare on that *she* is competent to judge or at least she alone has a right to decide. With respect to your own comfort you of course do right to consult it, that she has done so you ought to be more grateful than you appear. – But how can you demand as a right what has been generously conceded as a favor; you do right to consult your own comfort, but the whole world besides may surely be excused.

Neither the laws of Nature, nor of England have made children private property. –

Adieu, when next I hear from you, I hope that time will have liberalized your sentiments.

Your's truly
P. B. Shelley

WILLIAM WORDSWORTH to Robert Southey, 2 December 1812

William Wordsworth, 1770–1850, poet; Robert Southey, poet. Thomas, Wordsworth's third child by his wife Mary, was six and a half years old.

Wednesday Evening

My dear Friend,

Symptoms of the measles appeared upon my Son Thomas last Thursday; he was most favorable held till tuesday, between ten and eleven at that hour was particularly lightsome and comfortable; without any assignable cause a sudden change took place, an inflammation had commenced on the lungs which it was impossible to check and the sweet Innocent yielded up his soul to God before six in the evening. He did not appear to suffer much in body, but I fear something in mind as he was of an age to have thought much upon death a subject to which his mind was daily led by the grave of his Sister. My Wife bears the loss of her Child with striking fortitude. My Sister was not at home but is returned to day, I met her at Threlkeld. Miss Hutchinson also supports her sorrow as ought to be done. For myself dear Southey I dare not say in what state of mind I am; I loved the Boy with the utmost love of which my soul is capable, and he is taken from me – yet in the agony of my spirit in surrendering such a treasure I feel a thousand times richer than if I had never possessed it. God comfort and save you and all our friends and us all from a repetition of such trials – O Southey feel for me! If you are not afraid of the complaint, I ought to have said if you have had it come over to us! Best love from everybody – you will impart this sad news to your Wife and Mrs Coleridge and Mrs Lovel and to Miss Barker and Mrs Wilson. Poor woman! she was most good to him – Heaven reward her.

Heaven bless you
Your sincere Friend
W. Wordsworth

Will Mrs Coleridge please to walk up to the Calverts and mention these afflictive news with the particulars. I should have written but my sorrow over-powers me.

LADY HAMILTON to Sir Richard Puleston, 24 July 1813

Emma Hamilton, ?1765–1815, Nelson's mistress; Sir Richard Puleston, a benefactor. Nelson on his death had, to little effect, left Emma as a legacy to his country; she was committed to a debtor's prison for a second time early in 1813 and remained there for a year. The first of August was the anniversary of the Battle of the Nile, fought in 1798.

No. 12 Temple Place opposite the Surry Theatre – July 24, 1813

If you are in Town & will take a drive to see one who will ever love & respect you, you will make me happy. You will not see an ambassadress nor in splendor but you will ever find me firm & my mind uncorrupted. Shame on those who will let me and Nelson's daughter pass the first of August in anguish. Mrs. Francis has often called for you but did not see you. May God bless you. I am well.

E. H.

SAMUEL TAYLOR COLERIDGE to Joseph Cottle, 26 April 1814

Samuel Taylor Coleridge, 1772–1834, poet and critic; Joseph Cottle, the Bristol bookseller who had published *The Lyrical Ballads*. Cottle had written to Coleridge urging him to renounce the opium to which he was addicted, assuming that he could do so by a mere act of will.

April 26, 1814

You have poured oil in the raw and festering Wound of an old friend's Conscience, Cottle! but it is oil of Vitriol! I but barely glanced at the middle of the first page of your Letter, & have seen no more of it – not for resentment (God forbid!) but from the state of my bodily & mental sufferings, that scarcely permitted human fortitude to let in a new visitor of affliction. The object of my present reply is to state the case just as it is – first, that for years the anguish of my spirit has been indescribable, the sense of my danger *staring*, but the conscience of my GUILT worse, far far worse than all! – I have prayed with drops of agony on my Brow, trembling not only before the Justice of my Maker, but even before the

Mercy of my Redeemer. 'I gave thee so many Talents. What hast thou done with them'? – Secondly – that it is false & cruel to say, (overwhelmed as I am with the sense of my direful Infirmity) that I attempt or ever have attempted to *disguise* or conceal the cause. On the contrary, not only to friends have I stated the whole Case with tears & the very bitterness of shame; but in two instances I have warned young men, mere aquaintances who had spoken of having taken Laudanum, of the direful Consequences, by an ample exposition of it's tremendous effects on myself – Thirdly, tho' before God I dare not lift up my eyelids, & only do not despair of his Mercy because to despair would be adding crime to crime; yet to my fellow-men I may say, that I was seduced into the ACCURSED Habit ignorantly. – I had been almost bed-ridden for many months with swellings in my knees – in a medical Journal I unhappily met with an account of a cure performed in a similar case (or what to me appeared so) by rubbing in of Laudanum, at the same time taking a given dose internally – It acted like a charm, like a miracle! I recovered the use of my Limbs, of my appetite, of my Spirits – & this continued for near a fortnight – At length, the unusual Stimulus subsided – the complaint returned – the supposed remedy was recurred to – but I can not go thro' the dreary history – suffice it to say, that effects were produced, which acted on me by *Terror & Cowardice* of PAIN & sudden Death, not (so help me God!) by any temptation of Pleasure, or expectation or desire of exciting pleasurable Sensations. On the very contrary, Mrs Morgan & her Sister will bear witness so far, as to say that the longer I abstained, the higher my spirits were, the keener my enjoyments – till the moment, the direful moment, arrived, when my pulse began to fluctuate, my Heart to palpitate, & such a dreadful *falling-abroad*, as it were, of my whole frame, such intolerable Restlessness & incipient Bewilderment, that in the last of my several attempts to abandon the dire poison, I exclaimed in agony, what I now repeat in seriousness & solemnity – 'I am too poor to hazard this! Had I but a few hundred Pounds, but 200£, half to send to Mrs Coleridge, & half to place myself in a private madhouse, where I could procure nothing but what a Physician thought proper, & where a medical attendant could be constantly with me for two or three months (in less than that time Life or Death would be determined) then there might be Hope. Now there is none!' – O God! how willingly would I place myself under Dr Fox in his Establishment – for my Case is a species of madness, only that it is a derangement, an utter impotence of the *Volition*, & not of the intellectual Faculties – You bid me rouse myself – go, bid a man paralytic in both arms rub them briskly together, & that will cure him. Alas! (he would reply) that I cannot move my arms is my Complaint & my misery. –

  My friend, Wade, is not at home – & I sent off all the little money, I had – or I would with this have inclosed the 10£ received from you. –

    May God bless you
    &
    Your affectionate &
    most afflicted
    S. T. Coleridge. –

Dr Estlin, I found, is raising the city against me, as far as he & his friends can, for having stated a mere matter of fact, . . . – viz – that Milton had represented Satan as a sceptical Socinian – which is the case, & I could not have explained the excellence of the sublimest single Passage in all his Writings had I not previously informed the Audience, that Milton had represented Satan as knowing the prophetic & Messianic Character of Christ, but sceptical as to any higher Claims – & what other definition could Dr E. himself give of a sceptical Socinian? – Now that M. has done so, please to consult, Par. Regained, Book IV. from line 196. – & then the same Book from line 500. –

THE DUKE OF WELLINGTON to Lady Frances Webster, 19 June 1815

Arthur Wellesley, first Duke of Wellington, 1769–1852, Field Marshal; Lady Frances Webster, friend of Lord Byron. The Battle of Waterloo had been fought the previous day.

Bruxelles, 19th June, 1815,
½ past 8 in the morning.

My dear Lady Frances,

  Lord Mountnorris may remain in Bruxelles in perfect security. I yesterday, after a most severe and bloody contest, gained a complete victory, and pursued the French till after dark. They are in complete confusion; and I have, I believe, 150 pieces of cannon; and Blücher, who continued the pursuit all night, my soldiers being tired to death, sent me word this morning that he had got 60 more.

My loss is immense. Lord Uxbridge, Lord FitzRoy Somerset, General Cooke, General Barnes, and Colonel Berkeley are wounded: Colonel De Lancey, Canning, Gordon, General Picton killed. The finger of Providence was upon me, and I escaped unhurt.

Believe me, &c.,

Wellington.

JOHN BARROW to Admiral Lord Keith, 14 July 1815

Sir John Barrow, 1764–1848, Secretary of the Admiralty; George Keith Elphinstone, Viscount Keith, Commander-in-Chief of the Channel Fleet, later intermediary of the British Government in its dealings with Napoleon. The British Government was uncertain as to Napoleon's movements in the days after Waterloo: he had in fact reached Rochfort on 10 July, where he was negotiating with Captain Maitland of the *Bellerophon*. He surrendered to Maitland the day after this letter was written.

Admiralty 14th July 1815

My dear Lord

I fear we are more likely to reduce than encrease your Lordship's means of intercepting Bonaparte having ordered the York to Spithead to hold a Court Martial & I suppose to be paid off.

The opinion here seems to be that Bonaparte is not at Rochfort either with the Army or in Paris. Perhaps rather he is lurking about one part of the coast, from where he will endeavour to steal away in some small vessel. If the White flag should be flying at Rochfort I suppose our Ships will anchor in the roads – but with every precaution it will be exceedingly difficult if not impossible to stop him if he embarks, like Hamlet, 'naked and alone'. – Ministers are very anxious about getting him

I have the honor to be
Your Lordship's
most obt Servt
John Barrow

The Lord Keith

JAMES STANIER CLARKE to Jane Austen, 27 March 1816

James Stanier Clarke, ?1765–1834, Domestic Chaplain and Librarian to the Prince Regent; Jane Austen, novelist. The Prince Regent, who Jane Austen loathed, was a great admirer of her work and kept a set of her novels in each of his residences. He sent Clarke to visit her and show her around Carlton House, and gave her permission to dedicate her next book (*Emma*) to him.

Pavilion: March 27, 1816.

Dear Miss Austen,

I have to return you the thanks of His Royal Highness, the Prince Regent, for the handsome copy you sent him of your last excellent novel. Pray, dear Madam, soon write again and again. Lord St. Helens and many of the nobility, who have been staying here, paid you the just tribute of their praise.

The Prince Regent has just left us for London; and having been pleased to appoint me Chaplain and Private English Secretary to the Prince of Cobourg, I remain here with His Serene Highness and a select party until the marriage. Perhaps when you again appear in print you may chuse to dedicate your volumes to Prince Leopold: any historical romance illustrative of the history of the august House of Cobourg, would just now be very interesting.

Believe me at all times,

Dear Miss Austen,

Your obliged friend,

J. S. Clarke.

JANE AUSTEN to James Stanier Clarke, 1 April 1816

Jane Austen, 1775–1817, novelist; J. S. Clarke, Domestic Librarian and Chaplain to the Prince Regent. Following the spirit of his advice, Clarke published that year a sycophantic biography of James II for which he was rewarded with the further title, Historiographer to the King.

My dear Sir

I am honoured by the Prince's thanks and very much obliged to yourself for the kind manner in which you mention the work. I have also to acknowledge a former letter forwarded to me from Hans Place. I assure you I felt very grateful for the friendly tenor of it, and hope my silence will have been considered, as it was truly meant, to proceed only from an unwillingness to tax your time with idle thanks. Under every interesting circumstance which your own talents and literary labours have placed you in, or the favour of the Regent bestowed, you have my best wishes. Your recent appointments I hope are a step to something still better. In my opinion, the service of a court can hardly be too well paid, for immense must be the sacrifice of time and feeling required by it.

You are very very kind in your hints as to the sort of composition which might recommend me at present, and I am fully sensible that an historical romance, founded on the House of Saxe Cobourg, might be much more to the purpose of profit or popularlity than such pictures of domestic life in country villages as I deal in. But I could no more write a romance than an epic poem. I could not sit seriously down to write a serious romance under any other motive than to save my life; and if it were indispensable for me to keep it up and never relax into laughing at myself or other people, I am sure I should be hung before I had finished the first chapter. No, I must keep to my own style and go on in my own way; and though I may never succeed again in that, I am convinced that I should totally fail in any other.

I remain, my dear Sir,
Your very much obliged, and very sincere friend,

J. Austen

Chawton, near Alton, April 1, 1816.

CHARLES LAMB to William Wordsworth, [26 April 1816]

Charles Lamb, 1775–1834, essayist; William Wordsworth, poet. Lamb was at this time employed as a clerk in the East India House, and was correcting for the press Wordworth's patriotic Odes and his *Letter to a Friend of Burns*. He had been a friend of Coleridge since their schooldays at Christ's Hospital. Coleridge's 'Christabel' with 'Kubla Khan' and the 'Pains of Sleep' was published later that year: his play *Zapolya* had been submitted to the Drury Lane Theatre, but was not accepted for performance. He spent the rest of his life in the household of James Gilman of Highgate. Wordsworth's *Excursion* had been published two years earlier.

[26 April 1816]

Sir,

    Please to state the Weights and Amounts of the following Lots of sold   Sale, 181 for

Your obedient Servant,

Chas. Lamb.

Accountant's Office,
  26 Apr. 1816

Dear W. I have just finished the pleasing task of correcting the Revise of the Poems and letter. I hope they will come out faultless. One blunder I saw and shuddered at. The hallucinating rascal had printed *battered* for *battened*, this last not conveying any distinct sense to his gaping soul. The Reader (as they call 'em) had discovered it and given it the marginal brand, but the substitutory *n* had not yet appeared. I accompanied his notice with a most pathetic address to the Printer not to neglect the Correction. I know how such a blunder would 'batter at your Peace.' With regard to the works, the Letter I read with unabated satisfaction. Such a thing was wanted, called for. The parallel of Cotton with Burns I heartily approve; Iz. Walton hallows any page in which his reverend name appears. 'Duty archly bending to purposes of general benevolence' is exquisite. The Poems I endeavored not to understand, but to read them with my eye alone, and I think I succeeded. (Some people will do that when they come out, you'll say.) As if I were to luxuriate tomorrow at some Picture Gallery I was never at before, and going by to day by chance, found the door open, had but 5 minutes to look about me, peeped in, just such a *chastised* peep I took with my mind at the lines my luxuriating eye was coursing over unrestrained, – not to anticipate another day's fuller satisfaction. Coleridge is printing Xtabel, by Ld Byron's recommendation to Murray, with what he calls a vision, Kubla Khan – which said vision he repeats so enchantingly that it irradiates and brings heaven and Elysian bowers into my parlour while he sings or says it, but there is an observation 'Never tell thy dreams,' and I am almost afraid that Kubla Khan is an owl that won't bear day light, I fear lest it should be discovered by the lantern of typography and clear reducting to letters, no better than nonsense or no sense. When I was young I used to chant with extacy *Mild Arcadians ever blooming*, till somebody told me it was meant to be nonsense. Even yet I have a lingering attachment to it, and think it better than Windsor Forest, Dying Xtian's address &c. – C. has sent his Tragedy to D.L.T. – it cannot be acted this season, and by their manner of receiving it, I hope he will be able to alter it to make them accept it for next. He is at present under the medical care of a Mr.

Gilman (Killman?) a Highgate Apothecary, where he plays at leaving off Laud—m. I think his essentials not touched: he is very bad, but then he wonderfully picks up another day, and his face when he repeats his verses hath its ancient glory, an Archangel a little damaged.

Will Miss H. pardon our not replying at length to her kind Letter? We are not quiet enough. Morgan is with us every day, going betwixt Highgate and the Temple. Coleridge is absent but 4 miles, and the neighbourhood of such a man is as exciting as the presence of 50 ordinary Persons. 'Tis enough to be within the whiff and wind of his genius, for us not to possess our souls in quiet. If I lived with him or the *author of the Excursion*, I should in a very little time lose my own identity, and be dragged along in the current of other people's thoughts, hampered in a net. How cool I sit in this office, with no possible interruption further than what I may term *material*; there is not as much metaphysics in 36 of the people here as there is in the first page of Locke's treatise on the Human understanding, or as much poetry as in any ten lines of the Pleasures of Hope or more natural Beggar's Petition. I never entangle myself in any of their speculations. Interruptions, if I try to write a letter even, I have dreadful. Just now within 4 lines I was call'd off for ten minutes to consult dusty old books for the settlement of obsolete Errors. I hold you a guinea you don't find the Chasm where I left off, so excellently the wounded sense closed again and was healed.

N.B. Nothing said above to the contrary but that I hold the personal presence of the two mentioned potent spirits at a rate as high as any, but I pay dearer, what amuses others robs me of myself, my mind is positively discharged into their greater currents, but flows with a willing violence. As to your question about work, it is far less oppressive to me than it was, from circumstances; it takes all the golden part of the day away, a solid lump from ten to four, but it does not kill my peace as before. Some day or other I shall be in a taking again. My head akes and you have had enough. God bless you.

C. Lamb.

WILLIAM WORDSWORTH to Charles Lamb, 21 November [1816]

William Wordsworth, 1770–1850, poet; Charles Lamb, essayist. The 'W.H.' referred to is William Hazlitt who, as well as being a writer, was a portrait painter; 'Thomas de Q—' is Thomas de Quincey, author of the *Confessions of an English Opium Eater*, who later married the girl in question.

Rydal Mount 21st Novr

Dear Lamb,

Miss H. writes that you may *read*. – W. H. is much such a drawer of characters, as, judging from the specimens of art which he has left in this country, he is a portrait painter. He tried his hand upon me. My brother Richard happened to come into the room where his work was suspended, saw, stopt, I believe recoiled, and exclaimed *God Zounds*! a criticism as emphatic as it was concise. He was literally *struck* with the strength of the sign-board likeness; but never, till that moment, had he conceived that so much of the diabolical lurked under the innocent features of his quondam playmate, and respected Friend and dear Brother. Devils may be divided into two large classes, first, the malignant and mischievous, – those who are bent upon all of evil-doing that is prayed against in the Litany; and secondly those which have so thorough a sense of their own damnation, and the misery consequent upon it, as to be incapable of labouring a thought injurious to the tranquillity of others. The pencil of W. H. is potent in delineating both kinds of physiognomy. My Portrait was an example of the one; and a Picture of Coleridge, now in existence at Keswick (mine has been burnt) is of the other. This piece of art is not producable for fear of fatal consequences to married Ladies, but is kept in a private room, as a special treat to those who may wish to sup upon horrors. As H. served the person of Coleridge, fifteen years ago, now has he served his mind; a likeness, it must be acknowledged there is, but one takes refuge from the spectacle in detestation (in this latter instance) of the malevolence by which the monstrous caricature was elaborated.

By the bye, an event has lately occured in our neighbourhood which would raise the character of its population in the estimation of that roving God Pan, who some years ago made his appearance among us. You will recollect, and Mr Henry Robinson will more easily recollect, that a little Friend of our's was profuse in praises of the 'more than beauty' – 'the angelic sweetness' – that pervaded the features of a fair young Cottager dwelling upon the banks of Rydal mere. To be brief, Love and opportunity have wrought so much upon the tender frame of the terrestrial angel, that, to the surprize of Gods, Men, and Matrons, she has lately brought forth a Man child to be known, and honored, by the name of *William*, and so called after a deceased Brother of its acknowledging Father Thomas de Q—. Such, in these later times, are the fruits of philosophy ripening under the shelter of our Arcadian mountains. A marriage is expected by some; but, from the known procrastination of one of the parties, it is not looked for by others till the commencement of the millenium. In the meanwhile he has a proud employment in nursing the new-born.

Let me hear that the Shoemaker has not bullied you out of your intention of completing the meditated Essays. Southey, of whom H. affects to talk contemptuously, beats us all hollow in interesting and productive power. If he reads, if he talks, if he is talked to, he turns it all to account: behold! it is upon paper, it is in print; and the whole world reads, or many read it, sure of being always entertained, and often instructed. If the attainment of just notions be an evidence of ability, Southey will be cherished by posterity when the reputation of those, who now so insolently decry him, will be rotted away and dispersed upon the winds. I wish to hear from you, and not unfrequently. You are better off than we – inasmuch as London contains one person whose conversation is worth listening to – whereas here we are in an utter desert, notwithstanding we have a very amiable and edifying Parson; an intelligent Doctor; an honest Attorney (for he is without practice); a Lady of the Manor, who has a Spice of the romantic; Landscape Painters who are fraught with admiration, at least of their own works; Irish Refugees, and Liverpool Bankrupts, without number. – Have you seen a thing advertized called the *Poetic Mirror*? a parody which selects, as a Subject for my Muse, 'The flying Taylor'. You will call to mind that I told you there was a person, in this neighbourhood, who from his agility, had acquired this name – hence a thought crossed my mind that the Author of this *Skit* might be of your acquaintance; but as he has selected *three* Scotch Poets – Hogg, Scott, and Wilson – to the exclusion of English ones of near equal eminence and more merit, I conclude that he is some Sawney ayont the Tweed, who has been resident in this Country and probably about the time when the annual sports bring the flying Taylor into notice. To conclude – I remain, in good health, and not bad spirits notwithstanding the bad weather and hard times,

Your friend to command,
Wm Wordsworth

LORD BYRON to Thomas Moore, 28 February 1817

George Gordon, Lord Byron, 1788–1824, poet; Thomas Moore, poet, Byron's biographer. This letter survives only in the version given in Moore's life of Byron, from which passages have been omitted.

Venice, February 28th, 1817

You will, perhaps, complain as much of the frequency of my letters now, as you were wont to do of their rarity. I think this is the fourth within as many moons. I feel anxious to hear from you, even more than usual, because your last indicated that you were unwell. At present, I am on the invalid regimen myself. The Carnival – that is, the latter part of it – and sitting up late o'nights, had knocked me up a little. But it is over, – and it is now Lent, with all its abstinence and Sacred Music.

The mumming closed with a masked ball at the Fenice, where I went, as also to most of the ridottos, etc., etc.; and, though I did not dissipate much upon the whole, yet I find 'the sword wearing out the scabbard,' though I have but just turned the corner of twenty-nine.

> So we'll go no more a roving
> So late into the night,
> Though the heart be still as loving,
> And the moon be still as bright.
>
> For the sword outwears its sheath,
> And the soul wears out the breast,
> And the heart must pause to breathe,
> And Love itself have rest.
>
> Though the night was made for loving,
> And the day returns too soon,
> Yet we'll go no more a roving
> By the light of the moon.

I have lately had some news of litter*atoor*, as I heard the editor of the Monthly pronounce it once upon a time. I hear that W[edderburn] W[ebster] has been publishing and responding to the attacks of the Quarterly, in the learned Perry's Chronicle. I read his poesies last autumn, and amongst them found an epitaph on his bull-dog, and another on *myself*. But I beg to assure him (like the astrologer Partridge) that I am not only alive now but was alive also at the time he wrote it.

XXXX Hobhouse has (I hear, also) expectorated a letter against the Quarterly, addressed to me. I feel awkwardly situated between him and Gifford, both being my friends.

And this is your month of going to press – by the body of Diana! (a Venetian oath,) I feel as anxious – but not fearful for you – as if it were myself coming out in a work of humour, which would, you know, be the antipodes of all my previous publications. I don't think you have any thing to dread but your own reputation. You must keep up to that. As you never showed me a line of your work, I do not even know your measure; but you must send me a copy by Murray forthwith, and then you shall hear what I think. I dare say you are in a pucker. Of all authors, you are the only really *modest* one I ever met with, – which would sound oddly enough to those who recollect your morals when you were young – that is, when you were *extremely* young – I don't mean to stigmatise you either with years or morality.

I believe I told you that the E[dinburgh] R[eview] had attacked me, in an article on Coleridge (I have not seen it) – '*Et tu*, Jeffrey?' – 'there is nothing but roguery in villanous man.' But I absolve him of all attacks, present and future; for I think he had already pushed his clemency in my behoof to the utmost, and I shall always think well of him. I only wonder he did not begin before, as my domestic destruction was a fine opening for all the world, of which all, who could, did well to avail themselves.

If I live ten years longer, you will see, however, that it is not over with me – I don't mean in literature, for that is nothing; and it may seem odd enough to say, I do not think it my vocation. But you will see that I will do something or other – the times and fortune permitting – that, 'like the cosmogony, or creation of the world, will puzzle the philosophers of all ages.' But I doubt whether my constitution will hold out. I have, at intervals, ex*orc*ised it most devilishly.

I have not yet fixed a time of return, but I think of the spring. I shall have been away a year in April next. You never mention Rogers, nor Hodgson, your clerical neighbour, who has lately got a living near you. Has he also got a child yet? – his desideratum, when I saw him last. XXXXXXXX

Pray let me hear from you, at your time and leisure, believing me ever and truly and affectionately, &c.

LORD BYRON to Augusta Leigh, 17 May 1819

George Gordon, Lord Byron, 1788–1824, poet; Augusta Leigh, his half-sister. The 'infamous fiend' is Byron's estranged wife, who kept him apart from Augusta. Passages in the original of this letter have been censored by a later hand.

Venice [Monday] May 17th. 1819

My dearest Love – I have been negligent in not writing, but what can I say[.] Three years absence – & the total change of scene and habit make such a difference – that we have now nothing in common but our affections & our relationship. –

But I have never ceased nor can cease to feel for a moment that perfect & boundless attachment which bound & binds me to you – which renders me utterly incapable of *real* love for any other human being – what could they be to me after *you*? My own XXXX [Short word crossed out] we may have been very wrong – but I repent of nothing except that cursed marriage – & your refusing to continue to love me as you had loved me – I can neither forget nor *quite forgive* you for that precious piece of reformation. – but I can never be other than I have been – and whenever I love anything it is because it reminds me in some way or other of yourself – for instance I not long ago attached myself to a Venetian for no earthly reason (although a pretty woman) but because she was called XXXX [short word crossed out] and she often remarked (without knowing the reason) how fond I was of the name. – It is heart-breaking to think of our long Separation – and I am sure more than punishment enough for all our sins – Dante is more humane in his 'Hell' for he places his unfortunate lovers (Francesca of Rimini & Paolo whose case fell a good deal short of *ours* – though sufficiently naughty) in company – and though they suffer – it is at least together. – If ever I return to England – it will be to see you – and recollect that in all time – & place – and feelings – I have never ceased to be the same to you in heart – Circumstances may have ruffled my manner – & hardened my spirit – you may have seen me harsh & exasperated with all things around me; grieved & tortured with *your new resolution*, – & the soon after persecution of that infamous fiend who drove me from my Country & conspired against my life – by endeavouring to deprive me of all that could render it precious – but remember that even then *you* were the sole object that cost me a tear? and *what tears*! do you remember *our* parting?

I have not spirits now to write to you upon other subjects – I am well in health – and have no cause of grief but the reflection that we are not together – When you write to me speak to me of yourself – & say that you love me – never mind common-place people & topics – which can be in no degree interesting – to me who see nothing in England but the country which holds *you* – or around it but the sea which divides us. – They say absence destroys weak passions – & confirms strong ones – Alas! *mine* for you is the union of all passions & of all affections – Has strengthened itself but will destroy me – I do not speak of *physical* destruction – for I have endured & can endure much – but of the annihilation of all thoughts feelings or hopes – which have not more or less a reference to you & to *our recollections* –

Ever dearest
[Signature erased]

JOHN KEATS to J. H. Reynolds, 21 September 1819

John Keats, 1795–1821, poet; John Hamilton Reynolds, poet. While at Winchester Keats wrote the Ode 'To Autumn', his last major poem; *The Fall of Hyperion* remained unfinished at his death.

Winchester, Tuesday

My dear Reynolds,

I was very glad to hear from Woodhouse that you would meet in the Country. I hope you will pass some pleasant time together. Which I wish to make pleasanter by a brace of letters, very highly to be estimated, as really I have had very bad luck with this sort of game this season. I 'kepen in solitarinesse,' for Brown has gone a visiting. I am surprized myself at the pleasure I live alone in. I can give you no news of the place here, or any other idea of it but what I have to this effect written to George. Yesterday I say to him was a grand day for Winchester. They elected a Mayor – It was indeed high time the place should receive some sort of excitement. There was nothing going on: all asleep: not an old maid's sedan returning from a card party: and if any old woman got tipsy at Christenings they did not expose it in the streets. The first night tho' of our arrival here, there was a slight uproar took place at about 10 o' the

Clock. We heard distinctly a noise patting down the high Street as of a walking cane of the good old Dowager breed; and a little minute after we heard a less voice observe 'What a noise the ferril made – it must be loose' – Brown wanted to call the Constables, but I observed 'twas only a little breeze, and would soon pass over. – The side streets here are excessively maiden-lady like: the door steps always fresh from the flannel. The knockers have a staid serious, nay almost awful quietness about them. – I never saw so quiet a collection of Lions' & Rams' heads – The doors most part black, with a little brass handle just above the keyhole, so that in Winchester a man may very quietly shut himself out of his own house. How beautiful the season is now – How fine the air. A temperate sharpness about it. Really, without joking, chaste weather – Dian skies – I never lik'd stubble fields so much as now – Aye better than the chilly green of the spring. Somehow a stubble plain looks warm – in the same way that some pictures look warm – this struck me so much in my sunday's walk that I composed upon it. I hope you are better employed than in gaping after weather. I have been at different times so happy as not to know what weather it was – No I will not copy a parcel of verses. I always somehow associated Chatterton with autumn. He is the purest writer in the English Language. He has no French idiom, or particles like Chaucer – 'tis genuine English Idiom in English words. I have given up Hyperion – there were too many Miltonic inversions in it – Miltonic verse cannot be written but in an artful or rather artist's humour. I wish to give myself up to other sensations. English ought to be kept up. It may be interesting to you to pick out some lines from Hyperion and put a mark × to the false beauty proceeding from art, and one ‖ to the true voice of feeling. Upon my soul 'twas imagination I cannot make the distinction – Every now & then there is a Miltonic intonation – But I cannot make the division properly. The fact is I must take a walk: for I am writing so long a letter to George; and have been employed at it all the morning. You will ask, have I heard from George. I am sorry to say not the best news – I hope for better – This is the reason among others that if I write to you it must be in such a scraplike way. I have no meridian to date Interests from, or measure circumstances – To night I am all in a mist; I scarcely know what's what – But you knowing my unsteady & vagarish disposition, will guess that all this turmoil will be settled by tomorrow morning. It strikes me to night that I have led a very odd sort of life for the two or three last years – Here & there – No anchor – I am glad of it. – If you can get a peep at Babbicomb before you leave the country, do. – I think it the finest place I have seen, or – is to be seen in the South. There is a Cottage there I took warm water at, that made up for the tea. I have lately skirk'd some friends of ours, and I advise you to do the same, I mean the blue-devils – I am never at home to them. You need not fear them while you remain in Devonshire. there will be some of the family waiting for you at the Coach office – but go by another Coach. – I shall beg leave to have a third opinion in the first discussion you have with Woodhouse – just half way – between both. You know I will not give up my argument – In my walk to day I stoop'd under a rail way that lay across my path, and ask'd myself 'Why I did not get over' Because, answered I, 'no one wanted to force you under' – I would give a guinea to be a reasonable man – good sound sense – a says what he thinks, and does what he says man – and did not take snuff – They say men near death however mad they may have been, come to their senses – I hope I shall here in this letter – there is a decent space to be very sensible in – many a good proverb has been in less – Nay I have heard of the statutes at large being chang'd into the Statutes at Small and printed for a watch paper. Your sisters by this time must have got the Devonshire ees – short ees – you know 'em – they are the prettiest ees in the Language. O how I admire the middle siz'd delicate Devonshire girls of about 15. There was one at an Inn door holding a quartern of brandy – the very thought of her kept me warm a whole stage – and a 16 miler too – 'You'll pardon me for being jocular.'

Ever your affectionate friend
John Keats –

LORD BYRON to the Hon. Douglas Kinnaird, 26 October 1819

George Gordon, Lord Byron, 1788–1824, poet; Douglas Kinnaird, ninth Baron Kinnaird. Lady Noel was Byron's mother-in-law; the first two cantos of *Don Juan* had come out that year and greatly scandalized the critics. The 'life (in MS)' is the manuscript of his famous memoirs, burnt after his death.

Venice. Octr. 26th. 1818 [1819]

My dear Douglas – My late expenditure has arisen from living at a distance from Venice and being obliged to keep up two establishments, from frequent journeys – and buying some furniture and books as well as a horse or two – and not from any renewal of the EPICUREAN system as you suspect. I have been faithful to my honest liaison with Countess Guiccioli – and I can assure you that *She* has never cost me directly or indirectly a sixpence – indeed the circumstances of herself and family render this no merit. – I never offered her but one present – a broach of brilliants – and she sent it back to me with her *own hair* in it (I shall *not* say of *what part* but *that* is an Italian custom) and a note to say that she was not in the habit of receiving presents of that value – but hoped that I would not consider her sending it back as an affront – nor the value diminished by the enclosure. – I have not had a whore this half-year – confining myself to the strictest adultery.——Why should you prevent Hanson from making a *peer* if he likes it – I think the '*Garretting*' would be by far the best parliamentary privilege – I know of.——Damn your delicacy. – It is a low commercial quality – and very unworthy a man who prefixes 'honourable' to his nomenclature. If you say that I must sign the bonds – I suppose that I must – but it is very iniquitous to make me pay my debts – you have no idea of the pain it gives one. – Pray do three things – get my property out of the *funds* – get Rochdale sold – get me some information from Perry about *South America* – and 4thly. ask Lady Noel not to live so very long.——As to Subscribing to Manchester – if I do that – I will write a letter to Burdett – for publication – to accompany the Subscription – which shall be more radical than anything yet rooted – but I feel lazy. – I have thought of this for some time – but alas! the air of this cursed Italy enervates – and disfranchises the thoughts of a man after nearly four years of respiration – to say nothing of emission. – As to 'Don Juan' – confess – confess – you dog – and be candid – that it is the sublime of *that there* sort of writing – it may be bawdy – but is it not good English? – it may be profligate – but is it not *life*, is it not *the thing*? – Could any man have written it – who has not lived in the world? – and tooled in a post-chaise? in a hackney coach? in a Gondola? against a wall? in a court carriage? in a vis a vis? – on a table? – and under it? – I have written about a hundred stanzas of a third Canto – but it is damned modest – the outcry has frightened me. – I had such projects for the Don – but the *Cant* is so much stronger than *Cunt* – now a days, – that the benefit of experience in a man who had well weighed the worth of both monosyllables – must be lost to despairing posterity. – After all what stuff this outcry is – Lalla Rookh and Little – are more dangerous than my burlesque poem can be – Moore has been here – we got tipsy together – and were very amicable – he is gone on to Rome – I put my life (in M.S.) into his hands – (*not* for publication) you – or any body else

may see it – at his return. – It only comes up to 1816.——He is a noble
fellow – and looks quite fresh and poetical – nine years (the age of a
poem's education) my Senior – he looks younger – this comes of
marriage and being settled in the Country. I want to go to South America
– I have written to Hobhouse all about it. – I wrote to my wife – three
months ago – under care to Murray – has she got the letter – or is the
letter got into Blackwood's magazine?——You ask after my Christmas
pye – Remit it any how – *Circulars* is the best – you are right about
income – I must have it all – how the devil do I know that I may live a year
or a month? – I wish I knew that I might regulate my spending in more
ways than one. – As it is one always thinks that there is but a span. – A
man may as well break or be damned for a large sum as a small one – I
should be loth to pay the devil or any other creditor more than sixpence
in the pound. –

[scrawl for signature]

P.S. – I recollect nothing of 'Davies's landlord' – but what ever Davies
says – I will *swear* to – and *that's* more than *he* would. – So pray pay – has
he a landlady too? perhaps I may owe her something.——With regard to
the bonds I will sign them but – it goes against the grain.——As to the
rest – you *can't* err – so long as you *don't* pay.——Paying is executor's or
executioner's work.——You may write somewhat oftener – Mr. Galig-
nani's messenger gives the outline of your public affairs – but I see no
results – you have no man yet – (always excepting Burdett – & you &
H[obhouse] and the Gentlemanly leaven of your two-penny loaf of
rebellion) don't forget however my charge of horse – and commission for
the Midland Counties and by the holies. – You shall have your account in
decimals. – Love to Hobby – but why leave the Whigs?——

JOHN KEATS to Fanny Brawne, [? 24 February 1820]

John Keats, 1795–1821, poet; Fanny Brawne, his fiancée. Keats had suffered a
severe haemorrhage of the lungs on 3 February. While convalescing, he lived at
Wentworth Place, Hampstead, next door to Fanny Brawne and her mother, who
had rented the other half of the house; he had become engaged to Fanny late the
previous year.

My dearest Girl,

Indeed I will not deceive you with respect to my Health. This is the fact as far as I know. I have been confined three weeks and am not yet well – this proves that there is something wrong about me which my constitution will either conquer or give way to – Let us hope for the best. Do you hear the Th[r]ush singing over the field? I think it is a sign of mild weather – so much the better for me. Like all Sinners now I am ill I philosophise aye out of my attachment to every thing, Trees, flowers, Thrushes Sp[r]ing, Summer, Claret &c &c aye [e]very thing but you——my Sister would be glad of my company a little longer. That Thrush is a fine fellow I hope he was fortunate in his choice this year – Do not send any more of my Books home. I have a great pleasure in the thought of you looking on them.

> Ever yours
> my sweet Fanny
> J—K—

JOHN KEATS to Fanny Brawne, [? March 1820]

John Keats, 1795–1821, poet; Fanny Brawne, his fiancée. On 6 March Keats suffered from 'violent palpitations of the heart', although he was well enough to leave the house by the end of the month.

My dearest Fanny,

I slept well last night and am no worse this morning for it. Day by day if I am not deceived I get a more unrestrain'd use of my Chest. The nearer a racer gets to the Goal the more his anxiety becomes so I lingering upon the borders of health feel my impatience increase. Perhaps on your account I have imagined my illness more serious than it is: how horrid was the chance of slipping into the ground instead of into your arms – the difference is amazing Love – Death must come at last; Man must die, as Shallow says; but before that is my fate I feign would try what more pleasures than you have given so sweet a creature as you can give. Let me have another op[p]ortunity of years before me and I will not die without being remember'd. Take care of yourself dear that we may both be well in the Summer. I do not at all fatigue myself with writing, having merely to put a line or two here and there, a Task which would worry a stout state of the body and mind, but which just suits me as I can do no more.

Your affectionate
J. K—

PERCY BYSSHE SHELLEY to John Keats, 27 July 1820

Percy Bysshe Shelley, 1792–1822, poet; John Keats, poet.

Pisa – July 27. 1820

My dear Keats

I hear with great pain the dangerous accident that you have undergone, & Mr. Gisborne who gives me the account of it, adds that you continue to wear a consumptive appearance. This consumption is a disease particularly fond of people who write such good verses as you have done, and with the assistance of an English winter it can often indulge its selection; – I do not think that young & aimiable poets are at all bound to gratify its taste; they have entered into no bond with the Muses to that effect. But seriously (for I am joking on what I am very anxious about) I think you would do well to pass the winter after so tremendous an accident in Italy, & (if you think it as necessary as I do) so long as you could find Pisa or its neighbourhood agreable to you, Mrs. Shelley unites with myself in urging the request, that you would take up your residence with us. – You might come by sea to Leghorn, (France is not worth seeing, & the sea air is particularly good for weak lungs) which is within a few miles of us. You ought at all events to see Italy, & your health which I suggest as a motive, might be an excuse to you. – I spare declamation about the statues & the paintings & the ruins – & what is a greater piece of forbearance about the mountains the Streams & the fields, the colours of the sky, & the sky itself. –

I have lately read your Endymion again & ever with a new sense of the treasures of poetry it contains, though treasures poured forth with indistinct profusion. This, people in general will not endure, & that is the cause of the comparatively few copies which have been sold. I feel persuaded that you are capable of the greatest things, so you but will.

I always tell Ollier to send you Copies of my books. – 'Prometheus Unbound' I imagine you will receive nearly at the same time with this letter. The Cenci I hope you have already received – it was studiously composed in a different style 'below the *good* how far! but far above the *great*'. In poetry *I* have sought to avoid system & mannerism; I wish those who excel me in genius, would pursue the same plan. –

Whether you remain in England, or journey to Italy, – believe that you carry with you my anxious wishes for your health happiness & success, wherever you are or whatever you undertake, – & that I am

Yours sincerely

P. B. Shelley

JOHN KEATS to Percy Bysshe Shelley, 16 August [1820]

John Keats, 1795–1821, poet; P. B. Shelley, poet.

Hampstead August 16th

My dear Shelley,

I am very much gratified that you, in a foreign country, and with a mind almost over occupied, should write to me in the strain of the Letter beside me. If I do not take advantage of your invitation it will be prevented by a circumstance I have very much at heart to prophesy – There is no doubt that an english winter would put an end to me, and do so in a lingering hateful manner, therefore I must either voyage or journey to Italy as a soldier marches up to a battery. My nerves at present are the worst part of me, yet they feel soothed when I think that come what extreme may, I shall not be destined to remain in one spot long enough to take a hatred of any four particular bed-posts. I am glad you take any pleasure in my poor Poem; – which I would willingly take the trouble to unwrite, if possible, did I care so much as I have done about Reputation. I received a copy of the Cenci, as from yourself from Hunt. There is only one part of it I am judge of; the Poetry, and dramatic effect, which by many spirits now a days is considered the mammon. A modern work it is said must have a purpose, which may be the God – *an artist* must serve Mammon – he must have 'self concentration' selfishness perhaps. You I am sure will forgive me for sincerely remarking that you might curb your magnanimity and be more of an artist, and 'load every rift' of your subject with ore. The thought of such discipline must fall like cold chains upon you, who perhaps never sat with your wings furl'd for six Months together. And is not this extraordinary talk for the writer of Endymion? whose mind was like a pack of scattered cards – I am pick'd up and sorted to a pip. My Imagination is a Monastry and I am its Monk – you must explain my metaphysics to yourself. I am in expectation of Prometheus every day. Could I have my own wish for its interest effected you would have it still in manuscript – or be but now putting an end to the second act. I remember you advising me not to publish my first-blights, on Hampstead heath – I am returning advice upon your hands. Most of the Poems in the volume I send you have been written above two years, and would never have been publish'd but from a hope of gain; so you see I am inclined enough to take your advice now. I must express once more my deep sense of your kindness, adding my sincere thanks and respects for Mrs Shelley. In the hope of soon seeing you I remain

most sincerely yours,

John Keats –

JOHN KEATS to Charles Armitage Brown, 30 November 1820

John Keats, 1795–1821, poet; Charles Armitage Brown, the friend with whom Keats had lodged at Wentworth Place. Keats sailed for Italy in September in the hopes of recovering his health. George is his brother, then living in America; Severn, the young artist who looked after him in his final days; and Tom his younger brother who had died of consumption. This letter survives only in a transcript made by its recipient, from which several passages have been omitted. It is the last Keats was to write; he died in Rome of consumption on 23 February 1821.

Rome. 30 November 1820.

My dear Brown,

'Tis the most difficult thing in the world to me to write a letter. My stomach continues so bad, that I feel it worse on opening any book, – yet I am much better than I was in Quarantine. Then I am afraid to encounter the proing and conning of any thing interesting to me in England. I have an habitual feeling of my real life having past, and that I am leading a posthumous existence. God knows how it would have been – but it appears to me – however, I will not speak of that subject. I must have been at Bedhampton nearly at the time you were writing to me from Chichester – how unfortunate – and to pass on the river too! There was my star predominant! I cannot answer any thing in your letter, which followed me from Naples to Rome, because I am afraid to look it over again. I am so weak (in mind) that I cannot bear the sight of any hand writing of a friend I love so much as I do you. Yet I ride the little horse, – and, at my worst, even in Quarantine, summoned up more puns, in a sort of desperation, in one week than in any year of my life. There is one thought enough to kill me – I have been well, healthy, alert &c, walking with her – and now – the knowledge of contrast, feeling for light and shade, all that information (primitive sense) necessary for a poem are great enemies to the recovery of the stomach. There, you rogue, I put you to the torture, – but you must bring your philosophy to bear – as I do mine, really – or how should I be able to live? Dr Clarke is very attentive to me; he says, there is very little the matter with my lungs, but my stomach, he says, is very bad. I am well disappointed in hearing good news from George, – for it runs in my head we shall all die young. I have not written to x x x x x yet, which he must think very neglectful; being anxious to send him a good account of my health, I have delayed it from week to week. If I recover, I will do all in my power to correct the mistakes made during sickness; and if I should not, all my faults will be forgiven. I shall write to x x x to-morrow, or next day. I will write to x x x x x in the middle of next week. Servern is very well, though he leads so dull a life with me. Remember me to all friends, and tell x x x x I should not have left London without taking leave of him, but from being so low in body and mind. Write to George as soon as you receive this, and tell him how I am, as far as you can guess; – and also a note to my sister – who walks about my imagination like a ghost – she is so like Tom. I can scarcely bid you good bye even in a letter. I always made an awkward bow.

God bless you!
John Keats.

STENDHAL to the Baron de Mareste, 31 December 1820

Stendhal, pseudonym of Henri Beyle, 1783–1842, novelist; the Baron de Mareste, for a time a close friend. While living in Italy Stendhal came under suspicion of being a French spy; in an attempt to outwit the authorities, he took to writing in English and signing himself in a typically English manner.

Novate, 31 décembre 1820.

Dear Sir,

Write no more to me directly, by terror periculous. Write every fornight to M. Agustoni neg. te in Chiasso, every fornight. You can write as you will, but the names in English, by excess of prudence. You can also write to Domenico V[ismara]. We are now in what the French were in 1815 in the little reactionary towns of France. I pray you write every fornight. Give me your dear news with all the possible lib[erty].

Yours

Smith and Co.

GEORGE STEPHENSON to Robert Stevenson, 28 June 1821

George Stephenson, 1781–1848, railway engineer; Robert Stevenson, lighthouse engineer (grandfather of Robert Louis Stevenson). A scheme for a tramroad linking Stockton and Darlington was approved by Act of Parliament on 19 April 1819. Originally the cars were intended to carry only coals and to be drawn by horses: but on meeting the 'engine-wright' George Stephenson, Edward Pease, projector of the tramroad, was persuaded of the advantages of steam locomotives over horse traction and of malleable iron rails over the cast-iron ones which had always hitherto been used. The first rail of the Stockton to Darlington line, the world's first railway, was laid on 23 May 1823.

Killingworth 28th June 1821

Sir, – With this you will receive three copies of a specification of a patent malleable iron rail invented by John Birkinshaw of Bedlington, near Morpeth.

The hints were got from your Report on Railways, which you were so kind as to send me by Mr. Cookson some time ago. Your reference to Tindal Fell Railway led the inventor to make some experiments on malleable iron bars, the result of which convinced him of the superiority of the malleable over the cast iron – so much so, that he took out a patent.

Those rails are so much liked in this neighbourhood, that I think in a short time they will do away with the cast iron railways.

They make a fine line for our engines, as there are so few joints compared with the other.

I have lately started on a new locomotive engine, with some improvements on the others which you saw. It has far surpassed my expectations. I am confident a railway on which my engines can work is far superior to a canal. On a long and favourable railway I would stent my engines to travel 60 miles per day with from 40 to 60 tons of goods.

They would work nearly fourfold cheaper then horses where coals are not very costly.

I merely make these observations, as I know you have been at more trouble than any man I know of in searching into the utility of railways, and I return you my sincere thanks for your favour by Mr. Cookson.

If you should be in this neighbourhood, I hope you will not pass Killingworth Colliery, as I should be extremely glad if you could spend a day or two with me.

I am sir,
Yours most respectfully,
G. Stephenson

**PERCY BYSSHE SHELLEY to Thomas Love Peacock,
[?10] August 1821**

Percy Bysshe Shelley, 1792–1822, poet; Thomas Love Peacock, satirical novelist. The 'Elegy on Keats', to which Shelley refers, is his *Adonais*.

Ravenna, August, 1821.

My dear Peacock

I received your last letter just as I was setting off from the Bagni on a visit to Lord Byron at this place. Many thanks for all your kind attention to my accursed affairs. I am happy to tell you that my income is satisfactorily arranged, although Horace Smith having received it, and being still on his slow journey through France, I cannot send you, as I wished to have done, the amount of my debt immediately, but must defer it till I see him or till my September quarter, which is now very near. – I am very much obliged to you for your way of talking about it – but of course, if I cannot do you any good, I will not permit you to be a sufferer by me. –

I have sent you by the Gisbornes a copy of the *Elegy on Keats*. The subject, I know, will not please you; but the composition of the poetry, and the taste in which it is written, I do not think bad. You and the enlightened public will judge. Lord Byron is in excellent cue both of health and spirits. He has got rid of all those melancholy and degrading habits which he indulged at Venice. He lives with one woman, a lady of rank here, to whom he is attached, and who is attached to him, and is in every respect an altered man. He has written three more cantos of 'Don Juan'. I have yet only heard the fifth, and I think that every word of it is pregnant with immortality. I have not seen his late plays, except 'Marino Faliero', which is very well, but not so transcendently fine as the 'Don Juan'. Lord Byron gets up at *two*. I get up, quite contrary to my usual custom, but one must sleep or die, like Southey's sea-snake in 'Kehama', at 12. After breakfast we sit talking till six. From six till eight we gallop through the pine forests which divide Ravenna from the sea; we then come home and dine, and sit up gossiping till six in the morning. I don't suppose this will kill me in a week or fortnight, but I shall not try it longer. Lord B.'s establishment consists, besides servants, of ten horses, eight enormous dogs, three monkeys, five cats, an eagle, a crow, and a falcon; and all these, except the horses, walk about the house, which every now and then resounds with their unarbitrated quarrels, as if they were the masters of it. Lord B. thinks you wrote a pamphlet signed 'John Bull'; he says he knew it by the style resembling 'Melincourt', of which he is a great admirer. I read it, and assured him that it could not possibly be yours. I write nothing, and probably shall write no more. It offends me to see my name classed among those who have no name. If I cannot be something better, I had rather be nothing, and the accursed cause to the downfall of which I dedicated what powers I may have had – flourishes like a cedar and covers England with its boughs. My motive was never the infirm desire of fame; and if I should continue an author, I feel that I should desire it. This cup is justly given to one only of an age; indeed, participation would make it worthless: and unfortunate they who seek it and find it not.

I congratulate you – I hope I ought to do so – on your expected stranger. He is introduced into a rough world. My regards to Hogg, and Co[u]lson if you see him.

Ever most faithfully yours,
P. B. S.

After I have sealed my letter, I find that my enumeration of the animals in this Circean Palace was defective, and that in a material point. I have just met on the grand staircase five peacocks, two guinea hens, and an Egyptian crane. I wonder who all these animals were before they were changed into these shapes.

WILLIAM HAZLITT to P. G. Patmore, 31 May 1822

William Hazlitt, 1778–1830, essayist; Peter George Patmore, journalist, father of the poet Coventry Patmore. In 1819 Hazlitt had met and fallen violently in love with Sarah Walker, the daughter of his boarding-house landlord, a simple girl who, it seems, was at first flirtatious, then frightened, and finally bored by his obsession. This letter was written from Edinburgh, where he had travelled to finalize the divorce from his wife. He incorporated other letters to Patmore in his painfully revealing account of the affair, which met with much obloquy, published the next year under the title *Liber Amoris: or, The New Pygmalion*.

My dear friend,
I wrote yesterday by Scarborough to say that the iron had entered my soul – forever. I have since thought more profoundly about it than ever before, & am convinced beyond a doubt that she is a regular lodging-house decoy, who leads a sporting life with every one who comes in succession, & goes different lengths according as she is urged or inclined. This is why she will not marry, because she hankers after this sort of thing. She has an itch for being slabbered & felt, & this she is determined to gratify upon system, & has a pride in making fools of the different men she indulges herself with & at the same time can stop short from the habit of running the gauntlet with so many. The impudent whore to taunt me, that 'she had always told me she had no affection for me,' as a salve for her new lewdness – and how did she tell me this, sitting in my lap, twining herself round me, [letting me enjoy her through her petticoats] looking as if she would faint with tenderness & modesty, admitting all sorts of

indecent liberties & declaring 'however she might agree to her own ruin, she would never consent to bring disgrace upon her family,' as if this last circumstance only prevented her, & all this without any affection – is it not to write whore, hardened, impudent, heartless whore after her name? Her look is exactly this. It is that of suppressed lewdness & conscious & refined hypocrisy, instead of innocence or timidity or real feeling. She never looks at you, nor has a single involuntary emotion. For any one to suffer what she has done from me, without feeling it, is unnatural & monstrous. A common whore would take a liking to a man who had shewn the same love of her & to whom she had granted the same incessant intimate favours. But her heart is seared, as her eyes gloat, with habitual hypocrisy & *lech* for the mere act of physical contact with the other sex. 'Do you let any one else do so,' I said to her when I was kissing her. 'No, not now,' was her answer, that is, because there was nobody in the house to do it with her. While the coast was clear, I had it all my own way: but the instant Tomkins came, she made a dead set at him, ran breathless upstairs before him, blushed when his foot was heard, watched for him in the passage, & he going away either tired of her or without taking the hint, she has taken up in my absence with this quack-doctor, a tall stiff-backed able bodied half blackguard that she can make use of & get rid of when she pleases. The bitch wants a *stallion*, & hates a lover, that is, any one who talks of affection & is prevented by fondness or regard for her from going or attempting to go all lengths. I at present think she liked me to a certain extent as a friend but still I was not good enough for her. She wanted to be courted not as a bride, but as a common wench. 'Why, could we not go on as we were, & never mind about the word, *forever*?' She would not agree to 'a tie,' because she would leave herself open to any new pretender that answered her purpose better, & *bitch* me without ceremony or mercy, & then say – 'She had always told me she had no regard for me' – as a rea[son for] transferring her obscenities (for such they were without [doubt) from] me to her next favourite. Her addicting herself to Tomkins was endurable, because he was a gentlemanly sort of man, but her putting up with this prick of a fellow, merely for bore & measurement & gross manners, sets me low indeed. The monster of lust & duplicity! I that have spared her so often because I hoped better things of her & to make her my future wife, & to be refused in order that she may be the trull of an itinerant apothecary, a fellow that she made a jest of & despised, till she had nobody else in the way to pamper her body & supply her morning's meal of studied wantonness. 'That way madness lies.' I do not feel as if I can ever get the better of it: I have sucked in the poison of her seeming modesty & tenderness too long. I thought she was dreaming of her only love & worshipped her equivocal face, when she wanted only a codpiece & I ought to have pulled up her petticoats & felt her. But I could not insult the adored of my heart, & find out her real character; & you see what has become of me. I was wrong at first in fancy[ing] a wench at a lodging house to be a Vestal, merely for her demure looks. The only chance I had was the first day: after that my hands were tied & I became the fool of love. Do you know the only thing that soothes or melts me is the idea of taking my little boy whom I can no longer support & wandering through the country as beggars, not through the wide world, for I cannot leave the country where she is. Oh God! Oh God! The slimy, varnished, marble fiend to bring me to this when three kind words would have saved me! Yet if I only knew she was a whore, *flagrante delicto*, it would wean me from her, & burst my chain. Could you ascertain this fact for me, by any means or through any person (E. for example) who might try her as a lodger? I should not like her to be seduced by elaborate means, but if she gave up as a matter of course, I should then be no longer the wretch I am or the God I might have been, but what I was before [poor] plain,

W. H.

LUDWIG VAN BEETHOVEN to Charles Neate, 25 February 1823

Ludwig van Beethoven, 1770–1827, composer; Charles Neate, English pianist, Director of the Philharmonic Society. This letter was written in English by an amanuensis and signed by Beethoven. He was at this time thinking of beginning work on what were to become the late quartets; the overture referred to is the *Consecration of the House* and the 'new symphony', the Ninth. Beethoven never managed to visit England, but he maintained his links with the Philharmonic Society who, when he lay dying, sent him a gift of £100.

Vienna, February 25, 1823

My dear and valued Friend!

As Ries has written to tell me that you would like to have three quartets from me, I am writing to ask you to be so kind as to let me know when you would like to receive them. I am satisfied with the fee of 100 guineas which you offer. But, as soon as you hear from me that the quartets are ready, please send a draft for the 100 g[uineas] to a Viennese banking house *where I shall also deliver* the quartets and at the same time receive the 100 guin[eas]. – I trust that you are leading a pleasant and happy life in the bosom of your small family. But why are you not in Vienna so that I might have the pleasure of witnessing your happiness? – I have sent Ries a new overture for the Philharmonic Society; and I am only waiting for the arrival of the draft to dispatch immediately the new symphony from Vienna and, what is more, by an opportunity provided by our Imperial and Royal Embassy. The bearer of this letter is Herr von Bauer, who is as intelligent as he is amiable and who can tell you a good deal about me – If my health, which has been very poor for the last three years, should improve, I hope to go to London in 1824. Let me know what compositions the Philharmonic Society would like to have, for I would gladly compose for it. I should like to visit England and meet all the splendid artists there. Such a visit would benefit me materially too, for I shall *never* be able to achieve anything in Germany – You need only write my *name* on a letter to me and I shall certainly receive it – That all good and beautiful things may be your portion is the wish of your sincere friend

Beethoven

LORD BYRON to Goethe, 22 July 1823

George Gordon, Lord Byron, 1788–1824, poet; Johann Wolfgang von Goethe, poet, playwright and novelist. Byron had sent Goethe via Charles Sterling, son of the British Consul at Genoa, a note expressing his homage. The grateful Goethe – who had a collection of Byron memorabilia on display at Weimar – sent some verses in return. This letter of thanks was written when Byron was on his way to join the Greeks in their struggle for independence. He had set sail from Genoa on 16 July and, after putting in at Leghorn, reached Cephalonia on 3 August. He died the following year at Missolonghi on 19 April.

Leghorn. July 22d. 1823

Illustrious Sir – I cannot thank you as you ought to be thanked for the lines which my young friend Mr. Sterling sent me of yours, – and it would but ill become me to pretend to exchange verses with him who for fifty years has been the undisputed Sovereign of European literature. – You must therefore accept my most sincere acknowledgements in prose – and in hasty prose too – for I am at present on my voyage to Greece once more – and surrounded by hurry and bustle which hardly allow a moment even to Gratitude and Admiration to express themselves.——I sailed from Genoa some days ago – was driven back by a Gale of Wind – and have since sailed again – and arrived here (Leghorn) this morning to receive on board some Greek passengers for their struggling Country. ——*Here* also I found your lines and Mr. Sterling's letter – and I could not have had a more favourable Omen or more agreeable surprise than a word from Goethe written by his own hand.——I am returning to Greece to see if I can be of any little use there; – if ever I come back I will pay a visit to Weimar to offer the sincere homage of one of the many Millions of your admirers. – I have the honour to be ever & most respectfully

> yr. obliged adm[irer] & Se[rvant]
> Noel Byron

Aux Soins de Monsieur Sterling.

CHARLES LAMB to Henry Crabb Robinson, [29 March] 1825

Charles Lamb, 1775–1834, essayist; Henry Crabb Robinson, lawyer and diarist. This note announcing Lamb's retirement was shoved through Crabb Robinson's letter-box.

I have left the d—d India House for Ever!

> Give me great joy.
> C. Lamb.

WILLIAM BLAKE to George Cumberland, 12 April 1827

William Blake, 1757–1827, poet, painter and engraver; George Cumberland, a patron. The 'Little Card' which Blake designed for his friend Cumberland was to be his last engraving. The letter also refers to his illuminated books which he engraved, printed and coloured himself. His fellow painter, Flaxman, had died on 7 December the previous year.

Dear Cumberland,

I have been very near the Gates of Death & have returned very weak & an Old Man feeble & tottering, but not in Spirit & Life, not in The Real Man The Imagination which Liveth for Ever. In that I am stronger & stronger as this Foolish Body decays. I thank you for the Pains you have taken with Poor Job. I know too well that a great majority of Englishmen are fond of The Indefinite which they Measure by Newton's Doctrine of the Fluxions of an Atom, A Thing that does not Exist. These are Politicians & think that Republican Art is Inimical to their Atom. For a Line or Lineament is not formed by Chance: a Line is a Line in its Minutest Subdivisions: Strait or Crooked It is Itself & Not Intermeasurable with or by any Thing Else. Such is Job, but since the French Revolution Englishmen are all Intermeasurable One by Another, Certainly a happy state of Agreement to which I for One do not Agree. God keep me from the Divinity of Yes & No too, The Yea Nay Creeping Jesus, from supposing Up & Down to be the same Thing as all Experimentalists must suppose.

You are desirous I know to dispose of some of my Works & to make them Pleasin[g]. I am obliged to you & to all who do so. But having none remaining of all that I had Printed I cannot Print more Except at a great loss, for at the time I printed those things I had a whole House to range in: now I am shut up in a Corner therefore am forced to ask a Price for them that I scarce expect to get from a Stranger. I am now Printing a Set of the Songs of Innocence & Experience for a Friend at Ten Guineas which I cannot do under Six Months consistent with my other Work, so that I have little hope of doing any more of such things. The Last Work I produced is a Poem Entitled Jerusalem the Emanation of the Giant Albion, but find that to Print it will Cost my Time the amount of Twenty Guineas. One I have Finish'd. It contains 100 Plates but it is not likely that I shall get a Customer for it.

As you wish me to send you a list with the Prices of these things they are as follows

	£	s	d
America	6.	6.	0
Europe	6.	6.	0
Visions &c	5.	5.	0
Thel	3.	3.	0
Songs of Inn. & Exp.	10.	10.	0
Urizen	6.	6.	0

The Little Card I will do as soon as Possible but when you Consider that I have been reduced to a Skeleton from which I am slowly recovering you will I hope have Patience with me.

Flaxman is Gone & we must All soon follow, every one to his Own Eternal House, Leaving the Delusive Goddess Nature & her Laws to get into Freedom from all Law of the Members into The Mind, in which every one is King & Priest in his own House. God send it so on Earth as it is in Heaven.

> I am, Dear Sir, Yours Affectionately
> William Blake

12 April 1827
N 3 Fountain Court Strand

GEORGE RICHMOND to Samuel Palmer, [15 August 1827]

George Richmond, 1809–96, painter; Samuel Palmer, painter and etcher. George Richmond and Samuel Palmer were members of a group of young artists who revered Blake in his old age and who produced work of high quality under his influence. Blake had died on 12 August 1827.

> Wednesday Even.g

My Dr Friend,

Lest you should not have heard of the Death of Mr Blake I have Written this to inform you – He died on Sunday night at 6 Oclock in a most glorious manner. He said He was going to that Country he had all His life wished to see & expressed Himself Happy, hoping for Salvation through Jesus Christ – Just before he died His Countenance became fair. His eyes Brighten'd and He burst out into Singing of the things he saw in

Heaven. In truth He Died like a Saint as a person who was standing by
Him Observed – He is to be Buryed on Fridayay at 12 in morn.g. Should
you like to go to the Funeral – If you should there there will be Room in
the Coach.

Yrs affection.y
G. Richmond

Excuse this wretched scrawl

JOEY GRIMALDI to an unidentified correspondent, 20 December 1829

Joseph Grimaldi, 1779–1837, clown. Grimaldi's last appearance in public was at
his benefit performance held at Drury Lane on 27 June the previous year, when,
sitting on a chair because he was too weak to stand, he played a scene in the
character of Harlequin Hoax.

Sadlers Wells
Decr 20 1829

Dear Sir

It is with sorrow I am unable to do as you wish. Christmas is near –
but I shall be unable to accept your invite. I am extremely ill and hardly
able to stand with the cursed gout – no grinning *now* for poor old Joey –
none! I shall be with you in spirit dear Friend and as such shall think of all
your enjoyments & amusements. I do not think I shall see many more
Christmases – but Providence willing, next year I will if alive be with you.
Accept my hearty wishes for happiness and believe me

Your true old
        Friend
Joey Grimaldi
(now grin all day!)

WILLIAM HAZLITT to Francis Jeffrey, [September 1830]

William Hazlitt, 1778–1830, essayist; Francis Jeffrey, editor of the *Edinburgh Review*. Hazlitt died on 18 September 1830. One of those by his death-bed heard him speaking his last words in a voice 'resembling the faint scream I have heard from birds'.

Dear Sir,
 I am dying; can you send me 10£. & so consummate your many kindnesses to me?

W. Hazlitt

SYDNEY SMITH to Guillemard, 22 November 1833

The Revd Sydney Smith, 1771–1845, Canon of St Paul's, wit. The editor of Sydney Smith's letters states that the recipient of this letter cannot be identified: but it is nice to think that he could have been the Revd William Henry Guillemard (1815–87), subsequently Fellow of Pembroke College and responsible, so the *Dictionary of National Biography* tells us, for introducing the Oxford Movement to Cambridge.

November 22nd, 1833

Dear Guillemard,
 To go to St. Paul's is certain death. The thermometer is several degrees below zero. My sentences are frozen as they come out of my mouth, and are thawed in the course of the Summer, making strange noises and unexpected assertions in various parts of the church; but if you are tired of a world which is not tired of you, and are determined to go to St. Paul's, it becomes my duty to facilitate the desperate scheme. Present the enclosed card to any of the vergers, and you will be well placed.

Ever truly yours
Sydney Smith

CHARLES DICKENS to Thomas Beard, [11 January 1835]

Charles Dickens, 1812–70, novelist; Thomas Beard, a fellow-reporter. At this time Dickens was working as parliamentary reporter on the *Morning Chronicle*, a rival to *The Times*, a post to which his friend Beard had recommended him. A year and a half later *The Pickwick Papers* was to make him famous.

Black Boy Hotel – Chelmsford
Sunday Morning

Dear Tom.

I am more anxious than I can well express to know the result of your Interview with Hodgkin, having set my heart on its being favourable. If you are not engaged tomorrow, will you write me a line by Return of Post, and resolve my doubts. I go into Suffolk on Tuesday Morning early but my Head Quarters will be here, and I have no doubt I shall receive at once any letter that arrives, directed as above.

I wish of all things that you were with me – Barring the grime of Solitude I have been very comfortable since I left town and trust I shall remain so until I return, which I shall do about the latter end of the week, unless I receive orders from the Office to the contrary.

Owing to the slippery state of the roads on the morning I started, I magnanimously declined the honour of driving myself, and hid my dignity in the Inside of a Stage Coach. As the Election here had not commenced, I went on to Colchester (which is a very nice town) and returned here on the following morning. Yesterday I had to start at 8 OClock for Braintree – a place 12 miles off; and being unable to get a Saddle Horse, I actually ventured on a gig, – and what is more, I actually did the four and twenty miles without upsetting it. I wish to God you could have seen me tooling in and out of the banners, drums, conservative Emblems, horsemen, and go-carts with which every little Green was filled as the processions were waiting for Sir John Tyrell and Baring. Every time the horse heard a drum he bounded into the hedge, on the left side of the road; and every time I got him out of that, he bounded into the hedge on the right side. When he *did* go however, he went along admirably. The road was clear when I returned, and with the trifling exception of breaking my Whip, I flatter myself I did the whole thing in something like style.

If any one were to ask me what in my opinion was the dullest and most stupid spot on the face of the Earth, I should decidedly say Chelmsford.

Though only 29 miles from town, there is not a single shop where they sell Sunday Papers. I can't get an Athenæum, a Literary Gazette – no not even a penny Magazine. And here I am on a wet Sunday looking out of a damned large bow window at the rain as it falls into the puddles opposite, wondering when it will be dinner time, and cursing my folly in having put no books into my Portmanteau. The only book I have seen here, is one which lies upon the sofa. It is entitled 'Field Exercises and Evolutions of the Army by Sir Henry Torrens'. I have read it through so often, that I am sure I could drill a hundred Recruits from memory. There is not even anything to look at in the place, except two immense prisons, large enough to hold all the Inhabitants of the country – whom they can have been built for I can't imagine.

I fear among the gloomy reflections which will present themselves to my mind this day that of having entailed upon you the misery of decyphering such an unconnected mass as this, will not be the least. As I thought it very likely however, that you would never get beyond the first three sentences I have comprised in them, the whole object of my letter; knowing that whether you came to the end of it or not, you would believe without a written assurance that I am

Most Sincerely Yours
Charles Dickens

My best remembrances to all.

THE DUKE OF WELLINGTON to Miss A. M. Jenkins, 14 March 1840

Arthur Wellesley, first Duke of Wellington, 1769–1852, Field Marshal and Prime Minister; Miss A. M. Jenkins, a female admirer. Miss Jenkins was one of several young women with whom Wellington conducted lengthy correspondences. She was fond of offering him spiritual comfort which seems, at times, to have strained his patience. She endorsed the present letter, 'Let NOT him that girdeth on his harness *boast himself* as he that putteth it off. I Kings XX. II. / Alas! I tremble for you.'

London, March 14th, 1840.

The Duke of Wellington presents His Compliments to Miss J. He has just received Her Note of friday evening the 13th Inst.

The Duke is very sensible of Miss J.'s offer of Service in case the Duke should be sick or afflicted.

The Duke is much obliged to Her. He is quite well. He has no reason to believe that he will have occasion to trouble Her upon any object whatever.

CHARLES DICKENS to Daniel Maclise, 12 March 1841

Charles Dickens, 1812–70, novelist; Daniel Maclise, painter. This letter describes the last moments of one of the two ravens who were the originals of Grip in *Barnaby Rudge*. Stuffed, in a glass case, the bird fetched £126 at the sale of Dickens's effects after his death. The letter originally bore an enormous black seal on its envelope.

> Devonshire Terrace.
> Friday Evening
> March The Twelfth 1841.

My Dear Maclise.

You will be greatly shocked and grieved to hear that the Raven is no more.

He expired to-day at a few minutes after Twelve o'Clock at noon. He had been ailing (as I told you t'other night) for a few days, but we anticipated no serious result, conjecturing that a portion of the white paint he swallowed last summer might be lingering about his vitals without having any serious effect upon his constitution. Yesterday afternoon he was taken so much worse that I sent an express for the medical gentleman (Mr. Herring) who promptly attended, and administered a powerful dose of castor oil. Under the influence of this medicine, he recovered so far as to be able at 8 o'Clock p.m. to bite Topping. His night was peaceful. This morning at daybreak he appeared better; received (agreeably to the doctor's directions) another dose of castor oil; and partook plentifully of some warm gruel, the flavor of which he appeared to relish. Towards eleven o'Clock he was so much worse that it was found necessary to muffle the stable knocker. At half past, or thereabouts, he was heard talking to himself about the horse and Topping's family, and to add some incoherent expressions which are supposed to have been either a foreboding of his approaching dissolution, or some wishes relative to the disposal of his little property – consisting chiefly of halfpence which he had buried in different parts of the garden. On the clock striking twelve he appeared slightly agitated, but he soon recovered, walked twice or thrice along the coach-house, stopped to bark, staggered, exclaimed 'Halloa old girl!' (his favorite expression) and died.

He behaved throughout with a decent fortitude, equanimity, and self-possession, which cannot be too much admired. I deeply regret that being in ignorance of his danger I did not attend to receive his last instructions. Something remarkable about his eyes occasioned Topping to run for the doctor at Twelve. When they returned together our friend was gone. It was the medical gentleman who informed me of his decease. He did it with great caution and delicacy, preparing me by the remark that 'a jolly queer start had taken place', but the shock was very great notwithstanding.

I am not wholly free from suspicions of poison – a malicious butcher has been heard to say that he would 'do' for him – his plea was, that he would not be molested in taking orders down the Mews, by any bird that wore a tail – other persons have also been heard to threaten – among others, Charles Knight who has just started a weekly publication, price fourpence; Barnaby being, as you know, Threepence. I have directed a post mortem examination, and the body has been removed to Mr. Herring's school of Anatomy for that purpose.

I could wish, if you can take the trouble, that you would inclose this to Forster when you have read it. I cannot discharge the painful task of communication more than once. Were they Ravens who took Manna to somebody in the wilderness? At times I hope they were, and at others I fear they were not, or they would certainly have stolen it by the way. In profound sorrow, I am ever Your bereaved friend. CD.

Kate is as well as can be expected, but terribly low as you may suppose. The children seem rather glad of it. He bit their ancles. But that was play –

CHARLES DICKENS to Basil Hall, 27 April 1841

Charles Dickens, 1812–70, novelist; Capt Basil Hall, RN, author. Hall, whose mind gave way soon afterwards, was in the habit of offering Dickens scenarios for his novels. This note is written in the manner of Alfred Jingle from *The Pickwick Papers*.

Devonshire Terrace
April The Twenty Seventh 1841.

My Dear Hall.

Post just going – compression of sentiments required – Bust received – likeness *amazing* – recognizable instantly if encountered on the summit of the Great Pyramid – Scotch anecdote most striking and most distressing – dreamed of it – babbies well – wife ditto – yours the same, I hope? – Seaport sketches, one of those ideas that improves in promise as they are pondered on – *Good*, I am certain – Ever faithfully, and at present hastily –

Boz.

HENRY THOREAU to Lucy Brown, 2 March 1842

Henry David Thoreau, 1817–62, author of *Walden*; Mrs Lucy Brown, Emerson's sister-in-law. Thoreau's brother John had died suddenly on 11 January, followed by Emerson's son Waldo, Thoreau's favourite, on 27 January. The shock was profound, and for two months Thoreau wrote neither letters nor journal.

Concord March 2nd 1842.

Dear Friend,

I believe I have nothing new to tell you, for what was news you have learned from other sources. I am much the same person that I was, who should be so much better; yet when I realize what has transpired, and the greatness of the part I am unconsciously acting, I am thrilled, and it seems as if there were now a history to match it.

Soon after John's death I listened to a music-box, and if, at any time, that even had seemed inconsistent with the beauty and harmony of the universe, it was then gently constrained into the placid course of nature by those steady notes, in mild and unoffended tone echoing far and wide under the heavens. But I find these things more strange than sad to me. What right have I to grieve, who have not ceased to wonder?

We feel at first as if some opportunities of kindness and sympathy were lost, but learn afterward that any *pure grief* is ample recompense for all. That is, if we are faithful; – for a spent grief is but sympathy with the soul that disposes events, and is as natural as the resin of Arabian trees. – Only nature has a right to grieve perpetually, for she only is innocent. Soon the ice will melt, and the blackbirds sing along the river which he frequented, as pleasantly as ever. The same everlasting serenity will appear in this face of God, and we will not be sorrowful, if he is not.

We are made happy when reason can discover no occasion for it. The memory of some past moments is more persuasive than the experience of present ones. There have been visions of such breadth and brightness that these motes were invisible in their light.

I do not wish to see John ever again – I mean him who is dead – but that other whom only he would have wished to see, or to be, of whom he was the imperfect representative. For we are not what we are, nor do we treat or esteem each other for such, but for what we are capable of being.

As for Waldo, he died as the mist rises from the brook, which the sun will soon dart his rays through. Do not the flowers die every autumn? He had not even taken root here. I was not startled to hear that he was dead; – it seemed the most natural event that could happen. His fine organization demanded it, and nature gently yielded its request. It would have been strange if he had lived. Neither will nature manifest any sorrow at his death, but soon the note of the lark will be heard down in the meadow, and fresh dandelions will spring from the old stocks where he plucked them last summer. I have been living ill of late, but am now doing better. How do you live in that Plymouth world, now-a-days? – Please remember me to Mary Russell. – You must not blame me if I do *talk to the clouds*, for I remain.

Your Friend,
Henry D. Thoreau.

SYDNEY SMITH to Lady Holland, 13 September 1842

The Revd Sydney Smith, 1771–1845, Canon of St Paul's, wit; Lady Holland, Whig hostess. The poet Rogers, the historians Macaulay and Hallam, the critic Jeffery, editor of the *Edinburgh Review*, and Smith's brother Bobus were all regular guests at Holland House.

Combe Florey, Sept. 13th, 1842

My dear Lady Holland,

I am sorry to hear Allen is not well; but the reduction of his legs is a pure and unmixed good; they are enormous, – they are clerical! He has the creed of a philosopher and the legs of a clergyman; I never saw such legs, – at least, belonging to a layman.

Read 'A Life in the Forest,' skipping nimbly; but there is much of good in it.

It is a bore, I admit, to be past seventy, for you are left for execution, and are daily expecting the death-warrant; but, as you say, it is not anything very capital we quit. We are, at the close of life, only hurried away from stomach-aches, pains in the joints, from sleepless nights and unamusing days, from weakness, ugliness, and nervous tremors; but we shall all meet again in another planet, cured of all our defects. Rogers will be less irritable; Macaulay more silent; Hallam will assent; Jeffrey will speak slower; Bobus will be just as he is; I shall be more respectful to the upper clergy; but I shall have as lively a sense as I now have of all your kindness and affection for me.

Sydney Smith

SYDNEY SMITH to Mrs Meynell, 23 September 1842

The Revd Sydney Smith, 1771–1845, Canon of St Paul's, wit; Mrs Meynell, daughter of Smith's friend Mrs Pigou. Evelyn Waugh was later to spend the last ten years of his life in the isolation of Combe Florey.

Combe Florey, Sept. 23rd, 1842

Dearest Gee,

Nothing could exceed the beauty of the grapes, except the beauty of the pine-apple. How well you understand the clergy!

I am living, lively and young as I am, in the most profound solitude. I saw a crow yesterday, and had a distant view of a rabbit today. I have ceased to trouble myself about company. If anybody thinks it worth while to turn aside to the Valley of Flowers, I am most happy to see them; but I have ceased to lay plots, and to toil for visitors. I save myself by this much disappointment.

Sydney Smith

DR LIVINGSTONE to his parents, 16 December 1843

David Livingstone, 1813–73, missionary and explorer; his parents Neil and Agnes Livingston of Blantyre and Hamilton, Scotland. Livingstone had been sent to Africa by the London Missionary Society three years previously; the Moffats were fellow missionaries, whose daughter Mary he later married. Kuruman is in Bechuana, northern South Africa, where Livingstone had set up a missionary post. Certain passages in the original of this letter have been scored out by a later hand, no doubt in order to spare the victims of Livingstone's sarcasm; at this period Livingstone was still signing his name 'Livingston'.

Kuruman
16 Decr. 1843

My dear Parents,

I recieved the boxes you sent by Mr Moffat a few days ago, and have to inform you that a bill of which I advised you was not forwarded at the time I expected. It however will now go, & go to Mr Pyne, who will transmit the sums to the different individuals. The reason of the delay I need not mention, as it is connected with the character of Mr Williams.

I am sorry you sent so many things. It would have been much better had you kept the money for your own use. What on earth induced you to send large buckling combs to people who have no hair to buckle? The Bechuanas have all short curly hair, not more than an inch in length. If you get any more, bury them in the garden, as I shall do today, for they are of no earthly use; also pincushions & any other nonsense, bury them rather than send stuff. For the other articles I feel much obliged. I am only sorry you send when you have nothing to spare. If you can send to Charles it will be better bestowed. The caps & Janet's shawl I give to Mrs Bartlett. The straw hat won't look well on my head x x x If any one else asks leave to write to me, it will be better to say that I am public property and can be addressed by any one. I can then answer their letters or not as I like. My address is South Africa. Give it always in a general way. I never wear a hat; a common midshipman's cap covers my head, & I leave my complexion to take care of itself.

I write this in a great hurry, as we are packing up to go off for the formation of our new mission. I have not had time to read all my letters yet, as I must write back by the individuals who came & go back again to the Colony.

I went a good way to meet Mr Moffat. He does not seem at all spoiled by the honours which have been heaped on him at home. We hope the work will recieve a new impulse by the arrival of the newcomers. May the Spirit be poured out, & cause the wilderness and solitary place to be glad & blossom as the rose.

Mothers' cakes were like wormwood to the taste, but I must not say so lest it should offend. Will cakes keep well at home for a twelvemonth? Ought they to be sent to a warm climate where they very soon become like x x x ? I ask these questions only, I don't say send no more. I am very much obliged to Mother for her towels, handkerchiefs, &c &c, all which I cannot at present enumerate, as I have not got time to look yet. My kind love to her, & may the Lord bless her & keep her near to himself.

Many of the Bechuanas met Mr & Mrs Moffat with tears of joy. One poor Bushman who has been brought up by him wept aloud when he approached him; and as I had gone to meet him, I recieved many thanks for bringing him. They had believed he should never return. He is not, as I was informed by some who knew him, in the least opposed to Native agency. He is a warm friend to them, but his character has been sadly traduced by many who ought to have known better. He told me the reason of the slander brought against him was his having got an unworthy character turned out of that office. He has been sadly slandered by some in other & more tender points. This he must expect, for nearly all great men have their slanderers & traducers. He is truly a good man, & will shine when all his enemies are forgotten. Mrs Moffat is a good motherly woman. She takes a kind interest not only over her own family, but seems to consider Mr & Mrs Edwards & Mr Hamilton as her children too.

Inglis I suspect won't do for Africa. His heart is in Scotland, and he ought never to have been out of it. But I have not yet seen him, as he has gone to Griqua Town instead of coming here. If he is not a blessing he will be a curse. Mokoteri is likely to prove the latter from unbearable pride & vanity fostered by the good people in England.

All is quiet in the Interior. I have thought that tartan will make good jackets. Let me have some. If so, you can tell Mr Drummond I mean xxx.

I shall answer all letters as soon as I can, Janet's & everybody's. Give thanks to everybody, & greetings to all who deserve them. You know I write this in great haste.

Yours affectionately,
David Livingston

Thank Mr Naismith for the boots; they fit exactly. I shall write him. No letter from either Samuel or John Naismith, Jun., nor yet from Mr Drummond.

ROBERT BROWNING to Elizabeth Barrett, [10 January 1845]

Robert Browning, 1812–89, poet; Elizabeth Barrett, afterwards Browning, poet. This is the first in the famous series of love letters between the two poets. Browning was not to meet Elizabeth Barrett until 20 May. They married and eloped in the autumn of the following year.

New Cross, Hatcham, Surrey.

I love your verses with all my heart, dear Miss Barrett, – and this is no off-hand complimentary letter that I shall write, – whatever else, no prompt matter-of-course recognition of your genius, and there a graceful and natural end of the thing: since the day last week when I first read your poems, I quite laugh to remember how I have been turning and turning again in my mind what I should be able to tell you of their effect upon me – for in the first flush of delight I thought I would this once get out of my habit of purely passive enjoyment, when I do really enjoy, and thoroughly justify my admiration – perhaps even, as a loyal fellow-craftsman should, try and find fault and do you some little good to be proud of hereafter! – but nothing comes of it all – so into me has it gone, and part of me has it become, this great living poetry of yours, not a flower of which but took and grew – oh how different that is from lying to be dried and pressed flat, and prized highly and put in a book with a proper account at top and bottom, and shut up and put away . . . and the book called a 'Flora,' besides! After all I shall be need not give up the thought of doing that, too, in time; because even now, talking with whoever is worthy, I can give a reason for my faith in one and another excellence, the fresh strange music, the affluent language, the exquisite pathos and true new brave thought – but in this addressing myself to you – your own self, and for the first time, my feeling rises altogether. I do, as I say, love these books with all my heart – and I love you too: do you know I was once not very far from seeing – really seeing you? Mr. Kenyon said to me one morning 'Would you like to see Miss Barrett?' – then he went to announce me, – then he returned . . . you were too unwell – and now it is years ago – and I feel as at some untoward passage in my travels – as if I had been close, so close, to some world's-wonder in chapel or crypt, only a screen to push and I might have entered, but there was some slight . . . so it now seems . . . slight and just-sufficient bar to admission; and the half-opened door shut, and I went home my thousands of miles, and the sight was never to be!

Well, these Poems were to be – and this true thankful joy and pride with which I feel myself

Yours ever faithfully,

Robert Browning

THOMAS HOOD to an autograph collector, 19 March 1845

Thomas Hood, 1799–1845, humorous poet; G. B. Webb, an autograph collector. Hood's health had broken down that Christmas, and he died on 3 May.

Devonshire Lodge
New Finchley Road
St. John's Wood
19 March
1845.

Sir

I have much pleasure in acceding to your wish, though I did not write the lines on Mr. Bish, having at the time to fry some other fish.
As I am about going I know not where, if you want another Autograph,

you must apply to my Heir.
I am Sir
Yours most obeditly
Thos. Hood
G.B. Webb Esqre.

PATRICK BRANWELL BRONTË to John Brown, [1848]

Patrick Branwell Brontë, 1817–48, brother of Charlotte, Emily and Anne Brontë; John Brown, sexton at Haworth. Branwell had taught for a spell at Thorpe Green with his sister Anne and conceived a disastrous passion for his employer, Mrs Robinson. He returned to Haworth in 1845 and, while his sisters were writing their novels, drank himself to death.

Sunday, Noon.

Dear John,
I shall feel very much obliged to you if [you] can contrive to get me Five pence worth of Gin in a proper measure.
Should it be speedily got I could perhaps take it from you or Billy at the lane top, or, what would be quite as well, sent out for, to you.
I anxiously ask the favour because I know the good it will do me.
Punctually at Half-past Nine in the morning you will be paid the 5d. out of a shilling given me then. – Yours,

P. B. B.

CHARLES DICKENS to Thomas Beard, 10 May 1848

Charles Dickens, 1812–70, novelist; Thomas Beard, former colleague on the *Morning Chronicle*. Timber was the family dog; Dickens had formed his friends into an amateur acting company and they were due to put on a performance of *Every Man in His Humour* at the Haymarket Theatre the following Monday.

Devonshire Terrace
Wednesday Tenth May 1848.

My Dear Beard
Will you come and dine with us (alone) at 5 on Sunday? We can then crack a peaceful bottle of *the* Port, and arrange about next night.

Would you like to have a young unicorn, a little griffin, or a small dragon? Timber is at length giving such frightful and horribly unnatural tokens of virility, in connexion with an insignificant, drivelling, bleareyed little tame rabbit of the female sex, that I am in constant expectation of a litter of monsters. – Excuse me concluding abruptly, but he has just sneaked past the window, sniffing after this deplorable animal and making stupid attempts to mount – and I *must* go and whop him.

Ever affectionately

CD.

P.S. Having whopped him, I may mention that the Company are all nearly worked to death. Stone is affected with congestion of the kidneys, which he attributes to being forced to do the same thing twenty times over, when he forgets it once. Beads break out all over Forster's head, and *boil* there, visibly and audibly. Fred says upon his soul he never saw anything like it in all his life. And Leech is limp with being bullied.

PRINCE ALBERT to Lord Brougham, 15 June 1848

Albert of Saxe-Coburg-Gotha, 1819–61, Prince Consort; Henry Brougham, Lord Chancellor. 'The Year of Revolutions', 1848, saw the overthrow of Louis Philippe in France and the publication of the Communist Manifesto. Robert Owen of New Lanark, the socialist, knew Brougham through their common interest in educational reform.

My dear Lord Brougham

I have felt that I could with safety lay Mr Owen's memorial before the Queen as by so doing I commit neither Her Majesty nor myself to any expression of opinion upon the subject matter. I think you could, as from yourself, tell your old friend, that it is hardly by the appointment of a Commission to enquire into the *Theory* of Socialism that we can hope to arrive at a satisfactory result, but that the value of its principles could alone be tested by their practical adaptation. Such practical experiments have unfortunately hitherto been found to be *exceedingly expensive* to the Nation which tried them. However one upon large scale is now being carried on in France, which I think might be considered as a 'Monster Commission' for the instruction of the rest of Europe.

> Ever
> your's truly
> Albert

Buckingham Palace
June 15. 1848. –

CHARLOTTE BRONTË to W. S. Williams, 2 October 1848

Charlotte Brontë, 1816–55, novelist; W. S. Williams, reader at Smith & Elder and first admirer of *Jane Eyre*. Branwell Brontë had died on 24 September.

October 2nd, 1848.

My Dear Sir,

'We have buried our dead out of sight.' A lull begins to succeed the gloomy tumult of last week. It is not permitted us to grieve for him who is gone as others grieve for those they lose. The removal of our only brother must necessarily be regarded by us rather in the light of a mercy than a chastisement. Branwell was his father's and his sisters' pride and hope in boyhood, but since manhood the case has been otherwise. It has been our lot to see him take a wrong bent; to hope, expect, wait his return to the right path; to know the sickness of hope deferred, the dismay of prayer baffled; to experience despair at last – and now to behold the sudden early obscure close of what might have been a noble career.

I do not weep from a sense of bereavement – there is no prop withdrawn, no consolation torn away, no dear companion lost – but for the wreck of talent, the ruin of promise, the untimely dreary extinction of what might have been a burning and a shining light. My brother was a year my junior. I had aspirations and ambitions for him once, long ago – they have perished mournfully. Nothing remains of him but a memory of errors and sufferings. There is such a bitterness of pity for his life and death, such a yearning for the emptiness of his whole existence as I cannot describe. I trust time will allay these feelings.

My poor father naturally thought more of his *only* son than of his daughters, and, much and long as he had suffered on his account, he cried out of his loss like David for that of Absalom – my son! my son! – and refused at first to be comforted. And then when I ought to have been able to collect my strength and be at hand to support him, I fell ill with an illness whose approaches I had felt for some time previously, and of which the crisis was hastened by the awe and trouble of the death-scene – the first I had ever witnessed. The past has seemed to me a strange week. Thank God, for my father's sake, I am better now, though still feeble. I wish indeed I had more general physical strength – the want of it is sadly in my way. I cannot do what I would do for want of sustained animal spirits and efficient bodily vigour.

My unhappy brother never knew what his sisters had done in literature – he was not aware that they had ever published a line. We could not tell him of our efforts for fear of causing him too deep a pang of remorse for his own time misspent, and talents misapplied. Now he will *never* know. I cannot dwell longer on the subject at present – it is too painful.

I thank you for your kind sympathy, and pray earnestly that your sons may all do well, and that you may be spared the sufferings my father has gone through. – Yours sincerely,

C. Brontë

HENRY THOREAU to Ellen Emerson, 31 July 1849

Henry David Thoreau, 1817–62, author of *Walden*; Ellen, Emerson's eldest child (then ten).

Concord July 31st 1849

Dear Ellen,

I think that we are pretty well acquainted, though we never had any very long talks. We have had a good many short talks, at any rate. Dont you remember how we used to despatch our breakfast two winters ago, as soon as Eddy could get on his feeding tire, which was not always remembered, before the rest of the household had come down? Dont you remember our wise criticisms on the pictures in the portfolio and the Turkish book with Eddy and Edith looking on, – how almost any pictures answered our purpose, and we went through the Penny Magazine, first from beginning to end, and then from end to beginning, and Eddy stared just as much the second time as the first, and Edith thought that we turned over too soon, and that there were some things which she had not seen – ? I can guess pretty well what interests you, and what you think about. Indeed I am interested in pretty much the same things myself. I suppose you think that persons who are as old as your father and myself are always thinking about very grave things, but I know that we are meditating the same old themes that we did when we were ten years old, only we go more gravely about it. You love to write or to read a fairy story and that is what you will always like to do, in some form or other. By and by you will discover that you want what are called the necessaries of life only that you may realize some such dream.

Eddy has got him a fish-pole and line with a pin-hook at the end, which he flourishes over the dry ground and the carpet at the risk of tearing out our eyes; but when I told him that he must have a cork and a sinker, his mother took off the pin and tied on a cork instead; but he doubts whether that will catch fish as well. He tells me that he is five years old. Indeed I was present at the celebration of his birthday lately, and supplied the company with onion and squash pipes, and rhubarb whistles, which is the most I can do on such occasions. Little Sammy Hoar blowed them most successfully, and made the loudest noise, though it almost strained his eyes out to do it. Edith is full of spirits. When she comes home from school, she goes hop skip and jump down into the field to pick berries, currants, gooseberries, raspberries, and thimbleberries; if there is one of these that has thoughts of changing its hue by to-morrow morning, I guess that Edith knows something about it and will consign it to her basket for Grandmama.

Children may now be seen going a-berrying in all directions. The white-lillies are in blossom, and the john'swort and goldenrod are beginning to come out. Old people say that we have not had so warm a summer for thirty years. Several persons have died in consequence of the heat, – Mr Kendal, perhaps, for one. The Irishmen on the railroad were obliged to leave off their work for several days, and the farmers left their fields and sought the shade. William Brown of the poor house is dead, – the one who used to ask for a cent – 'Give me a cent?' I wonder who will have his cents now!

I found a nice penknife on the bank of the river this afternoon, which was probably lost by some villager who went there to bathe lately. Yesterday I found a nice arrowhead, which was lost some time before by an Indian who was hunting there. The knife was a very little rusted; the arrowhead was not rusted at all.

You must see the sun rise out of the ocean before you come home. I think that Long Island will not be in the way, if you climb to the top of the hill – at least, no more than Bolster Island, and Pillow Hill and even the Lowlands of Never-get-up are elsewhere.

Do not think that you must write to me because I have written to you. It does not follow at all. You would not naturally make so long a speech to me here in a month as a letter would be. Yet if sometime it should be perfectly easy, and pleasant to you, I shall be very glad to have a sentence

Your old acquaintance
Henry Thoreau

NATHANIEL HAWTHORNE to an autograph collector, 12 April 1851

Nathanial Hawthorne, 1804–64, novelist; the autograph collector unidentified.

Lenox, April 12th. 1851.
My dear Sir,

I ought to have answered your note some days ago; but to say the truth, having a particular repugnance to the use of pen and ink, I generally indulge myself with a delay of a week or so, in regard to all correspondence that does not absolutely require immediate attention. In the case of autographs, however, this course is somewhat dangerous; as the ephemeral nature of literary reputation may render the signature worthless before it comes to hand.

Respectfully,
Nathl Hawthorne.

ALFRED TENNYSON to Robert Monteith, [*c.* **24 April 1851**]

Alfred Lord Tennyson, 1809–92, poet; Robert Monteith, fellow undergraduate at Trinity and 'Apostle'.

My dear Robert

    I am quite sure you will feel with me. My poor little boy got strangled in being born. I would not send the notice of my misfortune to the Times and I have had to write some 60 letters. If you desire to know about it ask Edmund Lushington to show you that letter which I wrote to him. My wife has been going on very well since; but last night she lost her voice and I thought I should lose *her*: she is however free from all danger this morning according to my medical man. I have suffered more than ever I thought I could have done for a child still born: I fancy I should not have cared so much if he had been a seven months spindling, but he was the grandest-looking child I had ever seen. Pardon my saying this. I do not speak only as a father but as an Artist – if you do not despise the word from German associations. I mean as a man who has eyes and can judge from seeing.

    I refused to see the little body at first, fearing to find some pallid abortion which would have haunted me all my life – but he looked (if it be not absurd to call a newborn babe so) even majestic in his mysterious silence after all the turmoil of the night before.

    He was – not born, I cannot call it born for he never breathed – but he was released from the prison where he moved for nine months – on Easter Sunday. Awful day! We live close upon an English-church chapel. The organ rolled – the psalm sounded – and the wail of a woman in her travail – of a true and tender nature suffering, as it seemed intolerable wrong, rose ever and anon.

    But ask Edmund for the account and God bless you and your wife, dear Robert,

For ever and ever

A. Tennyson

    I sent part of your note (I mean about the Novel) to Moxon but he has taken no notice of it.

    I look over this note and I find I have written so obscurely that it is a chance whether you ever make it out: and perhaps it does not matter; I think that other written to Edmund is clearer. Ask for it. I don't remember what it was but I am sure there was more of me in it.

WALTER BAGEHOT to his mother, 8 May 1851

Walter Bagehot, 1826–77, economist; Edith Bagehot, his mother. The Great Exhibition opened at the Crystal Palace on 7 May 1851.

6 Great Coram St.
8 May 1851

My dearest Mother,

I took a start yesterday and went to see the Queen open the Exhibition. It went off very well though her Majesty looked matronly and aged and the ladies in attendance on her were an affecting spectacle. The only accurate idea that I can give you of the Exhibition is that it is a great fair under a cucumber frame: the booths very numerous and the glass case very well painted: only it must be one of the Swiss fairs where they sell everything from the best jewellery down to needles and thread. The day was most brilliant and the crowd enormous both of which were essential to the goodness of the spectacle as the palace would be cold and icy without inhabitants and sun is required for the proper apportionment of light and shade and the due appreciation of the painted roof. The form of the building is that of a cross – the long stroke from an analogy to Church architecture being called the nave, and the short stroke the transept. The Queen sat in the centre with the crowd around and behind her, and I was lucky enough to get a place in the front row of one of the galleries immediately overlooking the chair of state, and almost exactly over the head of your aged and infirm friend the Duke of Wellington. The proceedings were in the nature of pantomime as I could not hear a single syllable either of the address or the answer to it, and ninety-nine hundreds of the audience were similarly circumstanced: a great majority not being able to see anything either. I fancied that I caught two or three words of the archbishop's grace or benediction but I am not sure: at any rate I heard a sermonic tone of voice which was a great satisfaction. I suppose the Archbishop was inserted in the program to please the foreigners who are in the habit of consecrating railways and all sorts of secular places: otherwise I think he might as well have been left out as there was nothing there in keeping with him, – nobody minded him and the Queen looked as if she wished that he would leave off. The court looked brilliant enough as far as the men went: the foreign magnates very well got up, our Cabinet ministers like town criers and the Lord

Chancellor like a Butler on the stage – There was a strong light upon them, and a tree behind – a real tree growing in the ground and just coming into leaf – which threw them out well and was original and picturesque looking. I walked about for an hour or two when the Queen went. There is an immense amount of wealth industry and ingenuity and all that sort of thing: and I suppose the best of all things that can be manufactured is there: but no one thing can make much impression in such a mass: the point of the scene is their number and the good effect of the whole. In the exact centre is a stunning fountain of glass made by the Oslers of Oxford St. The foreign departments are much behindhand: the United States especially: indeed at present nothing satisfactory can be collected except that in that country they are extremely well off for soap. They have an immense compartment all to themselves at the end of the nave and nothing hardly in it except busts in soap of the Queen and other people. It must be amusing to wash yourself with yourself and a great relief from the wretchedness of the employment. There were a great many Americans in the crowd. Quain – with whom I went – got hold of one who swore he was member in Congress for California and looked like a Smithfield drover. Otherwise there were much fewer foreigners than I expected. They were certainly not a twentieth part of the crowd. There are a good many of questionable aspect in the streets, but few I take it that abound in coin. I hear that the house-letting people are at a low ebb in consequence. Hope you can read this scrawl. I write in a hurry as I want to go to bed –

> Yours affly
> W Bagehot

I shall go to Hampstead on Sunday. Love to all.

HERMAN MELVILLE to Nathaniel Hawthorne, 29 June 185[1]

Herman Melville, 1819–91, novelist; Nathaniel Hawthorne, novelist. Melville's masterpiece *Moby-Dick, or, The Whale* was in part inspired by Hawthorne's own achievement.

> Pittsfield June 29th 185[1]

My dear Hawthorne – The clear air and open window invite me to write to you. For some time past I have been so busy with a thousand things that I have almost forgotten when I wrote you last, and whether I received an answer. This most persuasive season has now for weeks recalled me from certain crotchetty and over doleful chimearas, the like of which men like you and me and some others, forming a chain of God's posts round the world, must be content to encounter now and then, and fight them the best way we can. But come they will, – for, in the boundless, trackless, but still glorious wild wilderness through which these outposts run, the Indians do sorely abound, as well as the insignificant but still stinging mosquitoes. Since you have been here, I have been building some shanties of houses (connected with the old one) and likewise some shanties of chapters and essays. I have been plowing and sowing and raising and painting and printing and praying, – and now begin to come out upon a less bustling time, and to enjoy the calm prospect of things from a fair piazza at the north of the old farm house here.

Not entirely yet, though, am I without something to be urgent with. The 'Whale' is only half through the press; for, wearied with the long delay of the printers, and disgusted with the heat and dust of the babylonish brick-kiln of New York, I came back to the country to feel the grass – and end the book reclining on it, if I may – I am sure you will pardon this speaking all about myself, – for if I *say* so much on that head, be sure all the rest of the world are thinking about themselves ten times as much. Let us speak, though we show all our faults and weaknesses, – for it is a sign of strength to be weak, to know it, and out with it, – not in [a] set way and ostentatiously, though, but incidentally and without premeditation. – But I am falling into my old foible – preaching. I am busy, but shall not be very long. Come and spend a day here, if you can and want to; if not, stay in Lenox, and God give you long life. When I am quite free of my present engagements, I am going to treat myself to a ride and a visit to you. Have ready a bottle of brandy, because I always feel like drinking that heroic drink when we talk ontological heroics together. This is rather a crazy letter in some respects, I apprehend. If so, ascribe it to the intoxicating effects of the latter end of June operating upon a very susceptible and peradventure feeble temperament.

Shall I send you a fin of the *Whale* by way of a specimen mouthful? The tail is not yet cooked – though the hell-fire in which the whole book is broiled might not unreasonably have cooked it all ere this. This is the book's motto (the secret one), – Ego non baptiso te in nomine – but make out the rest yourself.

H.M.

HERMAN MELVILLE to Nathaniel Hawthorne, [?17 November 1851]

Herman Melville, 1819–91, novelist; Nathaniel Hawthorne, novelist. *Moby-Dick* came out that year. This is the only known letter, apart from those to his family, which Melville signs with his Christian name.

Pittsfield, Monday afternoon.

My Dear Hawthorne, – People think that if a man has undergone any hardship, he should have a reward; but for my part, if I have done the hardest possible day's work, and then come to sit down in a corner and eat my supper comfortably – why, then I don't think I deserve any reward for my hard day's work – for am I not now at peace? Is not my supper good? My peace and my supper are my reward, my dear Hawthorne. So your joy-giving and exultation-breeding letter is not my reward for my ditcher's work with that book, but is the good goddess's bonus over and above what was stipulated for – for not one man in five cycles, who is wise, will expect appreciative recognition from his fellows, or any one of them. Appreciation! Recognition! Is love appreciated? Why, ever since Adam, who has got to the meaning of this great allegory – the world? Then we pygmies must be content to have our paper allegories but ill comprehended. I say your appreciation is my glorious gratuity. In my proud, humble way, – a shepherd-king, – I was lord of a little vale in the solitary Crimea; but you have now given me the crown of India. But on trying it on my head, I found it fell down on my ears, notwithstanding their asinine length – for it's only such ears that sustain such crowns.

Your letter was handed me last night on the road going to Mr. Morewood's, and I read it there. Had I been at home, I would have sat down at once and answered it. In me divine maganimities are spontaneous and instantaneous – catch them while you can. The world goes round, and the other side comes up. So now I can't write what I felt. But I felt pantheistic then – your heart beat in my ribs and mine in yours, and both in God's. A sense of unspeakable security is in me this moment, on account of your having understood the book. I have written a wicked book, and feel spotless as the lamb. Ineffable socialities are in me. I would sit down and dine with you and all the gods in old Rome's Pantheon. It is a strange feeling – no hopefulness is in it, no despair. Content – that is it; and irresponsibility; but without licentious inclination. I speak now of my profoundest sense of being, not of an incidental feeling.

Whence come you, Hawthorne? By what right do you drink from my flagon of life? And when I put it to my lips – lo, they are yours and not mine. I feel that the Godhead is broken up like the bread at the Supper, and that we are the pieces. Hence this infinite fraternity of feeling. Now, sympathizing with the paper, my angel turns over another page. You did not care a penny for the book. But, now and then as you read, you understood the pervading thought that impelled the book – and that you praised. Was it not so? You were archangel enough to despise the imperfect body, and embrace the soul. Once you hugged the ugly Socrates because you saw the flame in the mouth, and heard the rushing of the demon, – the familiar, – and recognized the sound; for you have heard it in your own solitudes.

My dear Hawthorne, the atmospheric skepticisms steal into me now, and make me doubtful of my sanity in writing you thus. But, believe me, I am not mad, most noble Festus! But truth is ever incoherent, and when the big hearts strike together, the concussion is a little stunning. Farewell. Don't write a word about the book. That would be robbing me of my miserly delight. I am heartily sorry I ever wrote anything about you – it was paltry. Lord, when shall we be done growing? As long as we have anything more to do, we have done nothing. So, now, let us add Moby Dick to our blessing, and step from that. Leviathan is not the biggest fish; – I have heard of Krakens.

This is a long letter, but you are not at all bound to answer it. Possibly, if you do answer it, and direct it to Herman Melville, you will missend it – for the very fingers that now guide this pen are not precisely the same that just took it up and put it on this paper. Lord, when shall we be done changing? Ah! it's a long stage, and no inn in sight, and night coming, and the body cold. But with you for a passenger, I am content and can be happy. I shall leave the world, I feel, with more satisfaction for having come to know you. Knowing you persuades me more than the Bible of our immortality.

What a pity, that, for your plain, bluff letter, you should get such gibberish! Mention me to Mrs. Hawthorne and to the children, and so, good-by to you, with my blessing.

Herman.

P.S. I can't stop yet. If the world was entirely made up of Magians, I'll tell you what I should do. I should have a paper-mill established at one end of the house, and so have an endless riband of foolscap rolling in upon my desk; and upon that endless riband I should write a thousand – a million – billion thoughts, all under the form of a letter to you. The divine magnet is on you, and my magnet responds. Which is the biggest? A foolish question – they are *One*.   H.

P.P.S. Don't think that by writing me a letter, you shall always be bored with an immediate reply to it – and so keep both of us delving over a writing-desk eternally. No such thing! I sh'n't always answer your letters, and you may do just as you please.

CHIEF SEATTLE to the President of the United States, [1854]

Seattle, c. 1784–1866, Chief of the Dwamish, Suquamish and allied Indian tribes; Franklin Pierce, President of the United States. This letter was presumably written with the help of an amanuensis. Seattle ceded his lands in Washington State by the Treaty of Point Elliot, signed on 22 January 1855. He was anxious that the new settlement should not be named after him, as he believed that after his death his spirit would be disturbed every time human lips uttered the syllables of his name; accordingly he used to solicit gifts from whites as a kind of tax to recompense himself in advance for his oft-broken sleep of eternity.

How can you buy or sell the sky, the warmth of the land? The idea is strange to us.

If we do not own the freshness of the air and the sparkle of the water, how can you buy them?

Every part of this earth is sacred to my people.

Every shining pine needle, every sandy shore, every mist in the dark woods, every clearing and humming insect is holy in the memory and experience of my people. The sap which courses through the trees carried the memories of the red man.

The white man's dead forget the country of their birth when they go to walk among the stars. Our dead never forget this beautiful earth, for it is the mother of the red man.

We are part of the earth and it is part of us. The perfumed flowers are our sisters; the deer, the horse, the great eagle, these are our brothers.

The rocky crests, the juices in the meadows, the body heat of the pony, and man – all belong to the same family.

So, when the Great Chief in Washington sends word that he wishes to buy our land, he asks much of us. The Great Chief sends word he will reserve us a place so that we can live comfortably to ourselves.

He will be our father and we will be his children. So we will consider your offer to buy our land.

But it will not be easy. For this land is sacred to us.

This shining water that moves in the streams and rivers is not just water but the blood of our ancestors.

If we sell you land, you must remember that it is sacred, and you must teach your children that it is sacred and that each ghostly reflection in the clear water of the lakes tells of events and memories in the life of my people.

The water's murmur is the voice of my father's father.

The rivers are our brothers, they quench our thirst. The rivers carry our canoes, and feed our children. If we sell you our land, you must remember, and teach your children, that the rivers are our brothers, and yours, and you must henceforth give the rivers the kindness you would give any brother.

We know that the white man does not understand our ways. One portion of land is the same to him as the next, for he is a stranger who comes in the night and takes from the land whatever he needs.

The earth is not his brother, but his enemy, and when he has conquered it, he moves on.

He leaves his father's graves behind, and he does not care. He kidnaps the earth from his children, and he does not care.

His father's grave and his children's birthright, are forgotten. He treats his mother, the earth, and his brother, the sky, as things to be bought, plundered, sold like sheep or bright beads.

His appetite will devour the earth and leave behind only a desert.

I do not know. Our ways are different from your ways.

The sight of your cities pains the eyes of the red man. But perhaps it is because the red man is a savage and does not understand.

There is no quiet place in the white man's cities. No place to hear the unfurling of leaves in spring, or the rustle of an insect's wings.

But perhaps it is because I am a savage and do not understand.

The clatter only seems to insult the ears. And what is there to life if a man cannot hear the lonely cry of the whippoorwill or the arguments of the frogs around a pond at night? I am a red man and do not understand.

The Indian prefers the soft sound of the wind darting over the face of a pond, and the smell of the wind itself, cleaned by a midday rain, or scented with the pinon pine.

The air is precious to the red man, for all things share the same breath – the beast, the tree, the man, they all share the same breath.

The white man does not seem to notice the air he breathes. Like a man dying for many days, he is numb to the stench.

But if we sell you our land, you must remember that the air is precious to us, that the air shares its spirit with all the life it supports. The wind that gave our grandfather his first breath also receives his last sigh.

And if we sell you our land, you must keep it apart and sacred, as a place where even the white man can go to taste the wind that is sweetened by the meadow's flowers.

So we will consider your offer to buy our land. If we decide to accept, I will make one condition: the white man must treat the beasts of this land as his brother.

I am a savage and I do not understand any other way.

I have seen a thousand rotting buffaloes on the prairie, left by the white man who shot them from a passing train.

I am a savage and I do not understand how the smoking iron horse can be more important than the buffalo that we kill only to stay alive.

What is man without the beasts? If all the beasts were gone, man would die from a great loneliness of spirit.

For whatever happens to the beasts, soon happens to man. All things are connected.

You must teach your children that the ground beneath their feet is the ashes of your grandfathers. So that they will respect the land, tell your children that the earth is rich with the lives of our kin.

Teach your children what we have taught our children, that the earth is our mother.

Whatever befalls the earth befalls the sons of the earth. If men spit upon the ground, they spit upon themselves.

This we know: the earth does not belong to man; man belongs to the earth. This we know.

All things are connected like the blood which unites one family. All things are connected.

Whatever befalls the earth befalls the sons of the earth. Man did not weave the web of life: he is merely a strand in it. Whatever he does to the web, he does to himself.

Even the white man, whose God walks and talks with him as friend to friend, cannot be exempt from the common destiny.

We may be brothers after all.

We shall see.

One thing we know, which the white man may one day discover – our God is the same God.

You may think now that you own Him as you wish to own our land; but you cannot. He is the God of man, and His compassion is equal for the red man and the white.

This earth is precious to Him, and to harm the earth is to heap contempt on its Creator.

The whites too shall pass; perhaps sooner than all other tribes. Contaminate your bed, and you will one night suffocate in your own waste.

But in your perishing you will shine brightly, fired by the strength of the God who brought you to this land and for some special purpose gave you dominion over this land and over the red man.

That destiny is a mystery to us, for we do not understand when the buffalo are all slaughtered, the wild horses are tamed, the secret corners of the forest heavy with scent of many men, and the view of the ripe hills blotted by talking wires.

Where is the thicket? Gone.

Where is the eagle? Gone.

The end of living and the beginning of survival.

LORD RAGLAN to the Light Brigade, [25 October 1854]

Lord Fitzroy Somerset, first Baron Raglan, 1788–1855, Commander-in-Chief of British troops in the Crimea. This is the order that launched the Charge of the Light Brigade. It was dictated by Raglan from the heights of Balaclava to General Airey, who signed it and gave it to his ADC, Captain Nolan. Raglan's intention was that the cavalry should prevent the Russians taking away some British naval guns from a position that they had captured, a relatively simple operation. After a dashing ride down into the valley, Nolan gave the order to Lord Lucan who commanded the cavalry. Lucan, who understood the message correctly, passed it on to Lord Cardigan, commander of the Light Brigade and his brother-in-law (with whom he was not on speaking terms). Lord Cardigan then led the Light Brigade in a murderous charge up the wrong valley. According to the first report published in *The Times*, of the 607 officers and men who rode with him (a figure later altered by Tennyson for metrical reasons), 198 returned.

Lord Raglan wishes the cavalry to advance rapidly to the front, follow the enemy and try to prevent the enemy carrying away the guns. Troop horse artillery may accompany. French cavalry is on your left. Immediate.

R. Airey

JOHN CLARE to James Hipkins, 8 March 1860

John Clare, 1793–1864, poet; James Hipkins, an admirer. Clare was committed to a private asylum in 1837; from 1841 till his death he was an inmate of the Northampton Asylum.

March 8th 1860

Dear Sir

    I am in a Madhouse & quite forget your Name or who you are   you must excuse me for I have nothing to commu[n]icate or tell of & why I am shut up I dont know   I have nothing to say so I conclude

yours respectfully John Clare

Mr J Hipkins

DANTE GABRIEL ROSSETTI to Alexander Gilchrist, 19 November 1861

Dante Gabriel Rossetti, 1828–82, Pre-Raphaelite painter and poet; Alexander Gilchrist, biographer of William Blake. Meredith, Swinburne and Rossetti later shared a house (with Rossetti's wombat) in Cheyne Walk.

My dear Gilchrist,

    Two or three blokes and coves are coming here on Friday evening at 8 or so – George Meredith I hope for one. Can you look in? I hope so. Nothing but oysters and of course the seediest of clothes.

    I trust your family anxieties are less every day now, and that your poor little Beatrice is more and more herself again.

I have been reading with much pleasure (and corresponding impatience to go on) the two first sheets of *Blake*, which I return herewith. By the bye I have ventured two red chalk surmises in margin. There is a Cloth of Gold picture by Holbein at Hampton – whether also at Windsor I know not. I thought Swinburne was more meteoric even than usual the other night – a point on which some light was eventually thrown by the geometrical curves which he described from time to time on the pavement as we walked home.

With kind remembrances to Mrs. Gilchrist,

I am yours sincerely,
D. G. Rossetti.

EMILY DICKINSON to T. W. Higginson, 26 April 1862

Emily Dickinson, 1830–86, poet; Colonel T. W. Higginson, critic. Higginson was the only professional critic to whom Emily Dickinson submitted her poems. He was intrigued, but wrote advising against publication (he was later to co-edit a posthumous selection).

April 26, 1862

Mr. Higginson,
Your kindness claimed earlier gratitude – but I was ill – and write today, from my pillow.

Thank you for the surgery – it was not so painful as I supposed. I bring you others – as you ask – though they might not differ –

While my thought is undressed – I can make no distinction, but when I put them in the Gown – they look alike, and numb.

You asked me how old I was? I made no verse – but one or two – until this winter – Sir –

I had a terror – since September – I could tell to none – and so I sing, as the Boy does by the Burying Ground – because I am afraid – You enquire my Books – For Poets – I have Keats – and Mr and Mrs Browning. For Prose – Mr Ruskin – Sir Thomas Browne – and the Revelations. I went to school – but in your manner of the phrase – had no education. When a little Girl, I had a friend, who taught me Immortality – but venturing too near, himself – he never returned – Soon after, my Tutor, died – and for several years, my Lexicon – was my only companion – Then I found I had one more – but he was not contented I be his scholar – so he left the Land.

You ask of my Companions Hills – Sir – and the Sundown – and a Dog – large as myself, that my Father bought me – They are better than Beings – because they know – but do not tell – and the noise in the Pool, at Noon – excels my Piano. I have a Brother and Sister – My Mother does not care for thought – and Father, too busy with his Briefs – to notice what we do – He buys me many Books – but begs me not to read them – because he fears they joggle the Mind. They are religious – except me – and address an Eclipse, every morning – whom they call their "Father." But I fear my story fatigues you – I would like to learn – Could you tell me how to grow – or is it unconveyed – like Melody – or Witchcraft?

You speak of Mr Whitman – I never read his book – but was told that he was disgraceful –

I read Miss Prescott's "Circumstances," but it followed me, in the Dark – so I avoided her –

Two Editors of Journals came to my Father's House, this winter – and asked me for my Mind – and when I asked them "Why?" they said I was penurious – and they, would use it for the World –

I could not Weigh myself – Myself –

My size felt small – to me – I read your Chapters in the Atlantic – and experienced honor for you – I was sure you would not reject a confiding question –

Is this – Sir – what you asked me to tell you?

Your friend,
E – Dickinson

EMILY DICKINSON to T. W. Higginson, [July 1862]

Emily Dickinson, 1830–86, poet; Colonel T. W. Higginson, critic. Higginson had asked her for a photograph.

Could you believe me – without? I had no portrait, now, but am small, like the Wren, and my Hair is bold, like the Chestnut Bur – and my eyes, like the Sherry in the Glass, that the Guest leaves – Would this do just as well?

It often alarms Father – He says Death might occur, and he has Molds of all the rest – but has no Mold of me, but I noticed the Quick wore off those things, in a few days, and forestall the dishonor – You will think no caprice of me –

You said 'Dark.' I know the Butterfly – and the Lizard – and the Orchis –

Are not those *your* Countrymen?

I am happy to be your scholar, and will deserve the kindness, I cannot repay.

If you truly consent, I recite, now –

Will you tell me my fault, frankly as to yourself, for I had rather wince, than die. Men do not call the surgeon, to commend – the Bone, but to set it, Sir, and fracture within, is more critical, and for this, Preceptor, I shall bring you – Obedience – the Blossom from my Garden, and every gratitude I know. Perhaps you smile at me. I could not stop for that – My Business is Circumference – An ignorance, not of Customs, but if caught with the Dawn – or the Sunset see me – Myself the only Kangaroo among the Beauty, Sir, if you please, it afflicts me, and I thought that instruction would take it away.

Because you have much business, beside the growth of me – you will appoint, yourself, how often I shall come – without your inconvenience. And if at any time – you regret you received me, or I prove a different fabric to that you supposed – you must banish me –

When I state myself, as the Representative of the Verse – it does not mean – me – but a supposed person. You are true, about the 'perfection.'

Today, makes Yesterday mean.

You spoke of Pippa Passes – I never heard anybody speak of Pippa Passes – before.

You see my posture is benighted.

To thank you, baffles me. Are you perfectly powerful? Had I a pleasure you had not, I could delight to bring it.

Your Scholar

W. M. THACKERAY to Dr Henry Bence Jones, [(?) 26 March 1863]

William Makepeace Thackeray, 1811–63, novelist; Dr Henry Bence Jones, Secretary to the Royal Institution. Thackeray (author of 'the Ballad of Bouillabaisse') records in his diary having dinner with Bence Jones on 27 March, when Browning was also present.

My dear Doctor

   I will come with pleasure tomorrow if you will promise not to have any bouillabaise.

      very faithfully yours

                              W M Thackeray

WALT WHITMAN to Mr and Mrs S. B. Haskell, 10 August 1863

Walt Whitman, 1819–92, poet; Mr and Mrs S. B. Haskell, parents of Erastus Haskell. Whitman served as a volunteer hospital orderly during the Civil War.

                  Washington   August 10   1863

Mr and Mrs Haskell,
         Dear friends, I thought it would be soothing to you to have a few lines about the last days of your son Erastus Haskell of Company K, 141st New York Volunteers. I write in haste, & nothing of importance – only I thought any thing about Erastus would be welcome. From the time he came to Armory Square Hospital till he died, there was hardly a day but I was with him a portion of the time – if not during the day, then at night. I had no opportunity to do much, or any thing for him, as nothing was needed, only to wait the progress of his malady. I am only a friend, visiting the wounded & sick soldiers, (not connected with any society – or State.) From the first I felt that Erasmus was in danger, or at least was much worse than they in the hospital supposed. As he made no

complaint, they perhaps thought him not very bad – I told the doctor of the ward to look him over again – he was a much sicker boy than he supposed, but he took it lightly, said, I know more about these fever cases than you do – the young man looks very sick, but I shall certainly bring him out of it all right. I have no doubt the doctor meant well & did his best – at any rate, about a week or so before Erastus died he got really alarmed & after that he & all the doctors tried to help him, but without avail – Maybe it would not have made any difference any how – I think Erastus was broken down, poor boy, before he came to the hospital here – I believe he came here about July 11th – Somehow I took to him, he was a quiet young man behaved always correct & decent, said little – I used to sit on the side of his bed – I said once, You don't talk any, Erastus, you leave me to do all the talking – he only answered quietly, I was never much of a talker. The doctor wished every one to cheer him up very lively – I was always pleasant & cheerful with him, but did not feel to be very lively – Only once I tried to tell him some amusing narratives, but after a few moments I stopt, I saw that the effect was not good, & after that I never tried it again – I used to sit by the side of his bed, pretty silent, as that seemed most agreeable to him, & I felt it so too – he was generally opprest for breath, & with the heat, & I would fan him – occasionally he would want a drink – some days he dozed a good deal – sometimes when I would come in, he woke up, & I would lean down & kiss him, he would reach out his hand & pat my hair & beard a little, very friendly, as I sat on the bed & leaned over him.

Much of the time his breathing was hard, his throat worked – they tried to keep him up by giving him stimulants, milk-punch, wine &c – these perhaps affected him, for often his mind wandered somewhat – I would say, Erastus, don't you remember me, dear son? – can't you call me by name? – once he looked at me quite a while when I asked him, & he mentioned over inaudibly a name or two (one sounded like Mr. Setchell) & then, as his eyes closed, he said quite slow, as if to himself, I don't remember, I dont remember, I dont remember – it was quite pitiful – one thing was he could not talk very comfortably at any time, his throat & chest seemed stopped – I have no doubt at all he had some complaint besides the typhoid – In my limited talks with him, he told me about his brothers & sisters by name, & his parents, wished me to write to his parents & send them & all his love – I think he told me about his brothers living in different places, one in New York City, if I recollect right – From what he told me, he must have been poorly enough for several months before he came to Armory Sq Hosp[ital] – the first week in July I think he told me he was at the regimental hospital at a place called Baltimore Corners not many miles from White House, on the peninsula – previous to that, for quite a long time, although he kept around, he was not at all well – couldn't do much – was in the band as a fifer I believe – While he lay sick here he had his fife laying on the little stand by his side – he once told me that if he got well he would play me a tune on it – but, he says, I am not much of a player yet.

I was very anxious he should be saved, & so were they all – he was well used by the attendants – poor boy, I can see him as I write – he was tanned & had a fine head of hair, & looked good in the face when he first came, & was in pretty good flesh too – (had his hair cut close about ten or twelve days before he died) – He never complained – but it looked pitiful to see him lying there, with such a look out if his eyes. He had large clear eyes, they seemed to talk better than words – I assure you I was attracted to him much – Many nights I sat in the hospital by his bedside till far in the night – The lights would be put out – yet I would sit there silently, hours, late, perhaps fanning him – he always liked to have me sit there, but never cared to talk – I shall never forget those nights, it was a curious & solemn scene, the sick & wounded lying around in their cots, just visible in the darkness, & this dear young man close at hand lying on what proved to be his death bed – I do not know his past life, but what I do know, & what I saw of him, he was a noble boy – I felt he was one I should get very much attached to. I think you have reason to be proud of such a son, & all his relatives have cause to treasure his memory.

I write to you this letter, because I would do something at least in his memory – his fate was a hard one, to die so – He is one of the thousands of our unknown American young men in the ranks about whom there is no record or fame, no fuss made about their dying so unknown, but I find in them the real precious & royal ones of this land, giving themselves up, aye even their young & precious lives, in their country's cause – Poor dear son, though you were not my son, I felt to love you as a son, what short time I saw you sick & dying here – it is as well as it is, perhaps better – for who knows whether he is not better off, that patient & sweet young soul, to go, than we are to stay? So farewell, dear boy – it was my opportunity to be with you in your last rapid days of death – no chance as I have said to do any thing particular, for nothing could be done – only you did not lay here & die among strangers without having one at hand who loved you dearly, & to whom you gave your dying kiss –

Mr and Mrs Haskell, I have thus written rapidly whatever came up about Erastus, & must now close. Though we are strangers & shall probably never see each other, I send you & all Erastus' brothers & sisters my love –

Walt Whitman

I live when home, in Brooklyn, N Y. (in Portland avenue, 4th door north of Myrtle, my mother's residence.) My address here is care of Major Hapgood, paymaster USA, cor 15th & F st, Washington DC.

CARDINAL NEWMAN to Monsignor Talbot, 25 July 1864

John Henry, Cardinal Newman, 1801–90, founder of the Birmingham Oratory, author; George Talbot, priest in Rome.

July 25. 1864

Dear Monsignor Talbot

I have received your letter, inviting me to preach next Lent in your Church at Rome, to 'an audience of Protestants more educated than could ever be the case in England.'

However, Birmingham people have souls; and I have neither taste nor talent for the sort of work, which you cut out for me: and I beg to decline your offer

I am &c J H N

ABRAHAM LINCOLN to General Ulysses S. Grant, 19 January 1865

Abraham Lincoln, 1809–65, President of the United States during the Civil War; Ulysses S. Grant, General-in-Chief of the Union forces, later President. Robert Todd Lincoln was appointed Captain on Grant's staff on 11 February, resigning his commission on 10 June.

Executive Mansion, Washington,
Jan. 19, 1865.

Lieut. General Grant:

Please read and answer this letter as though I was not President, but only a friend. My son, now in his twenty second year, having graduated at

Harvard, wishes to see something of the war before it ends. I do not wish to put him in the ranks, nor yet to give him a commission, to which those who have already served long, are better entitled, and better qualified to hold. Could he, without embarrassment to you, or detriment to the service, go into your Military family with some nominal rank, I, and not the public, furnishing his necessary means? If no, say so without the least hesitation, because I am as anxious, and as deeply interested, that you shall not be encumbered as you can be yourself. Yours truly

A. Lincoln

THOMAS CARLYLE to Ralph Waldo Emerson, 27 January 1867

Thomas Carlyle, 1795–1881, essayist and historian; Ralph Waldo Emerson, philosopher and poet. The death of Carlyle's wife Jane the year before was a blow from which he never recovered. Emerson thought Carlyle's massive life of Frederick the Great the 'wittiest book ever written'.

Mentone (France, Alpes Maritimes)
27 Janry, 1867

My dear Emerson,

It is a long time since I last wrote to you; and a long distance in space and in fortune, – from the shores of the Solway in summer 1865, to this niche of the Alps and Mediterranean today, after what has befallen me in the interim! A longer interval, I think, and surely by far a sadder, than ever occurred between us before, since we first met in the Scotch moors, some five and thirty years ago. You have written me various Notes, too, and Letters, all good and cheering to me, – almost the only truly *human* speech I have heard from anybody living; – and still my stony silence cd not be broken; not till now, tho' often looking forward to it, cd I resolve on such a thing. You will think me far gone, and much bankrupt in hope and heart; – and indeed I am, as good as without hope and without fear; a gloomily serious, silent and sad old man; gazing into the final chasm of things, in mute dialogue with 'Death Judgement and Eternity' (dialogue *mute* on *both* sides!) not caring to discourse with poor articulate-speaking fellow creatures on *their* sorts of topics. It is right of me; – & yet also it is not right. I often feel that I had better be dead than thus indifferent, contemptuous, disgusted with the world and its roaring nonsense, which I have no thought farther of lifting a finger to help, and only try to keep out of the way of, and shut my door against. But the truth is, I was nearly killed by that hideous Book on Friedrich, – 12 years in continuous wrestle with the nightmares and the subterranean hydras; – nearly *killed*, and had often thought I shd be altogether, and must die leaving the monster not so much as finished! This is one truth, not so evident to any friend or onlooker as it is to myself: and then there is another, known to myself alone, as it were; and of which I am best not to speak to others, or to speak to them no farther. By the calamity of April last, I lost my little all in this world; and have no soul left who can make any corner of this world into a *home* for me any more. Bright, heroic, tender, true and noble was that lost treasure of my heart, who faithfully accompanied me in all the rocky ways & climbings; and I am forever poor without her. She was snatched from me in a moment, – as by a death from the gods. Very beautiful her death was; radiantly beautiful (to those who understood it) had all her life been: *quid plura*? I shd be among the dullest & stupidest if I were not among the saddest of all men. But not a word more on all this.

All summer last, my one solacement in the form of work was writing, and sorting of old documents and recollections; summoning out again into clearness old scenes that had now closed on me without return. Sad, and in a sense sacred; it was like a kind of *worship*; the only *devout* time I had had for a great while past. These things I have half or wholly the intention to burn out of the way before I myself die: – but such continues still mainly my employment, – so many hours every forenoon; what I call the 'work' of my day: – to me, if to no other, it is useful; to reduce matters to writing means that you shall know them, see them in their origin & sequences, in their essential lineaments, considerably better than you ever did before. To set about writing my own *Life* wd be no less than horrible to me; and shall of a certainty never be done. The common impious vulgar of this earth, what has it to do with my Life or me? Let dignified oblivion, silence, and the vacant azure of Eternity swallow *me*; for my share of it, that, verily is the handsomest or one handsome way of settling my poor acct with the canaille of mankind extant and to come. 'Immortal glory,' is not that a beautiful thing, in the Shakespeare Clubs & Literary Gazettes of our improved Epoch? – I did not leave London, except for 14 days in August, to a fine and high old Lady-friend's in Kent; where, riding about the woods & by the sea-beaches and chalk cliffs, in utter silence, I felt sadder than ever, tho' a little less *miserably* so, than in the intrusive babblements of London, which I cd not quite lock out of doors. We read, at first, Tennyson's *Idyls*, with profound recognition of the finely elaborated execution, and also of the inward perfection of *vacancy*, – and, to say truth, with considerable impatience at being treated so very like infants, tho the lollipops were so superlative. We gladly changed for one Emerson's *English Traits*; and read that, with increasing satisfaction every evg; blessing Heaven that there were still Books for grown-up people too! That truly is a Book all full of thought like winged arrows (thanks to the Bowyer from us both): – my Lady-friend's name is Miss Davenport Bromley; it was at Wooton, in her Grandfather's House, in Staffordshire, that Rousseau took shelter in 1760; and 106 years later she was reading Emerson to me, with a recognition that wd have pleased the man, had he seen it.

About that same time, my health and humours being evidently so the Dowager Lady Ashburton (*not* the high Lady you saw, but a Successor of Mackenzie-Highland type), who wanders mostly about the Continent since her widowhood, for the sake of a child's health, began pressing & inviting to spend the black months of Winter, here in her Villa with her; – all friends warmly seconding and urging; by one of whom I was at last snatched off, as if by the hair of the head (in spite spite of my violent No, no!) on the eve of Xmas last, and have been here ever since, – really with improved omens. The place is beautiful as a very Picture, the climate superlative (today a sun & sky like very June); the *hospitality* of usage beyond example. It is likely I shall be here another six weeks at longest. If you plan to write me, the address is on the margin; and I will answer!

Adieu.   T. Carlyle

T. Carlyle Esqr
  Aux soins de Mylady Ashburton/Menton/France.

ROBERT BROWNING to William G. Kingsland, 27 November 1868

Robert Browning, 1812–89, poet; William G. Kingsland, an admirer. Browning was often accused of obscurity.

Upper Westbourne Terrace, W.
Nov. 27, '68.

My dear Sir,
      Will the kindness that induced you to write your very gratifying letter forgive the delay that has taken place in answering it? – an

unavoidable delay, for I have been far from well, and oppressed by work.

I am heartily glad I have your sympathy for what I write: intelligence, by itself, is scarcely the thing with respect to a new book, – as Wordsworth says (a little altered), 'you must like it before it be worthy of your liking.' In spite of your intelligence and sympathy, I can have little doubt but that my writing has been, in the main, too hard for many I should have been pleased to communicate with: but I never designedly tried to puzzle people, as some of my critics have supposed. On the other hand, I never pretended to offer such literature as should be a substitute for a cigar, or game at dominos to an idle man. So, perhaps on the whole I get my deserts and something over, – not a crowd but a few I value more. Let me remember gratefully that I may class you, and the friends you mention, among these: while you, in turn, must remember me as

> Yours, my dear Sir, very
> faithfully,
> Robert Browning.

DANTE GABRIEL ROSSETTI to Jane Morris, 4 February 1870

Dante Gabriel Rossetti, 1828–82, Pre-Raphaelite painter and poet; Jane Morris, Pre-Raphaelite model, wife of William Morris. Jane Morris inspired much of Rossetti's poetry and was his favourite model at this period: their intimacy seems to have met with Morris's approval.

> 16 Cheyne Walk, Chelsea
> Friday

Funny sweet Janey,

A bloke is coming here tomorrow with a frame, so I think I had better take the opportunity of sending you that chalk drawing as said bloke can hang it up. If he should happen not to come tomorrow, then I suppose he will on Monday, and I will send it then.

Dear Janey, I suppose this has come into my head because I feel so badly the want of speaking to you. No one else seems alive at all to me now, and places that are empty of you are empty of all life. And it is so seldom that the dead hours breathe a little and yield your dear voice to me again. I seem to hear it while I write, and to see your eyes speaking as clearly as your voice; and so I would write to you for ever if it were not too bad to keep reminding you of my troubles, who have so many of your own. It is dreadful to me to think constantly of a sudden while my mind longs for you, that perhaps at that moment you are suffering so much as to shut out even the possibility of pleasure if life had it ready for you in every shape. I always reproach myself with the comfort I feel despite all in the thought of you, when that thought never fails to present me also with the recollection of your pain and suffering. But more than all for me, dear Janey, is the fact that you exist, that I can yet look forward to seeing you and speaking to you again, and know for certain that at that moment I shall forget all my own troubles nor even be able to remember yours. You are the noblest and dearest thing that the world has had to show me; and if no lesser loss than the loss of you could have brought me so much bitterness, I would still rather have had this to endure than have missed the fulness of wonder and worship which nothing else could have made known to me.

When I began this I meant to try and be cheerful, and just see what vague and dismal follies I have been inflicting on you – I hope to look in tomorrow evening and see how you are, even if I only stay half an hour.

Your most affectionate
Gabriel

Mrs Morris
26 Queen Square
W.C.

CHARLES DICKENS to Charles Kent, 8 June 1870

Charles Dickens, 1812–70, novelist; Charles Kent, editor of the *Sun*. On 8 June, in violation of his normal habits, Dickens worked all day on *Edwin Drood*. That evening he came in from the garden chalet where he had been writing and before dinner wrote a few letters, including this note to Charles Kent in which he playfully quotes the admonition given by Friar Laurence to the young lovers in *Romeo and Juliet*. Minutes later at a little past six he suffered a massive stroke and died the following day without recovering consciousness.

> Gad's Hill Place,
> Higham by Rochester, Kent.
> Wednesday, Eighth June, 1870.

My Dear Kent,

To-morrow is a very bad day for me to make a call, as, in addition to my usual office business, I have a mass of accounts to settle with Wills. But I hope I may be ready for you at 3 o'clock. If I can't be – why, then, I shan't be.

You must really get rid of those Opal enjoyments. They are too overpowering:

'These violent delights have violent ends.'

I think it was a father of your church who made the wise remark to a young gentleman who got up early (or stayed out late) at Verona?

> Ever affectionately,
> C. D.

GEORGE ELIOT to the Hon. Mrs Robert Lytton, 8 July 1870

George Eliot, pseudonym of Marian Evans, 1819–80, novelist; Edith, wife of Robert Lytton, afterwards first Earl of Lytton, poet and Viceroy of India. This letter was written on the death of Mrs Lytton's uncle, Lord Clarendon (formerly Foreign Secretary) whom she had loved as a father.

I did not like to write to you until Mr Lytton sent word that I might do so, because I had not the intimate knowledge that would have enabled me to measure your trouble; and one dreads of all things to speak or write a wrong or unseasonable word when words are the only signs of interest and sympathy that one has to give. I know now, from what your dear husband has told us, that your loss is very keenly felt by you, – that it has first made you acquainted with acute grief, and this makes me think of you very much. For learning to love any one is like an increase of property, – it increases care, and brings many new fears lest precious things should come to harm. I find myself often thinking of you with that sort of proprietor's anxiety, wanting you to have gentle weather all through your life, so that your face may never look worn and storm-beaten, and wanting your husband to be and do the very best, lest anything short of that should be disappointment to you. At present the thought of you is all the more with me, because your trouble has been brought by death; and for nearly a year death seems to me my most intimate daily companion. I mingle the thought of it with every other, not sadly, but as one mingles the thought of some one who is nearest in love and duty with all one's motives. I try to delight in the sunshine that will be when I shall never see it any more. And I think it is possible for this sort of impersonal life to attain great intensity – possible for us to gain much more independence, than is usually believed, of the small bundle of facts that make our own personality.

I don't know why I should say this to you, except that my pen is chatting as my tongue would if you were here. We women are always in danger of living too exclusively in the affections; and though our affections are perhaps the best gifts we have, we ought also to have our share of the more independent life – some joy in things for their own sake. It is piteous to see the helplessness of some sweet women when their affections are disappointed – because all their teaching has been, that they can only delight in study of any kind for the sake of a personal love. They have never contemplated an independent delight in ideas as an experience which they could confess without being laughed at. Yet surely women need this sort of defence against passionate affliction even more than men.

Just under the pressure of grief, I do not believe there is any consolation. The word seems to me to be drapery for falsities. Sorrow must be sorrow, ill must be ill, till duty and love towards all who remain recover their rightful predominance. Your life is so full of those claims, that you will not have time for brooding over the unchangeable. Do not spend any of your valuable time now in writing to me, but be satisfied with sending me news of you through Mr Lytton when he has occasion to write to Mr Lewes.

I have lately finished reading aloud Mendelssohn's 'Letters,' which we had often resolved and failed to read before. They have been quite cheering to us, from the sense they give of communion with an eminently pure, refined nature, with the most rigorous conscience in art. In the evening we have always a concert to listen to – a concert of modest pretensions, but well conducted enough to be agreeable.

I hope this letter of chit-chat will not reach you at a wrong moment. In any case, forgive all mistakes on the part of one who is always yours sincerely and affectionately.

LEWIS CARROLL to Mary Talbot, 8 January 1872

Lewis Carroll, pseudonym of Charles Lutwidge Dogson, 1832–98, author; Mary Talbot, a child friend, later a foundation scholar at Lady Margaret Hall. *Through the Looking-Glass* and *What Alice Found There* had been published the previous month.

> 1. Little Alleys,
> Christmas Street,
> Lewes.
> Jan. 8/72

My dear Mary,

Thanks for your nice little note, though I am sorry to hear you find 'Through the Looking-glass' so uninteresting. You see I have done my best, so that it really isn't really *my* fault if you think Tweedledum & Tweedledee stupid, and wish that I had left out all about the train and the gnat. You see, if *all* the book is stupid, and if I leave out *all* the stupid parts, there really will be so *very* little left.

Please remember that you are *not* one of the 'dear children I have made friends with, whose faces I shall never see.' I consider that we *have* made friends, but you may tell your uncle I shall be seriously angry with him, if he doesn't soon invite you to Keble College, and then bring you to see me at Ch[rist] Ch[urch].

Your affectionate friend,
Lewis Carroll

HEINRICH SCHLIEMANN to Frank Calvert, 1 January 1873

Heinrich Schliemann, 1822–90, excavator of Troy; Frank Calvert, archaeologist. Frank Calvert pioneered the excavations at Hissarlik-Troy: Schliemann was generous in his acknowledgements when writing privately to him, although less so when writing for publication.

> Athens, 1 January 1873.

I have just made the important discovery that all the owls heads with helmet which I find on the trojan gobelets from 2 to 12 meters depth and all the owls faces which I find with the 2 female breasts and navel on the vases as well as the 2 female breasts and navel with which a vast number of vases are decorated and finally all the owls faces which I find on the numberless idols of hard white stone and on 2 of terracotta together with the never missing female girdle represent the ilian Minerva the protecting divinity of Troy and that consequently the common epithet of this goddess in Homer >γλαυκῶπις< does not signify with blue, sparkling or firy eyes, as it has been translated by scholars of all centuries, but it signifies >with the owls face<. The natural conclusion is that Homer knew very well that Minerva with the owls face was the protecting divinity of Troy and that consequently Troy existed and that it existed on the sacred premises which I am excavating and that further, when civilisation advanced, Minerva got a human face and from her former owls face was made her favorate bird, the owl, which as such is unknown to Homer. I have written about this a long article to the leading german journal, and this article will no doubt be reproduced by nearly all newspapers of the civilised world.

I avail myself of this opportunity to present to you, to your brothers and to their illustrious families my hearty congratulations with the change of the year in wishing you all sorts of prosperity and above all lasting good health, besides the joy to see soon ancient Troy's glorious ruins be brought to light by the efforts of yours very faithfully

H. Schliemann.

JACOB WAINWRIGHT to Lovett Cameron, October 1873

Jacob Wainwright, one of Livingstone's native African companions; Lieutenant Lovett Cameron, leader of the second Livingstone Relief Expedition. With this note came the first news to the outside world of Livingstone's death. He had been in the African interior since 1866, relieved only by his meeting with Stanley in 1871. He had died on the night of 30 April 1873 at Chitambo's village, Ilala, to the south of Lake Bangweolo (present-day Zimbabwe). His followers then carried his embalmed body to the east coast, meeting Cameron's expedition on the way and informing them of their master's death. Cameron wanted to bury the body, but they carried on (while Cameron went on into the interior), arriving at the coast in February 1874 – a journey of over 1000 miles through hostile country, undertaken in eleven months. Livingstone's body was then shipped to Zanzibar, and from there to England, and was finally buried at Westminster Abbey on 18 April.

Ukhonongo,
October, 1873.

Sir,
   We have heared in the month of August that you have started from Zanzibar for Unyenyembe, and again and again lately we have heared your arrival – your father died by disease beyond the country of Bisa, but we have carried the corpse with us. 10 of our soldiers are lost and some have died. Our hunger presses us to ask you some clothes to buy provision for our soldiers, and we should have an answer that when we shall enter there shall be firing guns or not, and if you permit us to fire guns then send some powder.
   We have wrote these few words in the place of Sultan or King Mbowra.
                              The writer Jacob Wainwright.
                              Dr. Livingstone Exeped.

FLORENCE NIGHTINGALE to Agnes Livingstone, 18 February 1874

Florence Nightingale, 1820–1910, nursing pioneer; Agnes Livingstone, Dr Livingstone's daughter. Sir Bartle Frere had accompanied Lovett Cameron and his second Livingstone Relief Expedition on their voyage to Zanzibar, where he negotiated a treaty with the Sultan for the suppression of the slave trade before returning to England.

London, Feb. 18, 1874.

Dear Miss Livingstone, – I am only one of all England which is feeling with you and for you at this moment.
   But Sir Bartle Frere encourages me to write to you.
   We cannot help still yearning to hear of some hope that your great father may be still alive.
   God knows; and in knowing that He knows who is all wisdom, goodness and power, we must find our rest.
   He has taken away, if at last it be as we fear, the greatest man of his generation, for Dr. Livingstone stood alone.
   There are few enough, but a few statesmen. There are few enough, but a few great in medicine, or in art, or in poetry. There are a few great travellers. But Dr. Livingstone stood alone as the great Missionary

Traveller, the bringer-in of civilisation; or rather the pioneer of civilisation – he that cometh before – to races lying in darkness.

I always think of him as what John the Baptist, had he been living in the nineteenth century, would have been.

Dr. Livingstone's fame was so world-wide that there were other nations who understood him even better than we did.

Learned philologists from Germany, not at all orthodox in their opinions, have yet told me that Dr. Livingstone was the only man who understood races, and how to deal with them for good; that he was the one true missionary. We cannot console ourselves for our loss. He is irreplaceable.

It is not sad that he should have died out there. Perhaps it was the thing, much as he yearned for home, that was the fitting end for him. He may have felt it so himself.

But would that he could have completed that which he offered his life to God to do!

If God took him, however, it was that his life was completed, in God's sight; his work finished, the most glorious work of our generation.

He has opened those countries for God to enter in. He struck the first blow to abolish a hideous slave-trade.

He, like Stephen, was the first martyr.

> He climbed the steep ascent of heaven,
>   Through peril, toil, and pain;
> O God! to us may grace be given
>   To follow in his train!

To us it is very dreary, not to have seen him again, that he should have had none of us by him at the last: no last word or message.

I feel this with regard to my dear father, and one who was more than mother to me, Mrs. Bracebridge, who went with me to the Crimean war, both of whom were taken from me last month.

How much more must we feel it, with regard to our great discoverer and hero, dying so far off!

But does he regret it? How much he must know now! how much he must have enjoyed!

Though how much we would give to know *his* thoughts, *alone with God*, during the latter days of his life.

May we not say, with old Baxter (something altered from that verse)? –

> My knowledge of that life is small,
> The eye of faith is dim;
> But 'tis enough that *Christ knows all*,
> And he will be with *Him*.

Let us think only of him and of his present happiness, his eternal happiness, and may God say to us: 'Let not your heart be troubled.' Let us exchange a 'God bless you,' and fetch a real blessing from God in saying so.

Florence Nightingale.

WILLIAM DEAN HOWELLS to Mark Twain, 5 November 1875

William Dean Howells, 1837–1920, novelist; Mark Twain, pseudonym of S. L. Clemens, author. At this time Howells was editing the *Atlantic Monthly*.

Nov. 5, 1875

My dear Clemens:

The type-writer came Wednesday night, and is already beginning to have its effect on me. Of course it doesn't work: if I can persuade some of the letters to get up against the ribbon they wont get down again without digital assistance. The treadle refuses to have any part or parcel in the performance; and *I* don't know how to get the roller to turn with the paper. Nevertheless, I have begun several letters to *My d ar lemans*, as it prefers to spell your respected name, and I don't despair yet of sending you something in its beautiful hand writing – after I've had a man out from the agent's to put it in order. It's fascinating, in the meantime, and it wastes my time like an old friend.

Don't vex yourself to provide a companion piece for the Literary Nightmare, though if you've anything ready, send it along. But it will do magnificently as it is. I've been reading it over, with joy.

I hope to get at the story on Sunday.   Yours ever

W. D. Howells.

ANTHONY TROLLOPE to G. W. Rusden, 8 June 1876

Anthony Trollope, 1815–82, novelist; George William Rusden, Australian administrator and historian. The actor W. C. Macready's posthumous *Reminiscences* had appeared in 1875, possibly prompting Trollope to write his own autobiography published after his death.

8 June 1876   39, Montagu Square.

My dear Rusden.

Your letter of 13 March which has I fear been on my table for more than a month, – so do I procrastinate the doing of things which are pleasant to do, but which will in their doing take some little time, – is very suggestive – So much so, that I could write volumes on each paragraph.

As to that leisure evening of life, I must say that I do not want it. I can conceive of no contentment of which toil is not to be the immediate parent. As the time for passing away comes near me I have no fear as to the future – I am ready to go. I dread nothing but physical inability and that mental lethargy which is apt to accompany it. Since I saw you I have written a memoir of my own life; – not as regards its activity but solely in reference to its literary bearing, as to what I have done in literature and what I have thought about it, – and now I feel as though every thing were finished and I was ready to go. No man enjoys life more than I do, but no man dreads more than I do the time when life may not be enjoyable.

Then, (in defending Macready,) you tell me of his beautiful humility before God! I do not prize humility before God. I can understand that a man should be humble before his brother men the smallness of whose vision requires self-abasement in others; – but not that any one should be humble before God. To my God I can be but true, and if I think myself to have done well I cannot but say so. To you, if I speak of my own work, I must belittle myself. I must say that it is naught. But if I speak of it to my God, I say, 'Thou knowest that it is honest; – that I strove to do good; – that if ever there came to me the choice between success and truth, I stuck to truth.' And I own that I feel that it is impossible that the Lord should damn me, and how can I be humble before God when I tell him that I expect from him eternal bliss as the reward of my life here on earth.

But the humility which you laud in a character such as that of Macready has always to me a certain falseness about it – I do not think myself to be a worm, and a grub, grass of the field fit only to be burned, a clod, a morsel of putrid atoms that should be thrown to the dungheap, ready for the nethermost pit. Nor if I did should I therefore expect to sit with Angels and Archangels. I must say that I judge a man by his actions with men, much more than by his declarations Godwards – When I find him to be envious, carping, spiteful, hating the successes of others, and complaining that the world has never done enough for him, I am apt to doubt whether his humility before God will atone for his want of manliness.

That doctrine which I broached before you and others at the Garrick as to the expediency of an artist working for money, I have always found it difficult to explain as I would have it explained. You ask me whether I would have willingly written for money any thing which would have been prejudicial to a reader. The same test may be given to a shoe-maker. His primary object is a living. But if he be an honest man he will prefer a poor living by good shoes, to a good living by bad shoes. It is the same with the authors, and with the lawyer, and the divine – But in each case bread and meat should be the rewards of work.

All of which things are almost too recondite for a letter.

> Yours always
> Most sincerely
> Anthony Trollope

IVAN TURGENEV to W. R. S. Ralston, 19 April 1877

Ivan Turgenev, 1818–83, novelist and playwright; W. R. S. Ralston, assistant librarian of the British Museum Library, translator of Turgenev's *Liza* (or *A Nest of Gentlefolk*). Turgenev himself had introduced the term nihilism. This letter refers to 'The Trial of the Fifty', who were mainly young Popularists, which took place in Moscow in March 1877.

Paris, 19 April 1877

My dear friend,

There is decidedly no French separate book about *nihilism* in Russia – but in the *Revue des Deux Mondes* there has appeared in 1876 or 75 an article intitulated 'Le Nihilisme en Russie' by Alf. Rambaud or Leroy-Beaulieu (I am not quite sure of the name of the author) – which I have read and found good and exact enough. I have not been able to put my hand on it. I have given to my bookseller the commission to find it out – but I have not yet received an answer. I imagine, it will be easy for you to find it in the bibliothèque of the British Museum.

The trial of the revolutionists is sad enough – certainly; but you are in a mistake if you imagine that the young girls resemble Mashurina rather than Marianna. Some of them are very handsome and interesting – and (as there still exists in our jurisprudence the barbarous custom of *a bodily* examination of prisoners accused of crimes) they have been found *all* in a state of virginity! There is matter of serious réflexion! I send you in this letter a very touching piece of verses by M-lle Figner, a very pretty blondine of 22 years – in the last stage of phthisis (that explains the last couplet but one) – she did not defend herself nor take an advocate – and was condemned to five years hard labour in Siberia – in the mines. Death will evidently soon release her. I send you likewise a letter (by Zsvilenef) which has been read during the trial – I received it from an unknown person with the remark that it could have been written by Solomine. Russian statesmen ought to think of all that – and come to the conclusion that the only way of stopping the progress of revolutionary propaganda in Russia – is to grant a constitutional reform. But all these considerations will now be swallowed by the turbid waves of war. My conviction is that we stand on the threshold of very dark times . . . There is nobody who can predict what shall come out of all this.

I leave Paris on 5 May – and come back – if nothing happens – in the middle of July.

Wishing you good health and good spirits, I remain

Yours very truly, Iv. Tourguéneff

ALFRED TENNYSON to the Governor of Witley Asylum, 21 October 1877

Alfred Lord Tennyson, 1809–92, poet. Tennyson himself came from a family afflicted by mental instability, described by him as 'the black bloodedness of the Tennysons'. His brother Edward was to die thirteen years later in the asylum to which he had been committed as a youth.

October 21, 1877

Mr. Alfred Tennyson presents his compliments to the Governor of Witley Hospital for Convalescent Lunatics, and requests him to be so kind as to take precautions that his patients should not pay visits at Aldworth, as two did yesterday (one describing himself as assistant librarian of the British Museum).

Mr. Tennyson is very glad if they in any way enjoy'd themselves here, and hopes that they did not suffer from their long walk.

GERARD MANLEY HOPKINS to Robert Bridges, 13 May 1878

Gerard Manley Hopkins, SJ, 1844–89, poet; Robert Bridges, later Poet Laureate. Hopkins's most ambitious poem, 'The Wreck of the Deutschland', had been inspired by the loss of the *Deutschland* in December 1875, which included among its passengers five Franciscan nuns exiled for their faith. He had submitted it to the Jesuit journal *The Month*, by whom it had been rejected as too difficult for its readers. An edition of Hopkins's poems, including 'The Wreck of the Deutschland', was first published by Bridges in 1918.

Stonyhurst College, Blackburn (or Whalley). May 13 1878.

Dearest Bridges, – Remark the above address. After July I expect to be stationed in town – 111 Mount Street, Grosvenor Square.

I hope your bad cold is gone.

I am very glad to hear the Rondeliers have come to see the beauty of your poetry. I have little acquaintance with their own. I have read a rondeau or rondel by Marzials in the *Athenaeum* beginning and ending 'When I see you': it was very graceful and shewing an art and finish rare in English verse. This makes me the more astonished about *Flop flop*. Is his name Spanish, Provençal, or what? Barring breach of confidence I wish I could have seen his letter and that of the habitually joyous. I think that school is too artificial and exotic to take root and last, is it not?

I enclose you my Eurydice, which the *Month* refused. It is my only copy. Write no bilgewater about it: I will presently tell you what that is and till then excuse the term. I must tell you I am sorry you never read the Deutschland again.

Granted that it needs study and is obscure, for indeed I was not over-desirous that the meaning of all should be quite clear, at least unmistakeable, you might, without the effort that to make it all out would seem to have required, have nevertheless read it so that lines and stanzas should be left in the memory and superficial impressions deepened, and have liked some without exhausting all. I am sure I have read and enjoyed pages of poetry that way. Why, sometimes one enjoys and admires the very lines one cannot understand, as for instance 'If it were done when 'tis done' sqq., which is all obscure and disputed, though how fine it is everybody sees and nobody disputes. And so of many more passages in Shakspere and others. Besides you would have got more weathered to the style and its features – not really odd. Now they say that vessels sailing from the port of London will take (perhaps it should be/used once to take) Thames water for the voyage: it was foul and stunk at first as the ship worked but by degrees casting its filth was in a few days very pure and sweet and wholesomer and better than any water in the world. However that maybe, it is true to my purpose. When a new thing, such as my ventures in the Deutschland are, is presented us our first criticisms are not our truest, best, most homefelt, or most lasting but what come easiest on the instant. They are barbarous and like what the ignorant and the ruck say. This was so with you. The Deutschland on her first run worked very much and unsettled you, thickening and clouding your mind with vulgar mudbottom and common sewage (I see that I am going it with the image) and just then unhappily you *drew off* your criticisms all stinking (a necessity now of the image) and bilgy, whereas if you had let your thoughts cast themselves they would have been clearer in themselves and more to my taste too. I did not heed them therefore, perceiving they were a first drawing-off. Same of the Eurydice – which being short and easy please read more than once.

Can you tell me who that critic in the *Athenaeum* is that writes very long reviews on English and French poets, essayists, and so forth in a style like De Quincey's, very acute in his remarks, provoking, jaunty, and (I am sorry to say) would-be humorous? He always quotes Persian stories (unless he makes them up) and talks about Rabelæsian humour.

My brother's pictures, as you say, are careless and do not aim high, but I don't think it would be much different if he were a batchelor. But, strange to say – and I shd. never even have suspected it if he had not quite simply told me – he has somehow in painting his pictures, though nothing that the pictures express, a high and quite religious aim; however I cannot be more explanatory.

Your bodysnatch story is ghastly, but so are all bodysnatch stories. My grandfather was a surgeon, a fellow-student of Keats', and once

conveyed a body through Plymouth at the risk of his own.
  Believe me your affectionate friend

Gerard M. Hopkins S.J.

JOHN RUSKIN to Thomas Carlyle, 23 June 1878

John Ruskin, 1819–1900, author, artist and social reformer; Thomas Carlyle, historian and essayist. This letter describes Ruskin's first serious attack of delirium: he was to suffer from several more and for the last ten years of his life was totally incapacitated.

Brantwood, Coniston
23rd June, '78

My dearest Papa,
  I have not written to you, because my illness broke me all to pieces, and every little bit has a different thing to say, – which makes it difficult in the extreme to write to any one whom one wants to tell things to, just as they are, and who cares very truly whether they are right or wrong. It was utterly wonderful to me to find that I could go so heartily & headily mad; for you know I had been priding myself on my peculiar sanity! And it was more wonderful yet to find the madness made up into things so dreadful, out of things so trivial. One of the most provoking and disagreeable of the spectres was developed out of the firelight on my mahogany bedpost – and my fate, for all futurity, seemed continually to turn on the humour of dark personages who were materially nothing but the stains of damp on the ceiling. But the sorrowfullest part of the matter was, and is, that, while my illness at Matlock encouraged me by all its dreams in after work, this one has done nothing but humiliate and terrify me; and leaves me nearly unable to speak any more except of the natures of stones and flowers.
  I have regained great part of my strength, and am not in bad *spirits*, – on the condition, otherwise absolutely essential, that I think of nothing that would vex me. But this means a very trifling form of thought and direction of work, throughout the day.
  Nevertheless, I am working out some points in the history and geography of Arabia which I think will be useful, and reading you, and

Gibbon! alternately – or Mahomet! I am going to stigmatize Gibbon's as the worst style of language ever yet invented by man – its affectation and platitude being both consummate. It is like the most tasteless water-gruel, with a handful of Epsom salts strewed in for flowers, and served with the airs of being turtle. Has Mary done any more Gotthelf – I never read him without renewed refreshment.

By the way, *you* are very unsatisfactory about Mahomet's death, – which I want to know all that may be known of; and also, in re-reading *Frederick*, the first book I got to, after I got my natural eyes again, I was worried of questions in his life – how far it was good for Silesia to be Prussian or Austrian – whether Silesia itself is Prussian or Austrian-tempered – and how its geography marks its relations to south and north. I might make out this from detached passages; but the great impression left on me was, how blessed it would have been for Silesia, Prussia, and Austria, if all their soldiers, generals, & Princes had been made at the first outbreak of the war one grand auto da fe of, in the style of – my recent scenic effects deduced from damp in the ceiling.

I can't write more today, but am ever your lovingest

J. Ruskin

LEO TOLSTOY to R. W. S. Ralston, 27 October 1878

Count Leo Tolstoy, 1828–1910, novelist; R. W. S. Ralston, Assistant Librarian of the British Museum, Russian scholar. Ralston had applied to Tolstoy for biographical information for an article he was writing; he eventually succeeded in getting the information from Turgenev. The article appeared in 1879 under the title 'Count Leo Tolstoy's Novels'.

Yasnaya Polyana, 27 October 1878

Dear Sir,

I am very sorry not to be able to give you a satisfactory answer to your letter. The reason of it is that I very much doubt my being an author of such importance as to interest by the incidents of my life not only the Russian, but also the European public. I am fully convinced by many examples of writers, of whom their contemporaries made very much of and which were quite forgotten in their lifetime, that for contemporaries it is impossible to judge rightly on the merits of literary works, and therefore, notwithstanding my wishes, I cannot partake the temporary illusion of some friends of mine, which seem to be sure that my works must occupy some place in the Russian literature. Quite sincerely not knowing if my works shall be read after a hundred years, or will be forgotten in a hundred days, I do not wish to take a ridiculous part in the very probable mistake of my friends.

Hoping that on consideration of my motives you will kindly excuse my refusal,

I am Yours faithfully,
Count L. Tolstoy

CHARLES DARWIN to an unidentified recipient, 24 November 1880

Charles Darwin, 1809–82, scientist, author of the *Origin of Species*. Although his evolutionary work argued for a natural, rather than divine, origin of species, Darwin was usually very reluctant to discuss his views on religion for fear of wounding the feelings of his family.

PRIVATE

Down,
Beckenham,
Kent.
Railway Station
Orpinton
S.E.R.

Nov. 24th 1880

Dear Sir
I am sorry to inform you that I do not believe in the Bible as a divine revelation, & therefore not in Jesus Christ as the son of God.

yours faithfully
Ch. Darwin

QUEEN VICTORIA'S PRIVATE SECRETARY
to William McGonagall, 17 October 1881

General Sir Henry Frederick Ponsonby, 1825–95, Private Secretary to Queen Victoria; William McGonagall, reputedly the world's worst poet. McGonagall had submitted a poem celebrating the military review held at Edinburgh in 1881, throughout which it rained so heavily that it became known as the 'Wet Review'. McGonagall's contribution begins:

> All hail to the Empress of India, Great Britain's Queen –
> Long may she live in health, happy and serene –
> That came from London far away,
> To review the Scottish Volunteers in grand array;
> Most magnificent to be seen,
> Near Salisbury Crags and its pastures green,
> Which will be long remembered by our gracious Queen –
>
> And by the Volunteers that came from far away,
> Because it rained most of the day.
> And with the rain their clothes were wet all through,
> On the 25th day of August, at the Royal Review.
> And to the Volunteers it was no lark,
> Because they were ankle-deep in mud in the Queen's Park,
> Which proved to the Queen they were loyal and true,
> To endure such hardship at the Royal Review . . .

General Sir Henry F. Ponsonby has received the Queen's commands to thank Mr McGonagall for sending the verses which were contained in his letter of the 10th instant, but to express Her Majesty's regret that they must be returned, as it is an invariable rule that offerings of this nature should not be received by the Queen.

17th October, 1881.

Privy Purse Office,
Buckingham Palace, S.W.

26 March 1882

H. M. STANLEY to Lieutenant Valcke, 26 March 1882

Sir Henry Morton Stanley, 1841–1904, African explorer; Lieutenant Valcke, European officer. The letter was written while Stanley was working to establish the Congo Free State.

Stanley Pool Station,
March 26th, 1882.

Sir,

If you are a member of the expedition du Congo I authorise you to seize upon any Zanzibari whether personal servant or otherwise who may be found at Vivi, or any place below Manyanga provided he does not belong to the boats plying between Manyanga and Isangila, and compel him to accompany you to Stanley Pool station, and report himself personally. If he is a cripple or otherwise on the sick list, of course he may be excused, but the plea that he is a personal servant of any European you will please disregard, and oblige me by conforming with the above request.

I have the honour to be your obed. servant,

H. M. Stanley.

ANTHONY TROLLOPE to G. N. Richardson, 7 October 1882

Anthony Trollope, 1815–82, novelist; G. N. Richardson, editor. *Fraser's Magazine* folded that October. Trollope had a stroke the following month, and died on 6 December.

Harting, Petersfield.

Oct. 7. 1882.
Dear Sir,

The Fraser's Magazine is I believe dead. At any rate I am not going to write a story for it.

Yours truly
Anthony Trollope

G. N. Richardson Esq.

A. C. SWINBURNE to Edward Burne-Jones, 26 December 1882

Algernon Charles Swinburne, 1837–1909, poet; Sir Edward Burne-Jones, painter. Archbishop Tait had died on 1 December, and Gladstone, whose grotesquely long-winded style Swinburne mocks, had yet to appoint a successor. Prevenient Grace can be defined as the Grace of God which precedes repentance and conversion: Swinburne's own repudiation of Christianity was famous.

The Pines
Putney Hill
S.W.
Dec. 26. 82.

My dear Ned

I feel that you may expect a few words of private explanation on a subject personal to myself, but not (I trust) indifferent to my friends. In case you should see in any of the 'Society' journals any account of the circumstances or any allusion to the fact of the refusal which I have felt myself compelled, by conscientious considerations, to return to the Premier's offer of the (recently) vacant Archbishopric, I think it well – shall I say, I think it due to myself? – to lay before you a simple statement of the Truth. Magna, my good friend, est veritas, et, we cannot without impiety question, praevalebit.

When, on the lamented decease – or shall I say, demise? of the late revered occupant of the highest station in our Church, the responsible advisors of the Crown felt it due to the country & themselves to submit for my consideration the question whether, in the interests of our holy religion, I was not bound – the Prime Minister's word was, bound – to accept the Primacy of all England (an office whose duties Mr. G. was good enough to express his opinion that no man could more efficiently discharge) I felt it my duty – having long foreseen, my very dear Sir, this obviously inevitable contingency, when ever it should please Almighty God to remove Archbishop Tait out of the cares (if I may so call them) of this troublesome world – I need not say whither I turned for counsel. It was not without prayer – it was not without searchings of the heart – that my mind was made up as to the inadvisability of accepting the responsible duties of a Primate while my opinion was not absolutely fixed on the subject of prevenient grace – while, indeed, it was not in perfect accordance with the doctrine laid down in the Articles of our Church on that most important of all subjects.

Have I done wrong?

Should I have done better to take into more serious consideration the arguments of the Premier, when he enlarged on the blow – 'blow' was his expressive phrase – which would be dealt, by my acceptance of the see of Canterbury, to Rationalism, Infidelity, Scepticism, & Dissent?

I cannot say.

My Christian friend will be pained to hear that when I laid this case of conscience before our mutual acquaintance Mr. Theodore Watts I found, with astonishment amounting to agony, that he did not know what prevenient grace was! I believe he thought it was a species of marshmallow.

Let us, my dear Sir, not attribute (if I may be allowed that endearing expression) to our imperfect selves the credit of the fact that we have been better grounded in the adorable mysteries of Divine Truth.

With every good spiritual wish appropriate to this hallowed season, alike for you & yours,

believe me
          Ever your affectionate
          A. C. Swinburne

EMILY DICKINSON to Mrs Sweetser, [late Autumn 1884]

Emily Dickinson, 1830–86, poet; Mrs J. Howard Sweetser, her aunt.

Dear Nellie,

I hardly dare tell you how beautiful your Home is, lest it dissuade you from the more mortal Homestead in which you now dwell – Each Tree a Scene from India, and Everglades of Rugs.

Is not 'Lead us not into Temptation' an involuntary plea under circumstances so gorgeous? Your little Note dropped in upon us as softly as the flake of Snow that followed it, as spacious and as stainless, a paragraph from Every Where – to which we never go – We miss you more this time, I think, than all the times before –

An enlarged ability for missing is perhaps a part of our better growth, as the strange Membranes of the Tree broaden out of sight.

I hope the Owl remembers me, and the Owl's fair Keeper, indeed the remembrance of each of you, were a gallant boon – I still recall your Son's singing, and when the 'Choir invisible' assemble in your Trees, shall reverently compare them – Thank you for all the Acts of Light which beautified a Summer now past to its reward.

Love for your Exile, when you write her, as for Love's Aborigines – Our Coral Roof, though unbeheld, it's foliage softly adds –

Emily, with Love.

GENERAL GORDON to Major Watson, 14 December 1884

Charles George Gordon, 1833–85, 'Chinese Gordon', Governor-General of the Sudan; Major Watson of the Royal Engineers, then stationed in Cairo. Gordon had been sent to the Sudan earlier that year in order to evacuate the Egyptian garrisons which had been placed under threat by the *jihad*, or holy war, led by the Mahdi. After Gordon had installed himself in Khartoum, and after considerable delay, a relief force was sent out to him. Unfortunately it made very slow progress. On 15 December Gordon sent his diary, a letter to his sister and the present letter out by steamer, and no more was heard from him. The town fell on the morning of 26 January.

Kartoum. 14.12.84

My dear Watson,

I think the game is up and send Mrs Watson, you & Graham my adieux. We may expect a catastrophe in the town, on or after 10 days time. this would not have happened (if it does happen) if our people had taken better precautions as to informing us, of their movements, but this is 'spilt milk'. Good bye, Mind & let my brother (68 Elm Park Road, Chelsea) know what I owe you.

Yours sincerely
C. G. Gordon.

PHINEAS T. BARNUM to President Ulysses S. Grant, 12 January 1885

Phineas T. Barnum, 1810–91, proprietor of 'The Greatest Show on Earth'; Ulysses S. Grant, Union general, President of the United States. Grant had recently gone bankrupt and had only six months to live. He had given all his trophies to W. H. Vanderbilt, and so declined Barnum's offer.

New York, 12 January 1885

Honored Sir:

The whole world honors and respects you. All are anxious that you should live happy and free from care. While they admire your manliness in declining the large sum recently tendered you by friends, they still desire to see you achieve financial independence in an honorable manner. Of the unique and valuable trophies with which you have been honored, we all have read; and all have a laudable desire to see these evidences of love and respect bestowed upon you by monarchs, princes, and people throughout the globe. While you would confer a great and enduring favor on your fellow men and women by permitting them to see these trophies, you could also remove existing embarrassments in a most satisfactory and honorable manner. I will give you one hundred thousand dollars cash, besides a proportion of the profits, if I may be permitted to exhibit these relics to a grateful and appreciative public, and I will give satisfactory bonds of half a million dollars for their safekeeping and return.

These precious trophies, of which all your friends are so proud, would be placed before the eyes of your millions of admirers in a manner and style at once pleasing to yourself and satisfactory to the best elements of the entire community. Remembering that the mementoes of Washington, Wellington, Napoleon, Frederick the Great, and many other distinguished men have given immense pleasure to millions who have been permitted to see them, I trust you will, in the honorable manner proposed, gratify the public and thus inculcate the lesson of honesty, perseverance, and true patriotism so admirably illustrated in your career.

I have the honor to be truly your friend and admirer,

P. T. Barnum

QUEEN VICTORIA to General Gordon's sister, 16 March 1885

Victoria, 1819–1901, Queen of Great Britain and Ireland, Empress of India; Augusta, General Gordon's sister. The Queen was particularly upset by Gordon's death for which she held Gladstone, whom she loathed, responsible.

Windsor Castle,
March 16, 1885.

Dear Miss Gordon,
    It is most kind and good of you to give me this precious Bible, and I only hope that you are not depriving yourself and family of such a treasure, if you have no other. May I ask you during how many years your dear heroic Brother had it with him? I shall have a case made for it with an Inscription and place it in the Library here with your letter and the touching extract from his last to you.
    I have ordered as you know a Marble Bust of your dear Brother to be placed in the Corridor here, where so many Busts and Pictures of our greatest Generals and Statesmen are, and hope that you will see it before it is finished, to give your opinion as to the likeness.
                Believe me always,
                   Yours very sincerely,
                       Victoria R. I.

JOHN RUSKIN to his correspondents, 30 March 1886

John Ruskin, 1819–1900, author, artist and social reformer. Ruskin, who had suffered from another attack of delirium, had this message printed and sent to all those who wrote to him at this time.

    Mr. Ruskin trusts that his friends will pardon his declining correspondence in Spring, and spending such days as may be spared to him in the fields, instead of at his desk.
    Had he been well, he would now have been in Switzerland, and begs

his correspondents to imagine that he *is* so; for there is no reason, because he is obliged to stop in England, that he should not be allowed to rest there.

Brantwood, Coniston, Lancashire.
30th March, 1886.

EMILY DICKINSON to Louise and Frances Norcross, [*c.* March 1886]

Emily Dickinson, 1830–86, poet; Louise and Frances Norcross, her cousins.

I scarcely know where to begin, but love is always a safe place. I have twice been very sick, dears, with a little recess of convalescence, then to be more sick, and have lain in my bed since November, many years, for me, stirring as the arbutus does, a pink and russet hope; but that we will leave with our pillow. When your dear hearts are quite convenient, tell us of their contents, the fabric cared for most, not a fondness wanting.

Do you keep musk, as you used to, like Mrs. Morene of Mexico? Or cassia carnations so big they split their fringes of berry? Was your winter a tender shelter – perhaps like Keats's bird, 'and hops and hops in little journeys'?

Are you reading and well, and the W[hitney]s near and warm? When you see Mrs. French and Dan give them a tear from us.

Vinnie would have written, but could not leave my side. Maggie gives her love. Mine more sweetly still.

Emily.

EMILY DICKINSON to Louise and Frances Norcross, [May 1886]

Emily Dickinson, 1830–86, poet; Louise and Frances Norcross, her cousins. During the second week in May 1886 Emily Dickinson probably came to know that she had but a short time to live, and this letter appears to be her last. She went into a coma on 13 May, and died on the 15th.

> Little Cousins,
> Called back.
> Emily.

VINCENT VAN GOGH to H. M. Livens, [late summer 1886]

Vincent Van Gogh, 1853–90, painter; Horace Mann Livens, painter. Livens, an English painter, had met Van Gogh when they were fellow students at the Antwerp Academy under Charles Verlat.

Paris

My dear Mr. Levens,

Since I am here in Paris I have very often thought of yourself and work. You will remember that I liked your colour, your ideas on art and literature and I add, most of all your personality. I have already before now thought that I ought to let you know what I was doing where I was. But what refrained me was that I find living in Paris is much dearer than in Antwerp and not knowing what your circumstances are I dare not say come over to Paris from Antwerp without warning you that it costs one dearer, and that if poor, one has to suffer many things – as you may imagine –. But on the other hand there is more chance of selling. There is also a good chance of exchanging pictures with other artists.

In one word, with much energy, with a sincere personal feeling of colour in nature I would say an artist can get on here notwithstanding the many obstructions. And I intend remaining here still longer.

[late summer 1886]

There is much to be seen here – for instance Delacroix, to name only one master. In Antwerp I did not even know what the impressionists were, now I have seen them and though *not* being one of the club yet I have much admired certain impressionists' pictures – *Degas* nude figure – *Claude Monet* landscape.

And now for what regards what I myself have been doing, I have lacked money for paying models else I had entirely given myself to figure painting. But I have made a series of color studies in painting simply flowers, red poppies, blue corn flowers and myosotys, white and rose roses, yellow chrysanthemums – seeking oppositions of blue with orange, red and green, yellow and violet seeking *les tons rompus et neutres* to harmonise brutal extremes. Trying to render intense colour and not a grey harmony.

Now after these gymnastics I lately did two heads which I dare say are better in light and colour than those I did before.

So as we said at the time: in *colour* seeking *life* the true drawing is modelling with colour.

I did a dozen landscapes too, frankly *green* frankly *blue*.

And so I am struggling for life and progress in art.

Now I would very much like to know what you are doing and whether you ever think of going to Paris.

If ever you did come here, write to me before and I will, if you like, share my lodgings and studio with you so long as I have any. In spring – say February or even sooner I may be going to the South of France, the land of the *blue* tones and gay colours.

And look here, if I knew you had longings for the same we might combine.

I felt sure at the time that you are a thorough colourist and since I saw the impressionists I assure you that neither your colour nor mine as it is developping itself, is *exactly* the same as their theories. But so much dare I say we have a chance and a good one finding friends. – I hope your health is all-right. I was rather low down in health when in Antwerp but got better here.

Write to me in any case. Remember me to Allen, Briet, Rink, Durant but I have not often thought of them as I did think of you – almost daily.

Shaking hands cordially.

Yours truly Vincent

My present address is
Mr. Vincent van Gogh
54 Rue Lepic, Paris.

200

With regard my chances of sale look here, they are certainly not much but still *I do have* a beginning.

At the present moment I have found four dealers who have exhibited studies of mine. And I have exchanged studies with many artists.

Now the prices are 50 francs. Certainly not much – but – as far as I can see one must sell cheap to rise and even at costing price. And mind my dear fellow, Paris is Paris. There is but one Paris and however hard living may be here, and if it became worse and harder even – the french air clears up the brain and does good – a world of good.

I have been in Cormons studio for three or four months but I did not find that so useful as I had expected it to be. It may be my fault however, anyhow I left there too as I left Antwerp and since I worked alone, and fancy that since I feel my own self more.

Trade is slow here. The great dealers sell Millet, Delacroix, Corot, Daubigny, Dupré, a few other masters at exorbitant prices. They do little or nothing for young artists. The second class dealers contrariwise sell those at very low prices. If I asked more I would do nothing, I fancy. However I have faith in colour. Even with regards the price the public will pay for it in the long run. But for the present things are awfully hard. Therefore let anyone who risks to go over here consider there is no laying on roses at all.

What is to be gained is *progress* and what the deuce that is, it is to be found here. I dare say as certain anyone who has a solid position elsewhere let him stay where he is. But for adventurers as myself, I think they lose nothing in risking more. Especially as in my case I am not an adventurer by choice but by fate, and feeling nowhere so much myself a stranger as in my family and country. – Kindly remember me to your landlady Mrs. Roosmalen and say her that if she will exhibit something of my work I will send her a small picture of mine.

17 August 1887

EMIN PASHA to General Gordon's sister, 17 August 1887

Eduard Schnitzer, Emin Pasha, 1840–92; Augusta, General Gordon's sister. Emin Pasha, one of the most enigmatic and accomplished of all African explorers, was a German who had converted to Islam and had served under Gordon as Governor of Equatoria (southern Sudan). After the fall of Khartoum he was cut off from the outside world in his headquarters at Wadelai in the Sudan. An expedition was mounted under Stanley to rescue him, which reached him several months after this letter was written.

Wadelai the 17th August 1887

Dear Miss Gordon,

I have the honor to acknowledge receipt of your kind letter of November 25th, 1886, arrived here at the end of June. I hasten to impress you my hearty thanks for your friendly words and for your request to write to you, a permission of which I shall be proud sometimes to avail me. As one who wanders over lonely paths, far off from the world and its turmoil, I cannot but deeply appreciate any token of interest in my doings. I can fully understand how grievously you have suffered by your brother's loss; if anyone I can bear testimony to the strong affection and love which he had for you. Many, many times in our wanderings or at the camp-fire he spoke of you and the day on which he received a letter from you, became a holiday. But the blow did not fall upon you alone; whoever had the honour of his intimacy will mourn him like a brother. He was one of those few privileged beings to whom God gave a child's heart in a man's body. Wherever he went he made friends, his unselfishness and ever ready bounty won him all hearts. The 'Colonel' as he was called, was adored like a saint before he died like a martyr. Permit me to thank you most heartily for the facsimile of his last words to you as well as for your very kind promise to send me a copy of his Khartoum journals. I shall certainly esteem it a priceless gift, its intrinsical value being enhanced by its comming from your hands.
Miss Felkin's letter to me must have been lost. It never reached here.

I am now busy to put things in order here. As I am determined to hold out and to stand by my people I am naturally anxious that our relations to the indigenous population should be most friendly ones. I am, therefore, always in the way. Unluckily, King Muanga has another time made war against Kabrega who would not listen to my advice and now he has to suffer for it. I had, nevertheless, the good chance to receive a little quantity of goods from Uganda justly before the outbreak. This piece of good luck has enabled me to supply my people with some clothes. On the whole we are all well and, thanks to God, we have no reason to complain. This letter leaving for Uganda by the man who brought our goods will, I hope, reach you safely. If in a lost moment you will answer it you shall deeply oblige.

Yours very sincerely,
Dr. Emin Pasha

W. B. YEATS to Katharine Tynan, 25 August [1888]

William Butler Yeats, 1865–1939, poet and playwright; Katharine Tynan, author, associated with Yeats in the Irish revival. Yeats was at this time busy transcribing Caxton's *The Fables of Aesop* (1484) for a reissue published in 1889. Churton Collins had published an attack showing up the carelessness of Edmund Gosse's scholarship; Kegan Paul was to bring out *The Wanderings of Oisin and Other Poems*, Yeats's first collection, in the following year. Yeats's spelling got even worse as he grew older.

Bedford Park
3 Blenheim Road
Turnham Green
August 25

My dear Miss Tynan

I have at last found time to write. Such works as I have had lately! These last two days I have had to take a rest quite worn out. There are still a hundred pages of Esope. When they are done I shall get back to my story in which I pour all my grievances against this meloncholy London – I sometimes imagine that the souls of the lost are compelled to walk through its streets perpetually. One feels them passing like a whif of air. I have had three months incessant work without a moment to read or think and am feeling like a burnt out taper. Will you write me a long letter all about your self and you[r] thoughts. When one is tired the tendril in ones nature asserts itself and one wants to hear about ones friends.

Did I ever tell you that a clairvoyant, who had never seen me before, told me months ago that I had made too many thoughts and that for a long time I should have to become passive. He told me besides in proof things he had know way of hearing of. Most passive I have been this long while, feeling as though my brain had been rolled about for centuries in the sea, and as I look on my piles of MSS, as though I had built a useless city in my sleep. Indeed all this last six months I have grown more and more passive ever since I finished Oisin and what an eater up of ideals is passivity for every things seems a vision and nothing worth seeking after.

I was at Oxford but was all day buisy with Esope. I dined two or three times with the fellows and did not take much to any one except Churten Collins who as you remember attacked Gosse so fiercely – he was there for a few days like myself – a most cheerful mild pink and white little man full of the freshest unreasonablest enthusiasms.

I wonder any body does any thing at Oxford but dream and remember the place is so beautiful. One almost expects the people to sing instead of speaking. It is all – the colleges I meen – like an Opera.

I will write again before long and give you some news. I merely write to you now because I want a letter, and because I am sad. My fairy book proofs are waiting correction.

Yours Always
W B Yeats

I saw Keegan Paul lately he will go on with my book now.

WINSTON CHURCHILL to his mother, 7 November 1888

Sir Winston Churchill, 1874–1965, Prime Minister and author; Jenny, Lady Randolph Churchill, his mother. This letter was written while Churchill was a schoolboy at Harrow, where he enjoyed a famously undistinguished career.

7 November 1888

Dearest Mamma,

I am going to write you a proper epistle, hoping you will forgive my former negligence. On Saturday we had a lecture on the

'Phonograph'

By 'Col Gouraud'. It was very amusing he astonished all sober-minded People by singing into the Phonograph

'John Brown Body lies—Mouldy in the grave
And is soul goes marching on
Glory, glory, glory Halleluja'

And the Phonograph spoke it back in a voice that was clearly audible in the 'Speech Room'
   He shewed us it in private on Monday. We went in 3 or 4 at a time.
   His boys are at Harrow.
   He fought at Gettysburg.
   His wife was at school with you.
   Papa gave him letter of introduction to India.
   He told me to ask Papa if he remembered the 'tall Yankee'.
   I want to be allowed to join the Harrow work shop for they then supply you wood and I want to make some scenery for the nursery if we have any Party. 3 or 4 scenes cost about ½ a sovereign and the man who is in charge thoroughly understands scenery making.

With love & kisses I remain
Winston S. Churchill

P.S. Will you write to say whether I may join as I have no imployment for odd half hours. W. C.

LAFCADIO HEARN to George M. Gould, [1889]

Lafcadio Hearn, 1850–1904, author, authority on Japan; Dr George M. Gould, author of *Concerning Lafcadio Hearn*. This letter was written while Hearn was living in America, working on two books about Martinique.

   Dear Gould – I feel like a white granular mass of amorphous crystals – my formula appears to be isomeric with Spasmotoxin. My aurochloride precipitates into beautiful prismatic needles. My Platinochloride develops octohedron crystals, – with a fine blue fluorescence. My physiological action is not indifferent. One millionth of a grain injected under the skin of a frog produced instantaneous death accompanied by an orange blossom odour. The heart stopped in systole. A base – $L_3 H_9 NG_4$ – offers analogous reaction to phosmotinigstic acid. Yours with best regards,

Phosmolyodic Lafcadio Hearn.

GOULD, – 'Concerning zombis, tell me all about them.'

HEARN, – 'In order to relate you that which you desire, it will be necessary first to explain the difference in the idea of the supernatural as existing in the savage and in the civilized mind. Now, I remember a very strange thing . . .'

GOULD, – 'I'll be back in a minute.' (*Strides across the street.*)

Violent agitation in the peripheral centres of Hearn, together with considerable acute anguish, owing to disintegration of cerebral tissue consequent upon the sudden arrest of nerve-force in discharge. (See Grant Allen on cause of pain, 'Physiological Æsthetics.')

Gould, suddenly reappearing: – 'Go on with that old story, now.'

(Resurrection of cerebral agitation in the ganglionic centres of inter-correlate cerebral fibres of Hearn. After desperate and painful research, the broken threads of memories and impulses are found again, and peripherally conjointed, and the wounded narrative proceeds, limping grievously.)

HEARN, – 'As I was observing, I recollect one very curious instance of emotional and fantastic – '

GOULD, – 'Yes, I'll be out in a moment – ' (*Disappears through a door.*)

– Brutal confusion established in the visual, auditory, gustatory, and olfactory ganglia of Hearn; – general quivering and strain of all the mnemonic current lines, and then a sense of inquisitorial torture going on in various brain-chambers, where the vital forces, suddenly arrested, flow back in a deluge and set all ideas afloat in drowning agony. Slow recovery as from concussion of the cerebellum.

ENTER GOULD, – 'Now proceed with that story of yours.'

HEARN, – pacifying the fury of the ganglionic centres with the most extreme possible difficulty, timidly observes, –

'But you don't care to hear it?'

GOULD, – moving with inconceivable rapidity, dynamically over-charged, –

'Of course, I do: I'm just dying to hear it.'

Hearn, running after him, skipping preliminaries in the anguish of 'hope deferred which maketh the heart sick,' –

'Well, it was in the Rue du Bois Morier, – one of the steepest and strangest streets in the world, full of fantastic gables, and the shadows of – '

GOULD, – 'Yes, I'll be out in a minute.'

(*Vanishes through a shop entrance.*)

(Inexpressible chaos and bewilderment of impulses afferent and efferent, – electrical collisions in the ganglia, – unspeakable combustion of tissue in the intercorrelated fibres, – paralysis of conflicting emotions, – unutterable anguish: coma followed by acute mania in the person of Hearn.)

GOULD, – emerging, 'Well, go on with that old yarn. . . .'

But Hearn is being already conveyed by two large Philadelphia Policemen to the Penn. Lunatic Asylum for Uncurables.

Astonishment of Gould.

ROBERT LOUIS STEVENSON to Henry James, [March 1889]

Robert Louis Stevenson, 1850–94, author; Henry James, novelist. Stevenson had gone to the South Seas the year before for the sake of his health. The letter to which he refers was one written with great affection from 'Ora A Ora, that is to say, Rui'.

Honolulu

My Dear James, – Yes – I own up – I am untrue to friendship and (what is less, but still considerable) to civilisation. I am not coming home for another year. There it is, cold and bald, and now you won't believe in me at all, and serve me right (says you) and the devil take me. But look here, and judge me tenderly. I have had more fun and pleasure of my life these past months than ever before, and more health than any time in ten long years. And even here in Honolulu I have withered in the cold; and this precious deep is filled with islands, which we may still visit; and though the sea is a deathful place, I like to be there, and like squalls (when they are over); and to draw near to a new island, I cannot say how much I like. In short, I take another year of this sort of life, and mean to try to work down among the poisoned arrows, and mean (if it may be) to come back again when the thing is through, and converse with Henry James as heretofore; and in the meanwhile issue directions to H. J. to write to me once more. Let him address here at Honolulu, for my views are vague; and if it is sent here it will follow and find me, if I am to be found; and if I am not to be found, the man James will have done his duty, and we shall be at the bottom of the sea, where no post-office clerk can be expected to discover us, or languishing on a coral island, the philosophic drudges of some barbarian potentate: perchance, of an American Missionary. My wife has just sent to Mrs. Sitwell a translation (*tant bien que mal*) of a letter I have had from my chief friend in this part of the world: go and see her, and get a hearing of it; it will do you good; it is a better method of correspondence than even Henry James's. I jest, but seriously it is a strange thing for a tough, sick middle-aged scrivener like R. L. S. to receive a letter so conceived from a man fifty years old, a leading politician, a crack orator, and the great wit of his village: boldly say, 'the highly popular M.P. of Tautira.' My nineteenth century strikes here, and lies alongside of something beautiful and ancient. I think the receipt of such a letter might humble, shall I say even – ? and for me, I would rather have received it than written *Redgauntlet* or the *Sixth Æneid*. All told, if my books have enabled or helped me to make this voyage, to know Rui, and to have received such a letter, they have (in the old prefatorial expression) not been writ in vain. It would seem from this that I have been not so much humbled as puffed up; but, I assure you, I have in fact been both. A little of what that letter says is my own earning; not all, but yet a little; and the little makes me proud, and all the rest ashamed; and in the contrast, how much more beautiful altogether is the ancient man than him of to-day!

Well, well, Henry James is pretty good, though he *is* of the nineteenth century, and that glaringly. And to curry favour with him, I wish I could be more explicit; but, indeed, I am still of necessity extremely vague, and cannot tell what I am to do, nor where I am to go for some while yet. As soon as I am sure, you shall hear. All are fairly well – the wife, your countrywoman, least of all; troubles are not entirely wanting; but on the whole we prosper, and we are all affectionately yours,

Robert Louis Stevenson

LAFCADIO HEARN to Professor Chamberlain, August 1891

Lafcadio Hearn, 1850–1904, author, authority on Japan; Basil Hall Chamberlain, formerly Professor of Japanese at Tokyo University. Hearn had moved to Japan the previous year, where he taught at Matsue and where he was to spend the rest of his life.

Matsue, August, 1891.

Dear Professor Chamberlain, – Having reached a spot where I can write upon something better than a matted floor, I find three most pleasant letters from you. The whole of the questions in them I cannot answer to-night, but will do so presently, when I obtain the full information.

However, as to cats' tails I can answer at once. Izumo cats – (and I was under the impression until recently that all Japanese cats were alike) – are generally born with long tails. But there is a belief that any cat whose tail is not cut off in kittenhood, will become an *obake* or a *nekomata*, and there are weird stories about cats with long tails dancing at night, with towels tied round their heads. There are stories about petted cats eating their mistress and then assuming the form, features, and voice of the victim. Of course you know the Buddhist tradition that no cat can enter paradise. The cat and the snake alone wept not for the death of Buddha. Cats are unpopular in Izumo, but in Hōki I saw that they seemed to exist under more favourable conditions. The real reason for the unpopularity of the cat is its powers of mischief in a Japanese house; – it tears the *tatami*, the *karakami*, the *shōji*, scratches the woodwork, and insists upon carrying its food into the best room to eat it upon the floor. I am a great lover of cats, having 'raised,' as the Americans say, more than fifty; – but I could not gratify my desire to have a cat here. The creature proved too mischievous, and wanted always to eat my uguisu.

The oscillation of one's thoughts concerning the Japanese – the swaying you describe – is and has for some time been mine also.

There are times when they seem so small! And then again, although they never seem large, there is a vastness behind them, – a past of indefinite complexity and marvel, – an amazing power of absorbing and assimilating, – which forces one to suspect some power in the race so different from our own that one cannot understand that power. And as you say, whatever doubts or vexations one has in Japan, it is only necessary to ask one's self: – 'Well, who are the best people to live with?'

For it is a question whether the intellectual pleasures of social life abroad are not more than dearly bought at the cost of social pettinesses which do not seem to exist in Japan at all.

Would you be horrified to learn that I have become passionately fond of *daikon*, – not the fresh but the strong ancient pickled *daikon*? But then the European Stilton cheese, or Limburger, is surely quite as queer. I have become what they call here a *jōgo*, – and find that a love of sake creates a total change in all one's eating habits and tastes. All the sweet things the *geko* likes, I cannot bear when taking sake. By the way, what a huge world of etiquette, art, taste, custom, has been developed by sake. An article upon sake, – its social rules, – its vessels, – its physiological effects, – in short the whole romance and charm of a Japanese banquet, ought to be written by somebody. I hope to write one some day, but I am still learning.

As to Dr. Tylor and the anthropological institute. If he should want any paper that I could furnish, I would be glad and consider myself honoured to please him. As for your question about the *o fuda*, why, I should think it no small pleasure to be mentioned merely as one of your workers and friends. Though the little I have been able to send does not seem to me to deserve your kindest words, it is making me very happy to have been able to please you at all. Whatever I can write or send, make always any use of you please.

About 'seeing Japan from a distance,' – I envy you your coming chance. I could not finish my book on the West Indies until I saw the magical island again through regret, as through a summer haze, – and under circumstances which left me perfectly free to think, which the soporific air of the tropics makes difficult. (Still the book is not what it ought to be, for I was refused all reasonable help, and wrote most of it upon a half-empty stomach, or with my blood full of fever.) But to think of Japan in an English atmosphere will be a delicious experience for you after so long an absence. I should not be surprised should the experience result in the creation of something which would please your own feelings as an author better than any other work you have made. Of course it is at the time one is best pleased that one does one's real best in the artistic line.

By the way, since you like those Shintō prints, – and I might get you others, – what about a possible edition of your 'Kojiki' illustrated by Japanese conceptions of this kind, colours and all? Such work can be so cheaply done in Japan! And an index! How often I wished for an index. I have made an imperfect one of my own. It is believed here that Hahaki is the ancient name of the modern Hōki. I was told this when I wanted to go to the legendary burial-place of Izanami.

As usual, I find I have been too presumptuous in writing offhand about cats' tails. On enquiring, I learn that there are often, born of the same mother, Izumo kittens with short tails, and kittens with long tails. This would show that two distinct species of cats exist here. The long-tailed kittens are always deprived when possible of the larger part of their caudal appendage. The short tails are spared. If an old cat be seen with a short tail, people say, – 'this cat is old, but she has a short tail: therefore she is a good cat.' (For the *obake* cat gets two tails when old, and every wicked cat has a long tail.) I am told that at the recent *bon*, in Matsue, cats of the evil sort were seen to dance upon the roofs of the houses.

What you tell me about those Shintō rituals and their suspicious origin seems to me quite certainly true. So the *kara-shishi* and the *mon* and the dragon-carvings and the *tōrōs*, – all stare me in the face as pillage of Buddhism. But the funeral rite which I saw and took part in, on the anniversary of the death of Prince Sanjō, struck me as immemorially primitive. The weird simplicity of it – the banquet to the ghost, the covering of the faces with white paper, the moaning song, the barbarian music, all seemed to me traditions and echoes of the very childhood of the race. I shall try to discover the genesis of the book you speak of as dubious in character. The Shintō christening ceremony is strictly observed here, and there are curious facts about the funeral ceremonies – totally at variance with and hostile to Buddhism.

By the way, when I visited a *tera* in Mionoseki after having bought *o fuda* at the Miojinja, I was told I must not carry the *o fuda* into the court of the *tera*. The Kami would be displeased.

For the moment, good-bye.

Ever faithfully,
Lafcadio Hearn.

OSCAR WILDE to Lord Alfred Douglas, [? January 1893]

Oscar Fingal O'Flahertie Wills Wilde, 1854–1900, author; Lord Alfred Douglas, his lover. This letter was stolen from Lord Alfred by a blackmailer. In an attempt to limit any damage that it might cause, and to give it the status of a work of art, it was translated into French by Pierre Louÿs and published as a sonnet in 1893. Wilde's fears were confirmed when it was produced as evidence at his trial and read out in court.

My Own Boy,

Your sonnet is quite lovely, and it is a marvel that those red rose-leaf lips of yours should have been made no less for music of song than for madness of kisses. Your slim gilt soul walks between passion and poetry. I know Hyacinthus, whom Apollo loved so madly, was you in Greek days.

Why are you alone in London, and when do you go to Salisbury? Do go there to cool your hands in the grey twilight of Gothic things, and come here whenever you like. It is a lovely place – it only lacks you; but go to Salisbury first. Always, with undying love, yours

Oscar

LAFCADIO HEARN to Sentarō Nishida, November 1893

Lafcadio Hearn, 1850–1904, author, authority on Japan; Sentarō Nishida, teacher of English at Matsue.

Kumamoto, November, 1893.

Dear Nishida, – A few days ago there came from Kizuki a little box addressed to me, – from Mr. Senke; and opening it, I found therein the robe of a *Kokuzō* – all black silk with the sacred *mon* of the temple worked into the silk. Accompanying the robe were two poems, very beautifully written upon vari-coloured paper. The robe was very curious in itself, and of course most precious as a souvenir. I hesitated to write at once; for I could not answer Mr. Senke's magnificent letter in a worthy way at all. It was a very long letter, written on fine paper and in large handsome characters. I have now tried to reply, but my answer reads very shabbily compared with Mr. Senke's gracious style.

I found I had forgotten, in writing you the other day, to speak about Kompira, as you asked me. What a pity I had not known about the real temple of Kompira, which I did not see at all. Yes, I did find the place interesting and very beautiful. But it was interesting because of the quaint shops and streets and customs; and it was beautiful *because the day happened to be very beautiful*. The vast blue light coloured everything, – walls, timbers, awnings, draperies, dresses of pilgrims; and the cherry-trees were one blaze of snowy blossoms; and the horizon was clear as crystal. In the distance towered Sanuki-Fuji – a cone of amethyst in the light. I wished I could teach in some school at Kompira *uchimachi*, and stay there always.

I like little towns. To live at Tadotsu, or at Hishi-ura in Oki, or at Yunotsu in Iwami, or at Daikon-shimain Naka-umi, would fill my soul with joy. I cannot like the new Japan. I dislike the officials, the imitation of foreign ways, the airs, the conceits, the contempt for Tempō, etc. Now to my poor mind, all that was good and noble and true was Old Japan: I wish I could fly out of Meiji forever, back against the stream of Time, into Tempō, or into the age of the Mikado Yūriaku, – fourteen hundred years ago. The life of the old fans, the old *byōbu*, the tiny villages – that is the *real* Japan I love. Somehow or other, Kumamoto doesn't seem to me Japan at all. I hate it.

Ever with best regards,

Lafcadio Hearn.

ROBERT LOUIS STEVENSON to Charles Baxter, [Autumn 1894]

Robert Louis Stevenson, 1850–94, author; Charles Baxter, Edinburgh friend and lawyer. 'Godkin' was William Mitchell, Baxter's senior partner. Stevenson died on 3 December that year.

[Samoa, received 15 September 1894]

My dear Charles,

I have thought well of the matter, and I judge thus: with your father and your sister gone, and the former loss, you would be horribly alone in

[Autumn 1894]

Edinr. The character of the Godkin or Godlet can scarce be accounted an alleviation. You have always wished to leave the place. Leave it in God's name!

At the same time, remember a change of this sort is, to a man of forty-five, a searching trial; and keep yourself well in hand whilst you make it – and after.

I will confess – going merely by instinctive physiognomical inferences – I am glad to be done with the Godlet. I wonder how your father, worthy man! ever looked twice at him. But he did not know *men*; three of his friends I condemned out of hand: Mitchell, Weir, the wine merchant, and Macdonald of Morar. The last justified me, I believe; the other two may not have, but they were insincere and dangerous men.

Well, there is no more Edmund Baxter now, and I think I may say I know how you feel. He was one of the best, the kindest, and the most genial men I ever knew; I shall always remember his brisk, cordial ways and the essential goodness which he showed me whenever we met with gratitude. And the always is such a little while now! He is another of the landmarks gone; when it comes to my own turn to lay my weapons down, I shall do so with thankfulness and fatigue, and whatever be my destiny afterward, I shall be glad to lie down with my fathers in honour. It is human at least, if not divine. And these deaths make me think of it with an ever greater readiness. Strange that you should be beginning a new life when I, who am a little your junior, am thinking of the end of mine. But I have had hard lines; I have been so long waiting for death, I have unwrapped my thoughts from about life so long, that I have not a filament left to hold by; I have done my fiddling so long under Vesuvius that I have almost forgotten to play, and can only wait for the eruption and think it long of coming. Literally no man has more wholly outlived life than I. And still it's good fun.

R. L. S.

214

OSCAR WILDE to Ada Leverson, [? 10 February 1895]

Oscar Fingal O'Flahertie Wills Wilde, 1854–1900, author; Ada Leverson, novelist. This letter was probably written a few days before the first performance of *The Importance of Being Earnest*, at the height of Wilde's fame, and not long before his ruin.

Hotel Avondale, Piccadilly

My dear Sphinx,

You were kind enough to say I might bring someone to dinner tonight, so, after carefully going over the list, I have selected a young man, tall as a young palm tree (I mean 'tall as two young palm trees'). His Christian name is 'Tom' – a very rare name in an age of Algies and Berties – and he is the son of Colonel Kennion, and lives at Oxford in the hopes of escaping the taint of modern education. I met him on Tuesday, so he is quite an old friend.

I could not get away last night. I am delighted to hear that the piece was tedious, but want to know what sort of dialogue you spoke between the acts. The critics say nothing about it. Why is this? Ever yours

Oscar

THE MARQUESS OF QUEENSBERRY to Oscar Wilde, [18 February 1895]

Sir John Sholto Douglas, eighth Marquess of Queensberry, 1844–1900, father of Lord Alfred Douglas; Oscar Fingal O'Flahertie Wills Wilde, author. This message, written on Lord Queensberry's card, was left at 4.30 p.m. on 18 February 1895 at the Albemarle Club, where it was handed to Wilde by the hall porter ten days later. Richard Ellmann, Wilde's biographer, surmises that Wilde read it as, 'To Oscar Wilde, ponce and Somdomite': in all events, it goaded him into taking the disastrous action against the Marquess for criminal libel which was to lead to his own prosecution and imprisonment for homosexual offences. Queensberry maintained in court that he had written 'posing as a Somdomite' (his misspelling of 'Sodomite').

To Oscar Wilde posing Somdomite

BERNARD SHAW to Arthur Clark, 18 May 1895

George Bernard Shaw, 1856–1950, playwright; Arthur S. Clark, aspiring playwright.

29 Fitzroy Square W
18th May 1895

Dear Sir

At thirtyeight you should have written half a dozen plays if you intend to become a dramatist by profession. And you must not write them with a view to reforming your fortune, or with any other view than the production of a work of art that satisfies your own judgment and fulfils the purpose created by your instinct as a dramatist. You are mistaken in supposing that plays are not read. Not only managers, but actors who are waiting to become managers until they have a few good plays in hand, spend their days in drudging through manuscripts, 99% of which are hopelessly bad. But they naturally turn first to the plays with promising titles; and 'The Vegetarian' is quite impossible. I have no hesitation in saying that unless that title is a purposely misleading one, the play *must* be a bad one. The only advice I can give you is not to waste any thought or anxiety on the play you have finished, but go on and write another, & then another & so on until you have either learnt the business or discovered that you have not the necessary turn for it. Refusals mean nothing: a play may be a masterpiece and yet not suit this or that particular manager. Besides the actual managers, you may take it that almost every 'leading man' in London – Fred Terry, Yorke Stephens, Forbes Robertson, Arthur Bourchier. &c. &c. &c. would read anything on the chance of picking up something good enough to start with. There is also a great demand for good one-act 'curtain raisers.'

yrs faithfully
G. Bernard Shaw

OSCAR WILDE to Ada Leverson, [20 May 1897]

Oscar Fingal O'Flahertie Wills Wilde, 1854–1900, author; Ada Leverson, novelist. The letter was written after Wilde's release from prison where he had served two years' hard labour. Robbie Ross and Reggie Turner were two friends who, like Ada Leverson, had stayed loyal to Wilde during his disgrace. Wilde's alias was taken from the novel *Melmoth the Wanderer* by the Revd Charles Maturin.

Hôtel Sandwich, Dieppe

Dear Sphinx,

I was so charmed with seeing you yesterday morning that I must write a line to tell you how sweet and good it was of you to be of the very first to greet me. When I think that Sphinxes are minions of the moon, and that you got up early before dawn, I am filled with wonder and joy.

I often thought of you in the long black days and nights of my prison-life, and to find you just as wonderful and dear as ever was no surprise. The beautiful are always beautiful.

This is my first day of real liberty, so I try to send you a line, and with kind regards to dear Ernest whom I was pleased to see again, ever affectionately yours

Oscar Wilde

I am staying here as Sebastian Melmoth – not Esquire but Monsieur Sebastien Melmoth. I have thought it better that Robbie should stay here under the name of Reginald Turner, and Reggie under the name of R. B. Ross. It is better that they should not have their own names.

OSCAR WILDE to Reggie Turner, 10 August [1897]

Oscar Fingal O'Flahertie Wills Wilde, 1854–1900, author; Reginald Turner, barrister. Leonard Smithers was to publish *The Ballad of Reading Gaol*, *The Importance of Being Earnest* and *An Ideal Husband*. He also published Aubrey Beardsley's drawings.

Tuesday 10 August

My dear Reggie,

Will you come over here on Saturday next, by the afternoon boat?

Robbie is here, and we want you so much. It is quite quiet and the weather is charming. Also last night acrobats arrived. Smithers, the publisher and owner of Aubrey, comes over on Sunday and we all dine with him: then we go to Berneval.

I do not know if you know Smithers: he is usually in a large straw hat, has a blue tie delicately fastened with a diamond brooch of the impurest water – or perhaps wine, as he never touches water: it goes to his head at once. His face, clean-shaven as befits a priest who serves at the altar whose God is Literature, is wasted and pale – not with poetry, but with poets, who, he says, have wrecked his life by insisting on publishing with him. He loves first editions, especially of women: little girls are his passion. He is the most learned erotomaniac in Europe. He is also a delightful companion, and a dear fellow, very kind to me.

You will on arrival proceed without delay to the *Café Suisse*, where Robbie and I will be waiting for you.

If you don't come I shall be quite wretched. I long to see you again.
Ever yours

Oscar

CONSTANCE WILDE to Arthur Humphreys, 27 February 1898

Constance Wilde, later Holland, 1858–98, Oscar Wilde's wife; Arthur Humphreys, manager of Hatchard's Bookshop, Piccadilly. Wilde's wife changed her name to Holland after her husband's disgrace. Wilde had been particularly lavish in the distribution of inscribed copies of *The Ballad of Reading Gaol*, published by Smithers that month. Deteriorating health made Constance unable to write by hand, and she was forced to type the entire letter including the signature. She died five weeks later on 7 April 1898.

Villa Elvira
Bogliasco
Riviera di Levante. 27.2.1898.

My dear Arthur,

Thank you a thousand times for the Millet which I am reading with immense pleasure and find most sympathetic. Also thank you for the three copies of the *Ballad* which came all right. I think I told you that I had had a copy from Robbie Ross, and that was perhaps the next best thing to getting one from the author, tho' not alas quite the same. I am afraid the sale will come to an end more or less rapidly! O. seems to have behaved badly to many of his true friends, and his punishment has not done him much good since it has not taught him the lesson he most needed namely that he is not the only person in the world! I did think that he was a true friend, but I am afraid I have had to change my mind about that as about many other things. Any way I have got my boys and more and more they become absolutely necessary to me and part of my life, as I find everything else fail. If I had not them I dread to think of what my life or rather my death would be! However we wont talk about that. It is very kind of you to think of me and to send me things, and I am sorry that I am able to do little. But I am not strong, as you know and less and less I seem able to do things as I used to do. But then I always did too much as you know and was very stupid.

Always affectionately yours,
Constance Holland.

AUBREY BEARDSLEY to Leonard Smithers, 7 March 1898

Aubrey Beardsley, 1872–98, illustrator; Leonard Smithers, his publisher. Beardsley, who had converted to Roman Catholicism, suffered a haemorrhage on 26 January and died on 16 March, five months short of his twenty-sixth birthday. His appeal, of course, was made in vain. Smithers is said to have further capitalized on his talents by later forging and selling copies of this letter.

Jesus is our Lord and Judge
Dear Friend,
I implore you to destroy *all* copies of *Lysistrata* and bad drawings. Show this to Pollitt and conjure him to do same. By all that is holy *all* obscene drawings.

Aubrey Beardsley

In my death agony.

LAFCADIO HEARN to Mitchell McDonald, July 1898

Lafcadio Hearn, 1850–1904, author, authority on Japan; Mitchell McDonald, Paymaster of the United States Navy.

Tokyo, July, 1898.

Dear McDonald, – We ran over somebody last night – and the train therefore waited in mourning upon the track during a decorous period. We did not see Tōkyō till after eleven considerably. But the waiting was not unpleasant. Frogs sang as if nothing had happened, and the breeze from the sea faintly moved through the cars; – and I meditated about the sorrows and the joys of life by turns, and smoked, and thanked the gods for many things, – including the existence of yourself and Dr. Hall. I was not unfortunate enough to see what had been killed, – or the consequences to friends and acquaintances; and feeling there was no more pain for that person, I smoked in peace – though not without a prayer to the gods to pardon my want of seriousness.

Altogether I felt extremely happy, in spite of the delay. The day had been so glorious, – especially subsequent to the removal of a small h—l, containing several myriads of lost souls, from the left side of my lower jaw.

Reaching home, I used some of that absolutely wonderful medicine. It was a great and grateful surprise. (I am not trying to say much about the kindness of the gift – that would be no use.) After having used it, for the first time, I made a tactile investigation without fear, and found –

What do you think?

Guess!

Well, I found that – *the wrong one had been pulled*, – No. 3 instead of No. 2.

I don't say that No. 3 didn't deserve its fate. But it had never been openly aggressive. It had struggled to perform its duties under disadvantageous circumstances: its character had been modest and shrinking. No. 2 had been, on the contrary, Mt. Vesuvius, the last great Javanese earthquake, the tidal wave of '96, and the seventh chamber of the Inferno, all in mathematical combination. It – Mt. Vesuvius, etc. – is still with me, and although to-day astonished into quiescence, is far from being extinct. The medicine keeps it still for the time. You will see that I have been destined to experience strange adventures.

Hope I may be able to see you again *soon*, – 4th, if possible. Love to you and all kind wishes to everybody.

Lafcadio.

JOSEPH CONRAD to Edward Garnett, 3 August 1898

Joseph Conrad, 1857–1924, novelist; Edward Garnett, author and publisher's reader.

3d Aug. '98.

My dear Garnett.

I am not dead tho' only half alive. Very soon I shall send you some MS. I am writing hopelessly – but still I am writing. How I feel I cannot express. Pages accumulate and the story stands still.

I feel suicidal.

Drop me a line and tell me where and how you are. If you could come down it would be an act of real friendship and also of charity.

My kind regards and Jessie's love to your wife. Jess is knocked up with the boy's teething performances. He has (and she has also) a rough time of it.

I am afraid there's something wrong with my thinking apparatus. I am utterly out of touch with my work – and I can't get in touch. All is darkness.

Ever yours

Jph. Conrad

JOSEPH CONRAD to John Galsworthy, [? **20 July 1900**]

Joseph Conrad, 1857–1924, novelist; John Galsworthy, novelist. The initials stand for *Man of Devon* by Galsworthy, and *Lord Jim*.

Pent Farm
Friday

Dearest Jack,

We are off in an hour – at last, and shall be back on the 16 or 17 Aug. to give their holidays to various children.

I've written to Blackwood mainly for the purpose of insinuating amongst other matters that a quick decision as to your story would be welcome. He has your address, but hurry of any sort is not in the tradition of the 'House.'

Meldrum professes great admiration for the *M. of D.* It is evident to me he has been struck plumb-centre, and I am glad to find him discriminative. This does not settle the question of publication, but his opinion has a certain weight with Mr. B'wood.

The end of *L. J.* has been pulled off with a steady drag of 21 hours. I sent wife and child out of the house (to London) and sat down at 9 A. M. with a desperate resolve to be done with it. Now and then I took a walk round the house, out at one door in at the other. Ten-minute meals. A great hush. Cigarette ends growing into a mound similar to a cairn over a dead hero. Moon rose over the barn, looked in at the window and climbed out of sight. Dawn broke, brightened. I put the lamp out and went on, with the morning breeze blowing the sheets of MS. all over the room. Sun rose. I wrote the last word and went into the dining-room. Six o'clock I shared a piece of cold chicken with Escamillo (who was very miserable and in want of sympathy, having missed the child dreadfully all day). Felt very well, only sleepy: had a bath at seven and at 1.30 was on my way to London.

Same day we journeyed to Slough and saw the children. They are improved, very much liked, very happy. That's a success. From there we rushed straight on to the poor Hopes, where we slept two nights. Yesterday morning check from B'wood arrived and to-day we are off to join the disconsolate and much enduring Hueffer. Address: *4 rue Anglaise, Bruges.*

I am still well. Jessie too. Notwithstanding the heat. Borys in great form but exceedingly naughty except when actually travelling, when he is simply angelic.

This is all that will go on this piece of paper.

Our love.

EDWARD ELGAR to A. E. Jaeger, 9 October [1900]

Sir Edward Elgar, 1857–1934, composer; August Jaeger, his publisher, subject of the 'Nimrod' variation. *The Dream of Gerontius* had received a disastrous first performance on 3 October.

Malvern
Oct. 9

My dear Jaeger,

I recd. the St. Francis this a.m. but no word with it: we hope you and yours are well and that you are recovering from the effects of last week: I was very well and not worried by the infernal music: we had however news of severe financial loss – (since partially amended to our great relief) and that made me very worried.

I hope *you* are all right: I have not seen the papers yet except one or two bits which exuberant friends insisted on my reading and I don't know or care what they say or do. As far as I'm concerned music in England is dead – I shall always write what I have in me of course.

I have worked hard for forty years & at the last, Providence denies me a decent hearing of my work: so I submit – I always said God was against art and I still believe it. anything obscene or trivial is blessed in this world and has a reward – I ask for no reward – only to live & to hear my work. I still hear it in my heart and in my head so I must be content. Still it is curious to be treated by the old fashioned people as a criminal because my thoughts and ways are beyond them.

I am very well and what is called 'fit'! I had my golf in good style yesterday & am not ill or pessimistic – don't think it, but I have allowed my heart to open once – it is now shut against every religious feeling and every soft, gentle impulse *for ever*.

Write soon,
Yrs. ever,
E.E.

BARON CORVO to Harry Bainbridge, [1902]

Frederick William Rolfe, 'Baron Corvo', 1860–1913, author of *Hadrian the Seventh*; Harry Bainbridge, his fellow lodger.

69 Broadhurst Gardens.
Hampstead.

Dear Bainbridge,
   Awfully sorry to worry you but can you make it a fiver by return of post. It's desperate.

Vty

R

BARON CORVO to Harry Bainbridge, [1902]

Frederick William Rolfe, 'Baron Corvo', 1860–1913, author of *Hadrian the Seventh*; Harry Bainbridge, his fellow lodger.

Tuesday

Dear Bainbridge,
   Many thanks. I instantly rushed out and wallowed in a Turkish Bath.
   Do come and see me when you will: but try to give me a day's notice; and don't come on Friday.

Vty

R.

JAMES JOYCE to Lady Gregory, 22 November 1902

James Augustine Aloysius Joyce, 1882–1941, novelist; Augusta, Lady Gregory, playwright and folklorist, promotor of the Irish Revival. Joyce went into his emblematic self-exile (paralleled by his hero Stephen Dedalus who must leave his own land in order 'to forge in the smithy of my soul the uncreated conscience of my race') on 1 December. He returned a few years later for his mother's death, but otherwise never settled in Ireland again.

22 November 1902

7 S. Peter's Terrace
Cabra, Dublin
22 Nov 1902

Dear Lady Gregory

I have broken off my medical studies here and I am going to trouble you with a history. I have a degree of BA from the Royal University and I had made plans to study medicine here. But the college authorities are determined I shall not do so, wishing, I daresay, to prevent me from securing any position of ease from which I might speak out my heart. To be quite frank I am without means to pay my medical fees and they refuse to get me any grinding or tuitions or examining – alleging inability – although they have done so and are doing so for men who were stuck in the exams I passed. I want to get a degree in medicine for then I can build up my work securely. I want to achieve myself – little or great as I may be – for I know that there is no heresy or no philosophy which is so abhorrent to the church as a human being. Accordingly I am leaving this country and am going to Paris. I intend to study medicine at the University of Paris supporting myself there by teaching English. I am going alone and friendless – I know of a man who used to live somewhere near Montmartre but I have never met him – into another country and I am writing to you to know can you help me in any way. I do not know what will happen to me in Paris but my case can hardly be worse there than it is here. I am leaving Dublin by the night boat on Monday, 1st December. I shall arrive in London on Tuesday morning and my train leaves Victoria Station for Newhaven the same night. I am not despondent however for I know that even if I fail to make my way such failure proves very little. I shall try myself against the powers of the world. All things are inconstant except the faith in the soul, which changes all things and fills their inconstancy with light but though I seem to be driven out of my country as a misbeliever I have found no man yet with a faith like mine

Faithfully Yours
Jas A Joyce

W. B. YEATS to James Joyce, [?25 November 1902]

William Butler Yeats, 1865–1939, poet and playwright; James Joyce, novelist. After receiving Joyce's letter, Lady Gregory passed his request for help on to her friend Yeats, then living in London.

Tuesday   18 Woburn Buildings, Euston Road

My dear Joyce,

I have just heard from Lady Gregory about your plan of going to Paris to study. It seems that you leave Dublin Monday night, and cross to Paris Tuesday night. If I am right I hope you will breakfast with me on Tuesday morning. I shall set my alarm clock and be ready for you as soon as the train gets in. You can lie down on my sofa afterwards and sleep off the fatigue of the journey. You can dine with me and catch your Paris train afterwards. I hope you will come to me as I should like a good talk. I think you should let me give you one or two literary introductions here in London as you will find it much easier to get on in Paris (where perhaps a great many people do not want to learn English) if you do some writing, book reviews, poems etc. for the papers here. This kind of work never did anybody any harm. Your poems will bring you something at once, I should think. Yours sincerely

W B Yeats

PS. I could get 'The Speaker' I have little doubt to take verse from you and to give you a chance of doing some reviewing. I brought them a young man a while back, whom they look upon as one of their best writers and I have no doubt they will be quite ready to expect as good from you. But we can talk over these things.

LEO TOLSTOY to Percy Redfern, 23 February 1903

Count Leo Tolstoy, 1828–1910, novelist; Percy Redfern, secretary of the Manchester Tolstoy Society.

Yasnaya Polyana, 23 February 1903

Dear Percy Redfern,

I think your friend who is against books and reading is quite right.

Lao-Tzu says: true words are not pleasant, pleasant words are not true. The wise are not learned, the learned are not wise.

The Brahmanes say that in their books there are many predictions of times in which it will rain. But press those books as strongly as you can, you can not get out of them a drop of water. So you can not get out of all the books that contain the best precepts the smallest good deed.

Ruskin says that the best men, those which have done the greatest good to humanity, are those that we do not know of.

The chief difference between words and deeds is that words are always intended for men for their approbation, but deeds can be done only for God.

Though it is possible to utter words only with the intention to fulfill the will of God, it is very difficult not to think about the impression which they will produce on men and not to form them accordingly. But deeds you can do quite unknown to men, only for God. And such deeds are the greatest joy that a man can experience.

As to his plan to live amongst prostitutes and tramps . . . I can not say that I approve of it. Rather not. I think that to change one's habitual life for such a one a man must be quite sure to be proof against the new temptations that will assail him in this new life.

This refers also to your doubts about your life.

I think that the changes in our life must come from the impossibility to live otherwise than accordingly to the demands of our conscience but not from our mental resolution to try a new form of life.

I was glad to hear all what you write about your society and yourself and thank you for your letter.

Your friend Leo Tolstoy

ORVILLE WRIGHT to his father, 17 December [1903]

Orville Wright, 1871–1948, brother of Wilbur Wright, aviator; Milton Wright, their father, bishop of the United Brethren Church. This telegram announces the first successful powered flight, made at Kitty Hawk Sands the same day. The Western Union Telegraph Company clerk has given the wrong figure for the longest flight (it was 59 not 57 seconds) and misspelt Orville's name.

176 C KA CS 33 Paid.   Via Norfolk Va
Kitty Hawk N C Dec 17
Bishop M Wright

7 Hawthorne St

Success four flights thursday morning all against twenty one mile wind started from Level with engine power alone speed through air thirty one miles longest 57 second inform Press home Christmas.   Orevelle Wright   525F

JAMES JOYCE to Nora Barnacle, [*c.* 1 September 1904]

James Joyce, 1882–1941, novelist; Nora Barnacle, later his wife. Written on Joyce's return to Dublin at the time of his mother's death.

7 S. Peter's Terrace, Cabra, Dublin

Sweetheart I am in such high good humour this morning that I insist on writing to you whether you like it or not. I have no further news for you except that I told my sister about you last night. It was very amusing. I am going out in half an hour to see Palmieri who wants me to study music and I shall be passing your windows. I wonder will you be there. I also wonder if you are there will I be able to see you. Probably not.

What a lovely morning! That skull, I am glad to say, didn't come to torment me last night. How I hate God and death! How I like Nora! Of course you are shocked at these words, pious creature that you are.

I got up early this morning to finish a story I was writing. When I had written a page I decided I would write a letter to you instead. Besides, I thought you disliked Monday and a letter from me might put you in better spirits. When I am happy I have an insane wish to tell it to everyone I meet but I would be much happier if you gave me one of those chirruping kisses you are fond of giving me. They remind me of canaries singing.

I hope you haven't that horrible pain this morning. Go out and see old Sigerson and get him to prescribe for you. You will be sorry to hear that my grant-aunt is dying of stupidity. Please remember that I have *thirteen* letters of yours at present.

Be sure you give that dragoon's stays to Miss Murphy – and I think you might also make her a present of the dragoon's entire uniform. Why do you wear these cursed things? Did you ever see the men that go round with Guinness's cars, dressed in enormous frieze overcoats? Are you trying to make yourself like one of them?

But you are so obstinate, it is useless for me to talk. I must tell you about my nice brother, Stannie. He is sitting at the table ½-dressed reading a book and talking softly to himself 'Curse this fellow' – the writer of the book – 'Who in the devil's name said this book was good' 'The stupid fuzzy-headed fool!' 'I wonder are the English the stupidest race on God's earth' 'Curse this English fool' etc etc

Adieu, my dear simple-minded, excitable, deep-voiced, sleepy, impatient Nora. A hundred thousand kisses.

Jim

CHARLES WRIGHT to Sherlock Holmes, 18 November 1904

Charles Wright, autograph collector; Sherlock Holmes, detective. One of several letters written to Holmes after it had been announced that he was retiring to take up beekeeping.

18 November 1904   9 Eriswell Road, Worthing

Dear Sir,

I trust I am not trespassing too much on your time and kindness by asking for the favour of your autograph to add to my collection.

I have derived very much pleasure from reading your Memoirs, and should very highly value the possession of your famous signature.

Trusting you will see your way to thus honour me, and venturing to thank you very much in anticipation.

I am, Sir, Your obedient Servant.

Charles Wright

P.S. Not being aware of your present address. I am taking the liberty of sending this letter to Sir A. Conan Doyle, asking him to be good enough to forward it to you.

Sherlock Holmes Esq.

ISADORA DUNCAN to Gordon Craig, Christmas Day 1904

Isadora Duncan, 1878–1927, dancer; Edward Gordon Craig, theatre designer.
Pre-Revolutionary Russia still followed the Julian Calendar, then thirteen days
behind the Gregorian Calendar adopted by Western Europe. Isadora Duncan
later married the poet Sergei Esenin, who was staying in the same hotel –
possibly even the same room – when he committed suicide in 1925.

GRAND HOTEL D'EUROPE
ST. PÉTERSBOURG
RUE MICHEL

Just arrived this morning –
Christmas morning
>   Here its
>   the *12* of December

My Darling –
   I don't like it at *all*. All the Chairs are staring at me in the most frightful
way – And there is a Lady on the Mantel piece who has taken a Great
objection to me – & I'm awfully scared –
This is no place for a person with a nice cheerful disposition like me – it
looks like those parlors in the Novels where they plot things –
All night long the train has been not flying over but going pim de pim
over Great fields of snow – vast plains of snow – Great bare Countries
covered with snow (Walt [Whitman] could have written 'em up fine) and
over all this the Moon shining – & across the window always a Golden
shower of sparks – from the locomotive – it was quite worth seeing and I
lay there looking out on it all & thinking of you – of you you dearest
sweetest best darling –
The City is covered in snow & little sleighs rushing madly about – All
things go in sliders of course. I sent you many little missives along the way
– Hope they arrived! –
I must go now & wash the soot off & have my Breakfast.
I say this is a fine way to spend one's Christmas – They brought me first
into the Great Bridal Suite here but I stoutly refused to stay in it – These
rooms are hung in Dark Dark Green. It would be an awfully good sort of
place to indulge any disposition to suicide lingering in an odd corner of
one's disposition.
Give my love to Dear Dear No. 11 – and to that nice musty little dear
Home No. 6 and for your dear self my heart is overflowing with just the
most unoriginal old fashionedest sort of love.

Write to me –
& tell me –
I go now to splash

    Your
      Isadora

JAMES JOYCE to his brother Stanislaus, 7 December 1906

James Joyce, 1882–1941, novelist; Stanislaus, his brother, author of *My Brother's Keeper*. The clutch of initials at the end of the letter stand for G. K. Chesterton, George Bernard Shaw, Sidney Lee, editor of the *Dictionary of National Biography*, Henry James and Grant Richards, his reluctant publisher. The other initials stand for the *Daily Mail* and George Moore.

7 December 1906 Tuesday evg   Rome

Dear Stannie, Since Saturday last we have slept in the hotel but I think this is our last night there. After immense difficulty I have succeeded in getting a room and, if all goes well, we move in there tomorrow evening. This pleasant interlude has cost me about £25. – I spent all Sunday going up and down staircases and Nora and Georgie went about during the day, as witness a letter enclosed which an usher of the bank brought me in yesterday evening. Happily it was enclosed in an envelope. Item: a case for Mr Thomas Hardy.

Tomorrow night I will go over my MS and send it to John Long. There is a publisher in London, name of Sisley, Ltd. He publishes 'daring' work. I saw a review in the heel of a D.M. column of a book by E. Temple Thurston, called 'The Realist'. It was very daring and unpleasant, D.M. said, but showed unmistakeable talent. I have ordered it from England: it is a book of short stories. Do you think I did right? I was going to read Hardy through but I have changed over to Octave Mirbeau instead. I have ordered a Danish Berlitz book from Berlin. It will be published in January. In six months I ought to be able to read the Danish writers. I would like to read some of those at whom Ibsen hints in The Master Builder. One is named Nansen, I think. I wish I could go to Denmark. Ferrero says that Abo, Stockholm and Copenhagen are the finest cities in Europe. G.M. has rewritten *The Lake*. D.M. praises his

artistic conscience. 'Very few writers &c.' The Maunsel Press has emitted
some booklets, also: poems of Ella Young: and a young gentleman
whom you may remember standing white-faced outside McGarvey's has
published verses in praise of, I think, the Sacred Heart.

Wed. morn. I am sitting in the office. The winter has begun. There are
no stoves, fire or pipes. My hands are cold. I blow my nose every three
minutes. I have just read an advt in the paper wanted a manager for some
place, salary L100 a month. What a beautiful country! Your friend H.J.
ought to get a running kick in the arse for writing his tea-slop about it. I
am damnably sick of Italy, Italian and Italians, outrageously, illogically
sick. Every time a pupil asks me how I like Rome I vent some sneering
remark. I hate to think that Italians ever did anything in the way of art.
But I suppose they did. What did they do but illustrate a page or so of the
New Testament! They themselves think they have a monopoly in the
line. I am dead tired of their bello and bellezza. A clerk here is named (he
is round, bald, fat, voiceless) Bartoluzzi. You pronounce by inflating
both cheeks and prolonging the u. Every time I pass him I repeat his
name to myself and translate 'Good day, little bits of Barto'. Another is
named Simonetti: They are all little bits of something or other, I think.
This is my first experience of clerks: but do they all talk for 5 minutes
about the position &c of a penwiper? I think the Irish are the most
civilised people in Europe, be Jesus Christ I do: anyway they are the least
burocratic. From the foregoing drivel you can judge the state of my mind
in this country where 'they drink nice wine not horrid black porter.'
Useless: too cold: stick hands in pocket.

Thurs. morn. We are in our new quarters. Expected a letter from you
this morning here (bank). (Address at end of letter) Today after lunch I
shall go over my MS for John Long.

Frid morn. No letter from you yet. Our room is quite small: one bed:
we sleep 'lying opposed in opposite directions, the head of one towards
the tail of the other'. Blasphemed often while correcting MS. Stories
dreadfully dull. When I get home at 10 o'clock after the bank and school
and have taken my dinner I am so tired that I can barely skim over the
Avanti or a page of a novel before my eyelids are heavy with the sleep
men have named etc. To make up I get up about 7 o'c and go out and read
in a café. I am reading *Sebastien Roch* by Mirbeau. The beginning deals
with life in a Jesuit college. It must be difficult to succeed in France where
nearly everyone writes well. I should like to read Zola but have not the
heart to attack his twenty volume history of France. Who called Moore
the English Zola? I wonder: he must have had large powers of

comparison. I think I will read Mirbeau and Hardy together alternately. What are you doing in this line at present? It is a very dark cloudy day, drizzling rain. I wish some power would lift me as far as, say, Talbot Street and let me walk about for an hour or so and then lift me back again. My imagination is so weak that I am afraid all the things I was going to write about have become uncapturable images. It is 9.30. I would like to go asleep at present. My glasses annoy me. They are crooked and there is a flaw in both the glasses. It is a bloody nuisance to have to carry bits of glass in your eye. A moment ago I was leaning my head upon my hand and writing when the banker rushed past me. He said something to me which I did not catch. I jumped up and went to his desk obediently: I had not heard what he said. He repeated it, however, smiling, it was 'Diritto, Signor Joyce. Non è bello così.' They are a funny lot, these bankers. There are four in all, two brothers Schumacher and father and son Nast-Kolb, also a younger one. One of them is like Ben Jonson with a big belly, walks sideways, wears a cap on his head, blinks his eyes. The brother is a little man white-haired with a pen behind his ear. These are the Schumacher brothers. One of them is (the elder) is consul for Austria-Hungary. The other family consists of father, who is very old, and bandy legged, with thick white eyebrows. Every morning he patters in here, stops, looks about him, says good-morning, and patters out again. The son, the brisk person, is like Curran in manner and complexion. Yesterday they put down carpets here: everyone said they were beautiful (How I hate that word). I suppose it would be the height of impudence if I said I think they are somewhat 'common' people. Anyway they talked a lot about the carpet.

Letter just received. What I have told you about rooms is painfully correct. I don't know why we were given notice by the landlady nor do I know whether it was the reason you suggest. I don't know anything except that I suppose I ought to cease grumbling and take up the white man's burden. Do you imagine you are corresponding with the indifferential calculus that you object to my vituperation on Italy and Rome. What the hell would I do? If you had to traipse about a city, accompanied by a plaintive woman with infant (also plaintive), run up stairs, ring a bell, 'Chi c'è?' 'Camera' 'Chi c'è?' 'Camera!' No go: room too small or too dear: won't have children, single man only, no kitchen. 'Arrivederla!' Down again. Rush off: give a lesson for $9\frac{1}{2}$d, rush back to bank, etc etc. Am sending MS to John Long by same post. Didn't change anything. No pen, no ink, no table, no room, no time, no quiet, no inclination. Never mind, it will be back in a week or so. Only I stuck in 'bloody' before the late lamented. How I should enjoy a night on Venetian waters with Miss Farchi's romance and reality. The Italian imagination is like a cinematograph, observe the style of my letter. Wurruk is more dissipating than dissipation. Thanks for Whitman's poems. What long flowing lines he writes. Kick in the arse for the following. G.K.C: G.B.S: S.L: H.J: G.R. Kicks in the arse all round, in fact. Write at once. Sent paper Sunday. Not surprised: Italian Post. Write. Via Monte Brianzo 51 IV° Rome

Jim

Tomorrow is a holiday!
   ,,   ,,   ,, ,,   ,,
   ,,   ,,   ,, ,,   ,,!

Deo Gratias!
   ,,   ,, !
   ,,   ,, !

J. M. SYNGE to Molly Allgood, 22 May 1907

John Millington Synge, 1871–1909, playwright; Molly Allgood, actress, his fiancée.

[Glendalough House, Glenageary]
Wednesday evening (late) 22.5.07

Dearest Heart

This is no less than *my third* letter to you today. What do you say to me now?

It is a wonderfully still beautiful evening and I feel as if I ought to write verses but I haven't the energy. There is nearly a half moon, and I have been picturing in my mind how all our nooks and glens and rivers would look, if we were out among them as we should be! Do you ever think of them? Ever think of them I mean not as places that you've been to, but as places that are there still, with the little moon shining, and the rivers running, and the thrushes singing, while you and I, God help us, are far away from them. I used to sit over my sparks of fire long ago in Paris picturing glen after glen in my mind, and river after river – there are rivers like the Annamoe that I fished in till I knew every stone and eddy – and then one goes on to see a time when the rivers will be there and the thrushes, and we'll be dead surely. It makes one grudge every evening one spends dully in a town, what wouldn't I give to be out with you now in this rich twilight coming down from Rockbrook or Enniskerry with strange smells and sounds, and the first stars, and the wonderful air of Wicklow? Is there anything in the world to equal the joy if it? And you, my poor changling, have to go to Birmingham next week, and I, poor divil, amn't well enough to go out to far-away places for even solitary walks. Write a nice *intimate* letter the next time and tell me how your little mind is feeling in its wandering.

I wrote to Jack Yeats today to ask if I might go there. I wonder shall I like it, if I go. I'll leave this now to see if there is anything new in the morning.

> Thursday morning

Nothing new except an American Magazine with an account of the Irish writers – poor stuff enough. I am to go to the dentist today and see what he can do for me before I go away.

Write me a nice letter

> Your old
> Tramp

LEO TOLSTOY to Aylmer Maude, 3 November 1910

Count Leo Tolstoy, 1828–1910, novelist; Aylmer Maude, his English translator and biographer. This is Tolstoy's last literary composition. He had fled his family with three companions on 31 October 1910, boarding a train bound for the Caucasus. That evening he developed a high temperature and they got off the train at Astapovo. Tolstoy was then installed in the station master's house. He was joined on 2 November by his secretary Chertkov, to whom he began dictating this note in English the next day (Aylmer Maude had written inquiring about his health and promising to send a copy of his biography). Tolstoy was too weak to finish it, and died on 7 November.

> Astapovo, 3 November 1910

On my way to the place where I wished to be alone I was taken ill

ROBERT FROST to Susan Hayes Ward, 10 February 1912

Robert Frost, 1874–1963, poet; Susan Hayes Ward, literary editor of the New York *Independent*.

10 February 1912   Plymouth

Dear Miss Ward:–

You should receive almost simultaneously with this your long-lost Sweet Singer. I ought to say that I don't think I laughed at her as much as I should have if I had been a hearty normal person, and not something of a sweet singer myself. She is only a little more self-deceived than I am. That she was not altogether self-deceived I conclude from the lines in which she declares it her delight to compose on a sentimental subject when it comes into her mind just right. There speaks something authentic anyway.

Two lonely cross-roads that themselves cross each other I have walked several times this winter without meeting or overtaking so much as a single person on foot or on runners. The practically unbroken condition of both for several days after a snow or a blow proves that neither is much travelled. Judge then how surprised I was the other evening as I came down one to see a man, who to my own unfamiliar eyes and in the dusk looked for all the world like myself, coming down the other, his approach to the point where our paths must intersect being so timed that unless one of us pulled up we must inevitably collide. I felt as if I was going to meet my own image in a slanting mirror. Or say I felt as we slowly converged on the same point with the same noiseless yet laborious strides as if we were two images about to float together with the uncrossing of someone's eyes. I verily expected to take up or absorb this other self and feel the stronger by the addition for the three-mile journey home. But I didn't go forward to the touch. I stood still in wonderment and let him pass by; and that, too, with the fatal omission of not trying to find out by a comparison of lives and immediate and remote interests what could have brought us by crossing paths to the same point in the wilderness at the same moment of nightfall. Some purpose I doubt not, if we could but have made it out. I like a coincidence almost as well as an incongruity. Enclosed is another in print. The Marion C. Smith you were talking of when I was with you I was very certain I had heard of somewhere, but I didn't know where. It must have [been] here. Heard of her? Yes it is almost as if I had met her in the pages of the [Youth's] Companion.

Nonsensically yours   Robert Frost

CAPTAIN SCOTT to Sir George Egerton, [March 1912]

Robert Falcon Scott, 1868–1912, Antarctic explorer; Sir George Egerton, his naval sponsor. This is one of the letters found with Scott's body, after he had perished on his return from the South Pole.

My dear Sir George,

I fear we have shot our bolt – but we have been to Pole and done the longest journey on record.

I hope these letters may find their destination some day.

Subsidiary reasons of our failure to return are due to the sickness of different members of the party, but the real thing that has stopped us is the awful weather and unexpected cold towards the end of the journey.

This traverse of the Barrier has been quite three times as severe as any experience we had on the summit.

There is no accounting for it, but the result has thrown out my calculations, and here we are little more than 100 miles from the base and petering out.

Good-bye. Please see my widow is looked after as far as Admiralty is concerned.

R. Scott.

My kindest regards to Lady Egerton. I can never forget all your kindness.

CAPTAIN SCOTT to Mrs Bowers, [March 1912]

Robert Falcon Scott, 1868–1912, Antarctic explorer; Mrs Bowers, mother of 'Birdie' Bowers. This is another of the letters found with Scott's body. Bowers was one of the two companions who perished with him.

My dear Mrs. Bowers,

I am afraid this will reach you after one of the heaviest blows of your life.

I write when we are very near the end of our journey, and I am finishing it in company with two gallant, noble gentlemen. One of these is your son. He had come to be one of my closest and soundest friends, and I appreciate his wonderful upright nature, his ability and energy. As the troubles have thickened his dauntless spirit ever shone brighter and he has remained cheerful, hopeful, and indomitable to the end.

The ways of Providence are inscrutable, but there must be some reason why such a young, vigorous and promising life is taken.

My whole heart goes out in pity for you.

Yours,
R. Scott.

To the end he has talked of you and his sisters. One sees what a happy home he must have had and perhaps it is well to look back on nothing but happiness.

He remains unselfish, self-reliant and splendidly hopeful to the end, believing in God's mercy to you.

D. H. LAWRENCE to Mrs Hopkin, 2 June 1912

David Herbert Lawrence, 1885–1930, novelist and poet; Sallie Hopkin, feminist. Lawrence had fallen in love with Frieda Weekley, wife of his old professor at Nottingham, and eloped with her to Germany.

bei Professor Alf. Weber, Icking, bei München
2 June 1912

Dear Mrs Hopkin,

Although I haven't heard from you, I'll get a letter off to you, because to people I like, I always want to tell my good news. When I came to Germany I came with Mrs Weekley – went to Metz with her. Her husband knows all about it – but I don't think he will give her a divorce – only a separation. I wish he'd divorce her, so we could be married. But that's as it is.

I came down from the Rhine land to Munich last Friday week. Frieda met me there in Munich. She had been living with her sister in a village down the Isar valley, next village to this. We stayed in Munich a night, then went down to Beuerberg for eight days. Beuerberg is about 40 kilometres from Munich, up the Isar, near the Alps. This is the Bavarian Tyrol. We stayed in the Gasthaus zur Post. In the morning we used to have breakfast under the thick horse-chestnut trees, and the red and white flowers fell on us. The garden was on a ledge, high over the river, above the weir, where the timber rafts floated down. The Loisach – that's the river – is pale jade green, because it comes from glaciers. It is fearfully cold and swift. The people were all such queer Bavarians. Across from the inn, across a square full of horsechestnut trees, was the church and the convent, so peaceful, all whitewashed, except for the minaret of the church, which has a black hat. Everyday, we went out for a long, long time. There are flowers so many they would make you cry for joy – alpine flowers. – By the river, great hosts of globe flowers, that we call bachelor's buttons – pale gold great bubbles – then primulas, like mauve cowslips, somewhat – and queer marsh violets, and orchids, and lots of bell-flowers, like large, tangled, dark-purple harebells, and stuff like larkspur, very rich, and lucerne, so pink, and in the woods, lilies of the valley – oh, flowers, great wild mad profusion of them, everywhere. One day we went to a queer old play done by the peasants – this is the Ober Ammergau country. One day we went into the mountains, and sat, putting Friedas rings on our toes, holding our feet under the pale green water of a lake, to see how they looked. Then we go to Wolfratshausen where Frieda's sister has a house – like a châlet – on the hill above the white village. Else – Dr Jaffé-Richthofen – is rather beautiful, but different from Frieda – you see, she's aesthetic – rather lovely. She's married – but has a lover – a professor Weber of Heidelberg, such a jolly fellow. Her husband, also a professor, but at Munich, doesn't mind. He lives mostly in their Munich flat.

Now Frieda and I are living alone in Professor Weber's flat. It is the top story of this villa – quite small – four rooms beside kitchen. But there's a balcony, where we sit out, and have meals, and I write. Down below, is the road where the bullock wagons go slowly. Across the road the peasant women work in the wheat. Then the pale, milk-green river runs between the woods and the plain – then beyond, the mountains, range beyond range, and their tops glittering with snow.

I've just had to run into the kitchen – a jolly little place – wondering what Frieda was up to. She'd only banged her head on the cupboard. So we stood and looked out. Over the hills was a great lid of black cloud, and the mountains nearest went up and down in a solid blue-black. Through, was a wonderful gold space, with a tangle of pale, wonderful mountains, peaks pale gold with snow and farther and farther away – such a silent, glowing confusion brilliant with snow. Now the thunder is going at it, and the rain is here.

I love Frieda so much I don't like to talk about it. I never knew what love was before. She wanted me to write to you. I want you and her to be friends always. Some time perhaps she – perhaps we – shall need you. Then you'll be good to us, won't you?

The world is wonderful and beautiful and good beyond one's wildest imagination. Never, never, never could one conceive what love is, beforehand, never. Life *can* be great – quite god-like. It *can* be so. God be thanked I have proved it.

You might write to us here. Our week of honeymoon is over. Lord, it was lovely. But this – do I like this better? – I like it so much. Don't tell anybody. This is only for the good to know. Write to us.

D. H. Lawrence

G. K. CHESTERTON to his wife, [*c.* 1912]

Gilbert Keith Chesterton, 1874–1936, author; Frances, his wife. Chesterton was famous for his absent-mindedness. He sent this telegram to his wife after having set off from home to give a lecture in some Midland town.

Am in Market Harborough. Where ought I to be?

D. H. LAWRENCE to Arthur McLeod, 4 October 1912

David Herbert Lawrence, 1885–1930, novelist and poet; Arthur McLeod, former teaching colleague at Croydon. 'Paul Morel' was to become *Sons and Lovers*.

> Villa Igéa, *Villa di Gargnano*, Lago di Garda. Italy
> Friday. Oct 1912

Dear Mac,

Your books came today, your letter long ago. Now I am afraid I put you to a lot of trouble and expense, and feel quite guilty. But thanks a thousand times. And F[rieda] thanks you too.

I have read *Anna of the Five Towns* today, because it is stormy weather. For five months I have scarcely seen a word of English print, and to read it makes me feel fearfully queer. I don't know where I am. I am so used to the people going by outside, talking or singing some foreign language, always Italian now: but today, to be in Hanley, and to read almost my own dialect, makes me feel quite ill. I hate England and its hopelessness. I hate Bennett's resignation. Tragedy ought really to be a great kick at misery. But *Anna of the Five Towns* seems like an acceptance – so does all the modern stuff since Flaubert. I hate it. I want to wash again quick, wash off England, the oldness and grubbiness and despair.

Today it is so stormy. The lake is dark, and with white lambs all over it. The steamer rocks as she goes by. There are no sails stealing past. The vines are yellow and red, and fig trees are in flame on the mountains. I can't bear to be in England when I am in Italy. It makes me feel so soiled. Yesterday F and I went down along the lake towards Maderno. We climbed down from a little olive wood, and swam. It was evening, so weird, and a great black cloud trailing over the lake. And tiny little lights of villages came out, so low down, right across the water. Then great lightnings spilt out. – No, I don't believe England need be so grubby. What does it matter if one is poor, and risks ones livelihood, and reputation. One *can* have the necessary things, life, and love, and clean warmth. Why is England so shabby.

The Italians here sing. They are very poor, they buy two pennorth of butter and a pennorth of cheese. But they are healthy and they lounge about in the little square where the boats come up and nets are mended, like kings. And they go by the window proudly, and they don't hurry or fret. And the women walk straight and look calm. And the men adore children – they are glad of their children even if they're poor. I think they haven't many ideas, but they look well, and they have strong blood.

I go in a little place to drink wine near Bogliaco. It is the living room of the house. The father, sturdy as these Italians are, gets up from table and bows to me. The family is having supper. He brings me red wine to another table, then sits down again, and the mother ladles him soup from the bowl. He has his shirt sleeves rolled up and his shirt collar open. Then he nods and 'click-clicks' to the small baby, that the mother, young and proud, is feeding with soup from a big spoon. The grandfather, white moustached, sits a bit effaced by the father. A little girl eats soup. The grandmother by the big, open fire sits and quietly scolds another little girl. It reminds me so of home when I was a boy. They are all so warm with life. The father reaches his thick brown hand to play with the baby – the mother looks quickly away, catching my eye. Then he gets up to wait on me, and thinks my bad Italian can't understand that a quarter litre of wine is 15 centesimi (1¼d) – when I give him thirty. He doesn't understand tips. And the huge lot of figs for 20 centesimi.

Why can't you ever come? You could if you wanted to, at Christmas. Why not. We should love to have you, and it costs little. Why do you say I sark you about your letters? – I don't, they *are* delightful. I think I am going to Salò tomorrow and can get you some views of the lake there. I haven't got the proofs of my poems yet. It takes so long. Perhaps I will send you the MS of Paul Morel – I shall alter the title – when it's done.

Thanks – je te serre la main.   D. H. Lawrence

RUPERT BROOKE to Cathleen Nesbitt, 31 May [1913]

Rupert Brooke, 1887–1915, poet; Cathleen Nesbitt, actress.

Broadway Central Hotel,
New York
Saturday, 31 May
6–7 p.m.

We got into dock at 8.30 this morning, and then there was a lot of loitering about the luggage: and finally I got here. And it's a beastly hotel: and I'm in a beastly room over a cobbled street where there's the Hell of a noise; and I've been tramping this damned city all day, and riding in its cars (when they weren't too full); and it's hot; and I'm very tired and cross; and my pyjamas haven't come; and my letters of introduction, which I left behind *en masse*, haven't come; and nothing's come; and I don't know a soul in New York; and I'm *very* tired; and I don't like the food; and I don't like the people's faces; and I don't like the newspapers; and I haven't a friend in the world; and nobody loves me; and I'm going to be extraordinarily miserable these six months; and I want to die.

There!

Oh, it's Saturday evening, and if I were in England I might be lying on the sofa in Kensington, or on the floor in Gray's Inn, and my head in your lap, and your face bent down over mine, and your hands about my head, and my eyes shut, and I only feeling your hands going to and fro in my hair and your kind lips wandering over my face. And I'm here in a dirty room and lonely and tired and ill, and this won't get to you for ten days.

I'm crying. I want you. I don't want to be alone.

Rupert

BERNARD SHAW to the Hon. Mrs Alfred Lyttelton, 5 July 1913

George Bernard Shaw, 1856–1950, playwright; Edith Lyttelton, née Balfour, one of the 'Souls'. Alfred Lyttelton, MP, to whom Edith had been married for twenty-one years, had died that day following surgery necessitated, apparently, by his exertions ten days previously in a charity cricket match.

10 Adelphi Terrace WC
5th July 1913

My dear DD

So Alfred has the start of us by a few years. He might have waited for you; but I suppose he couldn't help himself. We get our marching orders; and off we must go, leaving our wives and all our luggage behind. He will be at a loss without you for a while, and will fret like a lost child; but he will be so popular that he will have to marry some pushing angel or another out of sheer goodnature, and annoy her from time to time by telling her, with a sigh, how nice DD could be without wings.

Dont order any black things. Rejoice in his memory; and be radiant: leave grief to the children. Wear violet and purple. Dying is a troublesome business: there is pain to be suffered, and it wrings one's heart; but death is a splendid thing – a warfare accomplished, a beginning all over again, a triumph. You can always see that in their faces.

Be patient with the poor people who will snivel: they dont know; and they think they will live for ever, which makes death a division instead of a bond. And let the children cry a little if they want to: it is natural.

And come and close *my* eyes too, when I die; and see me with my mask off as I really was. I almost envy him.

yours, dear DD, still marching on
G.B.S.

GEORGE V to Lord March, 26 July 1914

George V, 1865–1936, King of Great Britain and Ireland, Emperor of India; Lord March, son of the Duke of Richmond. It was George V's custom to visit Goodwood races every year. On 26 July the Admiralty cancelled all leave and bade the fleet stand by at Portsmouth; the same day the King had an interview with Prince Henry, the Kaiser's brother, on the subject of Britain's possible neutrality in the coming war.

Buckingham Palace
July 26th. 1914

My dear March

I very much regret to say that I find it is quite impossible for me to leave London tomorrow to pay you my promised visit at Goodwood which I had been so much looking forward to. The political crisis is so acute with regard to the Irish question & now the probability of a general European war necessitates my remaining in London for the present & I much fear I should not be able to leave until the end of the week. if then. I am sure you will understand how disappointed I am. I hope you will have fine weather & that the racing will [be] good.

Believe me very sincerely yours
George R. I.

BERTRAND RUSSELL to the Editor of the *Nation*, 12 August 1914

Bertrand Russell, third Earl Russell, 1872–1970, philosopher. War had been declared on 4 August.

Sir

Against the vast majority of my countrymen, even at this moment, in the name of humanity and civilization, I protest against our share in the destruction of Germany.

A month ago Europe was a peaceful comity of nations; if an Englishman killed a German, he was hanged. Now, if an Englishman kills a German, or if a German kills an Englishman, he is a patriot, who has deserved well of his country. We scan the newspapers with greedy eyes for news of slaughter, and rejoice when we read of innocent young men, blindly obedient to the word of command, mown down in thousands by the machine-guns of Liège. Those who saw the London crowds, during the night leading up to the Declaration of War saw a whole population, hitherto peaceable and humane, precipitated in a few days down the steep slope to primitive barbarism, letting loose, in a moment, the instincts of hatred and blood lust against which the whole fabric of society has been raised. 'Patriots' in all countries acclaim this brutal orgy as a noble determination to vindicate the right; reason and mercy are swept away in one great flood of hatred; dim abstractions of unimaginable wickedness – Germany to us and the French, Russia to the Germans – conceal the simple fact that the enemy are men, like ourselves, neither better nor worse – men who love their homes and the sunshine, and all the simple pleasures of common lives; men now mad with terror in the thought of their wives, their sisters, their children, exposed, with our help, to the tender mercies of the conquering Cossack.

And all this madness, all this rage, all this flaming death of our civilization and our hopes, has been brought about because a set of official gentlemen, living luxurious lives mostly stupid, and all without imagination or heart, have chosen that it should occur rather than that any one of them should suffer some infinitesimal rebuff to his country's pride. No literary tragedy can approach the futile horror of the White Paper. The diplomatists, seeing from the first the inevitable end, mostly wishing to avoid it, yet drifted from hour to hour of the swift crisis, restrained by punctilio from making or accepting the small concessions that might have saved the world, hurried on at last by blind fear to loose the armies for the work of mutual butchery.

And behind the diplomats, dimly heard in the official documents, stand vast forces of national greed and national hatred – atavistic instincts, harmful to mankind at its present level, but transmitted from savage and half-animal ancestors, concentrated and directed by Governments and the Press, fostered by the upper class as a distraction from social discontent, artificially nourished by the sinister influence of the makers of armaments, encouraged by a whole foul literature of 'glory', and by every text-book of history with which the minds of children are polluted.

England, no more than other nations which participate in this war, can be absolved either as regards its national passions or as regards its diplomacy.

For the past ten years, under the fostering care of the Government and a portion of the Press, a hatred of Germany has been cultivated and a fear of the German Navy. I do not suggest that Germany has been guiltless; I do not deny that the crimes of Germany have been greater than our own. But I do say that whatever defensive measures were necessary should have been taken in a spirit of calm foresight, not in a wholly needless turmoil of panic and suspicion. It is this deliberately created panic and suspicion that produced the public opinion by which our participation in the war has been rendered possible.

Our diplomacy, also, has not been guiltless. Secret arrangements, concealed from Parliament and even (at first) from almost all the Cabinet, created, in spite of reiterated denials, an obligation suddenly revealed when the war fever had reached the point which rendered public opinion tolerant of the discovery that the lives of many, and the livelihood of all, had been pledged by one man's irresponsible decisions. Yet, though France knew our obligations, Sir E. Grey refused, down to the last moment, to inform Germany of the conditions of our neutrality or of our intervention. On August 1st he reports as follows a conversation with the German Ambassador (No. 123):

'He asked me whether, if Germany gave a promise not to violate Belgian neutrality, we would engage to remain neutral. I replied that I could not say that; our hands were still free, and we were considering what our attitude should be. All I could say was that our attitude would be determined largely by public opinion here, and that the neutrality of Belgium would appeal very strongly to public opinion here. I did not think that we could give a promise of neutrality on that condition alone.

The Ambassador pressed me as to whether I could not formulate conditions on which we would remain neutral. He even suggested that the integrity of France and her colonies might be guaranteed. I said I felt obliged to refuse definitely any promise to remain neutral on similar terms, and I could only say that we must keep our hands free.'

It thus appears that the neutrality of Belgium, the integrity of France and her colonies, and the naval defence of the northern and western coasts of France, were all mere pretexts. If Germany had agreed to our demands in all these respects, we should still not have promised neutrality.

I cannot resist the conclusion that the Government has failed in its duty to the nation by not revealing long-standing arrangements with the French, until, at the last moment, it made them the basis of an appeal to honour; that it has failed in its duty to Europe by not declaring its attitude at the beginning of the crisis; and that it has failed in its duty to humanity by not informing Germany of conditions which would insure its non-participation in a war which, whatever its outcome, must cause untold hardship and the loss of many thousands of our bravest and noblest citizens.

Yours, etc.

August 12, 1914   Bertrand Russell

D. H. LAWRENCE to Lady Cynthia Asquith, 30 January 1915

David Herbert Lawrence, 1885–1930, novelist and poet; Lady Cynthia Asquith, the Prime Minister's daughter-in-law.

Greatham, Pulborough, Sussex.
Sunday 30 Jan 1915

Dear Lady Cynthia,

We were very glad to hear from you. I wanted to send you a copy of my stories at Christmas, then I didn't know how the war had affected you – I knew Herbert Asquith was joined – and I thought you'd rather be left alone, perhaps.

We have no history, since we saw you last. I feel as if I had less than no history – as if I had spent those five months in the tomb. And now, I feel very sick and corpse-cold, too newly risen to share yet with anybody, having the smell of the grave in my nostrils, and a feel of grave clothes about me.

The War finished me: it was the spear through the side of all sorrows and hopes. I had been walking in Westmoreland, rather happy, with water-lilies twisted round my hat – big, heavy, white and gold water-lilies that we found in a pool high up – and girls who had come out on a spree and who were having tea in the upper room of an inn shrieked with laughter. And I remember also we crouched under the loose wall on the moors and the rain flew by in streams, and the wind came rushing through the chinks in the wall behind one's head – and we shouted songs, and I imitated music hall turns, whilst the other men crouched under the wall and I pranked in the rain on the turf in the gorse, and Kotilianski groaned Hebrew music – Ranani Sadekim Badanoi.

It seems like another life – we *were* happy – four men. Then we came down to Barrow in Furness, and saw that war was declared. And we all went mad. I can remember soldiers kissing on Barrow station, and a woman shouting defiantly to her sweetheart 'When you get at 'em, Clem, let 'em have it', as the train drew off – and in all the tram-cars 'War'. – Messrs Vickers Maxim call in their workmen – and the great notices on Vickers' gateways – and the thousands of men streaming over the bridge. Then I went down the coast a few miles. And I think of the amazing sunsets over flat sands and the smoky sea – then of sailing in a fisherman's boat, running in the wind against a heavy sea – and a French onion boat in with her sails set splendidly, in the morning sunshine – and the electric suspense everywhere – and the amazing, vivid, visionary beauty of everything, heightened up by immense pain everywhere.

And since then, since I came back, things have not existed for me. I have spoken to no one, I have touched no one, I have seen no one. All the while, I swear, my soul lay in the tomb – not dead, but with the flat stone over it, a corpse, become corpse cold. And nobody existed, because I did not exist myself. Yet I was not dead – only passed over – trespassé. And all the time I knew I should have to rise again.

Now I am feeble and half alive. On the downs on Friday I opened my eyes again, and saw it was daytime. And I saw the sea lifted up and shining like a blade with the sun on it. And high up, in the icy wind, an aeroplane flew towards us from the land – and the men ploughing, and the boys in the fields on the tablelands, and the shepherds, stood back from their work and lifted their faces. And the aeroplane was small and high in the thin, ice cold wind. And the birds became silent and dashed to cover, afraid of the noise. And the aeroplane floated high out of sight. And below, on the level earth away down, were floods and stretches of snow – And I knew I was awake. But as yet my soul is cold and shaky and earthy.

I dont feel so hopeless now I am risen. My heart has been as cold as a lump of dead earth, all this time, because of the war. But now I don't feel so dead. I feel hopeful. I couldn't tell you how fragile and tender the hope is – the new shoot of life. But I feel hopeful now about the war. We shall all rise again from this grave – though the killed soldiers will have to wait for the Last Trump.

There is my autobiography – written because you ask me, and because, being risen from the dead, I know we shall all come through, rise again and walk healed and whole and new, in a big inheritance, here on earth.

It sounds preachy, but I dont quite know how to say it.

Viola Meynell has lent us this rather beautiful cottage. We are quite alone. It is at the foot of the downs. I wish you would come and see us, and stay a day or two. It is quite comfortable – there is hot water and a bathroom, and two spare bedrooms. I dont know when we shall be able to come to London. We are too poor for excursions. But we *should* like to see you, and it *is* nice here.

auf wiedersehen   D. H. Lawrence

HENRY JAMES to W. B. Yeats, 25 August 1915

Henry James, 1843–1916, novelist; W. B. Yeats, poet. Yeats had contributed a poem, 'A Reason for Keeping Silent' (later called 'On Being Asked for a War Poem') to an anthology edited by James's friend, the novelist Edith Wharton. This letter Yeats gave to his friend Lady Gregory and later incorporated its central image into this poem 'In Memory of Major Robert Gregory', her son (see Introduction).

Telephone 2417 Kensington

21 Carlyle Mansions
Cheyne Walk
S.W.

August 25th
1915

My Dear Yeats,
   I rejoice to hear that you have kindly sent everything to Mrs. Wharton, who will value your extell (or whatever the proper name of your cluster of rhymes may be) in a high & grateful degree. The great thing is that you shldn't. be absent – & happy you poets who can be present & *so* present by a simple flicker of your genius, & not, like the clumsier race, have to lay a train & pile up faggots that may not after prove in the least combustible!
   I infer from your address that you may be able very kindly to recall me to the indulgent recollection of Lady Gregory. If you can tell her from me with what a special tenderness of felicity & sympathy I thought of her a while back – and still think of her, you will greatly serve
                    yours & hers most truly
                    Henry James

WALLACE STEVENS to his wife, 19 July 1916

Wallace Stevens, 1879–1955, poet; Elsie Kachel Stevens, his wife.

<u>Eminent Vers Libriste</u>
     <u>Arrives in Town</u>
<u>Details of Reception</u>

St Paul, Minn. July 19, 1916. Wallace Stevens, the playwright and barrister, arrived at Union Station, at 10.30 o'clock this morning. Some thirty representatives of the press were not present to greet him. He proceeded on foot to the Hotel St. Paul, where they had no room for him. Thereupon, carrying an umbrella and two mysterious looking bags, he proceeded to Minnesota Club, 4th & Washington-Streets, St. Paul where he will stay while he is in St. Paul. At the Club, Mr. Stevens took a shower-bath and succeeded in flooding not only the bath-room floor but the bed-room floor as well. He used all the bath-towels in mopping up the mess and was obliged to dry himself with a wash-cloth. From the Club, Mr. Stevens went down-town on business. When asked how he liked St. Paul, Mr. Stevens, borrowing a cigar, said, 'I like it.'

Dear Bud:
      The above clipping may be of interest to you. Note my address. I am waiting for some papers to be typed – ah! Give my best to the family.

With love,
Wallace

ROBERT GRAVES to Eddie Marsh, 7 August 1916

Robert von Ranke Graves, 1895–1985, author; Sir Edward Marsh, Secretary to Winston Churchill, promoter of the Georgian poets. Graves had been severely wounded on the Western Front and his family notified of his death. He had earlier submitted to an operation on his nose so that he could wear a new type of gas helmet.

7 August 1916

My dear Eddie,
    If I wasn't such a desperately honest chap I'd cover my wickedness by swearing that I'd written to you and that someone had forgotten to post the letter – but what really happened was I started writing then stopped because I was waiting to give you a bit of news which didn't arrive, then forgot and imagined I'd written. Such millions and billions and squadrillions of letters came condoling, inquiring, congratulating – I never knew I had so many friends. Mostly rather tedious. But three lovely ones today, the first from old Siegfried (whom by the way I always call 'Sassons' since Tommy was killed: he invented it) at Oxford and he's coming to see me in a week (Eddie, what *is* a spot on the lung? A wound, or tubercle or what?) and as I'm going to be able to travel in 'a week or ten days', the medico says, I'm going to lug him up to Harlech (I hope you liked the Harlech part of the Caucasus letter: I wrote it within 50 yards of the dead Bosche in Mametz Wood!) and we'll have high old primitive times together.

By the way, Mark Gertler would paint the Bosche so well: do ask him sometime.

To resume, next was your letter which I'm endeavouring to answer in a manner that will show my appreciation. Next, a wonderful composition from dear old Ralph Rooper starting: 'Oh my dear, dear Lazarus'; he has also been mourning me for a week. It's awfully jolly to have such friends: I'd go through it all again for those three letters I got today; straight I would.

I never knew S.S. was in England. I'm so relieved he's out of it.

I've had ridiculously little pain, the worst being when they tear the sticking plaster that holds my leg bandage in position . . . off the hairy part of my leg.

I had an immensely uncomfortable journey down to Rouen because they wouldn't risk tipping me off a stretcher onto a bed and a stretcher is agony after the first few minutes – no support for your back, if you can understand. Also, I sneezed by mistake this afternoon which was most painful. But I've not had a thousandth part of what I suffered when they cut my nose about at Millbank: that made this a beanfeast by contrast.

As a matter of fact, I did die on my way down to the Field Ambulance and found myself just crossing Lethe by ferry. I had only just time to put on my gas-helmet to keep off the fumes of forgetfulness but managed it and on arrival at the other side began to feel much better. To cut short a long story, old Rhadamanthus introduced himself as my judge but I refused to accept his jurisdiction. I wanted a court-martial of British officers: he was only a rotten old Greek. He shouted out: 'Contempt of Court' but I chucked a Mills bomb at him which scattered the millions of the mouthless dead in about two seconds and wounded old R. in the leg and broke his sceptre. Then I strode away, held a revolver to Charon's head, climbed into the boat and so home. I gave him a Rouen note for 50 cm. which I didn't want particularly. Remained Cerberus whose three heads were, I noticed, mastiff, dalmatian and dachshund. He growled furiously and my revolver was empty, and I'd no ammunition. Happy thought: honeyed cakes and poppy seed. But none was handy; however, I had an excellent substitute – Army biscuit smeared with Tickler's 'plum and apple' and my little morphia tablets carefully concealed in the appetizing conserve. He snapped, swallowed, slumbered. I tiptoed past him, a free man and found myself being lowered on the floor of the 99th Field Ambulance. The doctor was saying 'hopeless case' (and this part of the tale is true, truer even than the rest) and I winked at him and said 'dear old doctor' and went off again to sleep.

My sense of humour may have been enfeebled but I laughed till I was nearly ill yesterday over 100 copy lines which a Charterhouse master told my brother to write the other day, to the effect that he mustn't be a baby. I can't reproduce the original exactly, but the result was ludicrous and more so as it was written in the very choicest copper-plate handwriting. It went something like this for eight pages:

I must endeavour to emerge from my present phase of infantility.
The symptoms of babyhood must be eradicated from my composition.
It behoves me to comport myself in a manner less typical of extreme juvenility.
I am bound by a moral obligation to rid myself of the characteristics of a youthful and childish baby.
I must not be a baby. Oh God, save me from shrinking smaller and smaller, from boyhood to babydom and finally from vanishing completely away, etc., etc.

Don't you love the 'youthful and childish baby'? It has a wonderful naiveté about it. Is the thing so funny because it was shown up to a master, or what?

I'm longing to see you on Saturday. Try to bring Ivor Novello with you. I'd love to meet him, if he wouldn't be bored and you, busy man, could kill two birds with one stone by coming up and back with him.

Peter has promised thro' my brother to act on my suggestion and write his folk a tragic letter of cold pathos and reproach about my death for my country and the way they've treated him and me. He'll do it well; he's an artist. Charterhouse is at Camp on the Plain now.

I'm afraid, great as is the love I bear you, Jane Austen is too hard a nut to attempt to bite at with these weak jaws. Thanks awfully tho'. I have my Sorley here: he's my chief standby.

I see in the *Mail* today that a damnably nasty German cousin of mine has been killed flying. I remember once my sister in her young enthusiasm told him: 'Oh Wilhelm, what a lovely squirrel.' Up went his rifle and the squirrel fell dead at her feet. He couldn't understand her tears of rage. She'd admired the squirrel: he'd got it for her and was prepared to skin it then and there for her.

The brute used to climb up the only greengage tree in the orchard (this was Bavaria) and throw us down the stones. How I hated him! I was too young to climb trees myself.

I hope to hear from Ruth Mallory soon about George: I wrote to her yesterday. I've not heard a word since he left Havre.

I'm looking forward to Arthur Parry's letter.

Now goodbye till Saturday. I must write to Ralph ere they dout my light.

Ever yours affectionately   Robert

Funny that in 'The Queer Time' I should have talked about 'clutching at my right breast': it's just what I did on the 20th July!

SIEGFRIED SASSOON to Robert Graves, 19 October [1917]

Siegfried Sassoon, 1886–1967, poet and prose writer; Robert Graves, author. Sassoon had made a public protest against the war in July, and soon after was sent to Craiglockhart War Hospital for shell-shocked officers. At Craiglockhart he wrote some of his finest war poems and formed a friendship with Wilfred Owen, a fellow inmate, whose work he encouraged and brought to the attention of Graves and others.

19 October   Craiglockhart

Dearest Robert, I am so glad you like Owen's poem. I will tell him to send you on any decent stuff he does. His work is very unequal, and you can help him a great deal.

Seeing you again has made me more restless than ever. My position here is nearly unbearable, and the feeling of isolation makes me feel rotten. I had a long letter from Cotterill to-day. They had just got back to rest from Polygon Wood and he says the conditions and general situation are more bloody than anything he has yet seen. Three miles of morasses, shell-holes and dead men and horses through which to get the rations up. I should like the people who write leading articles for the *Morning Post* (about victory) to read his letter.

I have told Rivers that I will go back to France if they will send me (making it quite clear that my views are exactly the same as in July — only more so).

They will have to give me a written guarantee that I shall be sent back at once. I don't quite understand how it is that Rivers can do nothing but pass me for General Service as he says, because I am in the same condition as I was three months ago, and if I am fit for General Service now, I was fit then.

He says I've got a very strong 'anti-war' complex, whatever that means. I should like the opinion of a first-class 'alienist' or whatever they call the blokes who decide if people are dotty. However we shall see what they say. Personally I would rather be anywhere than here.

It's too b....y to think of poor old Joe [Cotterill] lying out all night in shell-holes and being shelled (several of the ration-party were killed) but, as he says, 'the Battalion got their rations'. What a man he is.

O Robert, what ever will happen to end the war? It's all very well for you to talk about 'good form' and acting like a 'gentleman'. To me that's a very estimable form of suicidal stupidity and credulity. You admit that the people who sacrifice the troops are callous b.....rs, and the same thing is happening in all countries (except some of Russia). If you had real courage you wouldn't acquiesce as you do.

Yours ever   Sassons

WILFRED OWEN to his mother, 31 December 1917

Wilfred Owen, 1893–1918, poet; Susan, his mother. Most of the poems for which Owen is remembered were written between the summer of 1917 and the autumn of the following year.

31 December 1917   Scarborough

My own dear Mother,

Just a short note to thank you for the message enclosed with forwarded letters. I guess you saw the Cards, from Johnny & Bobby; characteristic cards: pictures of monkeys & the motto: 'Times change, & we with Time, but not in ways of Friendship.' So they are unchanged – from the old shallow waggery, and the old deep affection. I haven't written to them since my arrival in England.

The other letter was from my *cher ami* in Bordeaux who, unlike Raoul, persists in his expressions of fidelity. What I taught him of English has got him a post as Interpreter to the <u>American</u> Y.M.C.A. at Bordeaux. (*verb. sap.*) I think Bordeaux is first on my post-war Visiting List. Many & various, strange & multitudinous are the friends that befriend me in this world. Yet I never found one false, or that did not surpass me in some virtue.

Some are very young, and some are already old, but none are middling.

And there are no dogs among my friends.

No dogs, no sorcerers, nor the other abominations on that list. For I have been bitten by the dogs of the world; and I have seen through the sorceries and the scarlet garments.

And so I have come to the true measure of man.

I am not dissatisfied with my years. Everything has been done in bouts:

Bouts of awful labour at Shrewsbury & Bordeaux; bouts of amazing pleasure in the Pyrenees, and play at Craiglockhart; bouts of religion at Dunsden; bouts of horrible danger on the Somme; bouts of poetry always; of your affection always; of sympathy for the oppressed always.

I go out of this year a Poet, my dear Mother, as which I did not enter it. I am held peer by the Georgians; I am a poet's poet.

I am started. The tugs have left me; I feel the great swelling of the open sea taking my galleon.

Last year, at this time, (it is just midnight, and now is the intolerable instant of the Change) last year I lay awake in a windy tent in the middle of a vast, dreadful encampment. It seemed neither France nor England, but a kind of paddock where the beasts are kept a few days before the shambles. I heard the revelling of the Scotch troops, who are now dead, and who knew they would be dead. I thought of this present night, and whether I should indeed – whether we should indeed – whether you would indeed – but I thought neither long nor deeply, for I am a master of elision.

But chiefly I thought of the very strange look on all faces in that camp; an incomprehensible look, which a man will never see in England, though wars should be in England; nor can it be seen in any battle. But only in Étaples.

It was not despair, or terror, it was more terrible than terror, for it was a blindfold look, and without expression, like a dead rabbit's.

It will never be painted, and no actor will ever seize it. And to describe it, I think I must go back and be with them.

We are sending seven officers straight out tomorrow.

I have not said what I am thinking this night, but next December I will surely do so.

I know what you are thinking, and you know me   Wilfred.

FATHER McCANN to Lady Grizel Hamilton, 1 April 1918

The Revd Isidore McCann, army chaplain; Lady Grizel Hamilton, widow of the Hon. Ralph Hamilton, Master of Belhaven. Hamilton lies buried in the Roman Catholic cemetery at Rouvrel in the Somme.

1st April 1918

Dear Lady Hamilton,
It is with deep regret that I have to communicate to you the sad death of your dear husband, who was killed yesterday at 12.25am by shell-fire. It came as a terrible blow to every one of us, but God knows the blow will be more terrible for you.

As far as his spiritual welfare is concerned, I have not the least fear, because he was indeed a good soul. I buried him last night, and the officers that could be spared came to the burial. This morning I arranged the grave and put some flowers on it, encircled with a little crown, for indeed he has well merited his crown, only a more glorious one.

Well, dear Lady Hamilton, I need not say that I shall never forget him in my Holy Mass, and also a little prayer for you, that God may give you strength to bear this terrible heavy cross.

I will obtain a photograph of the grave from the War Office. I am sure you would like it – that is, if we can possibly get it; circumstances may make it well-nigh impossible for the time being.

When I come on leave, I should like very much to call and see you. I come in May for a month's leave, if things are quiet by then.

Well, dear Lady Hamilton, kindly accept my deepest sympathy in this terrible loss of your dear husband and my old friend. May God bless and protect you and give you strength to bear this terrible blow. Please say a little prayer for me now and again.
I remain dear Lady Hamilton,
Your sincerely,
Rev Isidore McCann, O.F.M., C.F
H.Q. 106 Bds., R.F.A., B.E.F.

WALLACE STEVENS to Harriet Monroe, 8 April [1918]

Wallace Stevens, 1879–1955, poet; Harriet Monroe, founder of *Poetry: A Magazine of Verse.*

Hartford, April 8.

Dear Miss Monroe:
   I've had the blooming horrors, following my gossip about death, at your house. I have not known just what to do. I had hoped to set things right, personally; but find that I am not likely to see you in Chicago for some little time. Accordingly, so that you may not think I am unconscious of the thing, nor indifferent, I write this to let you know that I have been sincerely regretful and hope that you and your family will forgive me. The subject absorbs me, but that is no excuse: there are too many

people in the world, vitally involved, to whom it is infinitely more than a thing to think of. One forgets this. I wish with all my heart that it had never occurred, even carelessly.

Very truly yours,
Wallace Stevens

WILFRED OWEN to his mother, 31 October [1918]

Wilfred Owen, 1893–1918, poet; Susan, his mother. This is Owen's last letter: he was killed four days afterwards while crossing the Sambre Canal. The war ended a week later.

Thurs. 31 October 6.15 p.m.

Dearest Mother,

I will call the place from which I'm now writing 'The Smoky Cellar of the Forester's House'. I write on the first sheet of the writing pad which came in the parcel yesterday. Luckily the parcel was small, as it reached me just before we moved off to the line. Thus only the paraffin was unwelcome in my pack. My servant & I ate the chocolate in the cold middle of last night, crouched under a draughty Tamboo, roofed with planks. I husband the Malted Milk for tonight, & tomorrow night. The handkerchief & socks are most opportune, as the ground is marshy, & I have a slight cold!

So thick is the smoke in this cellar that I can hardly see by a candle 12 ins. away, and so thick are the inmates that I can hardly write for pokes, nudges & jolts. On my left the Coy. Commander snores on a bench: other officers repose on wire beds behind me. At my right hand, Kellett, a delightful servant of A Coy. in <u>The Old Days</u> radiates joy & contentment from pink cheeks and baby eyes. He laughs with a signaller, to whose left ear is glued the Receiver; but whose eyes rolling with gaiety shows that he is listening with his right ear to a merry corporal, who appears at this distance away (some three feet) nothing [but] a gleam of white teeth & a wheeze of jokes.

Splashing my hand, an old soldier with a walrus moustache peels & drops potatoes into the pot. By him, Keyes, my cook, chops wood; another feeds the smoke with the damp wood.

It is a great life. I am more oblivious than alas! yourself, dear Mother, of the ghastly glimmering of the guns outside, & the hollow crashing of the shells.

There is no danger down here, or if any, it will be well over before you read these lines.

I hope you are as warm as I am; as serene in your room as I am here; and that you think of me never in bed as resignedly as I think of you always in bed. Of this I am certain you could not be visited by a band of friends half so fine as surround me here.

Ever Wilfred x

BERNARD SHAW to Sylvia Beach, 10 October 1921

George Bernard Shaw, 1856–1950, playwright; Sylvia Beach, proprietor of the Shakespeare & Co Bookshop, Paris. Joyce's *Ulysses* had been published by Sylvia Beach on 2 February.

10 October 1921   10 Adelphi Terrace, London, W.C.2

Dear Madam, I have read several fragments of *Ulysses* in its serial form. It is a revolting record of a disgusting phase of civilisation; but it is a truthful one; and I should like to put a cordon round Dublin; round up every male person in it between the ages of 15 and 30; force them to read it; and ask them whether on reflection they could see anything amusing in all that foul mouthed, foul minded derision and obscenity. To you, possibly, it may appeal as art: you are probably (you see I don't know you) a young barbarian beglamoured by the excitements and enthusiasms that art stirs up in passionate material; but to me it is all hideously real: I have walked those streets and known those shops and have heard and taken part in those conversations. I escaped from them to England at the age of twenty; and forty years later have learnt from the books of Mr. Joyce that Dublin is still what it was, and young men are still drivelling in slackjawed blackguardism just as they were in 1870. It is, however, some consolation to find that at last somebody has felt deeply enough about it to face the horror of writing it all down and using his literary genius to force people to face it. In Ireland they try to make a cat cleanly by rubbing its nose in its own filth. Mr. Joyce has tried the same treatment on the human subject. I hope it may prove successful.

I am aware that there are other qualities and other passages in *Ulysses*: but they do not call for any special comment from me.

I must add, as the prospectus implies an invitation to purchase, that I am an elderly Irish gentleman, and that if you imagine that any Irishman, much less an elderly one, would pay 150 francs for a book, you little know my countrymen. Faithfully,

G. Bernard Shaw

DORA CARRINGTON to Gerald Brenan, undated

Dora Carrington, 1892–1932, painter; Gerald Brenan, author. '

> A BaD, CoLd
>   DuLL letter
> But we live in a
>   BaD DuLL coLD
>   climate
> and I've a cold, Bad, DuLL character
>
>   oh to be my Persian cat
>   lying snug upon the mat

A. E. HOUSMAN to Grant Richards, 14 October 1922

Alfred Edward Housman, 1859–1936, poet and classicist; Grant Richards, his publisher. The first edition in question is of his *Last Poems*, a sequel to *A Shropshire Lad*.

No, don't put in an errata slip. The blunder will probably enhance the value of the 1st edition in the eyes of bibliophiles, an idiotic class.

Yrs
A. E. Housman

14 Oct. 1922   Trin. Coll. Camb.

VIRGINIA WOOLF to Gwen Raverat, 11 March [1925]

Virginia Woolf, 1882–1941, novelist; Gwen Raverat, wood engraver, author of *Period Piece*. Gwen Raverat's husband Jacques had been suffering from a long and painful illness, and Virginia Woolf had taken the, for her, unprecedented step of sending him proofs of her unpublished novel, *Mrs Dalloway*. These were read to him by Gwen, and Jacques dictated a letter of appreciation which, Virginia Woolf recorded in her diary, 'gave me one of the happiest days of my life'. It arrived with the letter announcing his death.

52 Tavistock Square, W.C.1

11th March
Dearest Gwen,

Your and Jacques' letters came yesterday, and I go about thinking of you both in starts, and almost constantly underneath everything, and I don't know what to say. The thing that comes over and over is the strange wish I have to go on telling Jacques things. This is for Jacques, I say to myself; I want to write to him about happiness, about Rupert [Brooke], and love. It had become to me a sort of private life, and I believe I told him more than anyone, except Leonard; I become mystical as I grow older and feel an alliance with you and Jacques which is eternal, not interrupted, or hurt by never meeting. Then of course, I have now for you – how can I put it? – I mean the feeling that one must reverence? – is that the word – feel shy of, so tremendous an experience; for I cannot conceive what you have suffered. It seems to me that if we met, one would have to chatter about every sort of little trifle, because there is nothing to be said.

And then, being, as you know, so fundamentally an optimist, I want to make you enjoy life. Forgive me, for writing what comes into my head. I think I feel that I would give a great deal to share with you the daily happiness. But you know that if there is anything I could ever give you, I would give it, but perhaps the only thing to give is to be oneself with people. One could say anything to Jacques. And that will always be the same with you and me. But oh, dearest Gwen, to think of you is making me cry – why should you and Jacques have had to go through this? As I told him, it is your love that has forever been love to me – all those years ago, when you used to come to Fitzroy Square, I was so angry and you were so furious, and Jacques wrote me a sensible manly letter, which I answered, sitting at my table in the window. Perhaps I was frightfully jealous of you both, being at war with the whole world at the moment. Still, the vision has become to me a source of wonder – the vision of your face; which if I were painting I should cover with flames, and put you on a hill top. Then, I don't think you would believe how it moves me that you and Jacques should have been reading Mrs Dalloway, and liking it. I'm awfully vain I know; and I was on pins and needles about sending it to Jacques; and now I feel exquisitely relieved; not flattered: but one does want that side of one to be acceptable – I was going to have written to Jacques about his children, and about my having none – I mean, these efforts of mine to communicate with people are partly childlessness, and the horror that sometimes overcomes me.

There is very little use in writing this. One feels so ignorant, so trivial, and like a child, just teasing you. But it is only that one keeps thinking of you, with a sort of reverence, and of that adorable man, whom I loved.

Yours,
V.W.

ERNEST HEMINGWAY to F. Scott Fitzgerald, 1 July 1925

Ernest Hemingway, 1899–1961, novelist; F. Scott Fitzgerald, novelist.

Burguete, Spain, 1 July 1925

Dear Scott:

We are going in to Pamplona tomorrow. Been trout fishing here. How are you? And how is Zelda?

I am feeling better than I've ever felt – havent drunk anything but wine since I left Paris. God it has been wonderful country. But you hate country. All right omit description of country. I wonder what your idea of heaven would be – A beautiful vacuum filled with wealthy mono-gamists, all powerful and members of the best families all drinking themselves to death. And hell would probably [be] an ugly vacuum full of poor polygamists unable to obtain booze or with chronic stomach disorders that they called secret sorrows.

To me heaven would be a big bull ring with me holding two barrera seats and a trout stream outside that no one else was allowed to fish in and two lovely houses in the town; one where I would have my wife and children and be monogamous and love them truly and well and the other where I would have my nine beautiful mistresses on 9 different floors and one house would be fitted up with special copies of the Dial printed on soft tissue and kept in the toilets on every floor and in the other house we would use the American Mercury and the New Republic. Then there would be a fine church like in Pamplona where I could go and be confessed on the way from one house to the other and I would get on my horse and ride out with my son to my bull ranch named Hacienda Hadley and toss coins to all my illegitimate children that lived [along] the road. I would write out at the Hacienda and send my son in to lock the chastity belts onto my mistresses because someone had just galloped up with the news that a notorious monogamist named Fitzgerald had been seen riding toward the town at the head of a company of strolling drinkers.

Well anyway we're going into town tomorrow early in the morning. Write me at the /Hotel Quintana

Pamplona
Spain

Or dont you like to write letters. I do because it's such a swell way to keep from working and yet feel you've done something.

So long and love to Zelda from us both,

> Yours,
> Ernest

WINSTON CHURCHILL to T. E. Lawrence, 16 May 1927

Sir Winston Churchill, 1874–1965, Prime Minister and author; T. E. Lawrence, soldier and author. After his wartime adventures in Arabia, Lawrence had served as Churchill's adviser on the Middle East at the Colonial Office. He retired from public life in 1922, enlisting first as an aircraftsman and then as a private in the tank corps, later rejoining the air force which he left shortly before his death. The 'pot-boiler' which Churchill measures against Lawrence's *Seven Pillars of Wisdom* is *The World Crisis*.

16.v.27   Treasury Chambers, Whitehall, sw

My dear 'Lurens'
        I read with rapt attention the long letter you wrote to Eddie about my book. It is a poor thing, mainly a pot-boiler, & deriving a passing vogue from the tremendous events with wh it deals & the curiosity of the British public to know something about them. In fact, when I put down the <u>Seven Pillars</u>, I felt mortified at the contrast between my dictated journalism & yr grand & permanent contribution to English literature. I cannot tell you how thrilled I was to read it. Having gone on a three days' visit to Paris, I never left my apartment except for meals, & lay all day & most of the night cuddling yr bulky tome. The impression it produced was overpowering. I marched with you those endless journeys by camel, with never a cool drink, a hot bath, or a square meal except under revolting conditions. What a tale! The young Napoleon or Clive, if only the stupid 20th century had not made peace. No wonder you brood in haughty anticlimax! I think yr book will live with Gulliver's Travels & Robinson Crusoe. The copy wh you gave me, with its inscription, is in every sense one of my most valuable possessions. I detected one misprint, but to torture you I will not tell you where.

I am always hoping some day to get a letter from you saying that yr long holiday is finished, & that yr appetite for action has returned. Please do not wait till the Bolshevik Revolution entitles me to summon you to the centre of strife by an order 'from the Imperial Stirrup'!

All yr many friends always ask about you, & I wish I had more news to tell them.

> Yours ever,
> Winston S. Churchill

E. M. FORSTER to T. E. Lawrence, 3 May 1928

Edward Morgan Forster, 1879–1970, novelist; T. E. Lawrence, soldier and author. Thomas Hardy had died that January.

Station Comshall   West Hackhurst,
3–5–28   Abinger Hammer,
Dorking.

Dear T.E.

Enough scraps have accumulated to fill a sheet to you. Siegfried S[assoon] asks me to tell you that a special copy of his poems, printed on green paper is waiting for you. He has given me a white one.

Mrs. Hardy – I saw her the other day in London, looking pretty wretched and still worrying over the old man's burial. I have read the typescript of the first vol. of his life, and she has asked me to help her through the second, which I think I shall be able to do, secretarially speaking: her scheme doesn't leave open any other activity, and the completed work is bound to be weak. She has suffered, a good deal, she is naturally retiring, he was naturally retiring. I am naturally retiring. Que veux tu? But when I die and they write my life they can say Everything.

E. Palmer Esq. – I continue to be his banker, but other relationships are forbidden by Mrs. Palmer and Mrs. Palmer's mother. They say I have tried to pit him against them. This is true.

L/Cpt. Middleton. – A good letter every now and then.

Self. Am in Belfast – stopping with my friend Forrest Reid whose novels you may know. The place is as uncivilised as ever – savage black mothers in houses of dark red brick, friendly manufacturers too drunk to entertain you when you arrive. It amuses me till I get tired.

Life. – No, I've nothing to teach you about it for the moment. May be writing about it another week.

E.M.F.

DORA CARRINGTON to Julia Strachey, [? June 1930]

Dora Carrington, 1892–1932, painter; Julia, a cousin of Lytton Strachey. This letter was written when Lytton Strachey was away from Ham Spray, the house where he and Carrington lived. After his death she committed suicide.

Friday morning   Ham Spray House, Hungerford

Darling Julia,

I wish a hundred times you were here today. Just to weep tears on your shoulders? No but to drive away the melancholy of the drizzling Scotch mists that envelope the downs and the bitter west wind that batters against the window panes. It's all very well aiming at being a stoic, but a different matter carrying out one's philosophy. I woke up in an ecstasy of love this morning very early to find my mouth full of sheets which I was biting passionately. Tomorrow 'company' as the servants say, will arrive and I'll get over my despairs. I feel it dreadfully ignominious to mind living alone. But the difficulty is not to let one's mind wander off into abysses of gloom that lead but to munching sheets by moonlight in bed. I can't tell you how much I loved our bathing tea party. After the blinking tiles are finished I am going to paint a picture of the little child at the lodge. I saw her sitting in a little [word illegible] the other [word illegible] in her [word illegible] with a doll: if it comes off, fatal words again, you shall have it for your birthday sweetie. [word illegible] day I expect. I'll tell you on Monday or Tuesday about the chances of a visit with Lytton one week.

Your very loving   Tante C.

T. E. LAWRENCE to Sir Edward Elgar, 12 October 1932

Thomas Edward Lawrence, afterwards Shaw, 'Lawrence of Arabia', 1888–1935, soldier and author; Sir Edward Elgar, composer. The BBC had commissioned a Third Symphony from Elgar, for which he managed to prepare only a few sketches before his death.

12.X.32   Mount Batten, Plymouth

Dear Sir Edward,

In the one week I have had letters from you and from W. B. Yeats – and it is a little difficult for an ordinary mortal to say the happy things when public monuments round him come suddenly to speech. I have liked most of your music – or most that I have heard – for many years: and your 2nd Symphony hits me between wind and water. It is exactly the mode that I most desire, and so it moves me more than anything else – of music – that I have heard. But thousands of people share my liking for your music, and with better reason for they know more about it than I do: so this doesn't justify the kindness of the Shaws in bringing me with them that afternoon. The chance of meeting you is just another of the benefits that have accrued to me from knowing G.B.S., who is a great adventure.

There are fleas of all grades; and so I have felt the awkward feeling of having smaller creatures than myself admiring me. I was so sorry to put you to that awkwardness: but it was inevitable. You have had a lifetime of achievement, and I was a flash in the pan. However I'm a very happy flash, and I am continually winning moments of great enjoyment. That Menuhin-Concerto is going to be a pleasure to me for years: and the news of your 3rd Symphony was like a week's sunlight. I do hope you will have enough enthusiasm left to finish it. There are crowds of us waiting to hear it again and again.

Probably it feels quaint to you to hear that the mere setting eyes upon you is a privilege: but by that standard I want to show you how good an afternoon it was for me, in your house. Yours sincerely,

                                                                    T. E. Shaw.

CARL GUSTAV JUNG to James Joyce, [October 1932]

Carl Gustav Jung, 1875–1961, psychiatrist; James Joyce, novelist. Jung had written an article on Joyce's *Ulysses* which he sent to him with this covering letter. Joyce thought it 'imbecile'. A couple of years later Jung treated Joyce's schizophrenic daughter Lucia. He likened father and daughter to two people going to the bottom of a river, one diving and the other falling.

Küsnacht-Zürich, Seestrasse 228

Dear Sir,

Your Ulysses has presented the world such an upsetting psychological problem, that repeatedly I have been called in as a supposed authority on psychological matters.

Ulysses proved to be an exceedingly hard nut and it has forced my mind not only to most unusual efforts, but also to rather extravagant peregrinations (speaking from the standpoint of a scientist). Your book as a whole has given me no end of trouble and I was brooding over it for about three years until I succeeded to put myself into it. But I must tell you that I'm profoundly grateful to yourself as well as to your gigantic opus, because I learned a great deal from it. I shall probably never be quite sure whether I did enjoy it, because it meant too much grinding of nerves and of grey matter. I also don't know whether you will enjoy what I have written about Ulysses because I couldn't help telling the world how much I was bored, how I grumbled, how I cursed and how I admired. The 40 pages of non stop run in the end is a string of veritable psychological peaches. I suppose the devil's grandmother knows so much about the real psychology of a woman. I didn't.

Well I just try to recommend my little essay to you, as an amusing attempt of a perfect stranger that went astray in the labyrinth of your Ulysses and happened to get out of it again by sheer good luck. At all events you may gather from my article what Ulysses has done to a supposedly balanced psychologist.

With the expression of my deepest appreciation, I remain, dear Sir, Yours faithfully   C. G. Jung

NEVILLE CHAMBERLAIN to the Editor of *The Times*, 24 January 1933

Neville Chamberlain, 1869–1940, later Prime Minister. On 30 January, six days after the date of this letter, Hitler became Chancellor of Germany.

From the Chancellor of the Exchequer

Sir,

It may be of interest to record that, in walking through St James's Park today, I noticed a grey wagtail running about on the now temporarily dry bed of the lake, near the dam below the bridge, and occasionally picking small insects out of the cracks in the dam.

Probably the occurrence of this bird in the heart of London has been recorded before, but I have not myself previously noted it in the Park.

> I am your obedient servant,
> Neville Chamberlain

P.S. For the purpose of removing doubts, as we say in the House of Commons, I should perhaps add that I mean a grey wagtail and not a pied.

January 24, 1933

T. E. LAWRENCE to Siegfried Sassoon, 7 December 1934

Thomas Edward Lawrence, afterwards Shaw, 'Lawrence of Arabia', 1888–1935, soldier and author; Siegfried Sassoon, poet and prose writer. Heytesbury was Sassoon's house, and Cloud's Hill the cottage to which Lawrence hoped to retire after leaving the RAF.

> Ozone Hotel
> Bridlington
> Yorks.
> 7–XII–34

Dear S. S.

Notice that I am now hardly in the land of the living. Queer place, the Yorkshire coast in winter. I confess I prefer it to Bridlington crowded and sweating in the suns of August.

Here are ten R.A.F. boats to overhaul. I sit and watch over them all day. In February it's all over, and in February I leave this R.A.F. which has been for 12 years my Heytesbury. Address them Shaw, Clouds' Hill, Moreton, Dorset . . . which is my cottage of cottages. How ownership biasses judgement.

I am hoping that you are very well; and her too. And that you and she will roll down to my cottage some day (some fine day . . . your coming will ensure that, inside the cottage) complete with buns and thermos flask, for tea: or rather, to give me tea. I aim at having no food in the place.

Till then imagine me wintering in a summer resort: spacious, peaceful and inclement. Especially inclement. Cats and landladies' husbands keep me company: and the sea rolls up the sand like a Lyons swiss roll beneath the windows all day and night.

Yours ever,
T. E. Shaw

W. B. YEATS to Ethel Mannin, 24 June [1935]

William Butler Yeats, 1865–1939, poet and playwright; Ethel Mannin, novelist. Yeats had just celebrated his seventieth birthday. Norman Haire was the surgeon who had given Yeats the Steinach operation for rejuvenation the year before. This operation (now known as a vasectomy and in which, contrary to popular belief, monkey glands played no part) had an extraordinary psychological effect on Yeats, and ushered in his final great creative period, the period of his *Last Poems*.

Riversdale, Willbrook,
Rathfarnham, Dublin
June 24

My dear Ethel

It was so good of you to send me the telegram of congratulations signed 'Ethel'. I have put off answering from day to day. I have had endless letters & telegrams to answer that it is always the friend who will not misunderstand who is put off till tomorrow. Then too I have been correcting the proof of my book of philosophy & reading poets for my

4 August 1936

Oxford Book of Modern Verse. Every poet is a week's reading. I am forbidden all exercise, & all work that is a strain – congestion of the lung has left me an enlarged heart. Further more the doctor has enjoined 'for the present' complete celebacy. I said 'If I were a mathematician I could take to drink' he said 'yes they do drink but I will give you a bromide'. The bromide has come. I do not accept his diagnosis – he is young, theoretical & over incisive. However any captain in a storm. I shall probably obey him until I have seen Norman Haire. 'For the present', meaning until I get back my normal health, & I believe I can do that quicker than my doctor thinks possible. I am of a healthy long lived race, & our minds improve with age.

I have had to make an important decision. Have I written all the good poetry I can expect to write? Should I turn my measure of fame into money for the sake of my family? It was brought to a head by an offer from Harvard of a thousand pounds & about a hundred pounds travelling expenses for six lectures on poetry & some weeks residence in the university: I hesitated for days & then with my wife's approval refused. I am about to cut myself adrift, as far as I can, from all external circumstance (The Abbey Theatre will soon be able to go its own road), I want to plunge myself into impersonal poetry, to get rid of the bitterness, irritation & hatred my work in Ireland has brought into my soul. I want to write the last song, sweet & exultant, a sort of European *Geeta*, or rather my *Geeta* not doctrine but song.

> Yours affectionately
> W. B. Yeats

I feel very well, full of energy & life but am soon made breathless if I am not careful. I was worse before the operation.

EVELYN WAUGH to Laura Herbert, 4 August 1936

Evelyn Waugh, 1903–66, novelist; Laura Herbert, afterwards his wife.

> Grand Hotel Subasio,
Tuesday
> Assisi.

My Darling Laura
   How I wish you were here. It is a lovely little town – full of sun, you

would like that, and bulls and Giottos (he is a famous dead painter). A charming little hotel, a room with a big stone balcony giving onto an empty colonnaded square with directly opposite the church of St Francis. (He is a famous dead saint who put this town on the map.) Good cooking & wine on a terrace from which we can see the whole of Umbria. A delightful maître d'hôtel whom I found telling my full life story. Mosquitos all night. Otherwise perfect. If I ever marry I shall bring my wife here for a bit.

Sweet poppet it seems such a waste to see lovely things & not be with you. It is like being one-eyed & goggling out of focus. I miss you & need you all the time. Most of all when I'm happy.

E

DYLAN THOMAS to Caitlin Macnamara, [? late 1936]

Dylan Thomas, 1914–53, poet; Caitlin Macnamara, afterwards his wife.

Nice, lovely, faraway Caitlin my darling,

Are you better, and please God you aren't too miserable in the horrible hospital? Tell me everything, when you'll be out again, where you'll be at Christmas, and that you think of me and love me. And when you're in the world again, we'll both be useful if you like, trot round, do things, compromise with the They people, find a place with a bath and no bugs in Bloomsbury, and be happy there. It's that – the *thought* of the few, simple things we want and the *knowledge* that we're going to get them in spite of you know Who and His spites and tempers – that keeps us living I think. It keeps *me* living. I don't want you for a day (though I'd sell my toes to see you now my dear, only for a minute, to kiss you once, and make a funny face at you): a day is the length of a gnat's life: I want you for the lifetime of a big, mad animal, like an elephant. I've been indoors all this week, with a wicked cold, coughing and snivelling, too full of phlegm and aspirins to write to a girl in hospital, because my letter would be sad and despairing, & even the ink would carry sadness & influenza. Should I make you sad, darling, when you're in bed with rice pudding in Marlborough Ward? I want so very much to look at you again; I love you; you're weeks older now; is your hair grey? have you put your

hair up, and do you look like a real adult person, not at all anymore
beautiful and barmy like the proper daughters of God? You mustn't look
too grown-up, because you'd look older than me; and you'll never, I'll
never let you, grow wise, and I'll never, you shall never let me, grow
wise, and we'll always be young and unwise together. There is, I suppose,
in the eyes of the They, a sort of sweet madness about you and me, a sort
of mad bewilderment and astonishment oblivious to the Nasties and the
Meanies; you're the only person, of course you're the only person from
here to Aldebaran and back, with whom I'm free entirely; and I think it's
because you're as innocent as me. Oh I know we're not saints or virgins
or lunatics; we know all the lust and lavatory jokes, and most of the dirty
people; we can catch buses and count our change and cross the roads and
talk real sentences. But our innocence goes awfully deep, and our
discreditable secret is that we don't know anything at all, and our horrid
inner secret is that we don't care that we don't. I've just read an Irish
book called Rory and Bran, and it's a bad charming book: innocent Rory
falls in love with innocent Oriana, and, though they're both whimsy and
talk about the secret of the language of the hills and though Rory
worships the moon and Oriana glides about in her garden listening to the
legendary birds, they're not as mad as we are, nor as innocent. I love you
so much I'll never be able to tell you; I'm frightened to tell you. I can
always feel your heart. Dance tunes are always right: I love you body and
soul: – and I suppose body means that I want to touch you & be in bed
with you, & I suppose soul means that I can hear you & see you & love
you in every single, single thing in the whole world asleep or awake.

Dylan X

I wanted this to be a letter full of news, but there isn't any yet. It's just a
letter full of what I think about you and me. You're not empty, empty
still now, are you? Have you got love to send me?

SCOTT FITZGERALD to his daughter, 12 December 1936

F. Scott Fitzgerald, 1896–1940, novelist; Frances Scott Fitzgerald, his daughter.

Grove Park Inn
Asheville, North Carolina
December 12, 1936

Dear Scottie:

As I wired you, there is no question of having ninety people. The most you can possibly ask is about sixty people; and even that is counting on ten or twelve refusals. If I had thought that the Ethel Walker School was going to give you a peculiar idea of what your financial resources are, it would have been far, far better to send you to a modest school here in the Carolina mountains. You are a poor girl, and if you don't like to think about it, just ask me. If you don't make up your mind to being that, you become one of those terrible girls that don't know whether they are millionairesses or paupers. You are neither one nor the other. The dance for you in Baltimore is a very modest one. It will have dignity because it pretends to nothing that it isn't. It will give you a certain amount of whoopee and it will probably lack a certain amount of things that you would expect. For instance, I am determined to have a hurdy-gurdy for the orchestra – you know, an Italian with a monkey, and I think the children will be very content with that. They don't want much, children of sixteen or seventeen, and they will be amused by the antics of the monkey. Your idea of a swing orchestra seems zero to me.

However, in the next room I will have some of the older people with a swing orchestra that I have engaged, and from time to time you may bring some of your choice friends in there to dance.

– But remember that I expect you and your crowd to dance by the hurdy-gurdy during the whole afternoon, quietly and slowly and without swing music, just doing simple waltz dancing.

You can stay all night all you want with people up to the night of December 24th, when you and I are going to make a hop South.

With dearest love,

Daddy

P.S. You ask what to put on the cards. It should be about like this:

> Miss Frances Scott Fitzgerald
> F. Scott Fitzgerald

> December 22nd
> Four to six
> Hotel Belvedere   Dancing

MALCOLM LOWRY to Juan Fernando Marquez, [1937]

Malcolm Lowry, 1909–1957, novelist; Juan Fernando Marquez, an Oaxaque-nian-Zapotecan friend. This letter was written while Lowry was working on *Under the Volcano*.

[Oaxaca, Mexico]

Juan:

I am here because there is much hostility in my hotel.

I am trying to do some work here but my life is so circumscribed by your detectives who walk up and down the street and stand at the street corner as though there were nothing better to do than to spy on a man who is unable to do anything anyway and never had intentions of doing anything but be good and love and help where help was necessary that I am rapidly losing my mind. It is not drink that does this but Oaxaca.

Do you wish me to leave with the impression that Oaxaca, the most lovely town in the world and with some of the most lovely people in it, is a town consisting entirely of spies and dogs?

This is unfair to me but it is a hell of a sight unfairer to Oaxaca.

The English are sufficiently stupid but the stupidity and hypocrisy of your detectives and the motives which are behind their little eternal spying – their activities – completely transcend any criminality and stupidity I have ever encountered anywhere in the world. Have these guys nothing better to do than to watch a man who merely wants to write poetry? As if I had not enough troubles on my mind!

I do profoundly think that the Oaxaquenians are among the most courteous, sweetly gracious, and fundamentally decent people in the entire world. I think this too of your boss and of yourself and of this lovely town.

However, the whole damn thing is being raised to an insane state of suspicion.

People even camp outside my bloody door to see if I am drinking inside, and of course I probably am because it is so difficult or becoming so difficult to drink outside.

If I do not drink now a certain amount there seems no possible doubt that I shall have a nervous breakdown. If I have that, equally I shall find myself in that Goddamn jail to which I seem to be progressing almost geometrically, and as you know, when one goes there sober, one comes out drunk. It seems almost that I have a kind of fixation on the place because, like the novelist Dostoievsky, I have practically a pathological sympathy for those who do wrong (what others are there?) and get into the shit.

What I have absolutely no sympathy with is the legislator, the man who seeks, for his own profit, to exploit the weaknesses of those who are unable to help themselves and then to fasten some moral superscription upon it. This I loathe so much that I cannot conceivably explain how much it is.

Nor – for that matter – has any man a right to legislate upon a person (who has paid through the nose as I have, who has his house robbed, his wife taken away, in short everything taken away, simply to be in Mexico) for his own Goddamned stupid political reactionary reasons when anyhow it is only a country that he himself – I mean the legislator – has criminally stolen. You know what I mean, of course. Of course it is true that Montezuma – not the beer – may not have been much better than Cortez or Alvarado. However, this is another story.

Malcolm

LAWRENCE DURRELL to Henry Miller, [August 1938]

Lawrence Durrell, b. 1912, novelist and poet; Henry Miller, novelist. Miller was working on his *Tropic of Capricorn* at this time.

Corfu

Henry:

It's so quiet today, and the sea so blue, and now the garden wall is built and the floors a little polished, so we are getting a little settled.

I was thinking: you must come about the tenth of September; it will be very quiet and quite new to you. Drop everything and leave someone in charge of your mail. Just wrap *Capricorn* in a red wool shawl and bring your portable along with you. I can give you a deep cool room with two windows over the sea, bright rugs on the floor, a desk and some books, an encyclopaedia and dictionary. Bring a woman too with you; that would make it an even keel for the days which come and go quite silently. We could sail and bathe in the mornings, have a fine sunny lunch with wine, then a long afternoon siesta, bathe before tea and then four hours' work in a slow rich evening. Even if you did not touch *Capricorn* I think you would profit; the thing would be there and the invisible chisel would be jockeying it about as you slept. Get well set on an even base, and come to terms with the scenery. Then in the middle of October you could start lashing out for Crete, Lesbos and so on.

It is perhaps not so primitive. There is a lavatory, for example, and we might have a bath put in by that time; anyway we could motor into town every week and have a bath at the hotel there. No mosquitoes, or any vermin: your work-room would be as flyless as Villa Seurat; bathing in the sea; trips into prehistory. And I think all this, a lull in your streamlined life, might just provide the shifting of the stance that *Capricorn* demands; because after all one only lets people and things impose if one wants them to; and if things intervene it really means that the Roman Road to *Capricorn*, your biggest and most dazzling child, runs not so straight.

After contemplating the circle for a week I have evolved one or two new speculative ideas on the nature of classical art: as DETACHMENT not being synonymous with objectivity; as in writers every new effort being vitiated by rationalisation – whereas in sculpture you find your way sensually through your fingertips and leave the critical debris to Herb Read; as the next phase is a CLASSICAL phase, a form of diathermy, a writing on the womb-plasm with the curette. You see, today all writing is

278

pretending to be Classical (Eliot, Hemingway, Stein) whereas the origins of it are really ROMANTIC. Compare *Waste Land* with Baudelaire, Stein and Alfred de Musset.

Never mind. Cut it all out. It's too hot. But in *Capricorn* your new attitude will be definable (surely not) as CLASSICAL, in the sense that a circle is classical.

Listen, the British fleet is in: two huge grey monsters, really beautiful to look at. War is really a fine art, I feel, when you think of this flawlessness of ingenuity spent on steel to twist and rivet and smooth it. Guns like great pricks, sliding in and out and coiling on themselves. And little men like lice running about in groups by arithmetic. It's wonderful. One side of us responds to the aggregates: when you see these flawless dummies you feel it. No responsibility. The idiots dream of an ant world where giant pricks slide in and out and vomit steel semen, and a regiment could be licked off the walls of this tower and leave not even a blob of pus behind.

Now Henry, no more dilly-dallying. Tell me, shall it be definitely in September? I don't think you'll regret it for a second.

Skoal to Capricorn,

Larry

THOMAS WOLFE to Maxwell Perkins, 12 August 1938

Thomas Wolfe, 1900–1938, novelist; Maxwell Perkins, editor. Perkins, as Wolfe's editor at Scribner's, had greatly assisted him with his first two novels. After the first of these, *Of Time and the River*, had been edited, Wolfe fled to Europe to avoid the publicity surrounding its publication. When he returned on 4 July 1935 he was met at the dock by Perkins who told him of its success. Wolfe later changed publishers and abandoned Perkins. This is his last letter: he died on 15 September.

Providence Hospital
Seattle, Washington
August 12, 1938

Dear Max:

I'm sneaking this against orders, but 'I've got a hunch' – and I wanted to write these words to you.

1 March [1939]

I've made a long voyage and been to a strange country, and I've seen the dark man very close; and I don't think I was too much afraid of him, but so much of mortality still clings to me – I wanted most desperately to live and still do, and I thought about you all a thousand times, and wanted to see you all again, and there was the impossible anguish and regret of all the work I had not done, of all the work I had to do – and I know now I'm just a grain of dust, and I feel as if a great window has been opened on life I did not know about before – and if I come through this, I hope to God I am a better man, and in some strange way I can't explain, I know I am a deeper and a wiser one. If I get on my feet and out of here, it will be months before I head back, but if I get on my feet, I'll come back.

Whatever happens – I had this 'hunch' and wanted to write you and tell you, no matter what happens or has happened, I shall always think of you and feel about you the way it was that Fourth of July day three years ago when you met me at the boat, and we went out on the café on the river and had a drink and later went on top of the tall building, and all the strangeness and the glory and the power of life and of the city was below.

Yours always,
                                    Tom

E. B. WHITE to Eugene Saxton, 1 March [1939]

Elwyn Brooks White, 1899–1985, author; Eugene Saxton, editor at Harper & Brothers. *Stuart Little* was published in 1945.

                                    Hotel Gramercy Park
                                    New York
                                    1 March

Dear Gene:

Herewith an unfinished MS of a book called *Stuart Little*. It would seem to be for children, but I'm not fussy who reads it. You said you wanted to look at this, so I am presenting it thus in its incomplete state. There are about ten or twelve thousand words so far, roughly.

You will be shocked and grieved to discover that the principal character in the story has somewhat the attributes and appearance of a mouse. This does not mean that I am either challenging or denying Mr. Disney's genius. At the risk of seeming a very whimsical fellow indeed, I will have to break down and confess to you that Stuart Little appeared to me in dream, all complete, with his hat, his cane, and his brisk manner. Since he was the only fictional figure ever to honor and disturb my sleep, I was deeply touched, and felt that I was not free to change him into a grasshopper or a wallaby. Luckily he bears no resemblance, either physically or temperamentally, to Mickey. I guess that's a break for all of us.

Stop in here for a drink some fine afternoon. We are enjoying room service and would like to see you.

Andy White

SIGMUND FREUD to H. G. Wells, 16 July 1939

Sigmund Freud, 1856–1939, creator of psychoanalysis; H. G. Wells, author. Freud, who was suffering from cancer of the jaw, had been driven out of Vienna by Hitler's invasion of Austria and settled in London. He wanted to be granted British citizenship before he died, for which a residence of five years was needed. Unsuccessful attempts were being made in Parliament on his behalf to get the Government to waive this requirement. He died on 23 September.

20, Maresfield Gardens, London, N.W.3,
16. Juli 1939

Dear Mr. Wells
Your letter starts with the question how I am. My answer is I am not too well, but I am glad of the chance to see you and the Baroness again and happy to learn that you are intending a great satisfaction for me. Indeed, you cannot have known that since I first came over to England as a boy of eighteen years, it became an intense wish phantasy of mine to settle in this country and become an Englishman. Two of my half-brothers had done so fifteen years before.

But an infantile phantasy needs a bit of examination before it can be admitted to reality. Now my condition is the following: There are two judgements on my case. One of them, represented by my physicians, maintains the hope that the combined Radium and Xray treatment I am now undergoing will cure me of the last attack of my malignant growth and leave me free to meet other adventures in life. Perhaps they only say so officially. There is another party, much less hopeful, to which I myself adhere in view of my actual pains and troubles. Now let us suppose the fact that you know the affair of the Act of Parliament cannot go through before half a year or more. In such a case, I expect you would prefer to drop your intention. So I have an interest not only in seeing you but also in your seeing me. As regards the time available for your visit, I see that you are ready to call on me any afternoon except the 18th. Sunday afternoon after 4 o'clock would be best for me. If I should not be in a condition to see you, I would let you know Sunday morning by telephone.

With the expression of my heartiest thanks, and my compliments to the Baroness,

Yours sincerely   Sigm. Freud

ALBERT EINSTEIN to the President of the United States, 2 August 1939

Albert Einstein, 1879–1955, scientist; Franklin Delano Roosevelt, President of the United States. Einstein had been driven into exile in America by the Nazis. This is the letter which led to the construction of the world's first atomic bomb.

> Albert Einstein
> Old Grove Rd.
> Nassau Point
> Peconic, Long Island
> August 2nd, 1939

F. D. Roosevelt
President of the United States
White House
Washington, D.C.

Sir:

Some recent work by E. Fermi and L. Szilard, which has been communicated to me in manuscript, leads me to expect that the element uranium may be turned into a new and important source of energy in the immediate future. Certain aspects of the situation seem to call for watchfulness and, if necessary, quick action on the part of the administration. I believe, therefore, that it is my duty to bring to your attention the following facts and recommendations.

In the course of the last four months it has been made probable – through the work of Joliot in France as well as Fermi and Szilard in America – that it may become possible to set up nuclear chain reactions in a large mass of uranium, by which vast amounts of power and large quantities of new radium-like elements would be generated. Now it appears almost certain that this could be achieved in the immediate future.

This new phenomenon would also lead to the construction of bombs, and it is conceivable – though much less certain – that extremely powerful bombs of a new type may thus be constructed. A single bomb of this type, carried by boat or exploded in a port, might very well destroy the whole port together with some of the surrounding territory. However, such bombs might very well prove to be too heavy for transportation by air.

The United States has only very poor ores of uranium in moderate quantities. There is some good ore in Canada and the former Czechoslovakia, while the most important source of uranium is the Belgian Congo.

In view of this situation you may think it desirable to have some permanent contact between the administration and the group of physicists working on chain reaction in America. One possible way of achieving this might be for you to entrust with this task a person who has your confidence and who could perhaps serve in an unoffical capacity. His task might comprise the following:

(*a*) To approach government departments, keep them informed of further developments, and put forward recommendations for government action, giving particular attention to the problem of securing a supply of uranium ore for the United States.

(*b*) To speed up the experimental work which is at present being carried on within the limits of the budgets of the university laboratories, by providing funds, if such funds be required, through his contacts with private persons who are willing to make contributions for this cause, and perhaps also by obtaining the cooperation of industrial laboratories which have the necessary equipment.

I understand that Germany has actually stopped the sale of uranium from the Czechoslovakian mines which she has taken over. That she should have taken such early action might perhaps be understood on the ground that the son of the German Undersecretary of State, von Weizsäcker, is attached to the Kaiser Wilhelm Institute of Berlin, where some of the American work on uranium is now being repeated.

Yours very truly,
A. Einstein.

Index of letter-writers

Albert, Prince, 148
Austen, Jane, 105

Bagehot, Walter, 154
Barnum, Phineas T., 196
Barrow, Sir John, 104
Beardsley, Aubrey, 219
Beaumont, Sir Francis, 12
Beethoven, Ludwig van, 129
Blake, William, 88, 132
Brontë, Charlotte, 149
Brontë, Patrick Branwell, 147
Brooke, Rupert, 242
Browne, Sir Thomas, 37
Browning, Robert, 145, 173
Buckingham, George Villiers, first
    Duke of, 18
Burns, Robert, 84
Byron, George Gordon, sixth Baron,
    97, 111, 113, 116, 130

Carlyle, Thomas, 171
Carrington, Dora, 261, 267
Carroll, Lewis, 178
Cecil, Sir Robert, first Earl of
    Salisbury, 11
Chamberlain, Neville, 270
Charles I, 21
Charles II, 35
Chatterton, Thomas, 73, 74
Chesterfield, Philip Dormer
    Stanhope, fourth Earl of, 70
Chesterfield, Philip Stanhope, second
    Earl of, 30, 33
Chesterton, G(ilbert) K(eith), 240
Churchill, Sir Winston, 204, 265
Clare, John, 163
Clarke, James Stanier, 105

Coleridge, Samuel Taylor, 92, 93,
    101
Conrad, Joseph, 221, 222
Cook, Captain James, 77
Corvo, Baron (Frederick William
    Rolfe), 224
Cowper, William, 80, 86, 87
Cromwell, Oliver, 20

Daborne, Robert, 16
Darwin, Charles, 190
Defoe, Daniel, 51
Dickens, Charles, 136, 138, 140, 147,
    175
Dickinson, Emily, 164, 165, 194, 198,
    199
Donne, John, 15, 17
Dryden, John, 28, 49
Duncan, Isadora, 230
Durrell, Lawrence, 278

Einstein, Albert, 282
Elgar, Edward, 223
Eliot, George, 176
Elizabeth I, 5, 6
Emin Pasha (Eduart Schnitzer), 202
Etherege, Sir George, 48
Evelyn, John, 34

Fell, Dr John, 41, 45
Field, Nathan, 16
Fitzgerald, F. Scott, 275
Forster, E(dward) M(organ), 266
Franklin, Benjamin, 82
Freud, Sigmund 281
Frost, Robert, 236

Gainsborough, Thomas, 69, 79
George III, 78

George V, 244
Gordon, General Charles George, 195
Graves, Robert von Ranke, 251
Gray, Thomas, 60
Grimaldi, Joey, 134
Gwyn, Nell, 44

Halley, Edmund, 46
Hambleton, Lady Ann, 30
Hamilton, Lady Emma, 101
Hamlet, Prince of Denmark, 8
Hawthorne, Nathaniel, 152
Haydon, Benjamin Robert, 98
Hazlitt, William, 127, 135
Hearn, Lafcadio, 205, 209, 212, 220
Hemingway, Ernest, 264
Henley, Anthony, 57
Hogarth, William, 60
Hood, Thomas, 146
Hopkins, Gerard Manley, 186
Housman, A(lfred) E(dward), 262
Howells, William Dean, 182
Hume, David, 76

Ireland, William Henry, 6

James, Henry, 249
Johnson, Dr Samuel, 61, 81, 84
Joyce, James Augustine Aloysius, 225, 228, 231
Jung, Carl Gustav, 269

Keats, John, 114, 118, 119, 121, 122

Lamb, Charles, 106, 131
Lane, Sir Ralph, 3
Lawrence, D(avid) H(erbert), 238, 241, 247
Lawrence, T(homas) E(dward), 268, 270
Lincoln, President Abraham, 170
Livingstone, Dr David, 143
Lowry, Malcolm, 276
Lyttelton, William Henry, first Baron, 65

McCann, Revd Isidore, 257

Mary, Princess (Queen Mary II), 39
Massinger, Philip, 16
Melville, Herman, 155, 157
Montagu, John, second Duke of, 59
Montagu, Lady Mary Wortley, 53
Morland, George, 94
Mulgrave, John Sheffield, third Earl of, 47

Nelson, Horatio, Viscount Nelson, Duke of Brontë, 90, 95
Newman, John Henry, Cardinal, 170
Nightingale, Florence, 180

Osborne, Dorothy, 26
Owen, Wilfred, 256, 259

Penn, William, 43
Ponsonby, General Sir Henry Frederick, 191
Pope, Alexander, 56

Queensberry, Sir John Sholto Douglas, eighth Marquess of, 215
Queensbury, Charles Douglas, third Duke of, 75
Quiney, Richard, 7

Raglan, Lord Fitzroy Somerset, first Baron, 162
Ralegh, Sir Walter, 9
Richmond, George, 133
Rochester, John Wilmot, second Earl of, 36
Rossetti, Dante Gabriel, 163, 174
Ruskin, John, 188, 197
Russell, Bertrand, third Earl, 245

'Sam', 96
Sassoon, Siegfried, 254
Saunders, Esther, 74
Savile, Henry, 40
Schliemann, Heinrich, 178
Scott, Captain Robert Falcon, 237, 238
Seattle, Chief, 159
Shaw, George Bernard, 216, 243, 260
Shelley, Percy Bysshe, 90, 120, 125

Sidney, Sir Philip, 3, 5
Smart, Christopher, 74
Smith, Revd Sydney, 135, 142
Stanley, Sir Henry Morton, 192
Steele, Sir Richard, 50
Stendhal, 124
Stephenson, George, 124
Sterne, Laurence, 67
Stevens, Wallace, 250, 258
Stevenson, Robert Louis, 207, 213
Swift, Jonathan, 54
Swinburne, Algernon Charles, 193
Synge, John Millington, 234

Taylor, Jeremy, 31
Tennyson, Alfred Lord, 153, 185
Thackeray, William Makepeace, 167
Thomas, Dylan, 273
Thoreau, Henry David, 140, 150
Tolstoy, Leo, 189, 226, 235
Trollope, Anthony, 183, 192
Turgenev, Ivan, 184

V., Mr, 8
Van Gogh, Vincent, 199
Victoria, Queen, 197
Villiers, Barbara, 30

Voltaire, 68

Wainwright, Jacob, 179
Waller, Edmund, 19
Walpole, Horace, fourth Earl of
   Orford, 63, 66, 71
Walpole, Sir Robert, first Earl of
   Orford, 58
Waugh, Evelyn, 272
Wellington, Arthur Wellesley, first
   Duke of, 103, 137
White, E(lwyn) B(rooks), 280
Whitman, Walt, 167
Wilde, Constance (later Constance
   Holland), 218
Wilde, Oscar Fingal O'Flahertie
   Wills, 212, 215, 217
Willoughby, John, 9
Windsor, Thomas, seventh Baron, 33
Winstanley, Gerrard, 22
Wolfe, Thomas, 279
Woolf, Virginia, 262
Wordsworth, William, 100, 109
Wright, Charles, 229
Wright, Orville, 227

Yeats, William Butler, 203, 226, 271

Index of recipients

Ainslie, Robert, 84
Allgood, Molly, 234
Apsley, Frances, 39
Asquith, Lady Cynthia, 247
Austen, Jane, 105
autograph collectors, 146, 152

Bagehot, Edith, 154
Bainbridge, Harry, 224
Banks, Sir Joseph, 82
Barnacle, Nora, 228
Barrett, Elizabeth, 145
Barrett, William, 73
Baxter, Charles, 213
Beach, Sylvia, 260
Beard, Thomas, 136, 147
Becher, Revd John Thomas, 97
Boufflers, Comtesse de, 76
Bowers, Mrs, 238
Brawne, Fanny, 118, 119
Brenan, Gerald, 261
Bridges, Robert, 186
Brougham, Henry Peter, Lord, 148
Brown, Charles Armitage, 122
Brown, John, 147
Brown, Lucy, 140
Browne, Edward, 37
Burne-Jones, Sir Edward, 193
Burney, Dr Charles, 74

Calvert, Frank, 178
Cameron, Lovett, 179
Carlyle, Thomas, 188
Chamberlain, Professor Basil Hall, 209
Chatterton, Thomas, 71, 74
Chesterfield, Philip Dormer Stanhope, fourth Earl of, 61, 68

Chesterfield, Philip Stanhope, second Earl of, 30
Chesterton, Frances, 240
Churchill, Jenny, Lady Randolph, 204
Churchill, Charles, 58
Clark, Arthur S., 216
Clarke, James Stanier, 105
Corbet, Robert, 48
Cottle, Joseph, 101
Craig, Gordon, 230
Cumberland, George, 132

Douglas, Lord Alfred, 212
Dryden, Honor, 28

Edmondes, Sir Thomas, 11
Egerton, Sir George, 237
Elgar, Sir Edward, 268
Elgin, Thomas Bruce, seventh Earl of, 98
Elizabeth I, 5
Elphinstone, George Keith, Viscount Keith, 104
Emerson, Ellen, 150
Emerson, Ralph Waldo, 171
Emperor Old Hop, 65
Etherege, Sir George, 47
Evelyn, John, 31

Fairfax, Thomas, third Baron, 22
Fitzgerald, F. Scott, 264
Fitzgerald, Frances Scott, 275
Fourmantel, Catherine, 67
Frederick, Charles, 59

Galsworthy, John, 222
Garnett, Edward, 221
Garrick, David, 69

Gilchrist, Alexander, 163
Godwin, William, 92
Goethe, Johann Wolfgang von, 130
Goodyer, Sir Henry, 15, 17
Gordon, Augusta, 197, 202
Gould, Dr George M., 205
Graham, John, 94
Grant, General Ulysses S., 170, 196
Graves, Robert, 254
Gregory, Augusta, Lady, 225
Guillemard, William Henry, 135

Halifax, George Savile, first
  Marquess of, 40
Hall, Captain Basil, 140
Hamilton, Emma, Lady, 90, 95
Hamilton, Lady Grizel, 257
Harley, Robert, first Earl of Oxford,
  51
Haskell, Mr and Mrs S. B., 167
Hatton, Christopher, first Viscount,
  33
Hatton, Lady Elizabeth, 41, 45
Hawthorne, Nathaniel, 155, 157
Henslowe, Philip, 16
Herbert, Laura, 272
Higginson, Colonel T. W., 164, 165
Hipkins, James, 163
Hitchener, Thomas, 99
Hogarth, Jenny, 60
Holland, Elizabeth Vassall, Lady,
  142
Holmes, Sherlock, 229
Hopkin, Sallie, 238
Humphreys, Arthur, 218
Hyde, Laurence, 44

Jackson, William, 79
Jaeger, August E., 223
James I, 18
James, Henry, 207
Jeffrey, Francis, 135
Jenkins, Miss A. M., 137
Jones, Dr Henry Bence, 167
Jonson, Ben, 12
Joyce, James, 226, 269
Joyce, Stanislaus, 231

Keats, John, 120
Kent, Charles, 175
Kéroualle, Louise de, Duchess of
  Portsmouth, 35
Kingsland, William G., 173
Kinnaird, Douglas, ninth Baron, 116

Lamb, Charles, 109
Lawrence, T(homas) E(dward), 265,
  266
Leigh, Augusta, 113
Lenthall, William, 20
Leverson, Ada, 215, 217
Light Brigade, the, 162
Little Carpenter, 65
Livens, Horace Mann, 199
Livingston, Neil and Agnes, 143
Livingstone, Agnes, 180
Loveringe, Mistress Mary, 8
Lyttelton, Edith (the Hon. Mrs
  Alfred), 243
Lytton, Edith (the Hon. Mrs
  Robert), 176

McDonald, Mitchell, 220
McGonagall, William, 191
McLeod, Arthur, 241
Maclise, Daniel, 138
Macnamara, Caitlin, 273
Mannin, Ethel, 271
March, Lord, 244
Mareste, Baron de, 124
Marquez, Juan Fernando, 276
Marsh, Sir Edward, 251
Maude, Aylmer, 235
Meynell, Mrs, 142
Miller, Henry, 278
Molyneux, Edmund, 3
Monroe, Harriet, 258
Montagu, Edward Wortley, 53
Montagu, George, 63, 66
Monteith, Robert, 153
Moore, Thomas, 111
Morris, Jane, 174
Motte, Benjamin, 54

Nation, the (Editor of), 245
Neate, Charles, 129

Nesbitt, Cathleen, 242
Newton, Sir Isaac, 46
Newton, Revd John, 87
Nishida, Sentarō, 212
Norcross, Louise and Frances, 198, 199

Ophelia, 8
Owen, Susan, 256, 259

Palmer, Samuel, 133
Patmore, Peter George, 127
Peacock, Thomas Love, 125
Perkins, Maxwell, 279
Pierce, President Franklin, 159
Porter, Lucy, 84
Puleston, Sir Richard, 101

Ralegh, Elizabeth, 9
Ralston, W. R. S., 184, 189
Raverat, Gwen, 262
Redfern, Percy, 226
Reynolds, John Hamilton, 114
Richards, Grant, 262
Richardson, G. N., 192
Robinson, Henry Crabb, 131
Roosevelt, Franklin Delano, 282
Rose, Samuel, 86
Rupert, Prince, 21
Rusden, George William, 183

Sandwich, John Montagu, fourth Earl of, 77, 78
Sassoon, Siegfried, 270
Savile, Henry, 36
Saxton, Eugene, 280
Scurlock, Mary, 50
Shakespeare, William, 6, 7
Shelley, Percy Bysshe, 121
Sidney, Colonel Henry, 43
Sidney, Lady Lucy, 19
Sidney, Sir Philip, 3

Smithers, Leonard, 219
Southey, Robert, 100
Southwell, Lady Elizabeth, 5
Spurway, Humphrey, 9
Stanhope, Philip (later fifth Earl of Chesterfield), 70
Stevens, Elsie Kachel, 250
Stevenson, Robert, 124
Steward, Elizabeth, 49
Strachey, Julia, 267
Sweetser, Mrs J. Howard, 194
Swift, Jonathan, 56

Talbot, Monsignor George, 170
Talbot, Mary, 178
Temple, Sir William, 26
Thrale, Hester Lynch, 81
Times, The (Editor of), 270
Tobin, James West, 93
Trusler, John, 88
Turner, Reginald, 217
Twain, Mark, 182
Tynan, Katharine, 203

Unwin, William, 80

Valcke, Lieutenant, 192

Walpole, Horace, fourth Earl of Orford, 60
Ward, Susan Hayes, 236
Watson, Major, 195
Webb, G. B., 146
Webster, Lady Frances, 103
Wells, H(erbert) G(eorge), 281
Wilde, Oscar, 215
Williams, W. S., 149
Witley Asylum, Governor of, 185
Wordsworth, William, 106
Wren, Sir Christopher, 34
Wright, Milton, 227

Yeats, William Butler, 249

Index of selected subjects

aeronautics, 82, 227

Africa, 143, 179, 180, 192, 195, 197, 202

Alice Through the Looking-Glass, 178

America and Americans, 3, 43, 65, 66, 78, 82, 140, 150, 152, 154, 155, 157, 159, 164, 165, 167, 170, 171, 178, 182, 192, 194, 196, 198, 199, 204, 205, 207, 220, 227, 236, 242, 249, 250, 258, 264, 275, 276, 278, 279, 280, 282

American Civil War, 167, 170, 196, 204

American Indians, 3, 65, 150, 155, 159

anatomical curiosities, 37

animals – *see* birds and animals

archaeology, 150, 178

Assisi, 272

atheism, 92, 190

atomic bomb, 282

autograph hunters, 146, 152, 229

Autumn, 66, 114

ballooning, 82

begging letters, 7, 16, 18, 51, 135, 147, 224, 225

Belfast, 266

bibliomania, 262

birds and animals, domestic, 11, 18, 125, 138, 147, 164, 209

birds and animals, exotic, 18, 37, 125, 147

Birmingham, 170

Bridlington, Yorkshire, 270

Bristol, 21

cats, 209, 260, 261

Charterhouse School, 251

Chelmsford, 136

children and childhood, 9, 15, 31, 41, 49, 70, 88, 93, 99, 100, 150, 153, 178, 204, 262, 275

church and clergy, 56, 88, 135, 142, 170, 193

Communism and Socialism, 22, 148, 265

consolation and mourning, 5, 9, 17, 31, 41, 76, 100, 133, 138, 140, 149, 153, 167, 171, 176, 179, 180, 197, 202, 213, 243, 257, 262

costume, 9, 11, 33

damnation, 87

dances and entertainments, 33, 48, 59, 97, 111, 275

death, letters written before, 9, 76, 84, 95, 122, 132, 135, 146, 175, 195, 199, 213, 218, 219, 235, 237, 238, 259, 279

death, of children, 31, 41, 100, 153

dentistry, 220

depressive illness, 81, 87

Dictionary of the English Language, Johnson's, 61

diggers, 22

dolphins, methods of cooking, 37

Don Juan, 116

Dream of Gerontius, The, 223

drink, 12, 36, 40, 92, 147, 163, 209, 264, 276

drugs, 94, 101, 106, 251

Dublin, 225, 260

Dunciad, The, 56

education, 34, 70

Index of selected subjects

Elegy Written in a Country Church-Yard, 60
Elgin Marbles, 98
England, attitudes towards, 113, 129, 223, 241, 281
English Civil War, 20–2
exploration, 3, 77, 143, 179, 180, 192, 195, 197, 202, 237, 238

fan letters, 6, 130, 145, 265, 268
First World War, 244–59
food, 37, 49, 56, 86, 93, 163, 209, 251
forgeries, 6

Great Exhibition, 154
Gulliver's Travels, 54

Hamlet, 8, 104

ill health, 17, 30, 49, 76, 84, 86, 94, 100, 118, 119, 120, 121, 134, 142, 167, 188, 197, 198, 235, 251, 271, 273, 279, 281
Impressionism, 199
insanity, 163, 186, 188

Japan, 209, 212, 220
jewellery, 18

Lake District, 93, 109
letters and letter-writing, 3, 9, 15, 26, 28, 51, 53, 70, 76, 80, 106, 124, 136, 143, 152, 153, 194, 197, 207, 212, 228, 251, 261, 264, 268
life abroad, 18, 48, 111, 113, 116, 120, 122, 124, 143, 199, 125, 207, 209, 220, 230, 231, 238, 241, 242, 256, 259, 264, 272, 276, 278
Light Brigade, Charge of the, 162
literary composition and criticism, 12, 49, 63, 105, 109, 114, 116, 120, 121, 145, 155, 157, 164, 171, 173, 178, 183, 186, 203, 216, 221, 222, 225, 226, 231, 241, 249, 256, 260, 262, 264, 265, 269, 271, 276, 278, 280
London, 9, 12, 15, 33, 44, 45, 48, 67, 74, 135, 154, 203, 242, 270, 273

Lord Jim, 222
love letters, 8, 26, 28, 33, 35, 39, 50, 53, 60, 67, 74, 90, 95, 113, 118, 119, 145, 174, 228, 230, 234, 242, 272, 273

Market Harborough, 20, 240
marriage, 9, 15, 19, 74, 84
medicine, 37, 225
Mermaid Tavern, 12
Mexico, 276
Moby Dick, 155, 157
Mrs Dalloway, 262
music and musicians, 59, 79, 129, 223, 268, 275
Music for the Royal Fireworks, 59

Naseby, Battle of, 20
nature and landscape, 56, 58, 88, 92, 140, 142, 150, 159, 171, 212, 234, 238, 241, 247, 264
Newark, 40
New York, 242, 279
newspapers, letters to, 245, 270
nihilism, 184
ninth symphony (Beethoven), 129

Ode 'To Autumn', 114
office life, 50, 106, 131, 231
old age, 17, 19, 47, 142, 171, 271
ornithology, 270
Oxford, 203

painters and painting, 60, 69, 71, 79, 88, 98, 109, 132, 133, 163, 174, 199, 219, 261, 267
Paris, 199
Parliamentary elections, 40, 57, 136
patronage, 6, 46, 51, 59, 61, 68, 73, 74, 88, 105, 129
phonography, 204
piles, 86
plays, playwrights and players, 6, 7, 8, 12, 16, 47, 48, 50, 184, 196, 212, 215, 216, 217, 230, 234, 243, 260
politics, 22, 40, 43, 51, 58, 63, 66, 142, 148, 154, 184, 193, 196, 244, 245, 265, 270, 282

Principia Mathematica, 46
pseudonymous letters, 54, 124
publishing and printing, 46, 51, 54,
    56, 60, 61, 68, 86, 106, 155, 192,
    260, 279
put-downs, 19, 41, 57, 61, 74, 88, 99,
    105, 137, 170, 191, 192, 197

railways, 124, 220
reading, 15, 26, 49, 63, 86, 93, 120,
    121, 136, 150, 164, 171, 188, 218,
    226, 231, 236, 241, 260, 262, 266,
    269, 273
retirement, 58, 63, 79, 183
royalty, 3, 5, 18, 20, 21, 35, 37, 39,
    44, 59, 65, 78, 105, 148, 154, 191,
    197, 244
Russia and Russians, 184, 189, 226,
    230, 235

St Paul's Cathedral, 9, 135
Salisbury, 212
science and technology, 46, 82, 124,
    182, 204, 272, 282
servants, lectures to, 75
Seven Pillars of Wisdom, 265
Shakespeare, 6, 7, 8, 68, 69, 104, 175

Socialism – *see* Communism
South Seas, 77, 207, 213
Stuart Little, 280

telegrams, 227, 240
Third Symphony (Elgar), 268
Troy, 178
Tropic of Capricorn, 278
typewriters, 182

Ulysses, 260, 269
Under the Volcano, 276

verse quoted in letters, 8, 12, 28, 39,
    50, 60, 63, 86, 111, 180

war, 3, 5, 20, 21, 65, 66, 78, 82, 95,
    96, 103, 104, 130, 162, 167, 188,
    195, 196, 244, 245, 247, 251, 254,
    256, 257, 259, 265, 278, 282
Waterloo, Battle of, 103
Winchester, 114
'Wreck of the Deutschland, The', 186

zombies, 205

Sources

Introduction

Extract from the Melbourne Manuscript (text here modernized), attributed by the present editor to John Webster (to be published in The Cambridge Edition of the Works of John Webster, edited by David Carnegie, David Gunby and Antony Hammond)

Extract from Keats's journal – letter to George and Georgiana Keats, 14 February–3 May 1819, from *Letters of John Keats*, edited by Robert Gittings (Oxford University Press, 1970)

Richard Steele to his wife, from *The Correspondence of Richard Steele*, edited by Rae Blanchard (Oxford University Press, 1941)

Extract from a letter by Dora Wordsworth to her father, quoted in *Catalogue of Valuable Autograph Letters, Literary Manuscripts, Historical Documents and Literary Relics and Portraits*, lot 402 (Sotheby Parke Bernet & Co., 5–6 July 1977)

Extract from a letter by Henry James to W. B. Yeats, photocopy from the Gregory papers

W. B. Yeats from 'In Memory of Major Robert Gregory', *The Collected Poems of W. B. Yeats* (Macmillan, 1933)

The Letters 1578–1939

SIR PHILIP SIDNEY to Edmund Molyneux, 31 May 1578
  The Prose Works of Sir Philip Sidney, edited by Albert Feuillerant, iii (Cambridge University Press, 1912–26; reprinted 1963)

SIR RALPH LANE to Sir Philip Sidney, 12 August 1585
  The Roanoke Voyages, i (the Hakluyt Society, Second Series, No. CIV, 1950)

SIR PHILIP SIDNEY to Queen Elizabeth I, 10 November 1585
The Prose Works of Sir Philip Sidney, edited by Albert Feuillerant, iii
(Cambridge University Press, 1912–26; reprinted 1963)

QUEEN ELIZABETH I to the Lady Elizabeth Southwell, 16 October 1598
MS, Spiro Collection, New York

QUEEN ELIZABETH I to William Shakespeare, undated
John Mair, *The Fourth Forger* (Cobden-Sanderson, 1938)

RICHARD QUINEY to William Shakespeare, 25 October 1598
Sir Sidney Lee, *A Life of William Shakespeare*, New Edition (Smith, Elder
& Co., 1915)

'MR V.' to Mistress Mary Loveringe, [May 1599]
*Catalogue of Valuable Autograph Letters, Literary Manuscripts and
Historical Documents*, lot 69 (Sotheby Park Bernet & Co., 22 June 1976)

HAMLET, PRINCE OF DENMARK, to Ophelia, [summer or autumn 1599]
William Shakespeare, *The Tragedie of Hamlet, Prince of Denmark*, II. ii, in
the First Folio (1623)

JOHN WILLOUGHBY to Humphrey Spurway, 1 June 1600
Trevelyan Papers, Part III, edited by Sir Walter Calverley Trevelyan and Sir
Charles Edward Trevelyan (Camden Society, 1872)

SIR WALTER RALEGH to his wife Elizabeth, [December 1603]
Edward Edwards, *The Life of Sir Walter Ralegh . . . Together with his
Letters*, ii (Macmillan & Co., 1868)

SIR ROBERT CECIL to Sir Thomas Edmondes, 9 November 1605
Facsimiles of Autographs in the British Museum, edited by George F.
Warner (British Museum, 1899)

SIR FRANCIS BEAUMONT to Ben Jonson, undated [?between 1605 and
1613]
Francis Beaumont, *Poems* (1640)

JOHN DONNE to Sir Henry Goodyer, [*c.* 1609]
John Donne, *Complete Poetry and Selected Prose*, edited by John Hayward
(Nonesuch Press, 1929; tenth impression 1972)

NATHAN FIELD AND OTHERS to Philip Henslowe, [early July 1613]
W. W. Greg, *English Literary Autographs, 1550–1650*, xiii (b) (Oxford,
Clarendon Press, 1932)

Sources

JOHN DONNE to Sir H[?enry Goodyer], 4 October 1622
  John Donne, *Complete Poetry and Selected Prose*, edited by John Hayward
  (Nonesuch Press, 1929; tenth impression 1972)

THE DUKE OF BUCKINGHAM to James I, 25 April 1623
  Facsimiles of Autographs in the British Museum, edited by George F.
  Warner (British Museum, 1899)

EDMUND WALLER to Lady Lucy Sidney, July 1639
  Edmund Waller, *Poems* (Jacob Tonson, 1712)

OLIVER CROMWELL to the Speaker of the House of Commons, 14 June
  1645
  Facsimiles of Autographs in the British Museum, edited by George F.
  Warner (British Museum, 1899)

CHARLES I to Prince Rupert, 14 September 1645
  Civil War Papers, lot 30 (Sotheby's, 21 July 1980)

GERRARD WINSTANLEY to Lord Fairfax and the Army Council,
  8 December 1649
  The Clarke Papers, ii, edited by C. H. Firth (Camden Society 1894)

DOROTHY OSBORNE to Sir William Temple, [5 or 6 March 1653]
  Dorothy Osborne, *Letters to Sir William Temple*, edited by Kenneth Parker
  (Penguin Books, 1987)

JOHN DRYDEN to Honor Dryden, [May 1653 or 1655]
  The Letters of John Dryden, edited by Charles E. Ward (Duke University
  Press, 1942)

LORD CHESTERFIELD to an unknown correspondent, December 1656
  *Philip Stanhope, Second Earl of Chesterfield, his Correspondence with
  Various Ladies* (Franfrolico Press, 1930)

BARBARA VILLIERS AND LADY ANN HAMBLETON to
  Lord Chesterfield, 1657
  *Philip Stanhope, Second Earl of Chesterfield, his Correspondence with
  Various Ladies* (Franfrolico Press, 1930)

JEREMY TAYLOR to John Evelyn, 17 February 1658
  Diary of John Evelyn, iii, edited by William Bray (Bickers and Son, 1879)

LORD WINDSOR to Lord Hatton, [October 1658]
  Correspondence of the Family of Hatton, i, edited by Edward Maunde
  Thompson (Camden Society, 1878)

LORD CHESTERFIELD to an unknown lady, [*c.* 1660]
Philip Stanhope, Second Earl of Chesterfield, his Correspondence with Various Ladies (Franfrolico Press, 1930)

JOHN EVELYN to Sir Christopher Wren, 4 April 1665
Diary of John Evelyn, iii, edited by William Bray (Bickers and Son, 1879)

CHARLES II to Louise de Kéroualle, [*c.* 1670]
Goodwood: Royal Letters, edited by Timothy J. McCann (Trustees of the Goodwood Collections, 1977)

LORD ROCHESTER to Henry Savile, [1673–4]
The Letters of John Wilmot, Earl of Rochester, edited by Jeremy Treglown (Basil Blackwell, 1980; reprinted 1985)

SIR THOMAS BROWNE to his son Edward, 14 June [1676]
The Letters of Sir Thomas Browne, edited by Geoffrey Keynes (Faber and Faber, 1946)

PRINCESS MARY to Frances Apsley, [*c.* 1676]
Letters of Two Queens, edited by Benjamin Bathurst (Robert Holden, 1924)

HENRY SAVILE to his brother Lord Halifax, 16 April 1677
Savile Correspondence, edited by William Durrant Cooper (Camden Society, 1858)

DR FELL to Lady Hatton, 3 July [1680]
Correspondence of the Family of Hatton, i, edited by Edward Maunde Thompson (Camden Society, 1878)

WILLIAM PENN to Colonel Henry Sidney, 29 March 1681
Facsimiles of Autographs in the British Museum, edited by George F. Warner (British Museum, 1899)

NELL GWYN to (?) Laurence Hyde, [? May or June 1682]
The Camden Miscellany, Volume the Fifth, Letters from the Collection of Autographs in the Possession of William Tite (Camden Society, 1864)

DR FELL to Lady Hatton, 25 January [1684]
Correspondence of the Family of Hatton, i, edited by Edward Maunde Thompson (Camden Society, 1878)

EDMUND HALLEY to Isaac Newton, 22 May 1686
The Correspondence of Isaac Newton, ii, edited by H. W. Turnbull (Cambridge University Press, for the Royal Society, 1960)

Sources

LORD MULGRAVE to Sir George Etherege, 7 March 1687
The Letters of Sir George Etherege, edited by Frederick Bracher (University of California Press, 1974)

SIR GEORGE ETHEREGE to Robert Corbet, April 1687
The Letters of Sir George Etherege, edited by Frederick Bracher (University of California Press, 1974)

JOHN DRYDEN to Mrs Steward, 2 February 1699
The Letters of John Dryden, edited by Charles E. Ward (Duke University Press, 1942)

SIR RICHARD STEELE to Mary Scurlock, 1 September 1707
The Correspondence of Richard Steele, edited by Rae Blanchard (Oxford, Clarendon Press, 1941)

DANIEL DEFOE to Robert Harley, 11 September 1707
The Letters of Daniel Defoe, edited by George Harris Healey (Oxford, Clarendon Press, 1955)

LADY MARY WORTLEY MONTAGU, to Edward Wortley Montagu, 28 March 1710
The Complete Letters of Lady Mary Wortley Montagu, i, edited by Robert Halsband (Oxford, Clarendon Press, 1967)

JONATHAN SWIFT to Benjamin Motte, 8 August 1726
The Correspondence of Jonathan Swift, iii, edited by Harold Williams (Oxford, Clarendon Press, 1963)

ALEXANDER POPE to Jonathan Swift, 28 June 1728
The Correspondence of Alexander Pope, ii, edited by George Sherburn (Oxford, Clarendon Press, 1956)

ANTHONY HENLEY, MP, to his Constituents, [1734]
Notes and Queries, second series, xii, (1861), p. 107; present text (incorporating corrections) from John Julius Norwich, *Christmas Crackers* (Penguin Books, 1982)

SIR ROBERT WALPOLE to Charles Churchill, 24 June 1743
Contemporary transcript, private collection

THE DUKE OF MONTAGU to Charles Frederick, 9 April 1749
Otto Erich Deutsch, *Handel* (Adam and Charles Black, 1955)

WILLIAM HOGARTH to his wife, Jenny, 6 June 1749
Facsimile in A. M. Broadley, *Chats on Autographs* (T. Fisher Unwin, 1910)

THOMAS GRAY to Horace Walpole, 11 February 1751
Correspondence of Thomas Gray, i, edited by Paget Toynbee and Leonard
Whibley (Oxford, Clarendon Press, 1935)

SAMUEL JOHNSON to Lord Chesterfield, February 1755
The Letters of Samuel Johnson, i, edited by R. W. Chapman (Oxford,
Clarendon Press, 1952)

HORACE WALPOLE to George Montagu, 24 October 1758
The Yale Edition of Horace Walpole's Correspondence, ix, edited by W. S.
Lewis (Oxford University Press, 1941)

WILLIAM HENRY LYTTELTON to Emperor Old Hop and
the Little Carpenter, 22 May 1759
The Lyttelton Papers, lot 64 (Sotheby Parke Bernet & Co.,
12 December 1978)

HORACE WALPOLE to George Montagu, 21 October 1759
The Yale Edition of Horace Walpole's Correspondence, x,
edited by W. S. Lewis (Oxford University Press, 1941)

LAURENCE STERNE to Catherine Fourmantel, 8 March 1760
Letters of Laurence Sterne, edited by Lewis Perry Curtis (Oxford,
Clarendon Press, 1935)

VOLTAIRE to Lord Chesterfield, 5 August 1761
The Complete Works of Voltaire, vol. 107 (The Voltaire Foundation, 1972)

THOMAS GAINSBOROUGH to David Garrick, 22 August 1768
The Letters of Thomas Gainsborough, edited by Mary Woodall
(The Cupid Press, 1963)

LORD CHESTERFIELD to his godson, Philip Stanhope, 15 September 1768
*Letters of Philip Dormer Stanhope fourth Earl of Chesterfield to his Godson
and Successor*, edited by the Earl of Carnarvon (Oxford, Clarendon Press,
1890)

HORACE WALPOLE to Thomas Chatterton, 28 March 1769
The Yale Edition of Horace Walpole's Correspondence, xvi, edited by W. S.
Lewis (Oxford University Press, 1952)

THOMAS CHATTERTON to William Barrett, [February or March 1770]
The Complete Works of Thomas Chatterton, i, edited by Donald S. Taylor
with Benjamin B. Hoover (Oxford, Clarendon Press, 1971)

ESTHER SAUNDERS to Thomas Chatterton, with Chatterton's reply,
3 April 1770
The Complete Works of Thomas Chatterton, i, edited by Donald S. Taylor
with Benjamin B. Hoover (Oxford, Clarendon Press, 1971)

Sources

CHRISTOPHER SMART to Dr Burney, 26 April 1770
British Literary Manuscripts, Series I from 800 to 1800, edited by Verlyn Klinkenborg, Herbert Cahoon and Charles Ryskamp (Pierpont Morgan Library and Dover Publications, 1981)

THE DUKE OF QUEENSBERRY to his Negro servant, Soubise, 8 November 1772
Catalogue of Collection of Autograph Letters and Historical Documents formed . . . by Alfred Morrison, v (privately printed, 1891)

DAVID HUME to the Comtesse de Boufflers, 20 August 1776
The Letters of David Hume, ii, edited by J. Y. T. Greig (Oxford, Clarendon Press, 1932)

CAPTAIN COOK to Lord Sandwich, 26 November 1776
Photocopy in the Sandwich Papers, England

GEORGE III to Lord Sandwich, 3 August 1777
MS in the Sandwich Papers, England

THOMAS GAINSBOROUGH to William Jackson, 4 June [before 1778]
The Letters of Thomas Gainsborough, edited by Mary Woodall (The Cupid Press, 1963)

WILLIAM COWPER to William Unwin, 6 August 1780
The Letters and Prose Writings of William Cowper, i, edited by James King and Charles Ryskamp (Oxford, Clarendon Press, 1979)

DR JOHNSON to Mrs Thrale, 28 June 1783
The Letters of Samuel Johnson, iii, edited by R. W. Chapman (Oxford, Clarendon Press, 1952)

BENJAMIN FRANKLIN to Sir Joseph Banks, 27 July 1783
Original Letters of Eminent Literary Men, edited by Sir Henry Ellis (Camden Society, 1893)

SAMUEL JOHNSON to Lucy Porter, 2 December 1784
The Letters of Samuel Johnson, iii, edited by R. W. Chapman (Oxford, Clarendon Press, 1952)

ROBERT BURNS to Robert Ainslie, 3 March 1788
The Letters of Robert Burns, i, edited by J. De Lancey Ferguson (Oxford, Clarendon Press, 1931)

WILLIAM COWPER to Samuel Rose, 24 April 1792
The Letters and Prose Writings of William Cowper, iv, edited by James King and Charles Ryskamp (Oxford, Clarendon Press, 1984)

WILLIAM COWPER to John Newton, 11 April 1799
The Letters and Prose Writings of William Cowper, iv, edited by James King
and Charles Ryskamp (Oxford, Clarendon Press, 1984)

WILLIAM BLAKE to John Trusler, 23 August 1799
The Letters of William Blake, edited by Geoffrey Keynes (Rupert Hart-
Davis, 1956)

LORD NELSON to Lady Hamilton, 29 January–2 February [1800]
MS, Spiro Collection, New York; an inaccurate transcript of part of the
letter was published in a recent auction catalogue, and a paragraph printed
by Tom Pocock, *Nelson* (1987), p. 193 (where a date of 1799 is assigned to
the letter)

SAMUEL TAYLOR COLERIDGE to William Godwin, [3 March 1800]
The Collected Letters of Samuel Taylor Coleridge, i, edited by Earl Leslie
Griggs (Oxford, Clarendon Press, 1956)

SAMUEL TAYLOR COLERIDGE to James West Tobin, 25 July 1800
The Collected Letters of Samuel Taylor Coleridge, i, edited by Earl Leslie
Griggs (Oxford, Clarendon Press, 1956)

GEORGE MORLAND to John Graham, 6 May 1801
Facsimile in A. M. Broadley, *Chats on Autographs* (T. Fisher Unwin, 1910)

LORD NELSON to Lady Hamilton, 19 and 20 October 1805
Facsimile, private collection (from the original now in the British Library)

'SAM' to his father, [October or November 1805]
Modernized text first printed in *Naval Yarns*, edited by W. H. Long (1899);
this text from John Julius Norwich, *Christmas Crackers* (Penguin Books,
1982)

LORD BYRON to the Revd J. T. Becher, 26 February 1808
Byron's Letters and Journals, i, edited by Leslie A. Marchand (John
Murray, 1973)

BENJAMIN ROBERT HAYDON to Lord Elgin, December 1808
Benjamin Robert Haydon: Correspondence and Table-Talk, with a memoir
by his son Frederic Wordsworth Haydon (Chatto & Windus, 1876)

PERCY BYSSHE SHELLEY to Thomas Hitchener, 14 May 1812
The Letters of Percy Bysshe Shelley, i, edited by Frederick L. Jones
(Oxford, Clarendon Press, 1964)

Sources

WILLIAM WORDSWORTH to Robert Southey, 2 December 1812
The Letters of William and Dorothy Wordsworth, iii, edited by Ernest de
Selincourt, second edition revised by Mary Moorman and Alan G. Hill
(Oxford, Clarendon Press, 1970)

LADY HAMILTON to Sir Richard Puleston, 24 July 1813
MS, Spiro Collection, New York

SAMUEL TAYLOR COLERIDGE to Joseph Cottle, 26 April 1814
The Collected Letters of Samuel Taylor Coleridge, iii, edited by Earl Leslie
Griggs (Oxford, Clarendon Press, 1959)

THE DUKE OF WELLINGTON to Lady Frances Webster, 19 June 1815
The Duke of Wellington, *Supplementary Despatches, Correspondence,
and Memoranda*, x, edited by his son the Duke of Wellington
(John Murray, 1863)

JOHN BARROW to Admiral Lord Keith, 14 July 1815
Photocopy from the original in the National Maritime Museum, Greenwich:
a text (addressed to J. W. Croker) is published in *The Keith Papers*, iii,
edited by Christopher Lloyd (Naval Records Society, 1955)

JAMES STANIER CLARKE to Jane Austen, 27 March 1816
Jane Austen's Letters, second edition, edited by R. W. Chapman
(Oxford University Press, 1952)

JANE AUSTEN to James Stanier Clarke, 1 April 1816
Jane Austen's Letters, second edition, edited by R. W. Chapman
(Oxford University Press, 1952)

CHARLES LAMB to William Wordsworth, [26 April 1816]
The Works of Charles and Mary Lamb, vi, edited by E. V. Lucas
(Methuen, 1905)

WILLIAM WORDSWORTH to Charles Lamb, 21 November [1816]
The Letters of William Wordsworth: A New Selection, edited by Alan
G. Hill (Oxford University Press, 1984)

LORD BYRON to Thomas Moore, 28 February 1817
Byron's Letters and Journals, v, edited by Leslie A. Marchand
(John Murray, 1976)

LORD BYRON to Augusta Leigh, 17 May 1819
Byron's Letters and Journals, vi, edited by Leslie A. Marchand
(John Murray, 1976)

JOHN KEATS to J. H. Reynolds, 21 September 1819
Letters of John Keats, edited by Robert Gittings
(Oxford University Press, 1970)

LORD BYRON to the Hon. Douglas Kinnaird, 26 October 1819
Byron's Letters and Journals, vi, edited by Leslie A. Marchand
(John Murray, 1976)

JOHN KEATS to Fanny Brawne, [(?)24 February 1820]
Letters of John Keats, edited by Robert Gittings (Oxford University Press,
1970)

JOHN KEATS to Fanny Brawne, [(?) March 1820]
Letters of John Keats, edited by Robert Gittings (Oxford University Press,
1970)

PERCY BYSSHE SHELLEY to John Keats, 27 July 1820
The Letters of Percy Bysshe Shelley, ii, edited by Frederick L. Jones
(Oxford, Clarendon Press, 1964)

JOHN KEATS to Percy Bysshe Shelley, 16 August [1820]
Letters of John Keats, edited by Robert Gittings
(Oxford University Press, 1970)

JOHN KEATS to Charles Armitage Brown, 30 November 1820
Letters of John Keats, edited by Robert Gittings
(Oxford University Press, 1970)

STENDHAL to the Baron de Mareste, 31 December 1820
Stendhal: Correspondence, i, edited by V. del Litto and Henri Martineau
(Bibliothèque de la Pléade, 1962)

GEORGE STEPHENSON to Robert Stevenson, 28 June 1821
W. O. Skeat, *George Stephenson, the Engineer and his Letters*
(The Institution of Mechanical Engineers, 1973)

PERCY BYSSHE SHELLEY to Thomas Love Peacock, [?10] August 1821
The Letters of Percy Bysshe Shelley, ii, edited by Frederick L. Jones
(Oxford, Clarendon Press, 1964)

WILLIAM HAZLITT to P. G. Patmore, 31 May 1822
The Letters of William Hazlitt, edited by Herschel Sikes, W. H. Bonner and
Gerald Lahey (Macmillan, 1979)

LUDWIG VAN BEETHOVEN to Charles Neate, 25 February 1823
The Letters of Beethoven, iii, edited by Emily Anderson (Macmillan, 1961)

Sources

LORD BYRON to Goethe, 22 July 1823
Byron's Letters and Journals, x, edited by Leslie A. Marchand
(John Murray, 1980)

CHARLES LAMB to Henry Crabb Robinson, [29 March] 1825
The Works of Charles and Mary Lamb, vii, edited by E. V. Lucas
(Methuen, 1905)

WILLIAM BLAKE to George Cumberland, 12 April 1827
The Letters of William Blake, edited by Geoffrey Keynes
(Rupert Hart-Davis, 1956)

GEORGE RICHMOND to Samuel Palmer, [15 August 1827]
The Letters of William Blake, edited by Geoffrey Keynes
(Rupert Hart-Davis, 1956)

JOEY GRIMALDI to an unidentified correspondent, 20 December 1829
Facsimile in A. M. Broadley, *Chats on Autographs* (T. Fisher Unwin, 1910)

WILLIAM HAZLITT to Francis Jeffrey, [September 1830]
The Letters of William Hazlitt, edited by Herschel Sikes, W. H. Bonner and
Gerald Lahey (Macmillan, 1979)

SYDNEY SMITH to Guillemard, 22 November 1833
The Letters of Sydney Smith, ii, edited by Nowell C. Smith (Oxford,
Clarendon Press, 1953)

CHARLES DICKENS to Thomas Beard, [11 January 1835]
The Letters of Charles Dickens: the Pilgrim Edition, i, edited by Madeline
House and Graham Storey (Oxford, Clarendon Press, 1965)

THE DUKE OF WELLINGTON to Miss A. M. Jenkins, 14 March 1840
The Letters of the Duke of Wellington to Miss J., edited by Christine
Terhune Herrick (T. Fisher Unwin, 1924)

CHARLES DICKENS to Daniel Maclise, 12 March 1841
The Letters of Charles Dickens: The Pilgrim Edition, ii, edited by Madeline
House and Graham Storey (Oxford, Clarendon Press, 1969)

CHARLES DICKENS to Basil Hall, 27 April 1841
The Letters of Charles Dickens: The Pilgrim Edition, ii, edited by Madeline
House and Graham Storey (Oxford, Clarendon Press, 1969)

HENRY THOREAU to Lucy Brown, 2 March 1842
The Correspondence of Henry David Thoreau, edited by Walter Harding
and Carl Bode (New York University Press, 1958)

SYDNEY SMITH to Lady Holland, 13 September 1842
The Letters of Sydney Smith, ii, edited by Nowell C. Smith (Oxford, Clarendon Press, 1953)

SYDNEY SMITH to Mrs Meynell, 23 September 1842
The Letters of Sydney Smith, ii, edited by Nowell C. Smith (Oxford, Clarendon Press, 1953)

DR LIVINGSTONE to his parents, 16 December 1843
David Livingstone, Family Letters 1841–1856, i, edited by I. Schapera (Chatto & Windus, 1959)

ROBERT BROWNING to Elizabeth Barrett, [10 January 1845]
The Letters of Robert Browning and Elizabeth Barrett Browning 1845–1846, i, edited by Elvan Kintner (Harvard, Belknap Press, 1969)

THOMAS HOOD to an autograph collector, 19 March 1845
The Letters of Thomas Hood, edited by Peter F. Morgan (Oliver and Boyd, 1973)

PATRICK BRANWELL BRONTË to John Brown, [1848]
The Brontë Letters, edited by Muriel Spark (Peter Nevill, 1954)

CHARLES DICKENS to Thomas Beard, 10 May 1848
The Letters of Charles Dickens: The Pilgrim Edition, v, edited by Graham Storey and K. J. Fielding (Oxford, Clarendon Press, 1981)

PRINCE ALBERT to Lord Brougham, 15 June 1848
Catalogue of the Collection of Autograph Letters and Historical Documents formed . . . by Alfred Morrison, i (privately printed, 1891)

CHARLOTTE BRONTË to W. S. Williams, 2 October 1848
Clement Shorter, *The Brontës*, i (Hodder & Stoughton, 1908)

HENRY THOREAU to Ellen Emerson, 31 July 1849
The Correspondence of Henry David Thoreau, edited by Walter Harding and Carl Bode (New York University Press, 1958)

NATHANIEL HAWTHORNE to an autograph collector, 12 April 1851
The Centenary Edition of the Works of Nathaniel Hawthorne, xvi, *The Letters, 1813–1843*, edited by Thomas Woodson, L. Neal Smith and Norman Holmes Pearson (Ohio State University Press, 1984)

ALFRED TENNYSON to Robert Monteith, [c. 24 April 1851]
The Letters of Alfred Lord Tennyson, ii, edited by Cecil Y. Lang and Edgar F. Shannon Jr. (Oxford, Clarendon Press, 1987)

Sources

WALTER BAGEHOT to his mother, 8 May 1851
  The Collected Works of Walter Bagehot, xii, *The Letters*, edited by Norman
  St John-Stevas (*The Economist*, 1986)

HERMAN MELVILLE to Nathaniel Hawthorne, 29 June 1851
  The Letters of Herman Melville, edited by Merrell R. Davis and William H.
  Gilman (Yale University Press, 1960)

HERMAN MELVILLE to Nathaniel Hawthorne, [(?)17 November 1851]
  The Letters of Herman Melville, edited by Merrell R. Davis and William H.
  Gilman (Yale University Press, 1960)

CHIEF SEATTLE to the President of the United States, [1854]
  Transcript, private collection, London

LORD RAGLAN to the Light Brigade, [25 October 1854]
  Facsimile in Cecil Woodham-Smith, *The Reason Why* (Constable, 1953)

JOHN CLARE to James Hipkins, 8 March 1860
  The Letters of John Clare, edited by Mark Storey (Oxford,
  Clarendon Press, 1985)

DANTE GABRIEL ROSSETTI to Alexander Gilchrist, 19 November 1861
  Letters of Dante Gabriel Rossetti, ii, edited by Oswald Doughty and John
  Robert Wahl (Oxford, Clarendon Press, 1965)

EMILY DICKINSON to T. W. Higginson, 26 April 1862
  The Letters of Emily Dickinson, ii, edited by Thomas H. Johnson and
  Theodora Ward (Harvard, the Belknap Press, 1958)

EMILY DICKINSON to T. W. Higginson, [July 1862]
  The Letters of Emily Dickinson, ii, edited by Thomas H. Johnson and
  Theodora Ward (Harvard, the Belknap Press, 1958)

W. M. THACKERAY to Dr Henry Bence Jones, [(?)26 March 1863]
  Facsimile in *English Literature and History*, lot 153 (Sotheby's,
  22 and 23 July 1985)

WALT WHITMAN to Mr and Mrs S. B. Haskell, 10 August 1863
  The Collected Writings of Walt Whitman: The Correspondence, i edited by
  Edwin Haviland Miller (New York University Press, 1961)

CARDINAL NEWMAN to Monsignor Talbot, 25 July 1864
  The Letters and Writings of John Henry Newman, xxi, edited by Charles
  Stephen Dessain and Edward E. Kelly, S. J. (Nelson, 1971)

ABRAHAM LINCOLN to General Ulysses S. Grant, 19 January 1865
Facsimile in *Highly Important American Historical Documents, Autograph Letters and Manuscripts* the Sang Collection, Part Two, lot 501 (Sotheby Parke Bernet Inc., 14 November 1978)

THOMAS CARLYLE to Ralph Waldo Emerson, 27 January 1867
The Correspondence of Emerson and Carlyle, edited by Joseph Slater (Columbia University Press, 1964)

ROBERT BROWNING to William G. Kingsland, 27 November 1868
Facsimiles of Autographs in the British Museum, edited by George F. Warner (British Museum, 1899)

DANTE GABRIEL ROSSETTI to Jane Morris, 4 February 1870
Dante Gabriel Rossetti and Jane Morris: Their Correspondence, edited by John Bryson and Janet Camp Troxell (Oxford, Clarendon Press, 1976)

CHARLES DICKENS to Charles Kent, 8 June 1870
Facsimiles of Autographs in the British Museum, edited by George F. Warner (British Museum, 1899)

GEORGE ELIOT to the Hon. Mrs Robert Lytton, 8 July 1870
The George Eliot Letters, v, edited by Gordon S. Haight (Yale University Press, 1954)

LEWIS CARROLL to Mary Talbot, 8 January 1872
MS, private collection, England

HEINRICH SCHLIEMANN to Frank Calvert, 1 January 1873
Heinrich Schliemann Briefwechsel, i, edited by Ernst Meyer (Gebr. Mann, 1953)

JACOB WAINWRIGHT to Lovett Cameron, October 1873
R. J. Campbell, *Livingstone* (Ernest Benn, 1929)

FLORENCE NIGHTINGALE to Agnes Livingstone, 18 February 1874
William Garden Blaikie, *The Personal Life of David Livingstone* (John Murray, 1880)

WILLIAM DEAN HOWELLS to Mark Twain, 5 November 1875
Selected Mark Twain–Howells Letters, edited by Frederick Anderson, William M. Gibson and Henry Nash Smith (Harvard, the Belknap Press, 1967)

ANTHONY TROLLOPE to G. W. Rusden, 8 June 1876
The Letters of Anthony Trollope, ii, edited by N. John Hall and Nina Burgis (Stanford University Press, 1983)

Sources

IVAN TURGENEV to W. R. S. Ralston, 19 April 1877
   Turgenev's Letters, edited by A. V. Knowles (University of London,
   Athlone Press, 1983)

ALFRED TENNYSON to the Governor of Witley Asylum, 21 October 1877
   The Letters of Alfred Lord Tennyson, i (Preface p. xxx), edited by Cecil Y.
   Lang and Edgar F. Shannon Jr. (Oxford, Clarendon Press, 1982)

GERARD MANLEY HOPKINS to Robert Bridges, 13 May 1878
   The Letters of Gerard Manley Hopkins to Robert Bridges, edited by Claude
   Colleer Abbott (Oxford University Press, 1935)

JOHN RUSKIN to Thomas Carlyle, 23 June 1878
   The Correspondence of Thomas Carlyle and John Ruskin, edited by George
   Allen Cate (Stanford University Press, 1982)

LEO TOLSTOY to R. W. S. Ralston, 27 October 1878
   Tolstoy's Letters, i, edited by R. F. Christian (University of London,
   Athlone Press, 1978)

CHARLES DARWIN to an unidentified recipient, 24 November 1880
   Facsimile, courtesy Maggs Brothers Ltd.

QUEEN VICTORIA'S PRIVATE SECRETARY to William McGonagall,
   17 October 1881
   David Phillips, *No Poets' Corner in the Abbey* (David Winter and Gerald
   Duckworth, 1971)

H. M. STANLEY to Lieutenant Valcke, 26 March 1882
   H. M. Stanley: Unpublished Letters, edited by Albert Maurice
   (W. & R. Chambers, 1957)

ANTHONY TROLLOPE to G. N. Richardson, 7 October 1882
   The Letters of Anthony Trollope, ii, edited by N. John Hall and Nina Burgis
   (Stanford University Press, 1983)

A. C. SWINBURNE to Edward Burne-Jones, 26 December 1882
   MS, Bernard Quaritch Ltd.

EMILY DICKINSON to Mrs Sweetser, [late Autumn 1884]
   The Letters of Emily Dickinson, iii, edited by Thomas H. Johnson and
   Theodora Ward (Harvard, the Belknap Press, 1958)

GENERAL GORDON to Major Watson, 14 December 1884
   Facsimile in Anthony Nutting, *Gordon: Martyr and Misfit* (Constable, 1966)

PHINEAS T. BARNUM to President Ulysses S. Grant, 12 January 1885
Selected Letters of P. T. Barnum, edited by A. H. Saxon
(Columbia University Press, 1983)

QUEEN VICTORIA to General Gordon's sister, 16 March 1885
Facsimiles of Autographs in the British Museum, edited by George F.
Warner (British Museum, 1899)

JOHN RUSKIN to his correspondents, 30 March 1886
Facsimile in *Catalogue of Autograph Letters, Literary Manuscripts and
Historical Documents*, lot 297 (Sotheby Parke Bernet & Co., 24–5 July
1978)

EMILY DICKINSON to Louise and Frances Norcross, [*c.* March 1886]
The Letters of Emily Dickinson, iii, edited by Thomas H. Johnson and
Theodora Ward (Harvard, the Belknap Press, 1958)

EMILY DICKINSON to Louise and Frances Norcross, [May 1886]
The Letters of Emily Dickinson, iii, edited by Thomas H. Johnson and
Theodora Ward (Harvard, the Belknap Press, 1958)

VINCENT VAN GOGH to H. M. Livens, [late summer 1886]
The Complete Letters of Vincent van Gogh, ii, edited by J. van Gogh-
Bongerand and C. de Dood (Thames & Hudson, 1958)

EMIN PASHA to General Gordon's sister, 17 August 1887
MS, Spiro Collection, New York

W. B. YEATS to Katherine Tynan, 25 August [1888]
The Collected Letters of W. B. Yeats, i, edited by John Kelly and
Eric Domville (Oxford, Clarendon Press, 1986)

WINSTON CHURCHILL to his mother, 7 November 1888
Randolph S. Churchill, *Winston S. Churchill*, i, (Heinemann, 1966)

LAFCADIO HEARN to George M. Gould, [1889]
Elizabeth Bisland, *The Life and Times of Lafcadio Hearn*, i
(Constable-Houghton Mifflin, 1906)

ROBERT LOUIS STEVENSON to Henry James, [March 1889]
The Letters of Robert Louis Stevenson, ii, edited by Sidney Colvin
(Methuen, 1899)

LAFCADIO HEARN to Professor Chamberlain, [August 1891]
Elizabeth Bisland, *The Life and Times of Lafcadio Hearn*, ii
(Constable-Houghton Mifflin, 1906)

Sources

OSCAR WILDE to Lord Alfred Douglas, [? January 1893]
The Letters of Oscar Wilde, edited by Rupert Hart-Davis
(Rupert Hart-Davis, 1963)

LAFCADIO HEARN to Sentarō Nishida, November 1893
Elizabeth Bisland, *The Life and Times of Lafcadio Hearn*, ii
(Constable-Houghton Mifflin, 1906)

ROBERT LOUIS STEVENSON to Charles Baxter, [Autumn 1894]
Stevenson: Stevenson's Letters to Charles Baxter, edited by De Lancey
Ferguson and Marshall Waingrow (Yale-Oxford University Press, 1956)

OSCAR WILDE to Ada Leverson, [? 10 February 1895]
The Letters of Oscar Wilde, edited by Rupert Hart-Davis
(Rupert Hart-Davis, 1963)

THE MARQUESS OF QUEENSBERRY to Oscar Wilde, [18 February 1895]
The Letters of Oscar Wilde, edited by Rupert Hart-Davis
(Rupert Hart-Davis, 1963)

BERNARD SHAW to Arthur Clark, 18 May 1895
Bernard Shaw: Collected Letters, i, edited by Dan H. Laurence
(Max Reinhardt, 1965)

OSCAR WILDE to Ada Leverson, [20 May 1897]
The Letters of Oscar Wilde, edited by Rupert Hart-Davis
(Rupert Hart-Davis, 1963)

OSCAR WILDE to Reggie Turner, 10 August [1897]
The Letters of Oscar Wilde, edited by Rupert Hart-Davis
(Rupert Hart-Davis, 1963)

CONSTANCE WILDE to Arthur Humphreys, 27 February 1898
Photocopy, private collection, a brief extract is printed by Richard Ellmann,
Oscar Wilde (1987), p. 523

AUBREY BEARDSLEY to Leonard Smithers, 7 March 1898
The Letters of Aubrey Beardsley, edited by Henry Maas, J. L. Duncan and
W. G. Good (Cassell, 1971)

LAFCADIO HEARN to Mitchell McDonald, July 1898
Elizabeth Bisland, *The Life and Times of Lafcadio Hearn*, ii
(Constable-Houghton Mifflin, 1906)

JOSEPH CONRAD to Edward Garnett, 3 August 1898
Letters from Conrad, edited by Edward Garnett (Nonesuch Press, 1928)

JOSEPH CONRAD to John Galsworthy, [? 20 July 1900]
G. Jean-Aubry, *Joseph Conrad: Life & Letters*, i (Heinemann, 1927)

EDWARD ELGAR to A. E. Jaeger, 9 October [1900]
Letters to Nimrod, edited by Percy M. Young (Dennis Dobson, 1965)

BARON CORVO to Harry Bainbridge, [1902]
Frederick William Rolfe, Baron Corvo: Letters to Harry Bainbridge
(Enitharmon Press, 1977)

BARON CORVO to Harry Bainbridge, [1902]
Frederick William Rolfe, Baron Corvo: Letters to Harry Bainbridge
(Enitharmon Press, 1977)

JAMES JOYCE to Lady Gregory, 22 November 1902
MS, private collection, London; an innacurate text, taken from a typescript
sent by Lady Gregory to W. B. Yeats, is printed in *Letters of James Joyce*,
i, edited by Stuart Gilbert (Faber and Faber, 1957)

W. B. YEATS to James Joyce, [? 25 November 1902]
Letters of James Joyce, ii, edited by Richard Ellmann
(Faber and Faber, 1966)

LEO TOLSTOY to Percy Redfern, 23 February 1903
Tolstoy's Letters, ii, edited by R. F. Christian
(University of London, Athlone Press, 1978)

ORVILLE WRIGHT to his father, 17 December [1903]
The Papers of Wilbur and Orville Wright, i, edited by Marvin W. McFarland
(McGraw-Hill, 1953)

JAMES JOYCE to Nora Barnacle, [*c.* 1 September 1904]
Letters of James Joyce, ii, edited by Richard Ellmann
(Faber and Faber, 1966)

CHARLES WRIGHT to Sherlock Holmes, 18 November 1904
Letters to Sherlock Holmes, edited by Richard Lancelyn Green
(Penguin Books, 1985)

ISADORA DUNCAN to Gordon Craig, Christmas Day 1904
'*Your Isador*', edited by Francis Steegmuller (Macmillan and the New York
Public Library, 1974)

JAMES JOYCE to his brother Stanislaus, 7 December 1906
Letters of James Joyce, ii, edited by Richard Ellmann
(Faber and Faber, 1966)

J. M. SYNGE to Molly Allgood, 22 May 1907
The Collected Letters of John Millington Synge, i, edited by Ann
Saddlemyer (Oxford, Clarendon Press, 1983)

LEO TOLSTOY to Aylmer Maude, 3 November 1910
Tolstoy's Letter, ii, edited by R. F. Christian (University of London,
Athlone Press, 1978)

Sources

ROBERT FROST to Susan Hayes Ward, 10 February 1912
Selected Letters of Robert Frost, edited by Lawrence Thompson
(Jonathan Cape, 1965)

CAPTAIN SCOTT to Sir George Egerton, [March 1912]
Scott's Last Expedition, i, edited by Leonard Huxley (John Murray, 1913)

CAPTAIN SCOTT to Mrs Bowers, [March 1912]
Scott's Last Expedition, i, edited by Leonard Huxley (John Murray, 1913)

D. H. LAWRENCE to Mrs Hopkin, 2 June 1912
The Letters of D. H. Lawrence, i, edited by James T. Boulton
(Cambridge University Press, 1979)

G. K. CHESTERTON to his wife, [c. 1912]
Maisie Ward, 'Gilbert Keith Chesterton' in *The Dictionary of National
Biography: 1931–1940* (Oxford University Press, 1949)

D. H. LAWRENCE to Arthur McLeod, 4 October 1912
The Letters of D. H. Lawrence, i, edited by James T. Boulton
(Cambridge University Press, 1979)

RUPERT BROOKE to Cathleen Nesbitt, 31 May [1913]
The Letters of Rupert Brooke, edited by Geoffrey Keynes,
(Faber and Faber, 1968)

BERNARD SHAW to the Hon. Mrs Alfred Lyttelton, 5 July 1913
Bernard Shaw: Collected Letters, iii, edited by Dan T. Laurence
(Max Reinhardt, 1965)

GEORGE V to Lord March, 26 July 1914
Goodwood: Royal Letters, edited by Timothy J. McCann
(Trustees of the Goodwood Collections, 1977)

BERTRAND RUSSELL to the Editor of the *Nation*, 12 August 1914
Bertrand Russell, *The Autobiography of Bertrand Russell*, ii,
(George Allen and Unwin, 1968)

D. H. LAWRENCE to Lady Cynthia Asquith, 30 January 1915
The Letters of D. H. Lawrence, ii, edited by George J. Zytaruk and James
T. Boulton (Cambridge University Press, 1981)

HENRY JAMES to W. B. Yeats, 25 August 1915
Photocopy from the Gregory papers – courtesy of Colin Smythe

WALLACE STEVENS to his wife, 19 June 1916
Letters of Wallace Stevens, edited by Holly Stevens (Faber and Faber, 1966)

ROBERT GRAVES to Eddie Marsh, 7 August 1916
In Broken Images: Selected Letters of Robert Graves, 1914–1946, edited by Paul O'Prey (Hutchinson, 1982)

SIEGFRIED SASSOON to Robert Graves, 19 October 1917
Siegfried Sassoon Diaries 1915–1918, edited and introduced by Rupert Hart-Davis (Faber and Faber, 1983)

WILFRED OWEN to his mother, 31 December 1917
Wilfred Owen: Collected Letters, edited by Harold Owen and John Bell (Oxford University Press, 1967)

FATHER McCANN to Lady Grizel Hamilton, 1 April 1918
MS, private collection

WALLACE STEVENS to Harriet Monroe, 8 April [1918]
Letters of Wallace Stevens, edited by Holly Stevens (Faber and Faber, 1966)

WILFRED OWEN to his mother, 31 October [1918]
Wilfred Owen: Collected Letters, edited by Harold Owen and John Bell (Oxford University Press, 1967)

BERNARD SHAW to Sylvia Beach, 10 October 1921
Letters of James Joyce, iii, edited by Richard Ellmann (Faber and Faber, 1966)

DORA CARRINGTON to Gerald Brenan, undated
Carrington: Letters and Extracts from her Diaries, edited by David Garnett (Jonathan Cape, 1970)

A. E. HOUSMAN to Grant Richards, 14 October 1922
The Letters of A. E. Housman, edited by Henry Maas (Rupert Hart-Davis, 1971)

VIRGINIA WOOLF to Gwen Raverat, 11 March [1925]
The Letters of Virginia Woolf, iii, edited by Nigel Nicolson and Joanne Trautmann (Hogarth Press, 1977)

ERNEST HEMINGWAY to F. Scott Fitzgerald, 1 July 1925
Ernest Hemingway: Selected Letters, edited by Carlos Baker (Charles Scribner's Sons, 1981)

WINSTON CHURCHILL to T. E. Lawrence, 16 May 1927
MS, Spiro Collection, New York; also printed in *Letters to T. E. Lawrence*, edited by A. W. Lawrence (Jonathan Cape, 1962)

E. M. FORSTER to T. E. Lawrence, 3 May 1928
MS, Spiro Collection, New York

Sources

DORA CARRINGTON to Julia Strachey, [? June 1930]
Carrington: Letters and Extracts from her Diaries, edited by David Garnett
(Jonathan Cape, 1970)

T. E. LAWRENCE to Sir Edward Elgar, 12 October 1932
The Letters of Jonathan Cape, edited by David Garnett
(Jonathan Cape, 1938)

CARL GUSTAV JUNG to James Joyce, [October 1932]
Letters of James Joyce, iii, edited by Richard Ellmann
(Faber and Faber, 1966)

NEVILLE CHAMBERLAIN to the Editor of *The Times*, 24 January 1933
The First Cuckoo, edited by Kenneth Gregory (Times Books, 1976)

T. E. LAWRENCE to Siegfried Sassoon, 7 December 1934
MS, Spiro Collection, New York

W. B. YEATS to Ethel Mannin, 24 June [1935]
Typescript; to be published in *The Collected Letters of W. B. Yeats* (Oxford,
Clarendon Press), extracts have been published in *The Letters of W. B.
Yeats*, edited by Allan Wade (1954)

EVELYN WAUGH to Laura Herbert, 4 August 1936
The Letters of Evelyn Waugh, edited by Mark Amory (Weidenfeld and
Nicolson, 1980)

DYLAN THOMAS to Caitlin Macnamara, [? late 1936]
The Collected Letters of Dylan Thomas, edited by Paul Ferris
(J. M. Dent, 1985)

SCOTT FITZGERALD to his daughter, 12 December 1936
The Letters of F. Scott Fitzgerald, edited by Andrew Turnbull
(The Bodley Head, 1964)

MALCOLM LOWRY to Juan Fernando Marquez, [1937]
Selected Letters of Malcolm Lowry, edited by Harvey Breit and Margerie
Bonner Lowry (Jonathan Cape, 1967)

LAWRENCE DURRELL to Henry Miller, [August 1938]
Lawrence Durrell–Henry Miller: A Private Correspondence, edited George
Wickes (Faber and Faber, 1963)

THOMAS WOLFE to Maxwell Perkins, 12 August 1938
Selected Letters of Thomas Wolfe, edited by Elizabeth Nowell and Daniel
George (Heinemann, 1958)

E. B. WHITE to Eugene Saxton, 1 March [1939]
Letters of E. B. White, edited by Dorothy Lobrano Guth
(Harper & Row, 1976)

SIGMUND FREUD to H. G. Wells, 16 July 1939
Sigmund Freud: Briefe 1873–1939, edited by Ernst and Lucie Freud
(S. Fischer, 1968)

ALBERT EINSTEIN to the President of the United States, 2 August 1939
Ronald W. Clark, *Einstein: The Life and Times* (World Publishing, 1971)

Acknowledgements

For permission to reprint the letters in this volume the editor and publishers gratefully acknowledge the following:

Associated University Presses for *The Letters of Aubrey Beardsley*, edited by Henry Maas, J. L. Duncan and W. G. Good; The Athlone Press Ltd for *Tolstoy's Letters*, edited by R. F. Christian Copyright R. F. Christian 1978, *Turgenev's Letters*, edited by A. V. Knowles; A & C Black (Publishers) Ltd for *Handel* by Otto Erich Deutsch; Basil Blackwell Ltd for *The Letters of John Wilmot, Earl of Rochester*, edited by Jeremy Treglown; The British Library Board for Facsimile in Cecil Woodham-Smith and Facsimile in Anthony Nutting; Estate of Thomas Carlyle for *The Correspondence of Emerson and Carlyle*, edited by Joseph Slater; W & R Chambers Ltd for *H. M. Stanley: Unpublished Letters*, edited by Albert Maurice; Chatto & Windus Ltd for *David Livingstone, Family Letters 1841–1856*, i, edited by I. Schapera, *The Letters of Virginia Woolf*, iii, edited by Nigel Nicolson and Joanne Trautmann; The Cupid Press for *The Letters of Thomas Gainsborough*, edited by Mary Woodall; Curtis Brown Group Ltd on behalf of Lawrence Durrell for *Lawrence Durrell – Henry Miller: A Private Correspondence*, edited by George Wicks Copywright © Lawrence Durrell 1963; Curtis Brown Group Ltd on behalf of the Estate of Sir Winston Churchill for *Letters to T. E. Lawrence*, edited by A. W. Lawrence Copyright © Estate of Sir Winston Churchill 1962; Curtis Brown Group Ltd and C & T Publications Ltd for *Winston S. Churchill*, i, by Randolph S. Churchill Copyright © C & T Publications Ltd; J. M. Dent for *The Collected Letters of Dylan Thomas*, edited by Paul Ferris; Dobson Books Ltd for *Letters to Nimrod: Edward Elgar to August Jaeger 1897–1908*, edited by Percy M. Young; Dover Publications Inc and The Pierpont Morgan Library for *British Literary Manuscripts, Series I from 800 to 1800*, edited by V. Klinkenborg, H. Cahoon and C. Ryskamp; Duke University Press for *The Letters of John Dryden*, edited by Charles E. Ward; The Economist Publications Ltd for *The Collected Works of Walter Bagehot*, xii, *The Letters*, edited by Norman St John-Stevas; Editions Gallimard for *Stendhal: Correspondence*, i, edited by V. del Litto and Henri Martineau © Editions Gallimard, 1962; Faber and Faber Ltd for *Letters of James Joyce*, edited by Richard Ellmann, *The Letters of Rupert Brooke*, edited by Geoffrey Keynes, *Siegfried Sassoon Diaries 1915–1918*, edited and introduced by Rupert Hart-Davis; Sigmund Freud Copyrights, Colchester, for *Sigmund Freud: Briefe 1873–1939*, edited by Ernst and Lucie Freud; Estate of Robert Frost, Lawrence Thompson for *Selected Letters of Robert Frost*, edited by Lawrence Thompson; David Garnett Estate for *Carrington: Letters and*

Extracts from her Diaries, edited by David Garnett; Gebr. Mann for *Heinrich Schliemann Briefwechsel*, i, edited by Ernst Meyer; Estate of Thomas Wolfe for *Selected Letters of Thomas Wolfe*, edited by Elizabeth Nowell and Daniel George, Copyrights 1956, 1984; by courtesy of the Trustees of the Goodwood Collections and with acknowledgements to the West Sussex Record Office and the County Archivist for *Goodwood: Royal Letters*, edited by Timothy J. McCann; Hakluyt Society for *The Roanoke Voyages*; Harcourt, Brace and Jovanovich, Inc for *The Letters of Virginia Woolf*, iii, edited by Nigel Nicolson and Joanne Trautmann Copyright © 1977 by Quentin Bell and Angelica Garnett; Harper and Row Publications Inc for *Letters of E. B. White*, edited by Dorothy Lobrano Guth Copyright © 1976 by E. B. White; Harvard, the Belknap Press, for *The Letters of Robert Browning and Elizabeth Barrett Browning 1845 – 1846*, i, edited by Elvan Kintner, *The Letters of Emily Dickinson*, edited by Thomas H. Johnson and Theodora Ward, *Selected Mark Twain-Howells Letters*, edited by F. Anderson, W. M. Gibson, H. N. Smith; A. M. Heath on behalf of Francis Steegmuller for *Your Isador*, edited by Francis Steegmuller; The Hebrew University of Jerusalem, Israel, for *Einstein: The Life and Times* by Ronald W. Clark; Merlin Holland for Oscar Wilde's letter to Lord Alfred Douglas, January 1893, Oscar Wilde's letters to Ada Leverson, 10 February 1895 and 20 May 1897, Oscar Wilde's letter to Reggie Turner, 10 August 1897, Constance Wilde's letter to Arthur Humphreys, 27 February 1898; Henry Holt (USA) for *Selected Letters of Robert Frost*, edited by Lawrence Thompson, Copyright © 1964 by Lawrence Thompson, and Holt, Rinehart and Winston Inc., *Carrington, Letters and Extracts from her Diaries*, edited by David Garnett, Copyright © 1970, David Garnett, Sophie Partridge Trust; Herr Jung for *Carl Gustav Jung's letter to James Joyce, October 1932*; Alfred A. Knopf Inc for *The Letters of Wallace Stevens*, edited by Holly Stevens Copyright © 1966 Holly Stevens; Macmillan Publishing Company for *The Letters of Aubrey Beardsley*, edited by Henry Maas, J. L. Duncan and W. G. Good, Copyright © 1975 by Macmillan Publishing Company, originally published in UK by Cassell, and for *The Collected Poems of W. B. Yeats*; Marquess of Lothian for the extract from the Melbourne manuscript; John Murray and The Harvard University Press for *Byron's Letters and Journals*, i, v, vi, x, edited by Leslie A. Marchand; National Maritime Museum for *The Keith Papers*, edited by Christopher Lloyd; New York University Press for *The Letters of William Hazlitt*, edited by Herschel Sikes, W. H. Bonner and Gerald Lehey, *The Correspondence of Henry David Thoreau*, edited by Walter Harding and Carl Bode, *The Collected Writings of Walt Whitman: the Correspondence*, edited by Edwin Haviland Miller; New York Graphic Society for *The Complete Letters of Vincent van Gogh*, ii, edited by J. van Gogh-Bongerand and C. de Dood; New Directions Publishing Corporation for *Dylan Thomas, Selected Letters* Copyright © 1965, 1966 by the Trustees for the Copyrights of Dylan Thomas; Nathaniel Hawthorne to an unknown recipient (April 12, 1851) from Vol. XVI of *The Centenary Edition of the Works of Nathaniel Hawthorne: The Letters, 1843–1853*, p.419, edited by Thomas Woodson, L. Neal Smith, and Norman Holmes Pearson © 1985 by the Ohio State University; Oxford University Press for *The Correspondence of Richard Steele*, edited by Rae Blanchard, *The Dictionary of*

Acknowledgements

National Biography: 1931–1940, Jane Austen's Letters, edited by Alan G. Hill, *The Letters of Gerard Manley Hopkins to Robert Bridges*, edited by Claude Colleer Abbott, *The Letters of John Keats*, edited by Robert Gittings, *The Letters of William Blake*, edited by Geoffrey Keynes, *The Letters of William Wordsworth: A New Selection*, edited by Alan G. Hill, *Wilfred Owen: Collected Letters*, edited by Harold Owen and John Bell; Oxford, Clarendon Press, for *The Collected Letters of John Millington Synge*, edited by Ann Saddlemyer, *The Collected Letters of Samuel Taylor Coleridge*, edited by Earl Leslie Griggs, *The Collected Letters of W. B. Yeats*, edited by John Kelly and Eric Domville, *The Complete Letters of Lady Mary Wortley Montagu*, edited by Robert Halsband, *The Complete Works of Thomas Chatterton*, edited by Donald S. Taylor with Benjamin B. Hoover, *The Correspondence of Alexander Pope*, edited by George Sherburn, *The Correspondence of Jonathan Swift*, edited by Harold Williams, *The Correspondence of Thomas Gray*, edited by Paget Toynbee and Leonard Whibley, *Dante Gabriel Rossetti and Jane Morris: Their Correspondence*, edited by John Bryson and Janet Camp Troxell, *English Literary Autographs, 1550–1650*, by W. W. Greg, *The Letters and Prose Writings of William Cowper*, edited by James King and Charles Ryskamp, *The Letters and Writings of John Henry Newman*, edited by Charles Stephen Dessain and Edward E. Kelly, S. J., *The Letters of Alfred Lord Tennyson*, edited by Cecil Y. Lang and Edgar F. Shannon, *The Letters of Charles Dickens: the Pilgrim Edition*, edited by Graham Storey and K. J. Fielding, *The Letters of Daniel Defoe*, edited by George Harris Healey, *The Letters of Dante Gabriel Rossetti*, edited by Oswald Doughty and John Robert Wahl, *The Letters of David Hume*, edited by J. Y. T. Greig, *The Letters of John Clare*, edited by Mark Storey, *Letters of Laurence Sterne*, edited by Lewis Perry Curtis, *The Letters of Percy Bysshe Shelley*, edited by Frederick L. Jones, *Letters of Philip Dormer Stanhope fourth Earl of Chesterfield to his Godson and Successor*, edited by the Earl of Carnarvon, *The Letters of Robert Burns*, edited by J. De Lancey Ferguson, *The Letters of Samuel Johnson*, edited by R. W. Chapman, *The Letters of Sydney Smith*, edited by Nowell C. Smith, *The Letters of William and Dorothy Wordsworth*, edited by Earl Leslie Griggs; Penguin Books Ltd for *Letters to Sir William Temple*, edited by Kenneth Parker, *Christmas Crackers* by John Julius Norwich, collections Copyright © John Julius Norwich, 1980, *Letters to Sherlock Holmes*, edited by Richard Lancelyn Green, collection Copyright © Richard Lancelyn Green, 1985; A. D. Peters and Co. Ltd for *Selected Letters of Malcolm Lowry*, edited by Harvey Breit and Margerie Bonner Lowry; Laurence Pollinger Ltd and the Estate of Mrs Frieda Lawrence Ravagli for *The Letters of D. H. Lawrence*, i, edited by James T. Boulton; The Provost and Scholars of King's College, Cambridge, for E. M. Forster's letter to T. E. Lawrence, 3 May 1928; The Gracious Permission of Her Majesty the Queen to publish material which is subject to Copyright for George III's letter to Lord Sandwich, Queen Victoria's letter to General Gordon's sister and George V's letter to Lord March; Roth & Company for *Frederick William Rolfe, Baron Corvo: Letters to Harry Bainbridge*; The Council of The Royal Society of London for *The Correspondence of Isaac Newton*, ii, edited by H. W. Turnbull; Ruskin Literary Trust for *The Correspondence of Thomas Carlyle and John Ruskin*, edited by George Allen Cate Copyright © Ruskin Literary Trust 1988; Charles Scribner's Sons, an imprint of Macmillan Publishing Company for *The Letters of F. Scott Fitzgerald*, edited by Andrew Turnbull Copyright © 1963 by Francis Scott Fitzgerald Lanahan, *Ernest Hemingway: Selected Letters 1917 to 1961*, edited by Carlos Baker, Copyright © 1981 Carlos Baker and The Ernest Hemingway Foundation Inc; Sligo County Library, Ann and Michael Yeats, Oxford University Press for W. B. Yeats's letter to Ethel Mannin, 24 June 1935; The Society of Authors on behalf of the Bernard Shaw Estate for *Bernard Shaw: Collected Letters*, edited by Dan T. Laurence, on behalf of the Estate of Henry James for extracts from the Gregory papers, on behalf of the Estate of James Joyce for *Letters of James Joyce*, edited by Richard Ellmann; Sotheby's and Maggs Bros. Ltd, for extracts from catalogues listed; Times Books Ltd for *The First Cuckoo*, edited by Kenneth Gregory; Toronto University Press for *The Letters of Thomas Hood*, edited by Peter F. Morgan; Trustees of the Estate of Muriel Rose Trollope for *The Letters of Anthony Trollope*, ii, edited by N. John Hall and Nina Burgis; Trustees of the Seven Pillars of Wisdom Trust for T. E. Lawrence's letter to Siegfried Sassoon, 7 December 1934; Andrew Turnbull, the editor, for *The Letters of F. Scott Fitzgerald*; The Regents of the University of California Press for *The Letters of Sir George Etherege*, edited by Frederick Bracher; Unwin Hyman Ltd for *The Autobiography of Bertrand Russell*, ii; Viking Penguin for *Letters of James Joyce*, edited by Richard Ellmann; The Voltaire Foundation for *The Complete Works of Voltaire, Vol. 107*; A. P. Watt Ltd on behalf of the Executors of the Estate of Robert Graves and Paul O'Prey for *In Broken Images: Selected Letters of Robert Graves 1914–1946*, edited by Paul O'Prey; Weidenfeld and Nicolson Ltd for *The Letters of Evelyn Waugh*, edited by Mark Amory; The Yale University Press for *Robert Louis Stevenson: Stevenson's Letters to Charles Baxter*, edited by De Lancey Ferguson and Marshall Waingrow and *Horace Walpole's Correspondence*, ix, x and xvi, edited by W. S. Lewis.

Faber and Faber apologizes for any errors or omissions in the above list and would be grateful to be notified of any corrections that should be incorporated in the next edition of this volume.